Revolutionary Negotiations

JEFFERSONIAN AMERICA

Jan Ellen Lewis, Peter S. Onuf, and
Andrew O'Shaughnessy, *Editors*

REVOLUTIONARY NEGOTIATIONS

*Indians, Empires, and Diplomats
in the Founding of America*

Leonard J. Sadosky

University of Virginia Press   *Charlottesville and London*

University of Virginia Press
© 2009 by the Rector and Visitors of the University of Virginia
All rights reserved
Printed in the United States of America on acid-free paper

First published 2009
First paperback edition published 2026
ISBN 978-0-8139-5519-3 (paper)

1 3 5 7 9 8 6 4 2

THE LIBRARY OF CONGRESS HAS CATALOGED THE HARDCOVER EDITION AS FOLLOWS:

Sadosky, Leonard J.
Revolutionary negotiations : Indians, empires, and diplomats in the founding of America / Leonard J. Sadosky.
p. cm. — (Jeffersonian America)
Includes bibliographical references and index.
ISBN 978-0-8139-2864-7 (cloth : alk. paper)
ISBN 978-0-8139-2870-8 (e-book)
1. United States—Foreign relations—1775–1783. 2. United States—Foreign relations—1783–1865. 3. United States—Foreign relations—To 1775. 4. Indians of North America—Government relations—To 1789. 5. Indians of North America—Government relations—1789–1869. I. Title.
E249.S23 2010
973.3—dc22
2009024319

To Roberta Crowe Robb (1902–1982),
my great-grandmother and first history teacher

Contents

Acknowledgments ix

Introduction 1

Prologue   *The Cherokee Emperor*   13

1. "In the Nature of Ambassadors"
   North American Diplomacy within the British Empire   31

2. "In an Odd State"
   The American Decision to Leave the British Empire   59

3. "Are We Not . . . Independant States?"
   Imagining and Realizing an Independent America   90

4. "Rendering Us Great and Respectable in the Eyes of the World"
   The Diplomatic Imperative for the Federal Constitution   119

5. "To Be Considered as Foreign Nations"
   The Ambiguous Triumph of Federalist Statecraft   148

6. Enlarging "Our Association"
   The Triumph of the Diplomacy of Conquest   176

Epilogue   *The Cherokee Lawyer*   207

Notes   217

Bibliography   251

Index   267

Acknowledgments

In the course of writing this book, I have received the support of several different institutions. This book began life as a doctoral dissertation at the University of Virginia. Its production was assisted by several graduate fellowships from the University of Virginia, a short-term research fellowship from the David Library of the American Revolution, and a dissertation fellowship from the Robert H. Smith International Center for Jefferson Studies at Monticello. My work on the book manuscript was furthered by the support of Iowa State University's College of Liberal Arts and Sciences and its Center for Excellence in the Arts and Humanities. Two postdoctoral fellowships—the Gilder Lehrman Research Fellowship at Monticello's Robert H. Smith International Center for Jefferson Studies and the Patrick Henry Fellowship at Johns Hopkins University's Krieger College of Arts and Sciences—also proved vital in supporting the completion of this manuscript. I am grateful to all these institutions for their support.

Numerous individuals provided invaluable support during the many years of this book's composition. Foremost was my advisor and dissertation director at the University of Virginia, Peter Onuf. As an advisor and mentor, Peter's guidance, advice, and instruction were invaluable in so many ways—at Virginia and beyond, his moral support was as important as his scholarly advice in helping me find my voice to write this book and also staying on task to see it to completion. Thanks are also due to Peter for overseeing the Early American Seminar at Virginia, where almost every chapter in this book was hashed out in some form or another when it was a dissertation.

Special thanks are due to my master's advisor from Miami University

(Ohio), Andrew Cayton, whose mentorship helped get me on the path to being a professional historian and whose example as a scholar and teacher I continue to try to live up to.

At the University of Virginia, thanks are due to my dissertation readers, John C. A. Stagg, Sophie Rosenfeld, and James Sofka, and to the classroom experiences provided by Edward Ayers, the late Stephen Innes, Joseph Kett, Maurie McInnis, Erik Midelfort, and Olivier Zunz. I also owe thanks to several professors from my years at Miami University: Mary Kupiec Cayton, Jeff Kimball, Jack Temple Kirby, Michael O'Brien, and Robert Thurston.

I incurred many debts while this book was coming together at the University of Virginia Press. Special thanks to editor Dick Holway and to Raennah Mitchell, Susan Murray, and Ruth Steinberg. Thanks, too, to the manuscript readers, David Hendrickson and Dan Richter, for their helpful and insightful reviews of the manuscript at multiple stages of the production process.

During my seven years in Charlottesville at UVA and Monticello, numerous friends both inside and outside the scholarly world sustained me in so many ways. Thanks to Carl Bon Tempo and Kristin Celello, Benjamin Carp, Kate Destler and Johann Neem, Christa Dierksheide, Brian and Danica D'Onofrio, Elizabeth Fitton, Ken Forziati and Sharon Murphy, Valerie Garver, Ari Helo, Charles Irons, Sarah and Scott Meacham, Jennifer Creger Miller, Brian Murphy, Louisa Parker-Mattozi, Robert Parkinson, Linda Retallack, Jennifer Ross, Brian and Kelli Schoen, Eric Vettel, and Brian Yost. I also should acknowledge my supportive friends from Miami University—Eric Crockwell, Thomas Keefe, Michael Thompson, and, especially, the late Hedda Lautenschlager.

Colleagues and friends from other scholarly institutions have been invaluable in helping me refine and rework this project, as both a dissertation and book. From the Robert H. Smith International Center for Jefferson Studies, two Saunders Directors—James Horn and Andrew J. O'Shaughnessy—welcomed and supported my scholarship, as did research historians Gaye Wilson and Christine Coalwell McDonald, librarian Jack Robertson, and the entire staff of the Papers of Thomas Jefferson Retirement Series. I was fortunate to get to know many of the fellows who passed through the halls of Kenwood and the Jefferson Library, and thanks are due to Charlene and James Lewis, Peter Nicolaisen, Sandra Rebok, and Hannah Spahn for their ongoing friendship and support, with special thanks to Max Edling for his kind reading of, and comments on, chapter 5. It was as a graduate assistant at the Papers of James Madison that I first encountered many of the diplomatic history sources I explored in this book, and thanks to the editors and staff there, including Ellen Barber, Anne Colony, Mary Hackett, Martha King, David Mattern, and John Stagg for their kindness and camaraderie. Portions of chapter 4 were presented to the Omohundro Institute of Early American History and Culture in 2003—I thank Ronald Hoffman for the invitation to present there and all members of the Institute for their reception and suggestions. The summer of 2003 that I spent with the Lewis and Clark Trail Heritage Foundation in Great Falls, Montana, as the Portage Route Chapter's Scholar in Residence was a very special time for me, and personal thanks are due to Carol Bronson, Larry Epstein, Jill Jackson, Ella Mae Howard, and everyone from the Portage Route Chapter, and Jane Weber and the entire staff of the Lewis and Clark Interpretive Center in Great Falls.

After leaving Charlottesville, I took up at employment at Iowa State University. Thanks first go to the Department of History's excellent secretary, Jennifer Rivera. Supportive friends who joined me in indulging in the wonders of state-subsidized ethanol were Michael Bailey, Patrick and Melissa Barr-Melej, Deanne Brocato, Jana Byars, Katherine Mellen Charron, Christopher and Karen Curtis, Lina del Castillo, April Eisman, Carla Fehr, Kathy Hilliard, David Hollander and Lucy Martin, Sara Gregg and Ben Hayes, Jeffrey Houghtby and Lisa Hovis, John Monroe and Wendie Schneider, and Matthew and Janelle Stanley.

This book reached maturity while I was the Patrick Henry Fellow at Johns Hopkins University in 2006–7. My first note of thanks here has to go to Margaret Nuttle for endowing the fellowship. Thanks are also in order to all those who welcomed me into the scholarly community at Hopkins—Toby Ditz and Philip Morgan of the Early American Seminar, John Marshall of the Seminar in Moral and Political Thought, and History Department Chair Gabrielle Spiegel, who invited me to be a part of the working seminar for the Mellon Foundation Postdoctoral Fellows. Seminarians Kevin Attell, Stanford Carpenter, Bruce Hall, Viola Kolarov, Jesse Molesworth, Bibi Obler, and Herica Valladares read a first draft of chapter 6, and their comments helped me improve it greatly. Additional thanks in the Hopkins community are also due to Joe Adelman, Kate Murphy, Jessica Roney, Molly Warsh, and especially to Jessica Stern for her reading and comments on the prologue and chapter 1.

I will never believe anyone who says you cannot go home again, since that is where I have always found some of the strongest support for this and all my endeavors. Thanks to my friends Kristina Howard, Ann Marie Macdonald, Ann Paggioli, Heather Titus, and David Young for their support.

My final notes of thanks and love are for my family, without whose love and support nothing that I have done would have been possible. Thanks go to my father, Leonard J. Sadosky Jr., and the entire Sadosky family, including my Aunt Sharon and Uncle Phil. Thanks as well to the Robb family—my aunts and uncles, Hal and Rosi, Susan, and Allan and Michele; my cousins, Andy and Claire; and my grandparents, Samuel and Genevieve. Special thanks are due to my sister, Jennifer, her daughter, Shaylee, and her husband, Dan O'Neill, for supporting and inspiring me. My mother, Jo-Ann Robb Sadosky, deserves more thanks than I can convey for lovingly supporting me through my entire life, but especially during my graduate study and during the writing of this book, even when things were not going as smoothly or speedily as I would have liked. My last note of thanks is to the woman to whom this book is dedicated, my great-grandmother, Roberta Crowe Robb. Her home was the first place where I was encouraged to ask any question, and where I first heard stories about other places and times past. In so many ways, my exploration of history (and so many other things) began there under her guidance.

Revolutionary Negotiations

Introduction

This is a book about how the United States of America came to be. At the start of the twenty-first century, when the American nation-state commands a position of nearly unrivaled political, commercial, and military strength—what, in 1999, French foreign minister Hubert Védrine provocatively labeled *hyperpuissance*, or hyperpower—it is scarcely imaginable that the United States ever occupied a position of abject weakness. Yet history tells us this was indeed the case. Far from being a historical constant, preeminent and preponderant American power is a development of relatively recent origin.[1]

In the first four decades following the American Congress's declaration of independence, the United States, while a subject of curiosity for some, was for most only a marginal presence in the wider world.[2] In the estimation of the vast majority of the European powers, the United States was politically peripheral and militarily impotent. American commerce expanded or contracted more on the basis of the changing tastes of Atlantic consumers and the shifting policies of the European imperial powers, than on anything Americans themselves did. And for a good part of its early life the United States of America was not a nation-state in the modern sense, but a loose confederation of thirteen polities, each of which jealously guarded its (still emerging) sovereign power and prerogatives. Concerted action to ameliorate America's situation of weakness in the international system was difficult to imagine and even more difficult to bring to fruition. All told, the United States endured a fragile and contingent existence during its early life. From the rupture of the British Empire in the mid-1770s through the end of the Napoleonic Wars in 1815, the viability of this new entity, the United States of America, remained an open question.

When we reflect that so many developments of lasting importance for the American nation occurred against the backdrop of this struggle for survival, the question of how the United States navigated through this seemingly dark time calls for further investigation. The success of the American Revolution, the shaping of the American Constitution, the division of American public life into partisan factions (the so-called First American Party System), and the coalescence of the relationship between the American federal government and American Indian peoples into one of inequality and expropriation—all of these important historical developments are rendered more explicable, and their interconnections illuminated, through an appreciation and examination of the international context of the American Founding. Simply put, the American Revolution was an event *in* international history, and thus an event *with* an international history. Remembering that the United States once consisted of small and powerless new states in an anarchic world, itself in the midst of revolutionary change, sheds light on why the American Founding proceeded in the way that it did, and why, at least in part, the United States looks the way it does today.

Exploring the international history of the American Founding has the potential to explode conventional wisdom and cherished national mythology. Consider the alleged long-standing isolationist impulse in American culture and politics, usually traced back to President George Washington's Farewell Address, if not before.[3] Although it has often seemed to be a permanent part of the American political idiom, "isolationism" was, for the most part, not in the vocabulary of America's Founding Fathers. The American leaders of the eighteenth and early nineteenth centuries understood that, for a variety of reasons, they could not turn inward upon themselves and hope to survive. The American states had to engage with the world beyond their borders: allies were needed to win independence; foreign markets had to be opened for American produce; order was needed on the United States' North American borderlands. The rejection of isolationism (and, really, the inability to seriously conceive of it) had enormous implications.[4]

At the same time that we acknowledge the international history of the American Revolution and the American Founding, it is profitable to reconsider what exactly we mean when we use the term "international." During the Revolutionary Era, the leaders of the American states were forced to enter into negotiation with the leaders of a variety of sovereign polities: the monarchies and republics of European Christendom come first to mind, but American leaders also engaged the "Barbary Regencies" of the Islamic Mediterranean and the villages and confederations of the various indigenous peoples of North America.[5] But these relations have rarely been considered together. Traditionally, the study of American interaction with European (and North African) sovereigns has been the subject of diplomatic and political history, while American interaction with Native American communities has been the realm of ethnohistory, American Indian history, and the history of the American West.[6] Although they often treated geographically different realms and ethnically and racially different peoples with different assumptions and objectives, American policymakers of the late eighteenth and early nineteenth centuries were never able to keep the theaters of diplomatic activity as hermetically sealed from one another as twentieth-century historians, political scientists, and anthropologists have managed to do. But this interpretive tendency has begun to change. Modern scholars have come to recognize the complex interconnectedness of the early modern Atlantic world, and the traditional divide historians and historiography have maintained between European diplomacy and American Indian diplomacy can thus be reexamined with profit. Recent scholarship has made it almost a commonplace that the political systems of the North American borderlands were interpenetrated by the concerns and conflicts of the European political system, even as the long-standing and emergent structures of Native American political and cultural negotiation and accommodation militated against complete European domination. Maintaining a hard-and-fast boundary line between the European world and the Native American one is proving to be as difficult for historians as it was for the men and women of the eighteenth century. The full extent of the evolution of American statecraft during this period can only become evident when we consider the assumptions, practices, and methods American diplomatists brought to bear contemporaneously in *all* the arenas of negotiation in which they were involved. Thus, a truly international history of the American Revolution and Founding needs to take into account the United States' interaction with all nations—in both the Old World and the New.[7]

No matter in what direction they looked and where they attempted to negotiate, the work of Revolutionary Era American diplomatists was laden with anxiety. Whether, and to what extent, extranational polities (be they European or American Indian) would recognize the new American states' claims of sovereignty was not immediately clear. Complicating the questions of recognition and respect was the reality that both the definition of sovereignty and the rules by which sovereigns interacted with each other—the law of nations—remained nebulous and somewhat unfixed through the course of the eighteenth century. The law of nations (the precursor to modern international law) served two simultaneous functions in the eighteenth century. First, it provided a mechanism for sovereigns to interact with one another in an attempt to solve real-world disputes, while it simultaneously provided rules for war-making and eventual peace-making if conflict was not avoided. Second, these collective norms also provided a coherent vision of peaceful coexistence among states. The law of nations helped order the world as it was and pointed the way to the world as it could be.[8] However, the law of nations as a normative force was called into open question after the beginning of the French Revolution. The ideologies of revolution and reaction convinced most sovereigns to increasingly allow *raison d'état* to trump the normative law of nations. Thus, as the United States pleaded for entry into the wider world, it was attempting to become a full member of the European-centered transatlantic diplomatic system at a time when what constituted full membership in this system was unclear and the rules of the system were increasingly in flux.[9]

Just as important, the implications of Revolutionary Era diplomatic negotiations did not stop outside the borders of the American states. In the process of negotiating with extranational polities, and often because of it, the individual American states reassessed how they related to one another. The nature of sovereign power within the United States was called into question. Negotiation of the frame that held together the American union of states—its constitution—occurred in the context of the United States' negotiations with polities beyond its collective borders. Giving American diplomats the power and legitimacy needed to seriously negotiate became an imperative for a stronger American union—finally realized when the Constitution drafted in 1787 was ratified and thus superseded the Articles of Confederation. Yet strengthening the power of the central government to act in the international realm threatened to weaken or even obliterate the sovereignty of the individual American states—the newly empowered instrumentalities of the central government could be turned inward as well as outward. Sovereign power within the union, as well as beyond it, would also be renegotiated during the Revolutionary and Founding Eras. Thus, acts of diplomacy (broadly construed) defined the shape of the United States of America.[10]

But how best can we tell this story? *Revolutionary Negotiations* is not a comprehensive narrative of the political or diplomatic history of this period, but is an extended interpretative essay, combining primary source research with a synthesis of several diverse strains of historiography. Rather than a work of traditional political or diplomatic history (focused solely on motivations, actions, and outcomes), or a work of traditional intellectual history (focused on the evolving intricacies of various systems of ideas), *Revolutionary Negotiations* is a hybrid of both these types of history. It is a history of ideas in service of action, and, to a great extent, a history of ideas transformed by action. It is thus a history of political culture, where we define political culture as the (evolving) set of assumptions, methods, and practices of the conduct of politics.[11] And here, of course, we are concerned with a particular kind of politics—that of diplomatic negotiation. The subject herein is probably best labeled the *political culture of diplomacy*, or the slightly more elegant term favored by diplomatic historians and political scientists, *statecraft*. It should be noted that this book's subject differs somewhat from what historians have traditionally labeled the *culture of diplomacy* or *diplomatic culture*, which has usually denoted the study of diplomatic protocol and court etiquette. The performative aspect of the political culture of diplomacy is most interesting, but it constitutes only one element of the field under my consideration.[12] Political culture, more than just diplomacy, is this study's central focus, in large part because the political culture of domestic politics and the political culture of diplomacy overlapped in so many ways in eighteenth- and early nineteenth-century America.[13]

But we are not studying the political culture of early American diplomacy simply for its own sake—this study uses explorations of political culture to illuminate key structural changes that allowed the United States of America to emerge as independent sovereignties (and ultimately, a singular sovereignty). Modern political science, and in particular the branch of the discipline concerned with international relations, gives historians an interpretive framework and a terminology within which to think about and discuss all of these developments. Taking sovereign states as their fundamental unit of analysis, international relations scholars concern themselves with the way that states interact with one another. While international relations theorists differ over the principles that guide how states interact (realists assert anarchic relations between states; idealists of various stripes presume an inherent order or at least the potential for order), all assert that sovereign states exist in relation to each other. States are thus part of systems. For our purposes in this book, a "states system" is defined as a network of interacting polities, tied together via real and observable relationships of negotiation and exchange—relationships with the potential for mutual cooperation, or conflict and subsequent resolution. Relationships can exist between polities of both overlapping and divergent interests, and between polities of both relatively equal, as well as unequal, bases of power. Beyond these multifaceted structures that bind polities together, states systems are also defined by shared sets of norms that allow these relations of negotiation, exchange, conflict, and resolution to proceed. Both of these elements—structures and norms—are definitive of a system of states.[14]

In this book, we are concerned with the nature of relations between polities at the margins of an established states system. In particular, we are interested in one of the building blocks of the modern international order: the early modern European states system, usually known as the Westphalian system. Emerging in the wake of the Thirty Years' War (at the eponymous 1648 Peace of Westphalia), the Westphalian system was rooted in the principles of the inviolability of state sovereignty, territoriality, and state equality. In other words, despite their real-world power differences, states engaged in diplomacy within the Westphalian system acknowledged each other as equals, and also pledged to not interfere in any matters within another state's borders. Working with conceptions of sovereignty that were rooted in the writings of Thomas Hobbes and Jean Bodin (among others), Westphalian diplomatists had midwifed a system of diplomacy and state interaction that was, in structural terms, externally anarchic and internally reactionary. Cooperation between states was fleeting at best, and views of sovereign power within a state tended toward absolutism. The Westphalian system's norms, however, militated against these trends. As we have already noted, the theoretical underpinnings of early modern diplomacy, the law of nations, was rooted in understandings of natural law that took as its fundamental unit of analysis not the sovereign state, but the human individual. Naturally bearing a full panoply of rights and freedoms, human beings had surrendered the bulk of those rights to live in society, or, as early moderns put it, to live in a commonwealth, or *res publica*. Law-of-nations theorists saw Westphalian Europe not as an anarchic realm of a perpetual war of each against all, but a commonwealth of commonwealths, or a Republic of Europe. These two views—the antecedents to modern structural realism and liberal internationalism—have never been completely reconciled.[15]

With the colonization of the Americas, Europeans extended the sphere of their settlement and their claims to dominion across the Atlantic Ocean. The structures of the Westphalian system extended with them. However, the new settler communities and the existing villages, confederacies, and empires of the Americas' indigenous peoples fit roughly, if at all, into the established norms of the Westphalian states system. Relationships between European settlers, indigenous Americans, and, eventually, European metropolitan authorities evolved into a variant of the Westphalian system. At first, European conquerors exercised extravagant claims to dominion over the lands of the Americas and their Native peoples.[16] In most cases, conquest by decree proved untenable, and the structures of interaction between settlers and Natives came to be guided by sets of customary norms that borrowed from both European and indigenous systems of diplomacy. Likewise, as settler polities expanded in both size and number, their relationships with metropolitan authorities evolved into hybrids of established forms of governance particular to each state, and new customs, laws, and institutions were devised to govern transatlantic empires.[17] Together, the structures and norms that guided metropolitan, settler, and indigenous polities resembled the Westphalian system, but deviated from it in significant ways. On the North American borderlands, political structures remained emergent and inchoate, and systemic norms were polyglot and contingent.[18]

Ultimately, the North American borderlands were incorporated into the Westphalian system. This occurred not through the rationalization of the inchoate borderlands diplomatic regime, but via the construction of a subsystem of Westphalian-style states on the borderlands. With their 1776 Declaration of Independence, the new United States began to constitute what the political scientist Daniel Deudney has labeled the "Philadelphian system." The American union was the vehicle through which the self-proclaimed sovereign American states sought full and unconditional membership in the Westphalian system. At the same time, the norms of the new American states subsystem (or "states-union," in Deudney's phraseology) were consciously modeled to limit the tendency toward absolutism embedded in the larger Westphalian system. Somewhat ironically, the new American Constitution of 1787, in reorganizing the American union to give its members power and legitimacy in diplomatic negotiation, ultimately served to undermine the existing structures and norms of North American borderlands diplomacy. Within the British Empire, North American settlers had to deal with American Indian communities within the norms of the borderlands diplomacy and thus acknowledge, at least in part, Indian sovereignty and Indian interests. As the American union organized, centralized, and consolidated power during and after the American Revolution, Indian interests were marginalized and ignored, while Indian polities were either reduced to dependency or conquered outright. The evolution of colonial settler polities into something approaching a nation-state and the transit of this new entity (the United States) into the Westphalian system came, in large part, at the expense of the ability of North America's indigenous peoples to engage the wider world on a firm, secure, and sovereign footing.

Thus, as much as this book is about how the United States of America came to be, it is also about how many of the powerful and independent American Indian nations of eastern North America came to be much less than they once had been. The changing structures of power through which the American union, the Indian nations, and the European empires engaged one another permitted the triumph of a set of norms that downplayed and then denied the sovereignty of the Indian nations. It was this geopolitical transformation of North America, put into motion by the American Revolution, that set the stage for the vast dispossessions and removals of the Age of Jackson and beyond.[19] With the United States government's suzerainty over the bulk of the North American interior confirmed by treaty between 1815 and 1825, American Indian nations lost the ability to appeal to the aid of any European powers. Their ability to play European powers off of one another, already diminishing before the War of 1812, was now at the end. Chief Justice John Marshall confirmed what was already obvious when he labeled the American Indian polities "domestic dependent nations" in the landmark 1831 case *Cherokee Nation v. Georgia*, the discussion of which concludes this book.[20] Whereas the United States had once sought confirmation of its claims to sovereignty from Indian nations in the 1770s, by the 1830s the American government unilaterally dictated that the Indian nations were not all that sovereign after all. Given that the American Revolution had its origins in an argument over the extent of the sovereign powers of the American colonies, the fact that the full achievement of American sovereignty came at the expense of that of other nations is no small irony.

Revolutionary Negotiations tells this story in chapters that revolve around particular problems in political culture and political thought—problems whose explication helps unfold the larger narrative of the formation of the United States of America in the international context. The prologue, "The Cherokee Emperor," sets our baseline, by using the journey of a minor Scots nobleman named Alexander Cuming to illustrate the fluid and inchoate nature of polity relations in the early eighteenth-century Atlantic system. With no formal commission to negotiate an Indian treaty, Cuming arrived in South Carolina in late 1729, and months later led a small party in the Cherokee nation, where he designated one village leader, Moitoi of Tellico, to be "Emperor of the Cherokees," and then led a delegation of Cherokee warriors and leaders to London to negotiate a treaty. That an unofficial (and somewhat disreputable) figure like Cuming could play such a role in the relationship between a colony and an Indian nation is revealing.

Chapter 1, "'In the Nature of Ambassadors': North American Diplomacy within the British Empire," explores the attempts of some British North Americans to come to terms with the fluid structures and competing sets of norms that guided polity relations within and beyond the British Empire on the North American borderlands during the middle decades of the eighteenth century. A small group of writers and politicians known retrospectively as imperial reformers sought to describe and then change the relationship between the metropolitan government, the colonial provinces, and the Indian nations that bordered the British Empire in North America. Their vision was comprehensive and complicated—and it ultimately failed. The roots of this failure were numerous, but its culmination was the Imperial Crisis that ultimately led to the Thirteen Colonies seeking independence from the British Empire.

Chapter 2, "'In an Odd State': The American Decision to Leave the British Empire," charts the period between the spring of 1775 and the summer of 1776, as the American Continental Congress began to assume and accumulate the powers held by a sovereign state, the culmination of which was the Declaration of Independence of July 1776. This gradual accumulation of sovereign power occurred with an eye toward the Westphalian system, but also with an acknowledgment that the new American union was, in many ways, a states system unto itself. The Revolutionary leadership first imagined their colonial provinces as potential independent polities in order to gain leverage within the British Empire. However, the Continental Congress soon began to accrue, both consciously and unconsciously, the attributes of a sovereign government. In this retelling of the story of the run-up to the Declaration of Independence, the Declaration emerges as one step in an ongoing process of the Thirteen Colonies transitioning to sovereign status within the Westphalian system, rather than a momentous, sharp, and sudden break from the past.

Chapter 3, "'Are We Not . . . Independant States?': Imagining and Realizing an Independent America," describes that second part of the United States' transition from the Atlantic system and the British Empire into the Westphalian states system—the quest for recognition by other powers of the American states' sovereign status. Like the proverbial tree falling in the forest that requires a listener in order to make a sound, the United States needed a great power to recognize its independence in order to truly enter the community of sovereign states. This recognition ultimately came in February 1778 from the Kingdom of France. The reality of the Treaty of Alliance with France allowed the Congress to resist and reject the bold proposals of reconciliation put forward on behalf on the North ministry by the peace commission headed by the Earl of Carlisle. Yet once the Peace of Paris was concluded in 1783, the diplomats of the United States found their dreams for open commerce with the nations of Europe frustrated by the realities of interest-based geopolitical and geoeconomic calculations by the governments of the Great Powers.

Chapter 4, "'Rendering Us Great and Respectable in the Eyes of the World': The Diplomatic Imperative for the Federal Constitution," demonstrates how frustrations with the Continental Congress's inability to conduct meaningful diplomacy throughout the 1780s gave rise to a diplomatic imperative for reforming the Articles of Confederation and ratifying the resulting federal Constitution of 1787. Congress had difficulty negotiating with the Indian nations within its borders and difficulty keeping the individual states from negotiating with these Indian nations as well. To the east, in Europe, matters were even worse. Europe's great Atlantic powers—France, Great Britain, and Spain—either refused to negotiate commercial treaties with the Americans or offered to do so under the most exploitive and humiliating conditions. The need for a strong, central, superintending authority to stand behind American diplomats as they attempted to negotiate, both in European courts and in Native American council houses, became a major selling point for the Constitution that emerged from the Philadelphia Convention in September 1787.

Chapter 5, "'To Be Considered as Foreign Nations:' The Ambiguous Triumph of Federalist Statecraft," shows how the new diplomatic dispensation evolved in the 1790s. American political elites generally favored centralization in the Philadelphian system in order to allow the United States to better negotiate in Europe's Westphalian states system and in what remained of the borderlands diplomatic regime in North America. The actions of the First Congress of the United States illuminate the existence of a national consensus in the area of diplomatic powers. Led by James Madison, the Congress passed the Foreign Affairs Bill, which conceded most diplomatic powers to the executive branch, a development the secretary of state, Madison's friend Thomas Jefferson, wholeheartedly endorsed. As the Federalist policies of Alexander Hamilton and Henry Knox threatened constitutional balances within the federal union, and also seemed to tie the United States too closely to Britain, the Jeffersonian Republicans pushed back, arguing for a stricter construction of diplomatic powers. By the time of the negotiation of the Treaty of Colerain with the Creek Indians in 1796, the Jeffersonian Republican opposition party saw a nefarious design contained within Federalist statecraft. When, in the Republican mind, the Federalists attempted to turn another diplomatic crisis (the XYZ Affair and resulting Quasi-War with France) into an unconstitutional power grab (the Alien and Sedition Acts), the logical response was a recalibration of the balances of sovereign power within the federal union—the so-called "Principles of '98," embodied in the Kentucky and Virginia Resolutions. Ironically, once in power, the Jeffersonians were generally unwilling to give back the centralized diplomatic apparatus the Federalists had created.

Chapter 6, "Enlarging 'Our Association': The Triumph of the Diplomacy of Conquest," demonstrates how full acceptance of the United States into the European-centered states system came at the expense of the American Indian nations' even piecemeal participation in that system. During Jefferson's presidency, American producers and consumers continued to depend on access to European (and European colonial) markets. As the United States' ability to leverage the European conflict between Britain and

France to its own advantage diminished in the aftermath of the collapse of the Peace of Amiens, the Jeffersonian Republicans redeployed the power of the federal state to ensure that the geopolitical situation in North America would not threaten the survival of the United States. Jefferson and Madison negotiated dozens of treaties with Indian nations in eastern North America and the Mississippi Valley, securing access to strategically important waterways, but also adding vast tracts of land to the national domain that could be turned into new settler states when the time was right. The consumption of Indian land would go hand in hand with the consumption of European goods, and American diplomacy would be devoted to promoting and protecting white Americans' ability to engage in each. The war that erupted during Madison's presidency—the War of 1812 (1812–15)—was fought to preserve both modes of consumption. At the negotiating table in Ghent, Belgium, and on the battlefields of the American South, both John Quincy Adams and Andrew Jackson sought to limit the power of American Indian nations while preserving the United States' access to Atlantic markets.

Finally, the epilogue, "The Cherokee Lawyer," offers a reading of the condition of the states system in North America as the Era of the American Revolution drew to a close. Using William Wirt as a counterpoint to Alexander Cuming, I conclude that, in the "Age of Jackson," conditions were quite different from what they had been a century before. Indeed, nothing really captures the fundamental nature of the changed geopolitical dynamic in North America better than a simple observation—in order to protect their interests vis-à-vis their neighbors in 1730, the Cherokee nation sent diplomats to London to negotiate a treaty with King George II and the Board of Trade; in 1830, the Cherokee nation hired a lawyer to plead their case before the Supreme Court of the United States. Ironically, William Wirt was everything Alexander Cuming was not. A former attorney general of the United States, Wirt was one of the most accomplished lawyers in America, and brought the Cherokee cause honor, integrity, and prestige, as well as legal skill and intelligence. And it was not enough. By 1830, with the United States growing stronger every day, the shape of polity relations in North America was utterly different from what it had been a century before. Where there had been access, negotiation, and dialogue for American Indian nations dealing with settler polities, now there was little but subordination, subjection, and the unfettered sovereignty of the United States of America.

Prologue

The Cherokee Emperor

Our story begins, fittingly (as this is a book about America), with a dream. During the summer of 1729, the wife of a minor Scots nobleman named Sir Alexander Cuming awoke to inform her husband that she had dreamt he was to travel across the Atlantic Ocean and into the American wilderness, where he would find fame and fortune. Interpreting the Lady Cuming's dream as a call to action, Sir Alexander boarded a ship and left England in the middle of September 1729, arriving at the port of Charles Town, South Carolina, on 6 December. Almost from the moment he arrived in Carolina, Cuming acted equal parts aristocrat, military adventurer, and confidence man. He set about on a course of action that disrupted life in the province of South Carolina and transformed the internal and external politics of the neighboring Cherokee nation. Within five months, Cuming would become a leading financier for the colony, float his own currency, and then march into the Cherokee country, where he would (without any formal authority to do so) christen one Cherokee village chief the "Emperor of the Cherokees," dramatically reshaping South Carolina's—and the British Empire's—relations with the Cherokee Indians. While Cuming's voyage was precipitous and his conduct audacious, the forces and structures that gave rise to this adventure are far less mysterious than a spouse's dream.[1]

For the better part of a decade before he disembarked in Charles Town, Cuming had been thinking about the expanding British Empire on the western side of the Atlantic. While he would later record that it was during the early decades of the eighteenth century that he and others became familiar with the writings of various imperial promoters, which had "so

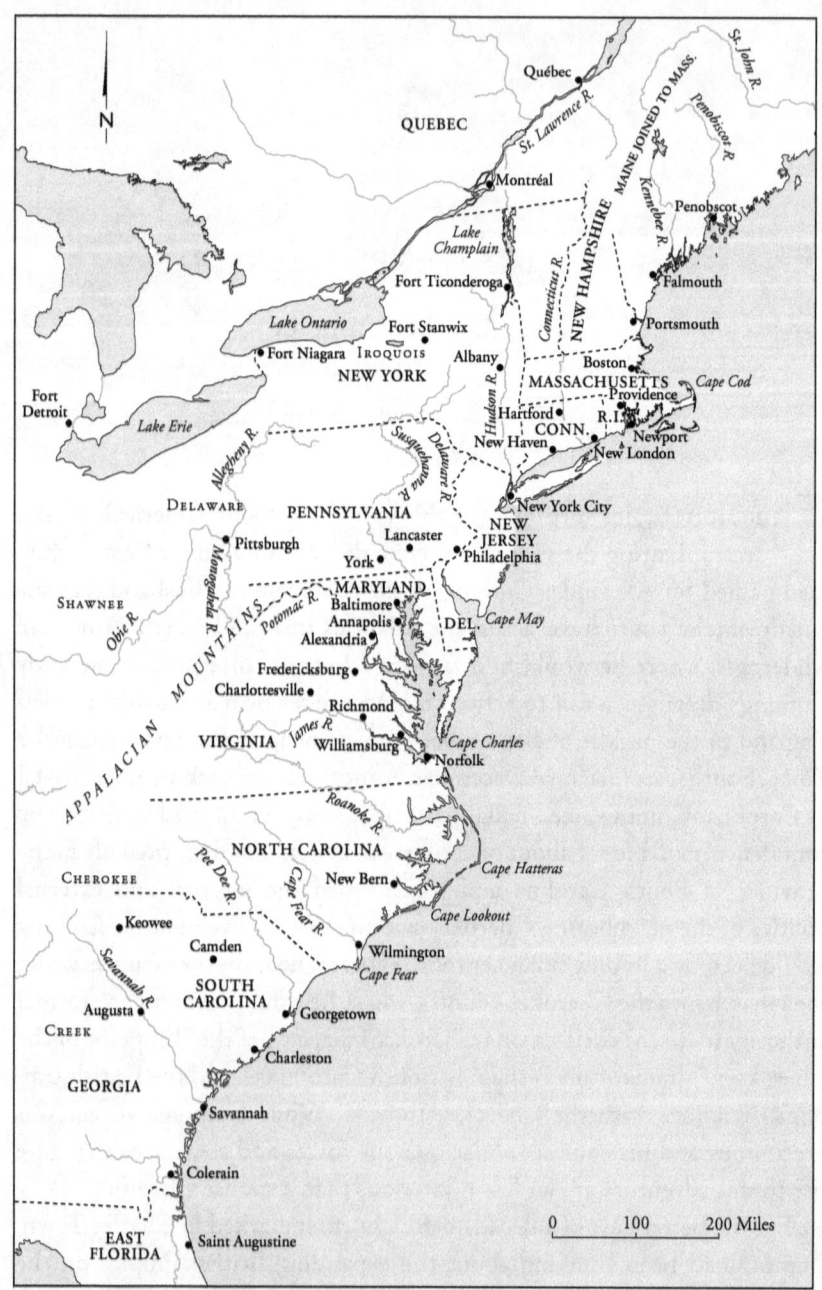

British North America in the Mid-Eighteenth Century

Prologue

The Cherokee Emperor

Our story begins, fittingly (as this is a book about America), with a dream. During the summer of 1729, the wife of a minor Scots nobleman named Sir Alexander Cuming awoke to inform her husband that she had dreamt he was to travel across the Atlantic Ocean and into the American wilderness, where he would find fame and fortune. Interpreting the Lady Cuming's dream as a call to action, Sir Alexander boarded a ship and left England in the middle of September 1729, arriving at the port of Charles Town, South Carolina, on 6 December. Almost from the moment he arrived in Carolina, Cuming acted equal parts aristocrat, military adventurer, and confidence man. He set about on a course of action that disrupted life in the province of South Carolina and transformed the internal and external politics of the neighboring Cherokee nation. Within five months, Cuming would become a leading financier for the colony, float his own currency, and then march into the Cherokee country, where he would (without any formal authority to do so) christen one Cherokee village chief the "Emperor of the Cherokees," dramatically reshaping South Carolina's—and the British Empire's—relations with the Cherokee Indians. While Cuming's voyage was precipitous and his conduct audacious, the forces and structures that gave rise to this adventure are far less mysterious than a spouse's dream.[1]

For the better part of a decade before he disembarked in Charles Town, Cuming had been thinking about the expanding British Empire on the western side of the Atlantic. While he would later record that it was during the early decades of the eighteenth century that he and others became familiar with the writings of various imperial promoters, which had "so

British North America in the Mid-Eighteenth Century

intoxicating an effect as to create an epidemical disaster which seemed to turn all the heads of Europe" in search of empire and wealth, his nation's empire was over a century old. Begun as the outgrowth of the activities of a handful of privateers and military adventurers during the reign of Elizabeth I, by Cuming's time the American empire controlled by England embraced nearly two dozen colonial provinces and outposts, stretching from the Grand Banks through the eastern seaboard of North America, to the islands of Caribbean. The 1707 Act of Union with Scotland transformed this realm into a truly British Empire, and opened the door to Scots like Cuming to participate in the enterprise of empire building and the risks and rewards that went with it. Thus a portion of his family's fortune had been lost in the 1720 financial collapse known as the South Sea Bubble. But Sir Alexander's desire to profit from the Empire was not sated. In 1725, after the death of his father and his accession to the baronetcy, he began to throw himself into schemes designed to further the British imperial project and augment his own personal fortune. Evincing an early interest in America's indigenous peoples, Cuming attached himself to a plan to establish a college on the island of Bermuda in order to educate American Indians. In short order, Sir Alexander offered himself as the logical choice for the governorship of Bermuda, and his name was backed by a number of noblemen. Yet despite their numerous petitions, no office was forthcoming, even after the accession of George II in 1727. By the time of his wife's dream in 1729, Cuming was still without a place. His voyage to South Carolina, whether the product of a dream or not, is thus more understandable as the act of a frustrated office-seeker who had long imagined finding new wealth in America, and who then (perhaps spurred on by an impatient spouse) finally took matters into his own hands. Of course, while Cuming was in many respects typical, his conduct upon arriving South Carolina was anything but.[2]

Traveling from Britain to South Carolina was one matter, but Cuming's ability to manipulate both local Carolina elites and the bulk of the Cherokee Indian nation with little besides the force of his own will was something else entirely. While in some respects the confidence man is a timeless figure, much of Sir Alexander Cuming's story could only have unfolded in the early eighteenth-century British Atlantic world. Although his confidence game was fairly exceptional, his rampant boundary crossing was far from uncommon in the decades abutting the great wars for empire in the middle of the eighteenth century.³ Alexander Cuming could cross seamlessly from Scotland to London to South Carolina to the Cherokee nation because, during the middle decades of the eighteenth century, the borders between the world of American Indian peoples, the world of British American settlers, and the world of the imperial metropolis in Great Britain were fluid ones. Early modern empires were held together through processes of negotiation between authorities and subject peoples, and political improvisation (even the disingenuous sort practiced by Cuming) was a frequent occurrence.⁴ And in a world in which communication was slow and inconstant and in which diverse cultures lived alongside one another, misunderstandings and misrepresentations, both intentional and unintentional, were the order of the day. It was for all these reasons that the historian Richard White eschewed the term "frontier" and christened the space where European empires and Native American communities came together as the "middle ground."⁵ But Cuming's story also reminds us that the borderlands were not a melting pot. Even at this moment there were stark lines separating these three worlds, and in some respects boundaries were sharpening rather than diffusing. In South Carolina of 1729–30, we can see British Americans and American Indians inhabiting an intercultural world at the same time we can see Britons, Americans, and Indians willing to commit unspeakable acts of violence against one another. Throughout the centuries-long project of colonization and empire building in the Americas, Europeans like Cuming retained a willingness to impose their own political forms on indigenous peoples and communities of which they had only the most cursory understanding. Only reality stood in the way of such schemes—and in the early eighteenth century, this reality was that in the affairs between metropolitan, settler, and indigenous communities, domination took a backseat to negotiation. A century later, the opposite would be the case: European-descended peoples would assert dominion over the Cherokee, and meaningful negotiation would be mostly a memory. But that is getting ahead of the story. There was chaos enough on the southeastern borderlands at the end of the 1720s.

In sailing to South Carolina, Alexander Cuming found ground ripe for sowing mischief. From its founding as a proprietary colony in 1670 through Cuming's arrival in 1729, South Carolina's interactions with its American

Indian neighbors had been a constant but uneasy part of life in the province. Before embracing rice cultivation and the widespread use of enslaved African labor that would, by the middle of the eighteenth century, make South Carolina's white master class the wealthiest in British North America, the early Carolina settlers (both white and black) subsisted modestly. The émigrés from Barbados and the British Isles developed a mixed economy based on cereal agriculture and livestock ranching. They also turned to the nearby American Indian communities for trade; imported English manufactured goods and liquor were exchanged for deerskins and other peltry. South Carolina's traders expanded the Indian slave trade, as they acquired individual captives from their near Indian neighbors.[6] However, most of the nearby Native communities had better-established trading links with the English colony of Virginia to the north, the Spanish colony of Florida to the south, or even the upstart French colony of Louisiana to the west. The traders of South Carolina found themselves in stiff competition with their neighboring European settlers for the commerce of neighboring Indian communities such as the Yamasee, Catawba, Savannah, and the Creek. After several decades of commerce and conflict, South Carolina's traders did finally manage to carve out a niche in the Indian trade for themselves, but the persistence of a variety of tensions led to a destructive conflict, the Yamasee War of 1715–17.[7]

The Yamasee War set the stage for Alexander Cuming's subsequent adventures by devastating the economy and infrastructure of South Carolina and cementing the province's alliance with the Cherokee nation. After years of unfair treatment at the hands of Carolina traders, the Yamasee Indians, along with their allies, the Catawbas, Choctaws, and the Lower Creeks, launched a series of raids against South Carolina's settlements, beginning in April 1715. After a Carolina counterattack put the enemy Indians on their heels, they still refused to treat for peace with the Carolina government. Governor Charles Craven turned to South Carolina's distant allies, the Cherokee Indians, with whom he had concluded a treaty of alliance in August 1715. An expedition from Carolina to the Cherokee country defeated an attempt by the Creek Indians to win the Cherokee to their side. With Cherokee intervention, the situation for the Yamasee and their allies became hopeless, and one by one, the belligerent nations concluded treaties with South Carolina over the course of the next year.[8] Two years of warfare had disrupted the colony's agriculture and forced the government into debt. Prolonged financial instability prompted the bulk of the white settlers to turn against the Lord Proprietors (the officers who managed the colony per its corporate charter) in 1719 and seek to become a Crown Colony. While the Crown appointed a temporary royal governor, formal negotiations to sell the colony's charter to the British government were not completed until 1729, and the sale was not confirmed by Parliament until 1730. The new royal governor, Robert Johnson, would not take charge until 1731. In the interim, local government in South Carolina had virtually collapsed. South Carolina's public treasury was bankrupt by 1730. Between 1727 and 1731, the South Carolina Assembly did not raise any taxes. During this same time period, the provincial treasurer, Alexander Parris, collected import duties and other fees, but used all of this money to pay off his personal debts. (When Johnson took office, Parris owed the colony £40,000.) It was into this anarchic world that Sir Alexander Cuming arrived.[9]

Soon after Cuming's ship landed at Charles Town harbor in early December 1729, he began to insinuate himself into the moribund financial life of the province. Sir Alexander immediately advertised (and likely embellished) his aristocratic pedigree and his land holdings back in Great Britain. Cuming began to issue bills of credit in his own name. He made sure to pay off any notes that were redeemed immediately. Given the state of public finances in South Carolina at the time, Cuming's reputation soared. The scale of Cuming's enterprise grew during the winter of 1729–30, as he set up his own loan office and issued "great Quantities of his Notes, and emitted them upon Loan at 10 per cent Interest." Cuming exchanged his handwritten notes for real agricultural produce and specie; he shipped the produce back to Britain for a profit and held the specie himself. (The total amount of specie was later estimated at £1,500 sterling.) He also made a show of purchasing several plantations, and "built a Stone House with Walls three foot thick, and strong Doors and Windows which he called his Treasury." (A search of the "Treasury" following Cuming's departure from Carolina would reveal it to be totally empty, except for "some empty Boxes, old Iron, and other Rubbish.") Within a few months, Cuming had cunningly established himself as a major player in the chaotic mercantile and financial situation of South Carolina. Then, in March 1730, he turned his attention westward toward the Cherokee nation.[10]

By the winter of 1729–30, the situation of South Carolina's borderlands had become unsettled once more. After the Yamasee War, the diplomacy of the colony's Indian agent, George Chicken, had established a framework for coexistence between the Carolinians, Creeks, and Cherokee, but tensions between the Indian communities and the Carolina settlers and traders had never truly abated. Cuming himself noted that most of the province's traders had grown nervous by the early months of 1730. "It was given out in the English Settlements that the Indians would rise in the Spring, so that the Traders would not venture to return again among them for fear of being murder'd," he recorded in his public journal. Cuming also learned from local informants of the potential for French encroachments into the region "by building Forts in the Creek nation for several Years past," and by sending agents into the Cherokee country "to seduce the Lower Cherokees to their Interest." While Cuming eventually presented himself as attempting to solidify South Carolina's trade with the Cherokee and thus halt French expansion into the British sphere of influence, whether this was the intent of his mission from its outset is unclear.[11] Citing his membership in the Royal Society, Cuming told the traders who escorted him that "he had no Errand but to see the Country."[12] Cuming and a small party of traders left Charles Town on 13 March 1730, and ten days later they arrived at Keowee, the closest of the Lower Towns to South Carolina. It was in Keowee that Cuming began his program of ersatz diplomacy.[13]

In Keowee, Cuming would have seen the intercultural structures of a borderlands community formed by Carolina traders and Cherokees living alongside one another. Whether he understood them is another matter—he certainly paid little attention to established customs of interaction between the Carolinians and the Cherokee. Decades later, one of those Carolina traders, Ludovick Grant, recalled the scene of Cuming's arrival in Keowee. An established trader, Grant then resided in Great Tellico (on the western slope of the Appalachians in the Overhill Towns), and was passing through Keowee on a return trip from Charles Town when he encountered Cuming's party. "We dined that day all together at the house of Joseph Baker Trader in Keowee," Grant remembered, "and at dinner some of the Traders mentioned, that these Indians was not in the best disposition." Cuming recorded that "Mr. Barker, a Trader," informed him "that last February there had been messengers from the lower Creeks" bearing offers of joining "the French interest" in exchange for "Presents." According to Cuming, Barker "expected that the Lower Cherokees would rise." (It is probable, but not certain, that

"Baker" and "Barker" were the same man.) With that warning forwarded, Cuming and the traders made their way through Keowee: "At night Wee went to the Town house where all the Indians men & women met every night when They are not out hunting even the Headmen go there to partake of the diversion." The town house was the large building located at the center of each Cherokee town. Capable of holding every member of a town within its seven-sided walls, the town house (or council house) was the center of each Cherokee town's political and cultural life, a place in which the non-Cherokee were expected to tread lightly. Not Sir Alexander Cuming. He marched into the Keowee town house carrying a gun and wearing two pistols and a cutlass. This was "a Circumstance pretty Extraordinary," Grant remembered. One did not go armed into a Cherokee town house, and the traders who accompanied Cuming told him "that the Indians never came there armed, and did not like that any should." Yet, the fully armed Cuming and his party now stood inside the Keowee town house, "where above 300 Indians were assembled." Through an interpreter, Cuming now laid down the gauntlet to the Cherokee.[14]

Alexander Cuming brazenly demanded a public oath of loyalty to King George II from the leaders of Keowee, a demand he would make to many other Cherokee leaders during the course of the next weeks. Cuming was careful to acknowledge that he acted without royal authority—Grant noted that he said "he was one of the Great King Georges Children but was not sent either by the Great King or any of his Governors—that he was no public person." Likely, the small arsenal that Cuming wore gave him enough "authority" in the minds of those he addressed. According to Grant, Cuming announced inside the town house "that he would Drink the King's health hoping that all persons would pledge him which he accordingly did upon his knee desiring us to follow his Example and Wee Desired the Indians to do so." Cuming's own account of the oath-taking omitted the role of drink in the process. He wrote that "he engaged the head Warriors to acknowledge his Majesty King George's Sovereignty over them on their Knee, and that they would obey him in every Thing; and that if they violated his Promise, they would become no People." When the leading men of Keowee acknowledged "King George's Sovereignty," Cuming then, according to his own record, "ordered Expresses immediately to be dispatched thro' the whole Cherokee Nation," directing that leaders "with full Powers" from the "upper Settlements," "middle Settlements," and "lower

Settlements" meet with him at Naquasse (in the Middle Towns) on 3 April. Cuming was so impressed with what he accomplished that he had all of the Carolina traders sign an affidavit swearing to the truth of what they had seen and heard. Cuming's "success" also generated a bit of smugness on his part. According to Grant, when his performance was complete, "Sir Alexander said it was easy to make them all good Subjects."[15]

While Cuming could attribute his diplomatic achievement to his bearing and persuasion, both his own account and Ludovick Grant's testify to the extent to which the threat of violence hung over the proceedings that night in Keowee. Cuming stressed his own prowess and audaciousness as the key to avoiding violence. He wrote that the traders who were with him "declared that what they heard and saw done that Night, was a thing itself so incredible, that they would not have believed it possible." Cuming's interpreter, the trader Joseph Cooper, said "that if he had known before hand what Sir Alexander would have order'd him to have said, he would not have ventured in the Town-House to have been the interpreter, . . . believing that none of them could have gone out of the Town-House without being murdered, considering how jealous that People had always been of their Liberties." Ludovick Grant was even more alarmed. He later testified that Cuming had "a Wild look" about him, and that he said "that his intention was if any of the Indians had refused the King's health [he would] have taken a brand out of the fire that Burns in the middle of the room and have set fire to the house," and that he then "would have guarded the door himself and put to death every one that endeavored to make their Escape that they might be consumed to ashes." Where Cuming imagined his unorthodox course of action had won him respect, Grant remembered that Cuming's conduct had caused the traders to view him as somewhat less than stable; many chose to remain in Keowee rather than follow Cuming deeper into the Cherokee nation.[16]

Grant escorted Cuming over the spine of the Appalachians to the town of Tellico in the Overhill Towns, where he then resided as a trader. It was at Tellico, in the shadow of "a great many Enemies Scalps, brought in and put upon Poles at the Warriors Doors," where Cuming "made a friend of the great Moytoy." According to Cuming, it was here that Moitoi confided to him "that it was talked among the several Towns last Year, that they intended to make him Emperor over the Whole; but that now it must be whatever Sir Alexander pleased." It is difficult to know what to make of this claim. The politics of the Cherokee nation did not provide a place for an "emperor," or anything resembling such an office. One possibility is that Cuming's interpreter mistranslated what Moitoi said, or that Cuming himself misrepresented what was said in his written account of the encounter. Another possibility is that Moitoi seized on Cuming's arrival to advance the interests of his town and himself. Neither of these possibilities is mutually exclusive, and even through the dark glass of the limited documentary record, we can see in outline form the actions of two men (Cuming and Moitoi) seizing on the inherent ambiguity of the moment of encounter to advance their own interests.[17]

Historians tend to interpret Moitoi's claim (and eventual acceptance) of the title of "emperor" as a product of a long-standing rivalry within the Overhill Towns between Tellico and Chota. With the establishment of Fort Toulouse by French authorities in the Creek country in 1717, and the gradual expansion of Carolina's trade with the Cherokee during the 1720s, the Overhill Towns were moving out of the far periphery and into the regular orbit of transatlantic commerce. The answer to the question of which of the Overhill Towns would be preeminent in dealing with European political and commercial agents would be of material and not just moral and spiritual interest. The sudden appearance of Alexander Cuming was an opportunity an ambitious war leader like Moitoi was not going to let pass by.[18] Whatever Moitoi's motivations, his claim of the title "emperor" also reveals much about Alexander Cuming. At this point in his journey, Cuming, through a combination of both deliberate conduct and accident, had begun to accrue a measure of prestige (or at least respect) in the eyes of some Cherokee; he was now imagined by town leaders like Moitoi to be a power broker of some sort. This was certainly an image he tried both to prepare himself for and to cultivate. Grant remembered that Cuming displayed an interest in learning about Cherokee political ceremony, and he was particularly fascinated with the crown (which "resembles a wig and is made of Possum's hair Dyed Red or Yellow") that Cherokee village leaders wore. Cuming's research yielded fruits, as Grant noted that "Sir Alexander had been informed of all the Ceremonies that are used in making a head beloved man, of which there are a great many in this nation." Cuming was also careful to note the name of every Cherokee he met and shook hands with: "Sir Alexander would take his name down in his pocket book saying that he had made a friend of him." Cuming was thus gathering knowledge about Cherokee politics that would allow him to play the role of power broker at Naquasse, and a compiling a written record of accomplishment that would give him standing at Charles Town and, most importantly, at London.[19]

The events that transpired between Cuming's meeting with Moitoi at Tellico and his arrival at Naquasse testify to the extent to which the two men hitched their fortunes to one another. The day after they met, Moitoi and another Tellico beloved man, Jacob the Conjurer, signaled their approbation of Sir Alexander. On the night of 30 March in Great Tellico, Cuming "was particularly distinguished in the Town-House by Moytoy, where the Indians sung Songs, danced, and stroaked his Head and Body over with Eagles Tails; after this a Consultation was held with Moytoy and Jacob the Conjurer, who determined to present him with the Crown of Tannassy."[20]

When Cuming left Tellico the next morning, both Moitoi and Jacob the Conjurer went with him. After two days' travel, they arrived at Tasetche, in the Valley Towns. According to Cuming's account, "Here the two head Men [Moitoi and Jacob the Conjurer], together with the Conjurer of the Place, declared in a private Conference their Agreement to what Moytoy had before resolved, in Relation to the Crown of Tannassy, as an Emblem of universal Sovereignty over the whole Cherokee nation." Again, Cuming's account is difficult to read. Certainly, town head men wore such "crowns" as markers of their positions of authority, but the notion that a single crown could convey the "universal Sovereignty" of all of the Cherokee towns was a novel interpretation, to say the least. Yet, with Moitoi in tow (or vice versa?), Cuming could win support for the assertion that the crown he now carried, in concert with his status as a British gentleman, gave him authority to mediate the relationship between the Cherokee nation and the distant British government. In this way, Cuming's embrace of Moitoi, and Moitoi's embrace of Cuming were mutually reinforcing acts of legitimation. Moitoi provided evidence that Cuming had mastered Cherokee politics, and when Cuming crowned Moitoi "emperor" at Naquasse, he gave the Tellico headman the imprimatur of (seemingly) being the Briton's chosen beloved man.[21]

Cuming's party arrived in Naquasse for the recently called meeting of many Cherokee leaders on 3 April 1730. Before arriving at Naquasse, Cuming had encountered a number of Carolina traders, including George Chicken, all of whom accompanied him to his congress with the Cherokee.

In his journal, Cuming called the festivities of 3 April "a Day of Solemnity the greatest that ever was seen in the Country," although where he derived the knowledge to justify his superlative is unclear. Certainly, what transpired was unprecedented, at least in Cherokee history. In addition to "Singing, Dancing, Feasting," and the "making of Speeches," the day also saw "the Creation of Moytoy Emperor." The coronation of Moitoi occurred

> with the unanimous Consent of all the head Men assembled from the different Towns of the Nation, a Declaration of their resigning their Crown, Eagles Tails, Scalps of their Enemies, as an emblem of their owning his Majesty King George's Sovereignty over them, at the Desire of Sir Alexander Cuming, in whom an absolute unlimited Power was placed, without which he could not be able to answer to his Majesty for their Conduct. The Declaration of Obedience was made on their Knees, in Order to intimate, that a Violation of their Promise made in so solemn a Manner, would be sufficient to make them no People.

In a conclusion to the ceremonies the next day, Cuming asked six "Chiefs" to meet him at Charles Town on 20 April, and travel with him to England to meet with the king. Six Cherokee delegates journeyed to Charles Town, and Cuming and the Cherokees departed at the end of the month. (The party included only one town headman, as well as a young warrior named Okoonaka, who would later be known as Attakullakulla, and as one of the beloved men of Chota would be a major player in Cherokee-British relations at midcentury.)[22]

The language Cuming chose to record his simultaneous deputization and empowerment is most interesting. The creation of a Cherokee "emperor," an embodiment of the singular sovereignty of the Cherokee nation, itself something entirely new and novel, only came with the simultaneous cession of Cherokee sovereignty to the king of Great Britain. Cuming had succeeded in getting the Cherokee headmen to give over to him what he believed they believed were markers of sovereign power and status—crowns, eagle feathers, trophies of war (enemy scalps)—to bring back to Britain. Only one crowned head, that of King George II, would rule the Cherokee now. Cuming also described his role as mediator in a way ("absolute unlimited Power") that reinforced the position of subjection to which the Cherokees were ostensibly agreeing in order to have the position of their new "emperor" confirmed. And the penalty for disobeying the new compact—that they would become "no People"—carried apocalyptic (if not genocidal) connotations. It is safe to assume that neither Moitoi nor any of the other Cherokee beloved men at the Naquasse congress believed they were reducing themselves to a status of subjection that Cuming's language described. Indeed, the treaty that the Cherokee leaders who went to London with Cuming in September 1730 eventually signed eschewed such totalizing language, describing "the Great King and the Cherokee Indians" being "fastn'd together by the Chain of Friendship."[23]

Arriving in Great Britain in June, the Cherokee delegation ultimately spent four months in the British capital. While the Cherokee delegation would be feted across London during their months in the capital, their appearance touched off a minor crisis among British policymakers. Upon arrival, Cuming himself dispatched a letter to the secretary of state for the Southern Department, Thomas Pelham-Holles, Duke of Newcastle, explaining what he had done and why he had brought this group of Cherokees to the capital. While the secretary of state for the Southern Department was the British cabinet minister charged with managing affairs in the American colonies, correspondence with the colonies and details of their administration were managed by a separate body known as the Board of Trade (formally, the Lords Commissioners for Trade and Plantations). It was the Board of Trade's advice that both the Duke of Newcastle and George II took when dealing with Cuming and the Cherokees; Cuming was ultimately marginalized.[24]

In advising Newcastle, the Board of Trade essentially sought to take advantage of circumstance—as Cuming had acted without sanction, no one in the current ministry had planned a new treaty with the Cherokees. The Board of Trade certainly felt now that the Cherokee delegation had arrived in London, they could not be sent home empty-handed. "For to return home again after so Solemn an Embassy without doing any thing of this sort, far from encreasing, would Weaken the Friendship at present subsisting between His Majesty's Subjects and these People," the board explained to Newcastle. To not conclude some kind of formal agreement would prove to be an embarrassment to the British and Cherokee alike.[25]

The Board of Trade's language in describing the importance and operation of such a treaty reflected the dual nature of the British (and by extension, all European imperial powers') relationship with all Native polities.

The Indian nations on the empire's borderlands were a vital part of the system of imperial defense and commerce, and like the provinces, they were, at least in name, dependents on the Crown. Yet at the same time the relations with American Indian communities were somehow different from the British metropole's other political relationships in America as well as being different with relations beyond the empire. The Board of Trade first reminded Newcastle of the alliance between the province of New York and the neighboring Iroquois Five Nations, saying, "It may be truly be said they are our Frontier Guards there, always ready to defend our Out Settlements and to make War upon any other Nation whenever we require them to do so." The alliance with the Iroquois was thus the model. "We conceive it is at present in our Power to put the Cherikees upon the same footing," the board offered, noting "certainly it would be of great Advantage to do so because they are a Warlike People and can bring three Thousand fighting Men upon Occasion into the Field." The officers of the Board of Trade here betrayed both knowledge and ignorance of the reality on the ground in North America. The alliance between the Iroquois and the British was indeed vital to the security and commercial interests of both New York (and to a lesser extent, many other northern colonies) and the Iroquois. Yet, the Board of Trade blithely assumed that the political structure of the Cherokee nation could be accommodated to a similar role vis-à-vis South Carolina as that existing between New York and the Iroquois Five Nations, when in fact the political structures that bound the different Native polities together were quite different (the Iroquois had a far more structured and formalized system of political confederation than the Cherokee did). The Board of Trade's prejudices and assumptions became clearer as they closed their letter to Newcastle, informing him that the formalities normally attendant to treaty negotiations could be superseded: "As this Treaty is to be only with Savages, we presume His Majesty's Orders signifyed to us by your Grace in a Letter, may be a sufficient Power for Us to act by on this Occasion."[26]

The treaty concluded on 7 September 1730 in the name of King George II and all the Cherokee people nonetheless served to further tie the Cherokees to the British interest. The relationship would only come fully unraveled two decades later during the Seven Years' War. And while the embassy would prove fruitful for the Cherokee delegation, Sir Alexander Cuming would come away frustrated. The negotiations between the Board of Trade and the Cherokee delegation were directed by the royal governor of South Carolina, Robert Johnson, and the former lieutenant governor of Pennsylvania, Sir William Keith. While the Cherokees inquired about Cuming's whereabouts during their negotiations, he was consistently marginalized during and after the negotiations. For years he continued to pepper Newcastle and the Board of Trade with letters proposing himself as the proper person to oversee British-Cherokee relations, as well as proposing schemes to reform the government of South Carolina. His fantastical scheming reached its height in 1748, when he proposed to the Pelham ministry to lead an effort to restore the Jewish homeland (as foretold by Scripture) in, of all places, the Cherokee country. Cuming eventually spent the years from 1755 to 1765 in debtors' prison and was committed to the Charterhouse Hospital from 1765 until his death in 1775.[27]

It is tempting to see Sir Alexander Cuming's journey from Britain to South Carolina to the Cherokee nation and back again as aberrant or trivial or both. Indeed, Cuming usually merits only a sentence or two and a footnote in even the most detailed histories of the southeastern borderlands. Spending less than a year in Carolina and lacking official sanction, Cuming seemingly lies outside established narratives of American Indian–European relations—neither a trader nor a commissioned colonial official, he defies easy categorization. Yet, he did reshape the relationship between the Cherokee nation and the British provinces of the Southeast, and by extension the Cherokee relationship with the British Empire as a whole. Between 1730 and 1760, subsequent beloved men of Great Tellico would claim the title of "emperor" following the passing of Moitoi; the title would be an important piece of leverage as Great Tellico, Chota, and other Cherokee towns jockeyed with one another for access to British commerce, not only with South Carolina, but also with the emergent colonies of Georgia and North Carolina. Although Alexander Cuming never achieved the fame and wealth he desired from his American adventure, his actions did leave their mark.[28]

But it is when we consider Alexander Cuming's actions in a larger and wider sense that they become most interesting. The world of Alexander Cuming was also the world of Moitoi of Tellico, Attakullakulla, Ludovick Grant, William Keith, and Robert Johnson. It was a world in which the boundaries between Great Britain, its colonial provinces, and their American Indian neighbors were, if not entirely fluid, certainly porous. And the fact that individuals and goods moved through these borders (although usually not as spectacularly as Cuming) forced those who held political power to negotiate with their counterparts and guide these exchanges as best they could. Cuming's journey reveals that both the structures and norms that guided and informed these myriad acts of negotiation in the early eighteenth-century British Atlantic were far from fixed. The customs that guided metropolitan/provincial/indigenous relations were still relatively new, and misunderstandings and improvisations were par for the course. This was what made polity relations in the North America borderlands different from those in the established Westphalian system. Structures of interaction were still emerging, and the norms of the system were a product of ongoing negotiation. In a way, two different sets of norms existed alongside one another. The independence and importance of Indian nations were recognized by many colonial subjects (especially those making policy) as well as the Board of Trade, but the form, manner, and significance of the negotiations between metropolitan and colonial authorities and the Indian nations was recognized to be somewhat different than that engaged in Europe. The position of the colonies themselves and the subjects who resided within their borders was also similarly nebulous. Some in Britain and America began to imagine that clarifying the norms that informed the negotiations between all of these polities might be a worthwhile task.

It was in the decades after Cuming's adventure, between the early 1730s through the mid-1750s, that a small number of commentators in British North America began to consider the structure of the British Empire and contemplate both the norms and structures of the Atlantic system. They began to speculate how this unwieldy system of polities might be rationalized. Interestingly, they looked to the American Indian polities to their west and saw challenges and opportunities that were similar in nature to those they saw when they looked at their own settler provinces. This small number of elite British Americans saw political, diplomatic, and commercial relationships, both in eastern North America's borderlands and on its seaboard, that served the interests of the British Empire as a whole. They believed that if properly managed and organized, the empire could redound to everyone's benefit. Sadly, they were proved horribly wrong. In the aftermath of the Seven Years' War, the British Empire in North America fractured irrevocably, and metropolitan authorities, colonial settlers, and the

Indians were involved, not in peaceful and prosperous coexistence, but in open warfare. To understand how this came to be, however, we need to first consider the world of the midcentury imperial reformers and thus the context—and the limitations—of their visions of the British Empire and the diplomatic regime of its borderlands.

I

"In the Nature of Ambassadors"

North American Diplomacy within the British Empire

> Now, if you were to pick out half a Dozen Men of good Understanding and Address, and furnish them with a reasonable Scheme and proper Instructions, and send them in the Nature of Ambassadors to the other Colonies, . . . I imagine such a Union might thereby be made and established; For reasonable sensible Men, can always make a reasonable Scheme appear such to other reasonable Men, if they take Pains, and have Time and Opportunity for it; unless from some Circumstances their Honesty and good Intentions are suspected.
>
> —Benjamin Franklin, 1751

In 1748, diplomats of the kingdoms of Great Britain and France negotiated the Treaty of Aix-la-Chapelle, leading the various European powers into ending the eight-year-long War of Austrian Succession. But in many quarters of the world touched by European power, there was little of the joy that usually comes with peace. In the British North American province of New York, the war's end only served to fill the colony's leading men with anxiety. Agents of the king of France remained firmly planted in Quebec, their alliances with the American Indian communities of the Great Lakes region as strong as ever. Some feared that if relations between New York and its American Indian neighbors continued the erosion that had been ongoing in the 1740s, the French would pounce on the situation, fatally compromising the frontiers of northern British America.[1] Among the most sober-minded of New Yorkers feeling these postwar anxieties was the port of New York's Crown-appointed collector of customs, Archibald Kennedy.

Having emigrated from Scotland to New York in 1710, Kennedy had served as the province's customs collector and receiver-general since the early 1720s. Like most provincial Britons, Kennedy reasoned that the peace of 1748 had truly resolved little. Given the manner in which European sovereigns made war and peace in the eighteenth century, it was logical to expect war between Great Britain and France would come again soon.[2]

Kennedy wanted to protect his colony's interests in the looming interimperial conflict, and he offered a program for doing so in a series of essays he wrote and had published in the early 1750s. With his intimate knowledge of New York's commerce, Kennedy understood intuitively that New York, as a commercial entrepôt, had interests that simultaneously extended in a multitude of directions. The city's commercial connections spread outward across the Atlantic to metropolitan markets and creditors, extended laterally with the nearby farming communities both within New York and in neighboring colonies, and moved into the interior via the Hudson River to European agricultural producers and the American Indian communities of Iroquoia. Beyond the realm of commerce, New York was also an important link in the emerging urban-centered, colonial public sphere. Cognizant of all of this, Kennedy imagined that the solution to New York's potential troubles was to organize and order all of these inter- and extracolonial relationships. In the five essays he published between 1750 and 1756, Kennedy proposed a military union of the colonies, which would include Indian nations, as well as a rationalization of the constitutional and legislative structures that regulated trade between the colonials and the metropolis. Taken together, his essays elaborated a sophisticated vision of an intercolonial union that could safeguard the interests of the majority of the colonies of British North America.[3]

Kennedy hoped to simultaneously rationalize the structures of the imperial union and the borderlands diplomatic regime. He thus saw New York's American Indian neighbors as an important part of his project to rationalize the structure of the British Empire in North America. It was in *The Importance of Gaining and Preserving the Friendship of the Indians to the British Interest, Considered*, published in 1751, that Kennedy most directly linked Indian relations, colonial security, imperial governance, and commercial prosperity. He argued that the commerce with the Indian nations enriched both Native Americans and Anglo-Americans. These commercial ties also served to cement political ties, which were eminently useful should the inevitable recurrence of interimperial warfare come to pass. Here Kennedy proposed the creation of an intercolonial union to organize a common defense, through a mutually supported requisition of troops and construction and garrisoning of forts. On the northern frontier, this defensive network should include the Iroquois towns (known to British colonists like Kennedy as "castles" for the palisaded compounds they had once possessed), which, although garrisoned by Indian men, should be armed by the British. (Three years later, Kennedy would suggest that these so-called "Indian Castles" could also function as "Truck or Trading-houses" and serve as commercial hubs in the Indian country.) The perspective conveyed throughout these essays is one where commerce between the colony and Indian communities, intraimperial commerce, economic development, and imperial organization were all interrelated and interdependent realms.[4]

As the printer James Parker prepared to set the type for *Importance*, he solicited commentary from Benjamin Franklin, who offered fairly enthusiastic comments. Parker duly appended Franklin's commentary to the published version of Kennedy's essay. Franklin affirmed Kennedy's main supposition that "securing the Friendship of the Indians is of the greatest Consequence to these Colonies; and that the surest means of doing it, are, to regulate the Indian Trade." But he was not so sure that Kennedy's intercolonial union, as proposed, would prove workable. The nature of colonial politics, with divergent interests present between as well as within colonies, tended to militate against the success of such grandiose projects. Many colonial governors, Franklin observed, had entertained similar plans, but "Governors are often on ill Terms with their Assemblies, and seldom are the Men that have the most Influence among them." Yet Franklin could imagine a chance for such a project of union if the usual channels between colonial governors and assemblies were superseded. Strictly local interests could be overlooked if business was conducted by plenipotentiaries. Relative to each other, the colonies each held a sovereignty of sorts within the imperial system. Each colony was jealous of its powers and liberties within the system that was the extended polity of the British Empire.[5] Could they not come together as other sovereigns do—in a diplomatic congress? Franklin imagined selecting "half a Dozen Men of good Understanding and Address," giving them "proper Instructions" and then sending "them in the Nature of Ambassadors to the other Colonies, where they might apply particularly to all the leading Men, where by being present they would have the Opportunity of pressing the Affair both in publick and private." A "voluntary Union entered into by the colonies themselves" would be a possibility, if it was pursued in a manner resembling something like a European diplomatic mission between colonies. Unfortunately, the somewhat unexpected culmination of Franklin's and Kennedy's projections, the Albany Congress of 1754, was not as successful as either man had hoped.[6]

The efforts, during the middle decades of the eighteenth century, of the small circle of provincial elites of which Franklin and Kennedy were a part to imagine and enact a program of rationalization and reform of the British Empire in North America met with failures similar to that of the Albany Congress. Kennedy and Franklin's pamphleteering had a counterpart in the southern colonies in the unpublished report Edmond Atkin prepared for the Board of Trade, and the reporting that Indian superintendents John Stuart and William Johnson dispatched to the Board of Trade and secretaries of state. In the 1750s and 1760s, both the public sphere and the official imperial correspondence were filled with a host of overlapping and reinforcing notions and projections about how to reorder the British Empire and its relations with its colonies and its Indian neighbors. The imperial reformers ran into two obstacles. The first, predicted by Franklin, was that self-interest on the part of the leadership of the various colonies, as well as Indian leaderships, would push back against any attempt to limit exploitative opportunities for one party for the benefit of the greater good. The second inherent problem was that the normative vision the imperial reformers had—where Indian nations and settler colonies could exist side by side in a British imperial framework and work together to first resist French aggression and then to promote general prosperity and welfare—was never widely held. The structures of the borderlands diplomatic regime and the imperial constitution were both customary arrangements rooted in mutual misunderstandings. But within each political system, actors brought to bear different sets of expectations. Thus, attempts to articulate the norms undergirding these structures of interaction exposed their inconsistencies and ironically made reform more difficult. The culmination of this resistance was the Imperial Crisis that followed the Seven Years' War and ultimately drove thirteen of the North American colonies out of the British Empire.

The Treaty of Lancaster and the Power of Intentional Misunderstandings

At the beginning of *The Importance of Gaining and Preserving the Friendship of the Indians*, Archibald Kennedy recapitulated, in a severely abridged and somewhat fanciful manner, the roots of the ongoing relationship between Europeans and American Indians. "When the first ship arrived here from *Europe*, the *Indians* it is said, were so well-pleased, that they would have tied her to a Tree, in order to better secure her," Kennedy wrote. But, "as Cables were subject to rot, they would have it an Iron Chain, and this to be continued into the *Indian* Countries, that they might be able to keep their Part of it clear from Rust, as we were to keep our Part." This so-called "Iron Chain" was, in Kennedy's explication, the basis of a cordial and mutually beneficial relationship between American Indians and European colonists. "If the *Indians* were in Distress or Want, the Call was, as it is in this Day, to come and make clean, or renew the Covenant Chain; and the Christians on their part, were to do the like: And accordingly we have assisted them in their Wars and Wants, and they have assisted us in our Wars, and we have their Furs." Kennedy was claiming to tell the story of the relations between all Europeans and all Indians, but in invoking the "Covenant Chain" and the "Iron Chain" he was actually referencing a very specific Native-European political relationship, the relationship between the colony of New York and the Iroquois Six Nations.[7] The Covenant Chain was the diplomatic alliance structure that tied the Iroquois Confederacy to a number of non-Iroquois nations as well as to New York and other settler colonies. The branch of this alliance structure that tied the Iroquois to the European settler colonies was often called the "Iron Chain" (when the alliance was with Dutch New Netherland) and the "Silver Chain" (when the English superseded the Dutch and rechristened as New York their colony in the Hudson Valley). Like Kennedy, most British colonial elites in the early 1750s would have perceived the central and important position played by Iroquois Six Nations. The fact that the language of Iroquois diplomacy had acquired a ubiquity among British North Americans at midcentury is but one testimony to the Iroquois' importance.[8]

While the Iroquois of the 1750s were not the militarily dominant force they had been a century before, the villages of the Mohawks, Oneidas, Tuscaroras, Onondagas, Cayugas, and Senecas continued to occupy a geopolitically crucial position between French Canada, the British seaboard colonies, and the various Indian nations of the Great Lakes basin and Ohio Valley. The Six Nations shrewdly maintained their political relevancy—and their own independence—through the perpetuation and deployment of one of the most effective shared political fictions in all of eighteenth-century North American diplomacy—the myth of Iroquois suzerainty over a host of "conquered" Indian communities. Rooted in a combination of misrepresentations and misunderstandings of the seventeenth-century history of the Iroquois' relations with their Indian neighbors, the notion that the Iroquois held title to the lands of other Indians nations they had conquered in previous wars proved eminently useful. The Iroquois could sell title to lands that they did not control and maintain sovereignty over the land they did, while colonial leaders could acquire (dubious but defensible) title to lands they coveted. Pamphleteers like Archibald Kennedy were not the only North Americans to traffic in a bowdlerized version of American Indian history in order to advance a particular political interest. Both Iroquois and British American negotiators utilized the fiction of Iroquois suzerainty to secure their interests throughout the early eighteenth century. One site where this mythology of conquest was deployed to great effect was at the treaty conference held at Lancaster, Pennsylvania, in 1744 between the Six Nations and the governments of the provinces of Pennsylvania, Maryland, and Virginia.

Like most myths, the fiction of Iroquois suzerainty had at its origins a grain of truth. A century before Lancaster, in the middle of the seventeenth century, the fur-bearing beaver had become virtually extinct in Iroquoia proper. In order to acquire valuable furs for trade in European goods, Iroquois raiding parties began to attack trappers from neighboring nations to the north. By the 1650s, during the so-called Beaver Wars, the Iroquois made several incursions into present-day Ontario, conquering or dispersing a number of substantial Great Lakes nations, including the Huron, the Neutral, and the Petun.[9] During the later part of the seventeenth century, however, matters took a turn for the worse for the Iroquois. As allies to British New York, they suffered greatly at the hands of the French, and in 1701 they adopted a pose of neutrality between the French and the British. This safeguarded the existence of the Iroquois Confederacy itself, but the world around the Iroquois began to change. Many other Indian nations felt increasing pressure on their lands during the early decades of the eighteenth century as the British colonies expanded from the Atlantic seaboard into the interior uplands. Communities of Shawnees, Delawares, Nanticokes, Tutelos, and Saponis all migrated into the environs of Iroquoia (mostly in present-day Pennsylvania, rather than present-day New York, where the Iroquois homelands were), where they sought Iroquois protection. In accordance with diplomatic protocols that predated European contact, the

Iroquois Confederacy (the temporal manifestation of the union of the Six Nations) allied itself with these nations and the Iroquois League (the spiritual manifestation) "adopted" these refugee communities, denoting them with a subordinate kinship relationship, and extended the protective alliance known as the Covenant Chain over them.[10]

A variant of the same Covenant Chain alliance that formally tied a variety of Ohio Valley, Susquehanna Valley, and Delaware Valley Indians to the Iroquois also united the Iroquois in formal relationships with New York and many of the other British colonies. Both colonial governments and the Iroquois themselves tacitly promoted the idea that the Covenant Chain gave the Iroquois suzerainty over a number of subject peoples and a vast amount of territory. This was the fiction. The Iroquois "conquest" of various Algonkian nations in the Great Lakes region consisted of the dispersal of villages, the taking of captives, and the adoption of the captives into the Confederacy's villages. For the Iroquois, "conquest" did not mean the seizure of territory as it did to colonial agents steeped in the European law of nations. And many Indian nations disputed the notion that they had been conquered in even this sense. Yet, at several key treaty negotiations, when colonials read Iroquois claims to rule over a number of subject peoples in this manner, the Iroquois did not protest all that much. In fact, in the 1730s and 1740s, the Iroquois had used claims to suzerainty as a selling point as they sought to break out of the hold New York had held over their relations with the other colonies. Nowhere was this more on display than at the treaty negotiations at Lancaster, Pennsylvania, in June and July 1744.[11]

The Treaty of Lancaster was a product of a confluence of the diverse interests of the Iroquois Confederacy and the colonies of Pennsylvania, Virginia, and Maryland. Since the 1720s, many Iroquois had grown increasingly unhappy with their alliance with New York. The Mohawks felt especially aggrieved: as the easternmost nation, they had been subject to encroachments by New York land speculators, and the establishment of a direct trading link between Albany and Montreal cut out the role of Mohawk middlemen. Thus, many in the Confederacy desired to diplomatically supersede New York, and geography rendered Pennsylvania the obvious place to turn. On the colonial side, Pennsylvania, Maryland, and Virginia were all anxious to treat, in large part to settle land disputes each had with the Six Nations. While both Pennsylvania and Virginia had signed treaties with the Confederacy before, New York held primacy over all the other colonies through the 1720s, and nearly every treaty council between the Iroquois and the colonials was held at Albany. Finally, some Iroquois had been recently murdered by a group of Virginians, and it was the responsibility of Virginia's government to "cover the dead" through the rituals of the condolence ceremony.[12]

The negotiations at Lancaster and the resultant treaty epitomize the give-and-take from all sides that characterized the terrain of the diplomatic middle ground between European colonizers and American Indians in the mid-eighteenth century. The protocol of the negotiations at Lancaster Court House were the mélange of Iroquoian and European forms that had been forged at Albany during the period of Dutch settlement and perfected in the hinterlands of Iroquoia during the ensuing century. Established customs of Iroquois-European diplomacy governed all aspects of the negotiation—the delegates' time and manner of arrival, their place of lodgings, the manner and timing of speeches, and the exchange of gifts and wampum. The overarching presence at the negotiations was Canasatego, one of the leading men of Onondaga and one of the Iroquois' leading speakers. The Lancaster negotiations served as a primer in Iroquois diplomacy for the delegation from Maryland, which had never treated with the Iroquois before, and as a review of sorts for Pennsylvania and Virginia, which had had only limited contact with the Iroquois during the decades of New York's ascendancy.[13]

The longest-lasting and arguably most important development to emerge from the Lancaster negotiations was the legitimization of Virginia's vast claim to the trans-Appalachian region. Iroquois suzerainty was, in this case, a useful fiction that was seized upon by both sides. In the years before Lancaster, Iroquois claims to represent communities that inhabited the Susquehanna Valley had gotten them a warm reception from Pennsylvanians, especially when the Iroquois took the side of the Pennsylvanians over the Delaware Indians in the aftermath of the controversial "Walking Purchase" of 1737. At Lancaster, Iroquois suzerainty was openly buttressed in a speech directed to the Virginia delegation by a war chief named Tocanontie.[14] "[Y]ou desire to know if we have any Right to the *Virginia* Lands, . . . and [to] tell you what Nations of *Indians* we conquered those Lands from," he stated. The answer to Virginia's challenge was a simple assertion, "We have the right of Conquest." Tocanontie continued: "All the World knows we conquered the several Nations living on the *Sasquahanna, Cohongoronta,* and on the Back of the Great Mountains in *Virginia*. [These nations] feel the Effects of our Conquests, being now a Part of our Nations, and their Lands at our Disposal." Finally, he dismissed the notion that Virginia had conquered the said nations and had some undisputed right to the trans-Allegheny region—"as to what lies beyond the Mountains, we conquered the Nations residing there, and that Land, if the *Virginians* ever get a good Right to it, it must be by us." Rather than feel reprobated by Tocanontie's assertions of Iroquois supremacy, Virginia's delegates, Thomas Lee and William Beverly, went along. By the time the Lancaster conference closed on 4 July 1744, they had gotten Canasatego's signature not only on the treaty, but also on an accompanying deed that ceded all of the Iroquois Confederacy's claims to what would become the Northwest Territory to the government of Virginia. That the Iroquois held anything approaching European-style dominion over the Ohio Valley was a ludicrous idea, yet it was a fiction that served both Iroquois and colonial ends. Such innovations, or shared fictions, allowed the machinery of North America's borderlands diplomatic regime to function and permitted British Americans and American Indians to work out a modus vivendi of coexistence and cooperation with one another.[15]

Indians and Empire in the Reformers' Imagination

The Treaty of Lancaster was but one of dozens of formal negotiations that drew British and American Indian diplomats together during the decades before the Seven Years' War. The fact that British Americans and American Indians came together on the diplomatic middle ground of places like the Lancaster Court House affected both structures and norms. Treaty negotiations produced new political outcomes, but they also, collectively and over time, reshaped the intellectual milieu within which colonial elites conceptualized the world in which they lived. Borrowing from American Indian vocabularies of politics in order to facilitate British-Indian diplomacy made possible the contemplation of the American Indian place in the system of diverse polities that was the British Empire. Provincial elites like Archibald Kennedy and Benjamin Franklin understood the role that the various Indian nations played in the imperial rivalries between Britain, France, and Spain, and they also understood the latent potential for conflict between American Indians and European settlers on the frontiers of settlement. Such understandings were a key motivator behind these men's desires to reform the structure of the British Empire in America.

In the late 1740s and early 1750s, the public sphere in North America and the networks of correspondence between London and America filled with tracts that analyzed the British Empire and offered prescriptions on how to make its structure even more efficient, rational, and beneficial to all of His Majesty King George II's subjects. Attempts to describe, understand, and modify the British imperial system could be found in the writings of not only Kennedy and Franklin, but also men such as New York Lieutenant Governor Cadwallader Colden, Northern Indian Agent Sir William Johnson, and Southern Indian Agent Edmond Atkin. These men all shared an understanding that maintaining and ordering commerce and diplomacy between the colonies and the various Indian polities, as well as more efficiently structuring intercolonial relations, were essential to imperial security in North America. The political and commercial relationships among the polities in America were, in turn, a vital part of the transatlantic British Empire.

The necessity of a functional empire was brought into sharp focus by the interimperial warfare of the 1740s and the prospect of renewed warfare in the 1750s. For Benjamin Franklin, the involvement of his country, Great Britain, in a war that threatened life and limb in his home province of Pennsylvania was the event that stirred his political conscience into action. Advocating for the more systematic and active defense of the province of Pennsylvania, Franklin wrote and published in 1747 one of his first overtly political pamphlets, *Plain Truth: Or, Serious Considerations on the Present State of the City of Philadelphia, and the Province of Pennsylvania*.[16] In setting the groundwork for Franklin's proposal of an association of volunteers to defend Philadelphia and Pennsylvania, *Plain Truth* emphasized the connectedness of Pennsylvania to both the British Empire and the world beyond its immediate borders. Franklin reminded his readers that "War, at this Time, rages over a great Part of the known World," and they all knew this, since "our News-Papers are Weekly filled with fresh Accounts of the Destruction it every where occasions." Franklin then mentioned that since Pennsylvania lay at the center of the American colonies, it had been so far spared significant depredations by Britain's French and Spanish enemies, but this central condition could, at any point, prove to be an Achilles' heel for the province. Naval raids could come from the ocean to the southeast;

raids by French-allied Indians could come from the west. Franklin wondered aloud about the security provided by the British colonies' long-standing alliance with the Six Nations Iroquois. "The French know the power and importance of the Six Nations, and spare no Artifice, Pains or Expence, to gain them to their interest," Franklin cautioned. "By their Priests they have converted many to their Religion, and these have openly espoused their cause." Franklin also worried that inattention to the maintenance of alliances with the Iroquois could result in their "Resentment" as well as a change of feelings among the Iroquois "thro' Disgust at our Usage, joined with Fear of the French Power, and greater Confidence in their Promises and Protection than in ours." Even indifference on the part of the Iroquois would expose the frontiers of both Pennsylvania and New York to "Ruin, Bloodshed and Confusion."[17]

Plain Truth explained to Pennsylvanians that, because of their membership in a transatlantic empire, distant wars could become local catastrophes quite easily and without much warning. Active efforts to defend the home province, coordination with other colonies, and maintenance of established alliances with neighboring Indian communities were all vital elements in preserving provincial security. The presence of a large population of pacifist Quakers gave Pennsylvania a unique set of challenges in organizing its defense, but overall the challenges seen by Franklin in Pennsylvania were quite similar to those confronted by all of the colonies of British North America. The population clusters of the British colonies existed along the Atlantic seaboard and had only begun to spread into the interior. Their security and viability was tenuous. North of the British colonies, along the St. Lawrence River, was the colony of New France, or Quebec. To the south of the young colony of Georgia lay the Spanish territories of East and West Florida. West of the Appalachian Mountains, the French claimed the entire drainage of the Mississippi River as the territory of Louisiana. In the overlapping War of Jenkins' Ear (began 1739) and War of Austrian Succession (1740–48), Great Britain had found itself at war with both Spain and France, respectively. The threat posed by the presence of Britain's imperial rivals on all of the colonies' flanks was not that rival armies would invade British territory, but the reality that Spain and (especially) France had been far more successful in forging alliances with the various American Indian nations of the interior. The fear that these alliances could be turned against the British settler populations was omnipresent.[18]

It was not only the prospect of a French-Spanish-Indian alliance falling upon British North America that instilled fear in the colonial heart, but an awareness of the tenuous nature of the British provincials' own alliances with their Indian neighbors. In *Plain Truth*, Franklin had noted that even the majority of the Iroquois, who had not fallen prey to French Jesuit priest-craft, "appear irresolute which Part to take; no Persuasions, tho' enforced with costly Presents having yet been able to engage them generally on our Side, tho' we had numerous Forces on their Borders, ready to second and support them." Franklin utilized this rhetoric primarily to spur Pennsylvanians to action; he was invoking a notion of Indian inconstancy in order to reinforce the need for Pennsylvanians to act for themselves and not to depend on distant allies or forces to defend them. At the same time, his assessment of numerous gifts given to the Iroquois in exchange for a relationship that appeared inconstant and thus unreliable testifies to a British view of Indian alliances, in which such alliances were seen as eminently necessary and yet were rife with misunderstandings on both sides.[19] What both the French and British saw as commercial exchanges, many Algonkians and Iroquois understood to be gift exchanges that cemented fictive kinships, the spiritual component that underlay any temporal alliance. For everyone, trade was a vital element of the intercultural "middle ground" in which day-to-day Indian-European relationships unfolded. Within this realm of negotiation, divergent cultural constructions of trade and exchange were directed toward mutually intelligible policy ends.[20]

Although colonial commentators like Franklin harbored some misgivings about the Indian trade, they generally saw the promotion and extension of commerce into the interior as important to the continued vitality of Britain's empire in America. In the Indian country, as in Europe, commerce and diplomacy went hand in hand. Alliances rooted in commerce would spell success for the British colonies for, as Archibald Kennedy observed, the "great advantage the English have over the French is there [sic] being able to furnish the Indians with goods at a cheaper rate than the French can." The French Empire in North America was rooted in its Indian alliances, and if these were turned to the British interest, the British Empire would be strengthened, and the French weakened. Kennedy observed that although the French had few settlers in Quebec ("there is hardly a Colony upon the Continent, but what is a Match for all *Canada*"), they, "by a proper Management of their *Indians*, keep us all, both in Time of peace and

War, in a constant Dread and Terror." Cadwallader Colden, Kennedy's fellow New Yorker, echoed these sentiments. Colden bluntly observed in 1751 that "The power of the British Colonies is so much superior to that of the French, that they could have no hopes of coping with us, in any regular attack with regular troops or militia; [and] consequently [they] had no other method of making war but by numerous of their Indians."[21] Kennedy saw his colony's Indian neighbors to be key. "Whatever Pretences may be made, it is absolutely true, that the Preservation of the whole Continent, depends upon a proper regulation of the *Six Nations*." Regulation, of course, meant constantly treating with the Iroquois and maintaining cordial political relations and thus successful commercial relations as well.[22]

In the aftermath of the War of Austrian Succession, British colonials actually did begin to aggressively counter French commercial and political preeminence in the North American interior. To counter this, the French pushed back into the Ohio Valley and into Iroquois lands in the years following the Treaty of Aix-la-Chapelle, attempting to secure commerce with the various Algonkian and Iroquoian communities to themselves. The zenith of this effort was the destruction of the Pennsylvania trading post at the Miami town of Pickawillany in the summer of 1752.[23] On the southern frontier, the French had established Fort Toulouse amidst the Upper Creek towns in 1717. While the British officials bemoaned the continued French presence into the 1750s, French agents increasingly found that the southern Indians—the Cherokees, the Creeks, the Choctaws, the Chickasaws—tended to prefer British trade goods; the French found their influence waning.[24] So, although British American commentators like Franklin, Colden, and Kennedy lamented their situation on the eve of the Seven Years' War, their strategic prospects were improving. Since British fortunes were improving slowly, however, and under no central design, this was not readily apparent.

It is worth noting that observers in different colonies need not have come to the same conclusions about the proper relationship between the British American colonies and their Indian neighbors. The observations and prescriptions of writers in Virginia, the Carolinas, and Georgia were shaped by close contact with the southern nations of the Cherokees and the Creeks, rather than the Iroquois Six Nations. Given the differences between the neighborhoods and situations of the northern and southern colonies, the congruence in the proposals from writers in different regions is striking. Notably, South Carolinian Edmond Atkin's 1755 report to the Board of Trade parallels the prescriptions of northern writers such as Kennedy and Colden.

Edmond Atkin observed the southern frontier at the same time as Kennedy and Colden observed the northern one, and Atkin's observations and projections echoed theirs. Part of this congruence of vision can be attributed to a shared outlook on the empire that was shaped by lived experience—Atkin's career was a rough parallel to that of Kennedy. Edmond Atkin was born in England in 1707 and had come to South Carolina as a boy. He and a likely relative named John Atkin established themselves as Charles Town merchants in the 1730s, and Edmond had won a seat on South Carolina's Governor's Council in 1738. Over the course of the next twelve years, Atkin became increasingly disgruntled with the South Carolina legislature's handling of Indian trade and diplomacy, and he left for Great Britain in 1750. While in England, Atkin wrote about Indian affairs, composing a lengthy report in which he offered observations on the state of British-Indian relations on the southern borderlands, as well as proposals for the reorganization of the Indian trade. Atkin found a sympathetic ear, and he returned to South Carolina in 1756 as the Indian agent and superintendant for the Southern Department.[25]

Edmond Atkin's extensive report to the Board of Trade, composed in 1754 and 1755, echoed contemporaneous writings by his northern counterparts. Atkin's observations illustrate how intertwined Indian relations were at midcentury with larger issues of empire. "The Importance of Indians is now generally known and understood," Atkin offered. "[A] Doubt remains not, that the prosperity of our Colonies on the Continent, will stand or fall with our Interest and favour among them." He noted that "While they are our Friends, they are the Cheapest and strongest Barrier for the Protection of our Settlements; when Enemies, they are capable by ravaging in their method of War, in spite of all we can do, to render those Possessions almost useless."[26] Atkin demonstrated a thorough working knowledge of the southern borderlands. He understood, at some level, the variations between the various villages and confederations of villages of the Cherokee ("The upper and lower Cherokee differ from each other, as much as two different Nations"), and he elaborated the vital strategic position commanded by the Cherokee ("the Cherokee Country is the best formed by Nature, for the dominion of the Inland Indian Nations on this side of the

Mississippi and the Lakes"). Atkin similarly, and deftly, unfolded his local knowledge of the Creeks, Catawbas, Chickasaws, and Choctaws.[27]

Beyond informing the Board of Trade of the state of affairs on the ground in the southern borderlands, the key argument behind Atkin's report was to emphasize the security threat posed by the French, who had made inroads in luring the Indian polities of the Southeast into their orbit during the 1740s. In Atkin's mind, the situation was insidious: the French were secretly trying to "establish a Claim of Possession" to all land east of the Mississippi.[28] Diagnosing the problem, Atkin felt that French friendship with the Indians of eastern North America was rooted in their presence among them—the French had built forts, staffed them with military officers and other agents of their government, including missionaries, and under this aegis conducted and expanded trade with the various Indian communities.[29] Like Kennedy, Atkin believed that trade was the strongest tie that bound Indian and European—"a friendly convenient and beneficial Commerce is the surest basis of Alliances with [the Indians]." And, shockingly, it was this element of intercultural interaction that *should* have given the British an advantage.

> [I]t is worth while to consider, whence it comes to Pass that, posses'd as we are of vastly superior Advantages, by Situation on the Ocean, by our Conveniences for the quick and easy introduction of our Goods to the Inland Parts, by the Quality and Cheapness of our Goods fit for Indians, and by the natural disposition of the Indians to prefer us, *from a greater similarity between their and our Government*, the French have notwithstanding, in spite of their own great disadvantages in all those Respects, made so rapid a Progress even among Nations nearest to our Settlements, as hath lately Suprized every Body.[30] (emphasis added)

Most tantalizing here is Atkin's observation about the "greater similarity" between Indian government and British government, as opposed to the French. While we could discount this as psychological projection or wishful thinking, it does conform to political images that held currency among contemporaries in other North American theaters. In the borderlands north of Virginia, the Iroquois image of the Covenant Chain was enthusiastically appropriated by colonial commentators to describe the links that bound northern Indian polities to the Six Nations, and these Indian polities to the colonies and the Crown. Additionally, the decentered, village-oriented political life of the Cherokees and Creeks may have had, in Atkin's British imagination, more in common with the amalgamated, composite British Empire, than with the highly centralized (at least in comparison) French monarchy and empire. Atkin was not drawing a sharp line between colonists and Indians, but emphasizing how much they had in common in the realm of politics, and how much they could benefit from one another in the area of commerce.

But how could the Indians not prefer superior British manufactures? How could the Indians not see the natural affinities between their polities and those of the British colonies? Atkin laid the blame at the feet of the French enemy.

> The French have accordingly taught the Indians *to consider our Colonies, as so many independent Communities,* having no Concern with each other. Whence it has arisen that Indians in Peace and Amity with one of them, have at the same time behaved as enemies towards the people of another. Some of the Colonies have no regulations at all in the Indian Affairs; others have made different ones, and some but seldom if at all sent proper Persons to look into them.[31] (emphasis added)

The political vision embedded in Atkin's observations is a most interesting one—the threat posed by one of Britain's imperial rivals was exacerbated by its ability to exploit the weaknesses of Britain's imperial constitution. Here Atkin was being a bit disingenuous. The French did not need to manipulate the Indians to get them to imagine a reality that Indians, colonists, and Atkin himself perceived so readily. Autonomous colonial governments often pursued divergent policies of trade, peace, and war with their Indian neighbors, often with disastrous results for all concerned. Only direction from the imperial center, and a concomitant adjustment of the imperial constitution, could change that reality.

Centralizing control over Indian trade and Indian diplomacy was the chief thrust of the plan Atkin offered to the Board of Trade. Atkin proposed taking control of Indian trade and diplomacy out of the hands of the individual colonies and appointing two superintendents, one for a northern district extending from Virginia to Nova Scotia, and a second for a southern district extending from North Carolina to Georgia.³² Beyond this large-scale structural adjustment, Atkin wanted stricter controls over traders' access to Indian towns, and a more permanent system of forts and outposts in the Indian country to keep out unapproved traders, resist French encroachments, distribute trade goods, and repair Indians' guns and other implements.³³ Finally, Atkin outlined a new geopolitical vision for eastern North America that he hoped his plan would help achieve. He wanted the French forts destroyed and the British to secure access to the Great Lakes and the Ohio, Tennessee, and Chattahoochee valleys. Finally, in prescribing changes to the methods of Indian diplomacy and commerce in North America, Atkin hoped, eventually, to facilitate the emergence of a replica of the Iroquois Confederacy in the South. He imagined the new superintendent could assist in "forming an *Union* among the Indian Nations of the Southern District, . . . like that of the Six united Nations of N York." This new union would be effected by a chain of treaties, originating with the 1730 treaty concluded between the Cherokee and the British in London. Such an Indian confederacy in the south could serve as a counterweight against the French, their Indian allies, or even the Iroquois themselves if they deserted the British cause.³⁴

Atkin's vision was complex. He saw the security of the British Empire threatened in the North American interior by the expansive policies of the French monarchy. Countering these moves required a reorganization of the British Empire. Power needed to be removed from individual colonies and placed in the hands of Crown agents. Indian policy directed from London would not seek to further the interests of a few—namely colonial merchants and land speculators—but to commercially and then politically tie the Cherokee, Creek, Choctaw, and Chickasaw polities into the extended system of polities that was the British Empire. It is most interesting that even though they were writing from perspectives over a thousand miles distant from one another, Edmond Atkin and Archibald Kennedy ended up saying many of the same things. With powerful Indian nations on their borders, both Atkin in South Carolina and Kennedy in New York knew that Indian polities could be either valuable allies or fierce foes, and that the security and prosperity of the British Empire hinged on its relations with these neighbors. But while commentators could identify the problem, effecting a solution was much more problematic. The question of how, and to what extent, Indian polities could be incorporated into the structure of the extended polity of the British Empire in a meaningful, lasting, and systematic way remained an open one.

Under "Our Common Father"?
The Divergence Begins

Not every British North American was as sanguine about the prospects of incorporating, in any fashion, the communities of the various American Indian peoples into the extended structure of the empire. Many wondered if it was really worth the trouble, or even at all possible. Attempting to write a comprehensive history of the American colonies in 1749, the Boston physician William Douglass offhandedly noted that "the *Aboriginal Americans* have no Honesty, no Honour, that is, they are of no Faith, but meer Brutes in that Respect," and that "Strictly speaking, they seem to have no Government, no Laws, and are only cemented by a Friendship and good Neighbourhood."[35] Douglass was certainly not the only denizen of British North America to hold American Indians in low esteem. And while elites like Douglass painted their disparaging portraits with pen and ink, thousands of Douglass's less refined fellows used rifles and blades to write their opinion of American Indians in blood. As sure as diplomacy could speak to the ability of Indian polities to function with the political structure of the extended polity of the British Empire, the lived experience of violence and warfare testified to different and darker possibilities. And war was never far away.[36]

In 1754, the fears of renewed war that had motivated the imperial reform projects of Atkin, Franklin, Kennedy, and others were confirmed. Warfare between France and Great Britain erupted in May when a small military expedition from the province of Virginia into the trans-Allegheny region skirmished along the Monongahela River with a French and Indian detachment from the newly constructed Fort Duquesne at the Forks of the Ohio. In order to stake Virginia's long-standing claim to the Forks (supported by its royal charter, as well as the Treaty of Lancaster), the Virginian commander, twenty-two year-old Colonel George Washington, ordered the Virginia Regiment to dig in. The Virginians constructed a makeshift fort, which Washington was forced to surrender to a French force in early July. Only eight years after the Treaty of Aix-la-Chapelle, interimperial war had come once again to North America. By 1756, the conflict that would come to be known as the Seven Years' War would be under way in Europe, with Prussia joining its ally Britain, and Austria, Russia, and (eventually) Spain joining France. Initially, the war did not go well for the British, with the defeat of Edward Braddock's expedition to the Forks in 1755 and the loss of Fort William Henry on the south shore of New York's Lake George in 1757 marking the nadir of the British war effort in the North American theater. The prudent administration of William Pitt the Elder enabled British victories by James Wolfe at Louisborg (1758) and Quebec (1759), and (following Wolfe's death) by Jeffrey Amherst at Montreal (1760). And the battles that culminated in the expulsion of France from North America constituted only one campaign among many. In what was truly a world war, British military and naval forces found themselves victorious all over the world. Britain and its ally Prussia held their own on the battlefields of the Holy Roman Empire, while the Royal Navy supported British victories in India (Plassey, 1757; Madras, 1758; and Pondicherry, 1761); the Philippines (Manila, 1762); and the Caribbean (Martinique, 1761–62; and Havana, 1762). The Treaty of Paris (1763) ended the Seven Years' War with Great Britain confirmed as the preeminent and preponderant power in the European world.[37]

In both how it was waged and how it was settled, the Seven Years' War would transform the structure of the British Empire in North America, setting in motion events that would lead to its dismemberment and diminution. On the surface, the Seven Years' War was a great triumph for the British Empire. British armies, along with their colonial subjects and Indian allies, had won all of eastern North America, expelling the French from the continent conditionally on the battlefield in 1760 and permanently under the terms of the 1763 peace treaty. North Americans could have imagined that peace and prosperity would surely follow under the aegis of the British Empire. This is certainly the impression one would take away from the negotiations that unfolded immediately at the close of the Seven Years' War at the Georgia frontier community of Augusta. In October and November 1763, the new superintendent of Indian affairs for the Southern Department, John Stuart, convened a general congress of Creek, Cherokee, Choctaw, and Chickasaw village leaders along with the colonial governors of Georgia, South Carolina, North Carolina, and Virginia. The leaders of all the major polities in southern North America that were part of the British imperial system were brought together under the authority of an agent of the British Crown. It was a signal, symbolic moment. But although the negotiations of the Augusta Congress testified to the potential for colonial-Indian unity via metropolitan guidance, a close examination of the congress and its aftermath reveals the persistence of an ad hoc system of borderlands diplomacy that could, and did, easily fall apart.

At the moment of the Augusta Congress, recent history on the southeastern borderlands certainly called for a moment of healing. The Seven Years' War had unfolded in southern North America without the intensity felt in the Great Lakes region, Canada, and New England, but with a conflict—the Anglo-Cherokee War—erupting nonetheless. The Cherokee nation began the Seven Years' War allied with the British Empire in its fight against the Kingdom of France. In 1757, a party of Cherokee warriors traveled through the Carolinas and Virginia to assist with the defense of the northern Virginia frontier at Fort Loudon. Despite the British-Cherokee alliance, the warriors' movement through the backcountry of the Carolinas and Virginia raised tensions, and violence and death on both sides resulted. Neither the acting governor of Virginia, Francis Fauquier, nor South Carolina governor William Henry Lyttelton were proactive in lowering tensions among the Virginians, South Carolinians, or the Cherokees. The man holding the newly created office of superintendent of Indian affairs for the Southern Department could have intervened in theory, but in reality he could not. The new superintendent was Edmond Atkin, the same man whose 1754 report to the Board of Trade had precipitated the creation of this new office. The board had adopted only part of Atkin's recommendations, however, and he and his northern counterpart, Sir William Johnson, were not given any power over local governors. Rather than fulfill the dreams of Atkin and Archibald Kennedy, and rationalize colonial-Indian relations within the British Empire, the new office of the Indian superintendent had, at least initially, provided only jurisdictional confusion. With the war on, the presence of the regular army with its attendant commander in chief further muddied the waters of who, exactly, was in charge of managing relations between the colonies and the Indians. A drift into low-intensity warfare on the southern borderlands was a result.[38]

Neither Atkin nor the British military commander John Forbes was timely in pursuing negotiations with the Cherokee. South Carolina governor William Henry Lyttelton took matters into his own hands and led an expedition against the Cherokee towns in October 1759, which ultimately caused the outbreak of a full-scale war between the Cherokees and the colonists. The origins and progress of the Anglo-Cherokee War confirmed Atkin's 1754 analysis of the troubles, jurisdictional rivalry foremost among them, plaguing British-Indian relations. Both Georgia and Virginia were pursuing negotiations with the Cherokee. Governor's Lyttelton's fears at having South Carolina's privileged position vis-à-vis the Cherokee usurped, in concert with pressures from backcountry residents, drove him to adopt his aggressive stance.[39] Only intervention and negotiation under Colonel James Grant of the British army regulars ultimately halted the war almost two years later. Although Atkin had failed in his attempts at negotiation, and then passed from the scene with his death, the vision of his report had been vindicated. Successful management of relations between the Indian villages of the interior and the colonies of the coast came only with the interposition of agents of the Crown. With Atkin's untimely death, it was left to his successor as superintendent, John Stuart, to rebuild the British imperial system on the southern borderlands in the aftermath of war. The convocation of the Congress of Augusta was the first step in rebuilding Indian-colonial relations after the brief Anglo-Cherokee War.[40]

The experience of trying to wage a world war was the shock to the system that convinced authorities in London to take heed of the calls for imperial reorganization and rationalization that had been emanating from the American colonies for well over a decade. The initiative for the Augusta Congress came not from Charles Town or even from Stuart's office, but directly from Whitehall and the secretary of state for the Southern Department, Charles Wyndham, Earl of Egremont. Beginning even before the final Peace of Paris was ratified, Egremont began shaping a policy of imperial rationalization. In North America, he put into motion policies that would disentangle the individual colonies from the management of Indian relations, solidify a border between colonist and Indian, and manage relations between all polities concerned via Crown-appointed superintendents.[41] Although this was, more or less, what the late Atkin had proposed in 1755, with the French gone from North America, the geopolitical context had changed. Now, all the Indian polities east of the Mississippi (as well as colonial populations in Canada and Florida) were unambiguously in the British imperial orbit. Changed geopolitical dynamics brought new policies that, of course, implied a new constitutional arrangement.[42]

This was not immediately apparent. In form, the Augusta Congress, as managed by Stuart, seemed to confirm and reaffirm the old balances and relationships of the British imperial system. Acting on orders he had received from Whitehall in June, Stuart, a Scots-born merchant resident in the Southeast since 1748, spearheaded the organization of the general congress during the summer of 1763.[43] The Augusta Congress brought together the leadership of all of the major polities of southern British North America. Lieutenant-Governor Francis Fauquier of Virginia (then acting governor), Governor Arthur Dobbs of North Carolina, Governor Thomas Boone of South Carolina, and Governor James Wright of Georgia led delegations from their respective colonies. From the Cherokee villages came fifteen leading men, including the influential leaders Attakullakulla, of the town of Chota, and Ostenaca, of the town of Tomotly. Delegations from a portion of the Creek towns, from the more distant Choctaws and Chickasaws, and from the small community of Catawbas were all also in attendance.[44]

Lasting for about a week in November, the formal sessions of the Augusta Congress ultimately produced a treaty, to which the five Indian nations and four colonies were all signatories. Interestingly, despite the size and diversity of the congress, the Treaty of Augusta itself brought little revolutionary change to British-Indian relations. Many of the major areas of discontent, such as those underlying the Anglo-Cherokee War of 1760–61, had already been negotiated.[45] The boundary between the Creeks and the colony of Georgia was adjusted, and commitments to continue and regularize trade between the colonials and the various Indian communities were made, but for the most part the treaty was merely a commitment on the part of all the parties to coexist peacefully under the aegis of King George III.[46]

The spectacle of Augusta, with its diversity of participants and interests, provides a window onto the complexity of the political, commercial, and cultural relationships that defined life on the pre-Revolutionary southern borderlands. For example, when Cherokee leader Attakullakulla rose to speak several days into the Congress, he delivered a speech to the four colonial governors. Here, he spoke not only for himself, but also for fellow Chota Cherokee Occonostota, the "Great Warrior," who was not present. Attakullakulla then presented beads and wampum from several towns that could not make the journey to Augusta. Attakullakulla's actions speak to the reality of the Cherokee nation decades after the creation of the notional "emperor"—each Cherokee town retained a good deal of independence, and each town felt the need to address British colonial governors individually. Attakullakulla then turned and addressed the other Indian leaders, and the Creeks in particular, assuring them that "his people bear no ill-will to the Southward Indians." The Augusta Congress witnessed not simply white leaders talking (or dictating) to Indian leaders, but whites addressing Indians, Indians addressing whites, Indians addressing each other, and whites doing the same. The congress provided a space where all could, at least ceremonially, come together.[47]

It was John Stuart's opening address to all the negotiators that set the tone for Britons and Indians to imagine that they could still come together. "Friends and brothers," he said, "We come here in the name, and by the command of the great King George, who, under God, the master and giver of breath, is your and our common father and protector. The talk you are now to hear, is from the great king, and ordered to be delivered to you by four governors of different provinces, and the superintendent, who is equally connected with all." Stuart assured the Indians that "Our words, our hearts, our intentions are the same; as our respective provinces join together, so are interests are inseparable." The ritual homage to the father/king and empire that opened the congress was, like the invocation of the Covenant Chain at Albany, a form that all parties could adhere to and accept, as each party's political cosmology accorded the figure of "king" or "father" an overarching position of respect. There was a cultural middle ground that allowed negotiation to proceed. This image of colonial governments and Indian villages and communities coexisting under the direction of the agents of the Crown would, however, ultimately prove to be an illusory one. As metropolitan authorities finally approached the project of imperial rationalization and reorganization with seriousness (and in large part because of this), the leaders and then the people of the settler colonies began to push back and resist.[48]

Few in North America—Indian leaders, traders, colonial governors, or colonial legislatures—desired to have their prerogatives limited by one man with one office, which was exactly what John Stuart and William Johnson wanted. Stuart hoped to build on the comity displayed at Augusta and reorder and rationalize political and commercial relationships on the southern borderlands. All interests would be subordinated to those of the empire. According to the most recent student of Stuart's policies, he was "committed to [a] vision of Indians and whites as imperial subjects with a common interest," and he advocated policies that would restrain frontier whites while "integrating the Indians as full members of the empire and subjects of the king."[49] Stuart's program, as he articulated it in the course of his correspondence between 1763 and 1768, drew heavily on the ideas articulated by Kennedy, Atkin, and Franklin in the 1750s, and set into motion by the secretary of state for the Southern Department in the mid-1760s, the Earl of Egremont. The Proclamation of 1763 and the Board of Trade's unofficial "Plan for the Future Management of Indian Affairs" of 1764 provided Stuart with a coherent intellectual framework on which to build a policy. Stuart advocated for controls over Indian traders through a centralized licensing process, and he wanted a firm boundary line, like that of the Proclamation of 1763, to be drawn and enforced. He wanted lawless frontier whites to be restrained, and colonial legislative policies on land and Indian trade, which often blatantly served private, local interests, to be modified and drained of any appearance of corruption. The Indian policy Stuart advocated would mean real changes in the long-established ways of politics practiced in the American colonies. Not surprisingly, it met with resistance.[50]

Colonial authorities either attempted to modify or refused to go along with Stuart's plans of reforming colonial-Indian relations. In 1767, Georgia's Governor James Wright insisted that his instructions to Indian commissaries and traders held primacy over Stuart's orders. He allowed that Georgian agents in the Indian country could adhere to Stuart's instructions only to the extent that such instructions did not violate his own.[51] Virginia's government was quite hostile to Stuart's attempts to regulate colonial-Indian commerce. In 1767, the Virginia legislature appointed its own Indian commissioners and resolved that they would not "be subjected to any Regulations or Restrictions whatsoever."[52] In general, imperial officials, notably the commander in chief in the colonies, General Thomas Gage, approved of Stuart's plans, as did the majority of Creek and Cherokee leaders. Colonial elites, operating through their legislatures and influencing the colonial governors, consistently provided resistance to Stuart's plans to centralize control of Indian trade and diplomacy in the hands of his office. Colonial interests had voices in London, and moves were soon afoot within the ministry itself to transform British policies toward the West and the Indians.[53]

The manner in which British policy toward colonial-Indian relations changed is revealing of the convoluted structure of imperial governance and the perhaps insurmountable challenge an Indian superintendent faced during the 1760s and 1770s. The plans for centralized control over the Indian trade and Indian-colonial relations, which Egremont and the Board of Trade had put forward at the end of the Seven Years' War, met with resistance not only in the colonies' legislatures and governors' halls, but also in Whitehall itself. The concern about financing the debts incurred by the British government during the war, as well as the continued garrisoning of North America, led not only to the controversial revenue legislation of the Stamp Act and the Townshend Duties, but also to all manner of proposals to slash the size of the imperial budget. Secretary at War William Wildman, Viscount Barrington, was particularly concerned about decreasing military expenditures. Barrington proposed evacuating all of the western garrisons and pulling back the army to the east side of the Appalachian Mountains. Egremont's successor as secretary of state for the Southern Department, Lord Shelburne, disagreed with Barrington. But Shelburne wanted to keep the British army in the trans-Appalachian region in order to facilitate land sales from the Indians and promote the formation of new colonies in the West. Both men wanted to cast aside the policies of careful management of Indian-colonial commercial and political relations that Egremont had put forward and that Stuart and Johnson, working on the ground in America, had endorsed. The Board of Trade was skeptical of both sets of ideas, as was Lord Jeffrey Amherst, who had seen firsthand how the presence of the army and a soft diplomatic touch were necessary in order to maintain order in the North American borderlands. Shelburne's opinions lost out, as in 1768 responsibility for American shifted from the secretary of state to the newly created office of American secretary.[54]

The new American secretary, Wills Hill, Earl of Hillsborough, was committed to Barrington's point of view—he wanted to cut imperial costs and limit colonial expansion. Following Hillsborough's and Barrington's lead, the Board of Trade decided in March 1768 to remove control of Indian trade from the superintendents and return it to the colonial legislatures themselves. Hillsborough explained the situation succinctly to Gage. "It appears to his Majesty that, in the present state of this kingdom, its future safety and welfare do in great measure depend upon the relieving it from every expense that is not of absolute necessity," he stated. But with the changing geopolitical dynamics in North America, new (and less expensive) administrative options were possible. Hillsborough noted that "his Majesty applauds the motives which induced the first institution of the present plan of superintendency for Indian affairs, which was evidently calculated to regain the confidence and combine the force of the savages against a then powerful enemy," but with the enemy gone, "his majesty trusts the continuance of it is rendered the less necessary, at least in its full extent, and that whatever regulations may be proper, they are more desirable for the sake of commerce than necessary for public security." The superintendents would have the power to negotiate for the Crown and mediate between Indians and the colonies when more than one colony was involved, but the broad authority they had been given over one of the most central elements of colonial-Indian relations was gone. Hillsborough tried to put the best light on the matter, telling Gage that "his Majesty concurs in opinion with his Board of Trade, that the laying aside that part of [the superintendents' duties] which relates to Indian trade and entrusting the entire management of that trade to the colonies themselves, will be of public utility and advantage as a means of avoiding much difficulty, and saving much expense to this country, both in present and in future." But a moment to bring regularity and order to the empire had passed.[55]

From 1768 forward, British imperial policy, such as it now was, developed at cross-purposes, with the colonial governments eager to acquire land titles and the Indian superintendents looking to maintain peace and order. William Johnson and John Stuart remained empowered as Indian superintendents in the North and the South, respectively. Their extensive contacts with the Indian leaders in their departments, their continued access to trade goods, and their knowledge of how to negotiate with the Indian peoples of trans-Appalachia guaranteed that they would continue to play an important role in Indian-colonial relations. But rather than guiding a singular policy for ordering polity relations in British North America, the superintendents would be working in a more ad hoc fashion, attempting to smooth out friction between the settler colonies and the Indian nations. Rather than perpetuate diplomatic structures that could provide for the continued coexistence of Indians and settlers, Johnson and Stuart more often facilitated land transfers between Indians and colonial governments, thus tipping the balance in favor of the settler colonies. The most obvious example of the emerging reality was the 1768 Treaty of Fort Stanwix, which Johnson was instrumental in brokering. Gathering near modern-day Rome, New

York, between late September and 24 October 1768 were over three thousand Indians, including members of the Iroquois Six Nations, as well as Delaware and Shawnee Indians. Official representatives of the colonies of Pennsylvania, New Jersey, and Virginia were also present, as were "sundry" gentlemen from a variety of colonies. Johnson had been instructed by the Board of Trade to negotiate a firm boundary between the Iroquois and the other Indians of the Ohio Valley and Great Lakes region on the one side and the colonists on the other—on the surface, a similar policy to that put forward in 1763. But with a diminished power base, Johnson had to also take colonial interests, and not just imperial instructions, into account. Johnson had been instructed to negotiate a boundary between the Indian and settler lands that extended from the eastern limits of Iroquoia, down the Susquehanna River to the village of Shamokin, and then westward across the Allegheny to the Ohio River, down to the mouth of the Great Kanawha River. Johnson eventually extended the boundary all the way to the mouth of the Tennessee River. While this was ostensibly done to honor the Iroquois claims of "conquest" over the Indians of that regions in the seventeenth century, historians attribute the expanded land cession to the behind-the-scenes lobbying of Virginia commissioner Dr. Thomas Walker, who was also working secretly as an agent for a group of Virginia land speculators. The Treaty of Fort Stanwix gave the colony of Virginia defensible title to almost all of the territory that would become Kentucky. Like the Treaty of Lancaster over two decades before, the Treaty of Fort Stanwix trafficked in a dubious claim of Iroquois "conquest" to transfer land title to a vast tract of the interior to the colonies. Land hunger, rather than an overarching plan for coexistence between Native and settler polities, was now driving British imperial policy in the interior.[56]

The weakened position of John Stuart and William Johnson to shape events in the borderlands of North America after 1768 is testimony to the increasing complexity of imperial governance in the 1760s and early 1770s. From London, the interests of the empire as a whole appeared quite different than they did in Charles Town or Albany. Reducing expenses and increasing revenue were the primary concerns, so while the Board of Trade devolved control of British-Indian commerce on to the colonial legislatures, Parliament continued to pass new and ever more refined revenue legislation. For many in the colonies, it was the actions of Parliament, rather than those of the Board of Trade, that loomed largest. Colonial desires to preserve individual and corporate British liberties seemed to be a more pressing concern than refining the machinery of imperial governance. Interestingly, the "conspiracy" imagined by many in the colonies, manifesting itself both in Grenville's and Townshend's revenue legislation as well as the remaining centralizing activities of the Indian superintendents, was not a concerted course of action at all. London's ham-handed push for imperial fiscal responsibility gave the colonial governments a slightly freer hand in the West, while clamping down on colonial liberty at the colonies' ports, with the various attempts to collect commercial duties. Neither course of action pleased the colonies. Gage reported that, in the aftermath of the 1768 change of regulations, colonists soon complained about frontier violence, but still bristled at the ministry's attempts to get the colonies to actually pay for the upkeep of the empire. Parliament's 1774 attempt to clamp down on frontier disorder, the incorporation of the Ohio Valley and the Great Lakes region into the province of Quebec via the Quebec Act, coming on the heals of the Coercive Acts, further angered many of the colonists. The difficulties of imperial governance—rivalry between colonies, rivalries within colonies, and rivalries between the colonies and the Crown—remained as formidable as they had been in 1751, when Benjamin Franklin questioned the efficacy of Archibald Kennedy's bold plans for imperial reform. But by the end of 1774, even though the problems of empire remained, the stakes of resolving them had increased considerably.[57]

2

"In an Odd State"

The American Decision to Leave the British Empire

> Dr. Franklin has been very constant in his Attendance on Congress from the Beginning. . . . He thinks us at present in an odd State, neither in Peace nor War, neither dependent nor independent. But he thinks that We shall soon assume a Character more decisive.
>
> —John Adams to Abigail Adams, July 1775

British North America had been turned upside down. At least this was the view from Philadelphia, the city that was emerging as the de facto capital of the Thirteen Colonies, where the Second Continental Congress convened on 10 May 1775. While the delegates of the First Continental Congress had promised to reassemble, if necessary, when they adjourned their ad hoc body the previous October, they could not have imagined how necessary such a meeting would be. The context in which Congress now came together was far more portentous than the previous year's controversy over the so-called Intolerable Acts had ever been.[1] Weeks before, on the morning of 19 April 1775, a detachment of British regular troops sent by General Thomas Gage from Boston to seize a rumored munitions stockpile of the Massachusetts Provincial Congress in Concord had met with armed resistance at village of Lexington. Fighting between the British regulars and the newly formed Massachusetts militia continued during the day as the regulars retreated back to Boston. While commentators would debate for centuries to come who exactly fired the first shot on the Lexington Green, for a majority of British North Americans there was no ambiguity. Provincials in Massachusetts and beyond perceived the British army—and by extension the king and the ministry—as the aggressors. Militiamen first from all over Massachusetts, and then from the rest of New England and other northern colonies, assembled and began to travel to Boston to support the local population's resistance. Gage's troops were trapped on the Boston peninsula as the city was quickly surrounded by provincial forces. A crossroads in the decade-old Imperial Crisis had been reached. The Continental Congress now directed its attention to providing a unified intercolonial response to this novel situation.[2]

Among the delegates to Congress who felt the tension—and excitement —of the moment most acutely was Massachusetts's John Adams. A lawyer of middling background from Braintree, Adams had risen to prominence in the Revolutionary movement in Massachusetts as an attorney in the legal case arising out of the 1770 "Boston Massacre," but it was Adams's works as a writer and a legislator that won him his seat in Congress. As author of the *Novanglus* essays in the *Boston Gazette* in 1774 and 1775, Adams had articulated one of the more cogent and ringing critiques of the constitutional doctrine of Parliament's unlimited supremacy over the colonies. However, in the aftermath of Lexington and Concord, Adams began, in private, to move away from one of the bedrock principles that undergirded *Novanglus* —the notion that the North American colonies and the British metropolis could continue to exist within the same empire.[3]

But as Adams contemplated the disintegration of the British Empire and the independence of the colonial provinces of British North America, a host of challenges soon revealed themselves. The colonies' relationship with the province of Canada; their relations with their American Indian neighbors; the prospects for commerce (and, of necessity, diplomacy) with the other sovereign powers of Europe; and the potential viability of a union among the sprawling, diverse thirteen colonies of eastern North America— each of these political relationships could, as they continued to develop, shipwreck the colonies' united resistance to the North ministry's legislation. Each could then, in turn, handicap an eventual bid for American independence. On 7 June, Adams described to James Warren that there was much discussion in the Continental Congress about "what we ought to do, with the Canadians and Indians." It was an unsettling question. The Thirteen Colonies were bordered by the province of Quebec to the north and west (under the capacious boundaries authorized by the 1774 Quebec Act) and at the same time surrounded by fairly powerful American Indian nations, such as the Iroquois, the Cherokee, and the Creek. Neither the Canadian settler population nor the majority of Native Americans displayed any inclination, in the late spring of 1775, to take a side in the emerging conflict, but the fear that both the Canadians and the Indians could chose to ally with the ministry was a real one among the American Revolutionaries. Rather than being worried only about a single force of regulars entirely surrounded in Boston, the Congress and the colonies feared that they would find themselves also dealing with conflicts on both their northern and western flanks. From almost the moment it began, the American Revolution simultaneously implicated, and was threatened by, peoples and polities beyond its borders.[4]

As the prospect of dealing with the Thirteen Colonies' near neighbors arose, the question of how to engage with distant neighbors—the other sovereign powers of Europe—soon followed. The American colonies' potential relationships with the European powers figured within Congress's major public statements published in response to the crisis arising in the aftermath of Lexington and Concord—the Declaration of the Causes and Necessity of Taking up Arms of 6 July 1775 and the Olive Branch Petition of 8 July 1775. The Declaration of Causes reiterated the American provincials' long-standing grievances against the ministry and then focused on the events of that spring in Massachusetts. It drew to a conclusion and a crescendo with a startlingly assured set of proclamations: "Our cause is just. Out union is perfect. Our internal Resources are great, and, if necessary, foreign Assistance is undoubtedly available." And while Congress insisted in the Declaration's following paragraph that "We have not raised Armies with ambitious Designs of separating from Great-Britain, and establishing Independent States," its earlier boast had given away the fact that at least some in Congress had contemplated the Thirteen Colonies' position (as well as Great Britain's) in the wider world of European sovereigns.[5]

Even if the majority of Congress was not willing to consider formal independence in July 1775—a reality to which the Olive Branch Petition's calls for reconciliation certainly testified—many of the leaders of the American resistance were pushing Congress to get the American colonies to begin to think and act like sovereign states. This process would both continue and accelerate through 1775 and into 1776. While the Declaration of Independence is (quite rightly) seen as a turning point in the process of the

American colonies moving from their status as British provinces to becoming fully sovereign participants in the Westphalian system, it was also one episode in a larger continuum. When Delegate Richard Henry Lee proposed on 7 June 1776 that Congress draft a declaration of independence, he simultaneously called for the Thirteen Colonies to draft a plan of confederation and to also consider measures for making foreign alliances. Potential articles of confederation were drafted and debated by Congress in July and August (and ultimately tabled until the following year), while a "Plan of Treaties" (drafted by John Adams himself) was approved in September 1776. The Declaration of Independence was but one pillar among many in the construction of the foundation of the sovereign United States. And American sovereignty was not the product of a singular event, but the product of a process that took a year and a half to unfold.

The story of the eighteen months between Lexington and the so-called "Model Treaty" is a crucial one. It would be a mistake to read the year and a half between the convening of the Second Continental Congress and the approval of the Plan of Treaties as an inevitable and unbroken march toward an independent United States. While some men (and women) agreed with John Adams and quickly wished for American independence, many were reluctant to break with the king and Parliament. These moderate voices (such as Benjamin Franklin) and conservative voices (such as John Dickinson) still believed through most of 1775 that the colonies could get what they wanted within the British Empire. They hoped that measures such as raising an army, issuing currency, and creating a de facto central government would provide leverage that would ultimately force the king and Ministry to redress long-standing imbalances and ambiguities within the British imperial constitution in favor of the vision and interests of the colonies. These cautionary voices also saw what Adams and those others who desired independence saw—that the Thirteen Colonies existed in a precarious geopolitical position. Altering the power dynamics within the British Empire (itself both an extended polity and a system of polities) was difficult to imagine without contemplating changed relationships with the Thirteen Colonies' near neighbors—American Indian Nations and the British Empire's loyal provinces—as well as with the other European powers. Congress and the Thirteen Colonies slowly (and, in part, unthinkingly) constructed the pillars of sovereign power during the course of 1775 and early 1776. And when American public opinion turned toward support of independence in the early months of 1776, the institutions were in place to allow the Thirteen Colonies to move from being provinces within the British imperial system to sovereign states within the European-centered states system. The choices made during these eighteen months also established the limits beyond which the American Revolutionary movement would not extend. Cognizant of the complexities of the wider world around them, the American Revolutionaries understood that in declaring independence they were more involved in the act of transposing preexisting polities from a imperial composite state to a larger states system than they were in creating new states from whole cloth.[6]

Benjamin Franklin's Negotiations

Shortly after the Continental Congress approved both the Declaration of the Causes and Necessity for Taking up Arms and the Olive Branch Petition in July 1775, John Adams noted to his wife, Abigail, the particular importance of one delegate to Congress, Pennsylvania's Benjamin Franklin. Among the most famous of British Americans in the middle of the eighteenth century, Franklin had returned from Great Britain and his duties as a colonial agent in early May 1775. He was almost immediately chosen by the Pennsylvania General Assembly to serve as one of the colony's delegates to Congress. Given Franklin's reputation, many (including Abigail Adams) wondered what Franklin's role in the Congress would be. "The People of England, have thought that the Opposition in America, was wholly owing to Dr. Franklin: and I suppose their scribblers will attribute the Temper, and Proceedings of this Congress to him," John Adams observed, "but there cannot be a greater Mistake." Rather than "take the lead" in shaping the debates and discussions in Congress, Franklin was "composed and grave and in the Opinion of many Gentlemen very reserved." Most surprisingly, Adams felt that Franklin had "discovered a Disposition entirely American." While modern readers generally imagine Benjamin Franklin to have been the American Patriot par excellence, in mid-1775 Franklin was something of a wild card, and regarded not without a bit of suspicion in many quarters of America. Franklin had devoted the bulk of his public career in the previous decade in attempting to soften the rough edges of the colonial opposition movement in order to end the Imperial Crisis through reconciliation.[7]

Through the summer of 1775, Franklin believed that the constitution of the British Empire could be reformed to both assuage colonial grievances and keep the empire whole. From his retirement from the printing trade in 1748 and his embrace of public life, Benjamin Franklin came to understand, better than most of his contemporaries, the challenges any advocate for the reform of the structure of the British Empire faced. Franklin experienced firsthand the peculiarities of colonial governance, the manner in which Indian polities and the colonial governments interacted with one another, and how Parliament and the ministry mishandled the questions surrounding the governance of the colonies. He thus had a capacious and flexible understanding of the potentialities for the structure of the British Empire—a fact that allowed him to hold out hope of reconciliation longer than most British Americans. When he abandoned the prospect of peacefully ending the Imperial Crisis, a major milestone on the path toward American independence had been passed. And Franklin would be an important ally for those who favored independence. His understanding of America's place in the empire guided his choice to embrace the movement for independence, and also undergirded his conception of how an independent American confederation could fit within the established European states system. Franklin's knowledge of the political structures of both the British Empire and the wider European world would prove invaluable in giving the American Revolutionaries the perspective they needed as they moved toward independence.[8]

One constant in Franklin's political thought was his recognition of the distinctiveness of America. Franklin's vision of the British Empire had coalesced in the 1740s and 1750s at the same time many of his colleagues, such as Archibald Kennedy, Edmond Atkin, and Cadwallader Colden, were also thinking about the empire and devising schemes to rationalize the various relationships it contained. Seeing the colonies and the mother country as distinct entities, Franklin understood that they had distinct interests. And he saw that the American colonies occupied an important—if not vital—position in the transatlantic geopolitical and political economic schema of the empire. As he articulated in his 1751 essay "Observations Concerning the Increase of Mankind," and on many subsequent occasions, Franklin believed that the American colonies' rising population and extensive land area made them the logical suppliers of agricultural sustenance for the British Isles and for a larger portion of Europe. Economically, the relationship between the mother country and the colonies was mutualistic and symbiotic, and Franklin thought that the constitutional arrangements between the two should reflect that as well. Economic self-interest combined with a shared history, resulting in mutual "affection," all of which also served to tie America and Britain to one another. Breaking this bond would be unnatural and unwise. Deep into the Imperial Crisis, Franklin maintained his view that the imperial system was flexible enough to handle the challenges caused by the divergent interests and understandings of the imperial constitution entertained by both colonial and metropolitan actors. This faith in the efficacy of the British Empire placed Franklin in a difficult position, especially during the moments when the Imperial Crisis became most heated—the colonial response to the Stamp Act in 1765, the debate over the Townshend Duties in 1767, and the violent response to the Tea Act, the Boston "Tea Party" of 1773.[9]

While Franklin believed that there was no reason that the British Empire could not accommodate both colonial and metropolitan interests for the mutual prosperity of all, commentators in both England and North America increasingly disagreed. After the Stamp Act Crisis of 1765, the majority of those who had the favor of George III (and who would compose the bulk of the subsequent British ministries) supported a policy and a constitutional vision of Parliamentary supremacy. This policy was embodied in the Declaratory Act (1766) and affirmed by every piece of legislation subsequent to it (until Parliament put forward the conciliatory proposals guiding the Carlisle Commission in 1778). Franklin's vision of a more federal imperial structure was untenable in the minds of most British policymakers. Similarly, as Franklin worked as a colonial agent in London during the 1760s and early 1770s, he found his perspective becoming more distant from that of the leaders of the Revolutionary movement in America. Colonial opposition leaders (especially in Massachusetts) put forward a vision of the British imperial constitution in which Parliament had no right at all to legislate for the colonies; the colonies' own legislatures were the only representative bodies with the right to pass laws and enact taxes on their respective colonies. Downplaying this fundamental difference, Franklin held out hope for reconciliation between Britain and America even though many Americans (especially those leading the opposition movement) had long abandoned such hopes.[10]

Franklin's writings in the spring and summer of 1775 reveal a man embracing the mood of the American political vanguard—that of strong protests against the actions at Lexington and Concord and a willingness to contemplate moves toward independence. Upon his return to America, Franklin quickly grasped the gravity of situation. "All America is exasperated by [Thomas Gage's] conduct, and more firmly united than ever," he reported to Joseph Priestley. "The breach between the two countries is grown wider, and in danger of becoming irreparable." The actions of Gage in particular, and the ministry in general, obviously exasperated Franklin personally, as his unsent missive of 5 July 1775 to his friend William Strahan ("you are my enemy and I am yours") clearly testifies. As Congress promulgated the Declaration of Causes and finished the Olive Branch Petition, Franklin wrote to two English correspondents, Joseph Priestley and Jonathan Shipley, and made it clear to both that he despaired of the prospects of reconciliation between the British government and the Thirteen Colonies and that he clearly placed the blame with the ministry. To Priestley, Franklin reflected on the "perfidy of General Gage" in marching on Lexington and Concord and the subsequent attack on Charlestown, Massachusetts ("She has begun to burn our seaport towns") as evidence the ministry had no real interest in "recovering the friendship of the colonies." To Shipley, he remarked that he felt that Britain "has neither the Temper nor Wisdom enough to seize the Golden Opportunity" for reconciliation provided by the Olive Branch Petition. Given his utter pessimism about the willingness of king, Parliament, and ministry to engage in good-faith negotiations to resolve the crisis and openly discuss the place of America in the empire, the beginning moves toward independence, such as raising an army, only made sense.[11]

Although Franklin accepted the moves toward independence, he continued to hope that the British imperial system could remain a useful vehicle for resolving the Imperial Crisis. Sometime before 21 July 1775 (when the articles were presented before Congress), Franklin composed draft articles of confederation for the American colonies. Franklin's draft articles were not the first attempt made at imagining an American confederation, and they differ in important ways from the Articles of Confederation that were eventually put forward to bind together the independent United States in 1777.[12] Unlike the later Articles, Franklin's confederation would have built on the existing structure of the British Empire, explicitly offered a role for American Indian polities, and left open the possibility of the colonies' reunification with Great Britain. Franklin's plan illuminates the complexity of the geopolitical situation in which the Thirteen Colonies found themselves as they moved toward independence and also underscores the transitional nature of this move.

Franklin's proposed confederation would mediate between the individual colonies and their neighbors while protecting their sovereignty. His thirteen articles bound the "United Colonies" into a "firm League of Friendship" while providing that "each Colony shall enjoy and retain as much as it may think fit of its own present Laws, Customs, Rights, Privileges, and peculiar Jurisdictions within its own limits." The point of any confederate structure was to safeguard the colonies' sovereignty, not obliterate or dilute it. At the same time, the "General Congress" would be the body that shepherded the relationship between the individual colonies and the world of the Westphalian system beyond. The Congress would have the "Power and Duty" of "Determining on War and Peace," of "sending and receiving Ambassadors," "entering into Alliances," eventually handling "the Reconciliation with Great Britain," as well as "Settling all Disputes and Differences between Colony and Colony." Congress would also have the responsibility of overseeing "the Planting of new Colonies when proper." Franklin envisioned articles of confederation that would respect the established legal position and standing of the colonies, as the colonials saw it, while protecting the colonies from the vicissitudes of the Westphalian states system.[13]

Franklin's proposed articles were quite broad in imagining a community of allies for the American Revolutionary project. Franklin sought peace, if not alliance, with the Indian polities neighboring the colonies. His proposed Article X placed the power to "engage in an offensive War with any Nation of Indians" squarely in the hands of the Congress, "who are first to consider the Justice and Necessity of such War." The following article was even more explicit about the potential for American-Indian relations. Article XI stated that "A perpetual Alliance offensive and defensive, is to be entered into as soon as may be with the Six Nations; their Limits ascertained and secur'd to them; their Land not to be encroach'd on." Franklin wanted no private land sales between colonials and the Iroquois, as the only contracts "were to be made between the Great Council of the Indians at Onondaga and the General Congress." And Franklin wanted similar boundary guarantees established between the colonies and "all other Indians." Finally, he proposed appointing officials or agents to reside in the Indian country to manage trade and maintain the alliance system. Clearly, Franklin was evoking memories of the Albany Congress and the entire history between the colonies and the Iroquois, as well as the system of interaction that British-American imperial writers had first articulated in the 1740s and 1750s. Franklin wanted to preserve the customary framework of interaction between colonial and Indian polities, not do away with it.[14]

Franklin's proposed confederation kept not only its western doors open, but also its eastern ones. Article XIII offered that "Any and every Colony from Great Britain upon the Continent of North America not at present engag'd in our Association, may upon Application and joining the said Association be receiv'd into this Confederation." Evincing a rather capacious definition of North America, "Ireland, the West India Islands, Quebec, St. Johns [now Prince Edward Island], Nova Scotia, Bermudas, and the East and West Floridas" were all "entitled to the Advantages of our Union, mutual Assistance and Commerce." Certainly, Franklin and other British Americans perceived a commonality of interests between the Thirteen Colonies and the other British "plantations" of the Atlantic rim; it is reasonable to assume that Franklin hoped that the colonial movement would find sympathizers, if not allies, in the other colonies. At the same time, Franklin's confederation was, at least officially, a temporary construct. Once the "Terms of Reconciliation proposed in the" Olive Branch Petition of 8 July 1775 were met, "the Colonies are to return to their former Connections and Friendship with Britain." Of course, "on Failure thereof this Confederation is to be perpetual."[15]

As much as Franklin's proposed articles were a precursor to a frame of government, they can also be understood as an attempt to tweak the mechanisms of the diplomatic systems of the British Empire to the colonials' advantage using measures just short of a full declaration of independence. By bringing the Iroquois Six Nations and the North American and Atlantic island colonies into the fold of the colonial movement, Franklin's plan was to pull the entire structure of the British Empire out from under the metropolitan authorities. Should that not work, the confederation had full diplomatic powers to go beyond the British Empire and send and receive ambassadors from other European sovereigns. Franklin's proposed articles show just how flexible the emerging Philadelphian states system was—at this point, the nascent American union could be folded back into the British Empire or petition for membership in the larger Westphalian states system. The Thirteen Colonies remained on the cusp of two systems of polities, and had yet to cross the threshold into the realm of sovereign states.

The Drift toward Sovereignty

The Olive Branch Petition arrived in Great Britain in the middle of August 1775, and was quickly delivered to the secretary of state for the colonies, William Legge, Earl of Dartmouth. The documents' bearers, Richard Penn and Arthur Lee, were soon informed by Dartmouth that King George III would not respond, since he had not formally received the petition "on the throne." The closest Congress received to a formal response of any kind was George III's 26 October speech opening the new session of Parliament. George III essentially labeled the petition a ruse. "The authors and promoters of this desperate conspiracy have, in the conduct of it, derived great advantage from the difference of their intention and ours," he told Parliament. "They mean only to amuse, by vague expressions of attachment to the parent state, and the strongest protestations of loyalty to me, whilst they were preparing for a general revolt." The congressional leaders' intentions were obvious in the mind of the British monarch: "They have raised troops, and are collecting a naval force: they have seized the public revenue, and assumed to themselves legislative, executive, and judicial powers, which they already exercise in the most arbitrary manner over the persons and properties of their fellow subjects." These actions were products of those who had "infuse[d] into their minds a system of opinions repugnant to the true constitution of the colonies," and they had only one logical endpoint: "The rebellious war now levied is become more general, and is manifestly carried on for the purpose of establishing an independent empire." George III thus looked at the ongoing actions of the American Continental Congress in the months following Lexington and Concord and saw the actions of a political elite taking the steps toward establishing a sovereign state or confederation of sovereign states. Eight months before the Declaration of Independence, the British king saw Congress's ultimate decision to make the Thirteen Colonies independent as a foregone conclusion.[16]

The irony of George III's observation was that while he was sure the colonial leadership was pursuing a course toward independence, such certainly was not echoed by many of the colonials. After the dispatch of the Olive Branch Petition, John Adams paraphrased Benjamin Franklin in a letter to Abigail. "He thinks us at present in an odd State, neither in Peace nor War, neither dependent nor independent," Adams wrote. "But he thinks that We shall soon assume a Character more decisive." How soon "soon" was, however, remained an open question.[17] By the time Adams had described the situation confronting the Thirteen Colonies, the Continental Congress had already constructed one necessary pillar of a sovereign state—an army. The Continental Army was created by a resolution of the Congress on 14 June 1775, and George Washington appointed its commanding general the following day. A second pillar followed a week later. On 22 June, Congress not only expanded the size of the Continental Army, appointing eight brigadier generals, but it also resolved to emit $2 million worth of bills of credit.[18] Before even offering the king the proverbial "Olive Branch," the Continental Congress had created both an American army and an American currency. Yet, the Thirteen Colonies remained "neither dependent nor independent" into the autumn and winter of 1775. Unanswered was an interesting and ultimately contentious question—what marked the divide between dependence and independence? As they proceeded to assume the powers of an independent state, what was the tipping point? When would the colonial leadership assume enough power and authority that the Thirteen Colonies would become sovereign states? And when would they publicly declare that this sovereignty had been achieved?[19]

George III did not cite a theoretical definition of sovereignty in his October speech before Parliament, but rather a practical one. His conclusion that the colonials aimed at creating an "independent empire" was based on their raising an army, issuing currency, and adopting the legislative, executive, and judicial prerogatives—all actions that were definitive of a sovereign state.[20] Yet, while George III counted the Thirteen Colonies as gone, the most ardent advocates for American independence believed the Continental Congress had not done nearly enough. Congress still publicly hoped for reconciliation and refused to consider a declaration of independence. Days before the king's speech in England, Joseph Ward (cousin and aide-de-camp to Massachusetts's leading general, Artemus Ward) dispatched a fiery note to John Adams from one of the Continental Army's encampments outside Boston. "I expect soon to hear that the Continental Congress have published the Confederacy of the Colonies—completed the republic of America—and formed a *commercial* alliance with France and Spain," Ward wrote. "Such tidings will be musick in my ears, as I apprehend nothing short of such a plan will secure our Liberties," he continued, "and if America should be enslaved it is probable freedom will expire thro the World." Prefiguring sentiments that would be used by Thomas Paine only months later in *Common Sense*, Ward laid out the stakes for American independence to Adams, proclaiming that "It is a great and glorious Prize which the Americans contend for, the *happiness of all future ages, and the freedom of the World* as the Liberties of all Nations may in some degree be connected with ours."[21]

Joseph Ward was not alone; other colonial commentators echoed his sentiments—both in what was at stake with the question of American independence, but also that American independence depended on rationalizing and fortifying the Thirteen Colonies' connections with the world of sovereign states beyond the British Empire. As he surveyed the stores of lead available to the Revolutionaries in Massachusetts for John Adams in early November, Massachusetts Brigadier General Joseph Palmer digressed from his report to complain of Congress's recalcitrance in proclaiming what seemed obvious and necessary from his position—American independence. "How long is this Continent to hope for a reconciliation with G B?" he wondered. "When will be the proper time to open our Ports to one or more other Nations? How long are we to be embarrassed and plagued with our vile Monarchical Charters?" Finally, Palmer asked Adams, "And when will the Congress give leave to all the United Colonies to take any form of Government they may respectively best like, not inconsistant with the General Union, of which the Congress to judge?"[22] Days after Palmer's letter, James Warren wrote John Adams similar sentiments. "Capital, and Effectual strokes" by Congress were needed. He, of course, meant independence. "It is said that the delicacy of modern Civilization will not admit of foreign powers while you continue to Acknowledge A dependency on Britain or Britains King, having any Connection with you," Warren observed. "Let us so far accomodate ourselves to their small policy as to remove this obstacle," he suggested. "I want to see Trade (if we must have it) open, and a Fleet here to protect it in opposition to Britain." And if that was a French fleet, that was fine with Warren. He left the most vociferous entreaty of the letter to be written by his wife. ("She sits at the table with me, and will have a paragraph of her own.") In an interesting and somewhat overt challenge to their masculinity, Mercy Otis Warren told Adams that he and Congress "should no longer *piddle* at the Threshold." She then exclaimed that it was "Time to

Leap into the *Theatre* and unlock the Barrs, and open every Gate that impedes the rise and Growth of the American ~~Empire~~ Republic, and then let the Giddy Potentate [George III] send forth his puerile Proclamations to France, to Spain, and to all the Commercial World who may be United in Building up an Empire he cannot prevent."[23] Ward, Palmer, the Warrens, and other Americans who urged Congress to declare American independence did so for many reasons, but one of the foremost among them was the perceived necessity of rationalizing, regularizing, and legalizing the Thirteen Colonies' relationships with the other sovereign powers of the European-centered world.

By the closing months of 1775, many elite Americans expressed an open desire to be free of the imperial connection to Great Britain. The desire for independence was not only rooted in a desire to have the local self-governing authority and control over the colonies' internal affairs restored, but also to engage the polities of the wider Atlantic world. Writing from eastern Massachusetts, both Joseph Palmer and James Warren believed that the Thirteen Colonies needed to be open to commerce from nations other than Great Britain—a wish no doubt driven both by the logic of Revolutionary ideology and the reality of subsisting under a blockade of trade for the better part of a year.[24] In December 1775, Benjamin Hinchborn reported from Lexington, Massachusetts, that the ongoing blockade of trade had kept "many thousands of our Merchants and Mechanics" "now idle in the Country," and that "a very numerous Body" were "now a burthen upon the Community." A declaration of independence would reopen American commerce and promised to provide employment for thousands of young men.[25] As more men and women involved in the Revolutionary movement imagined an independent and sovereign America, they did not imagine their polities floating in a void. They were well aware that independence would break an existing connection and provide opportunities for their polities to form new connections. Thus Mercy Otis Warren could imagine France, Spain, and "all the Commercial World" forging connections with the independent American states ("Building up an Empire"). And where Warren imagined these developments would redound to the embarrassment of George III and foster the growth of a rising American republic, others imagined more prosaic ends—increased American commerce and the employment of American sailors, merchants, and mechanics. Nonetheless, no matter what end one imagined, the acknowledgment of the position of the

Thirteen Colonies in an international system and the need to maximize that position was a given for all concerned. The American Revolution, as it was emerging, was a project with obvious international implications.

At the same time as the Warrens' and Hinchborn's pleas for a declaration, events on the northern borderlands of the Thirteen Colonies brought home the fully international context of the American Revolutionary project. By December, American troops had captured Montreal and stood on the outskirts of the city of Quebec. Although the American invasion of Canada would come to naught by the New Year, many, including Thomas Jefferson, began to contemplate the expansion of the American union to include Canada.[26] Yet December also reminded the Continental Congress what many had imagined early in the summer—that the constituent communities of the British imperial system could turn on and devour the Revolutionary project. Concern flowed from the pen of General Philip Schuyler in Albany, who was charged not only with the coordination of General Richard Montgomery's invasion into Canada, but also with the maintenance of cordial relations with the Iroquois Six Nations. In July 1775, shortly after Congress had created separate and distinct Indian departments to manage diplomacy and commerce with the various American Indian nations, it had drafted instructions and a speech to be given the Iroquois as soon as possible. Appointed a commissioner for the Northern Department, Schuyler had received the speech and his instructions shortly thereafter and had called for a treaty conference with the leaders of the Six Nations. After a preliminary meeting at German Flats, Schuyler oversaw a full-fledged treaty conference at Albany from 23 August to 1 September 1775. The Iroquois had promised neutrality in what Congress had instructed Schuyler to claim was a "family quarrel" between the British father and his American children.[27]

As reassuring as Schuyler's reports from Albany in the late summer had been, now came cause for nervousness. On 12 December during a subsequent conference at Albany, a group of Indians "related the Substance of all the Conferences [British Indian Superintendent] Colo: [Guy] Johnson had with them the last Summer." At a final conference at Montreal, Johnson had "delivered to each of the Canadian Tribes a War Belt and the Hatchet, who accepted It," Schuyler noted, "after which they were invited to feast on a Bostonian and drink his Blood." An ox was roasted, a "Pipe of Wine" consumed, and "the War Song was Sung." An unnamed leader of the Six

Nations reported all of this and gave the war belt to Schuyler. He then summarized the point of this intelligence to John Hancock (the president of Congress) with the conclusion that "We have now a full Proof that the Ministerial Servants have attempted to engage the Savages against Us."[28] In reality, nothing so dramatic had happened at Montreal; the accounts Schuyler related were exaggerated rumors. Nonetheless, Samuel Adams recounted these horrifying details in a subsequent letter to John Adams; word of the alleged ministerial perfidy was quickly disseminated across North America, as the Congress ordered the relevant paragraph from Schuyler's letter published.[29] While many delegates to Congress were as shocked and horrified as Schuyler intended them to be at the thought of a British Indian superintendent authorizing the consumption of an imagined American provincial's body, the larger message of Schuyler's letter was not news to anyone. Just as relations with the European powers could propel or sink the American Revolutionary project, relations with the several American Indian nations would also prove a crucial determinant in the outcome of the Thirteen Colonies' resistance to the plans of George III and the North ministry. From the first month the Second Continental Congress convened, it sought to appropriate a key pillar of sovereign power that had fallen within the purview of the British imperial state—the power and authority to negotiate and treat with North America's Indian nations.

The position of the bordering American Indian nations was never far from the minds of the delegates to the Continental Congress as they set about responding to Lexington and Concord and constructing the foundations of American sovereignty. John Adams conveyed the mood of many in early June 1775 when he observed to James Warren that the "Nations of Indians inhabiting the Frontiers of the Colonies are numerous and warlike." He noted hopefully that "They seem disposed to Newtrality," and that "None have yet taken up the Hatchet against us." Also boding well was the fact that "We have not obtained any certain Evidence that Either [Canadian Governor Guy] Carlton or [Indian Superintendent Guy] Johnson have discreetly attempted to persuade them to take up that Hatchet." Yet Adams also noted, "Some Suspicious Circumstances there are."[30] Congress created a committee to study the question of how to approach Indian relations on 16 June, and the body was soon known as the Committee on Indian Affairs. Worried that the Ministry "will spare no pains to excite the several Nations of Indians to take up arms against these colonies," the

Committee on Indian Affairs recommended on 12 July that "Commissioners be appointed ... to superintend Indian affairs" and that three Indian departments—northern, middle, and southern—be created in order to subdivide the responsibilities of the several commissioners. The following day the Committee for Indian Affairs presented language to be used in a speech to be given to the Six Nations, language that Schuyler would use, with some modifications, a month and a half later in the conference at Albany.[31]

The Continental Congress's actions in the realm of Indian relations—in the creation of the Indian departments, in the appointment of Indian commissioners, and in the drafting of language to be presented at Indian treaty councils—all were deliberate appropriations of powers exercised by the British imperial authorities. Not only was Congress appropriating powers that were once the obvious purview of the British Empire—and, in doing so, undermining the local legitimacy of British rule—but Congress was also attempting to regulate the relationship between provincial and Native polities in North America and affect the political and commercial relationships between the indigenous communities and the wider Atlantic world.

The plan put forward by Congress's Committee on Indian Affairs to manage relations between the Indian nations and the colonies resembled the customary and legal system that was existence in British North America, but also went beyond it in ways that found the Revolutionaries following in the footsteps of the imperial reformers of a generation before. Noting that "the Indians depend on the Colonists for arms, ammunition, and cloathing, which are become necessary to their subsistence," the committee recommended that "Commissioners be appointed by this Congress, to superintend Indian affairs of behalf of their colonies." The appointed commissioners would not range all over the eastern half of North America—"there would be three departments of Indians, the northern, middle, and southern." The divisions were not all that innovative. The Northern Department would encompass the Six Nations and the Indian nations to north of them; the Southern Department would embrace the Cherokees and the nations south of them; the Middle Department would simply "contain the Indian Nations that lie between the other departments." The division roughly paralleled that enacted by the ministry in the 1750s, when northern and southern Indian superintendents were appointed; the prominence and significance of the Cherokee and the Iroquois were specifically acknowledged. The disaggregation of the various nations of the Ohio Valley into the Middle Department was likely an implicit acknowledgment of the prominence to which Ohio Valley nations like the Shawnee had risen and also of the rising value of the lands held by these nations. Unlike the ministerial strategies for organizing settler-Native relations, power to treat with Indian leaders was more diffuse. Rather than singular superintendents, Congress was required to appoint multiple commissioners for each department (five for the Southern, and three for the Middle and Northern). The committee recommended that "the commissioners have the power to treat with the Indians in their respective departments, in the name, and on behalf of the united colonies, in order to preserve peace and friendship with the said Indians, and to prevent their taking any part in the present commotions." Like their British imperial predecessors, the commissioners would also have the "power to take to their assistance gentlemen of influence among the Indians, in whom they can confide," as well as the power "to appoint Agents, residing near or among the Indians, to watch the conduct of the [British] superintendants and their emissaries." With a few minor adjustments, Congress planned to re-create the system of bureaucratic oversight that had guided relations between the British metropolis, its colonial provinces, and the Indian polities of eastern North America for the previous two decades.[32]

The Revolutionary leadership's cognizance of the power relationships that defined the British imperial version of the diplomatic system that bound Indians, provincials, and metropolitans was revealed not only in how they constructed their replacement diplomatic regime, but also in how they justified the new system and how they imagined it would be deployed. Congress's willingness to appoint commissioners and allow them to depute agents to manage the commerce in "arms, ammunition, and cloathing" demonstrated an awareness that the political relationships with the Indian nations that they hoped to massage depended on the distribution of useful trade goods. Aware of the expensive nature of this form of diplomacy, $10,000 was authorized for the commissioners of the Southern Department, and $6,666.66 each was budgeted to the commissioners of the Middle and Northern departments. And the need to actively supersede the existing imperial diplomatic structures was made explicit. The commissioners in each department were to appoint agents, not only to manage trade, but also "to watch the conduct of the superintendants and their emissaries." If any nefarious activity was found—"in case the Commissioners for the respective districts, shall have satisfactory proof, that the King's superintendants, their deputies or agents, or any other person whatsoever, are active in stirring up or inciting the Indians"—Congress gave the commissioners permission to "seize" and detain the said offenders against the Continental interest. This was an extraordinary grant of police power to the Indian commissioners, but one that testified to the magnitude of what Congress imagined to be at stake. At the start of the resolution creating the Indian departments, Congress had declared that "securing and preserving the friendship of the Indian Nations, appears to be a subject of the utmost moment to these colonies," especially given that there was "too much reason" to believe that the ministry would "spare no pains" to "excite the several Nations of Indians to take up arms against" the Thirteen Colonies.[33] A month and a half later at Albany, Philip Schuyler presented the Congress's message explaining the conflict between Congress and the king and his ministers as a "family quarrel" between Britain and America and asked the Six Nations to remain neutral. This was a request that was heard, accepted, and, at first, honored.[34] Ultimately, the rumors Schuyler conveyed in December of Guy Johnson's diplomacy at Montreal served to reawaken previously existing anxieties. In constructing the Indian departments and drafting a preliminary raison d'être for appointing Indian commissioners, the Continental Congress acknowledged the nature of the existing political relations between the colonial governments, the metropolitan authorities, and the Indian nations while they simultaneously sought to insert themselves in the position currently held by the agents of the ministry, even authorizing the physical seizure of those agents. The construction of another element of sovereign power—with an explicit eye toward reworking the established borderlands diplomatic system—is obvious.

Just as Congress appropriated power to manage the diplomacy of the Thirteen Colonies to the west, it was during the last months of 1775 that it made the first steps to manage diplomacy to the east and open communication with sovereign states that were not Great Britain. Historians of early American diplomacy have often recounted the fortuitous coincidence that the Kingdom of France's first agent to the Continental Congress (a minor nobleman then residing in the Caribbean named Julien-Alexandre Achard de Bonvouloir) arrived in America shortly after Congress had created its first body to manage relations with the European powers, the Committee of

Secret Correspondence.[35] Charged with "the sole purpose of corresponding with our friends in Great Britain, Ireland, and other parts of the world," and initially composed of John Dickinson and Benjamin Franklin (of Pennsylvania), Benjamin Harrison (of Virginia), John Jay (of New York), and Thomas Johnson (of Maryland), the committee was to eventually (in 1777) be rechristened the Committee of Foreign Affairs. The creation of the Committee of Secret Correspondence, with its express powers to both correspond and to dispatch agents, was, most historians agree, the Congress's first concrete step in formally appropriating diplomatic powers.[36]

While the creation of the Committee of Secret Correspondence was an important milestone in the Thirteen Colonies' transition to fully sovereign states, a closer look at the business it and its members conducted during its first months reveals its actions to be just that—transitional. Letters were sent to Virginian Arthur Lee, one of the few remaining colonial agents in London who still corresponded with the Continental Congress, on 30 November and then again on 12 December 1775. In December, Lee was asked to discover and report "the Disposition of Foreign Powers towards us," a task the committee reminded Lee would require "great Circumspection and impenetrable Secrecy." Congress wanted no open acknowledgment that the Thirteen Colonies had begun to explore the possibility of forming political relationships outside of the British Empire. The committee's official dispatch to Lee also mentioned that Franklin had contacted a friend in the Netherlands, Charles-Guillaume-Frédéric Dumas, with a request to gather information for the committee and serve as a conduit for Lee's correspondence back to America, if he could not send such letters directly.[37] The Americans' relationship with Dumas during the course of the War of the American Revolution would prove beneficial; Dumas would serve both as a source of intelligence and a contact for American diplomats operating in the Netherlands. That said, Franklin's letter to Dumas and his initial request for him to serve the American interest merit further consideration.

The message conveyed by Franklin to Dumas was that the Thirteen Colonies were a group of polities on the precipice of declaring their independence and joining the wider community of nations. Franklin thanked Dumas for his gift (sent in July) of three copies of Emmerich de Vattel's *The Law of Nations*. "It came to us in good season," Franklin wrote, "when the circumstances of a rising state make it necessary frequently to consult the law of nations." Franklin updated Dumas on the events of the previous months, describing the Congress's ongoing attempts to coordinate resistance to the ministry's political and military efforts to enforce the Coercive Acts and maintain the integrity of the empire. Franklin expected war to continue and noted to Dumas that "we may find it necessary to ask the aid of some foreign power." Recalling Dumas's earlier observation that "all of Europe" (*toute l'Europe*) hoped the Americans maintained their liberties, Franklin used this as a jumping-off point from which to request further and more detailed information. "But we wish to know whether any one of" the European powers, "from principles of humanity, is disposed magnanimously to step in for the relief of an oppressed people," he wondered. Beyond that, "if, as it seems likely to happen, we should be obliged to break off all connection with Britain, and declare ourselves an independent people," Franklin asked if "there is any state in Europe, who would be willing to enter into an alliance with us for the benefit of our commerce"? (A commerce "which amounted before the war, to near seven millions sterling per annum, and must continually increase, as our people increase most rapidly.") American independence and American entry into the European-centered diplomatic and commercial system were imagined simultaneously.[38]

That Franklin subsequently made it clear that "We have hitherto applied to no foreign power" only underscored the delicacy of the moment and the importance of the queries he was putting to Dumas. These were not idle questions posed for intellectual curiosity. Knowing how inextricably linked the American Revolutionary project was to the ability of the Thirteen Colonies to exist and thrive in the world of sovereign states, the need for accurate and reliable intelligence about how the colonies would be received into that world was vital. Franklin's requests for information became more detailed, and they served to implicate Dumas in the American Revolutionary project. He asked Dumas whether he would be willing to make discrete inquiries (he was urged to proceed with "caution") to the resident ambassadors at the Hague (where Dumas lived) who might be open to a connection with the American colonies. Realizing that Dumas would receive inquiries in return about the state of the American resistance effort, Franklin gave him a encapsulation of the military situation in North America that put the congressional forces in the best light—"we have had on foot . . . an army of near twenty-five thousand men" and yet the Congress could "spare considerable detachments for an invasion of Canada." In short, the Thirteen Colonies were in a strong position and getting stronger.

Franklin ultimately allowed that if discussions developed in a serious direction, Dumas could "show them this letter as your credential" in order to provide support for such discussions and give them a more official cast.[39] Thus the letter to Dumas itself was an important milestone on the march to sovereignty in a twofold way—not only in the ideas that it contained and expressed, but also in its physicality, the very fact it was written and sent.[40]

It was when the Committee of Secret Correspondence dispatched its own agent from America to Europe to take the work it had asked Dumas and Arthur Lee to begin a step further—effectively commissioning a diplomat—that the Thirteen Colonies made arguably the penultimate step before declaring independence. On 2 March 1776, the Committee of Secret Correspondence issued instructions to Silas Deane, a Connecticut merchant and former delegate, on a secret mission to the Kingdom of France to purchase war materiel and sound out the French government about other ways it might aid the American cause. "On your arrival in France, you will for some time be engaged in the business of providing goods for the Indian trade," began the instructions. While suggestive of the interconnectedness of the colonies' diplomatic and commercial connections to the west and east, the proposed disguise was seen as eminently practical. The committee reasoned that such a pose "will give good countenance to your appearing in the character of a merchant, which we wish you to continually retain among the French, in general, it being probable that the court of France may not like it should be known publickly, that any agent from the Colonies is in that country."[41] Congress's instructions testify that Deane's mission to France began laced with ambiguity, reflective of the liminal position the United Colonies were in during the first half of 1776. Deane could not claim to be an official representative of a sovereign state seeking formal diplomatic contact and communication. Yet it was obvious to nearly everyone who observed him in France that he was something more than a mere merchant. By the time Deane crossed the Atlantic, the Continental Congress and the majority of the political public of the Thirteen Colonies were ready and eager for American independence. When Deane arrived in Paris in June 1776, he began initiating secret contacts with men in and around the court of Louis XVI (more because of the actions of French foreign minister Comte de Vergennes than because of any action of Deane's), and in doing so he would pave the way for France's eventual recognition of American independence. All that remained was for America to declare it.[42]

The Declaration and Its Limits

The Continental Congress did not formally begin to consider declaring independence until 7 June 1776, when Richard Henry Lee, speaking for the Virginia delegation, put forward a resolution that declared that "these United Colonies are, and of right ought to be, free and independent States." Lee's resolution further asserted that the United Colonies "are absolved from allegiance to the British Crown, and that all political connection between them and the State of Great Britain is, and ought to be, totally dissolved."[43] In taking up discussion of the resolution the next day, Congress set the United States on the final path toward a formal declaration of independence. But a formal declaration was only one part of the equation of independence that Lee presented to Congress on 7 June. Following its call for the dissolution of the bonds between Britain and America, Lee's resolution called on Congress "to take the most effectual measures for forming foreign Alliances," and then put forward a third necessity. The resolution declared the need for "a plan of confederation" between the thirteen individual colonies and asked that one "be prepared and transmitted to the respective Colonies for their consideration and approbation."[44] At the moment Congress began considering it, independence was predicated on not one, but on three distinct yet interrelated actions—a formal declaration of independence; the formation of official diplomatic relationships with foreign sovereign powers; and a formal rationalization of the relationship between the now-sovereign thirteen American states.[45]

The day after it was proposed, Congress began to debate Lee's resolution. While many delegates questioned the propriety of a declaration of independence, the validity of Lee's implicit threefold rubric of sovereignty was not brought into question. Indeed, the nature of the debate among the delegates confirms how interrelated the three concerns—declaration, diplomacy, and confederation—were. The detailed notes of the proceedings of Congress kept by Virginia delegate Thomas Jefferson testify to the myriad concerns that many delegates harbored about a declaration. A group led by John Dickinson, Robert Livingston, Edward Rutledge, and James Wilson worried that a precipitous declaration was contrary to the "voice of the people" at this moment, especially in "the middle colonies," where public sentiments "were not yet ripe for bidding adieu to British connection." The public in Pennsylvania, Delaware, New Jersey, and New York, in the thinking of those who counseled delaying a declaration, "had not yet accommodated their minds to a separation from the mother country," and many of these colonies had expressly forbid their delegates from voting for a declaration of independence. Should a majority of states in Congress push through a declaration now, the delegates from many of the middle colonies would have to withdraw with Congress, and "possibly their colonies might secede from the Union." This would be a disaster for the American cause. The delegates worried on the one hand that "such a secession would weaken us more than could be compensated by any foreign alliance," while on the other, they feared that a loss of the union would make the prospect of treaties with foreign powers even more unlikely in the first place. Even worse, any treaty the remaining American colonies contracted would likely be "proportionably more hard & prejudicial" than one they could contract as a single union of thirteen polities. Thus, those who opposed the declaration of independence called for in Lee's resolution did not reject his threefold framework for asserting American independence and sovereignty. Far from it. Their opposition was rooted in the fact that they saw a declaration, acts of diplomacy, and a permanent confederation as so interconnected, that a misstep on the first measure would doom the future of the other two.[46]

Despite these protests, Congress proceeded to appoint committees to handle all three of the tasks that Lee's resolution has suggested. On 11 June 1776, Thomas Jefferson, John Adams, Benjamin Franklin, Roger Sherman, and Robert Livingston were appointed to begin the drafting of a declaration of independence. That same day, it was resolved to appoint committees to draft a plan of treaties and articles of confederation. The next day those committee assignments were filled—Adams, Franklin, Dickinson, Benjamin Harrison, and Robert Morris were given the task of drafting a plan for treaties with foreign powers, while thirteen delegates (one for each colony) were charged with the drafting of a plan of confederation.[47] Congress undertook to answer the three great questions embedded in Lee's resolution—independence, international relations, and union—simultaneously. The Declaration of Independence was not drafted in a vacuum, but as one among a suite of documents that would attempt to answer the complicated question of how this new creature—the United States of America—would enter into the world of its would-be fellows.

That the Declaration was written with an eye to the international system—that it was a foreign policy document—is a historical reality that historians had largely forgotten until very recently.[48] The historian David Armitage has convincingly described how the Declaration served as what international lawyers describe as a "general manifesto"; in the international context, the Declaration was a diplomatic document issued to every sovereign government announcing a set of principles and justifying a course of action. In this context, the most substantive portions of the Declaration were not in its famous articulation of the principles of natural law found in the second paragraph ("all men are created equal"), but in its "statements of what the United States intended to become" and "what they could do once they had achieved that goal," found in its beginning and conclusion.[49] The Declaration's ultimate purpose was to announce that "these United Colonies are, and of Right ought to be Free and Independent States," that "all political connection between them and the State of Great Britain" was "totally dissolved," and that "as Free and Independent States, they have full Power to levy War, conclude Peace, contract Alliances, establish Commerce, and do all other Acts and Things which Independent States may of right do."[50] The Declaration defined what an independent sovereignty was, and forthrightly claimed that mantle on behalf of the thirteen United States. It was a definition rooted, not on the states' internal constitutions, but on how they related to the community of sovereigns around them. It would be the responsibility of the Declaration's companion documents to flesh out and confirm how these relationships would unfold.

Although work began on the Plan of Treaties (also known as the Model Treaty) and the Articles of Confederation at almost the same time as the drafting of Declaration, their gestation periods were longer and, especially in the case of the Articles, much more problematic.[51] The Plan of Treaties was the less controversial of the two. Drafted initially by John Adams, the Plan was supposed to serve as a blueprint for a commercial treaty with France. Adams, like many in Congress, wanted a binding commercial connection with France, but hoped to keep any potential political connection as limited as possible. Working with two published collections of European treaties, Adams modified or copied language from earlier treaties that France had concluded with other powers (including Great Britain). Adams likely believed that using established language only increased the chances that Louis XVI and his ministers would agree to the articles that the Americans were proposing. At the same time, however, Adams's work is revealing of the transitional, and almost conservative, nature of the political transformation the Americans hoped to achieve. The desire, expressed eloquently in the Declaration, was that the United States would assume "the separate and equal station" of any other sovereign state. The Plan of Treaties imagines that the transition of the thirteen colonial polities from the British imperial system into the community of sovereign states will be almost seamless. The principles of commercial reciprocity (or "most-favored-nation" status), respect for established maritime law, and definitions of contraband that France had agreed to with other powers would now extend to the United States. The trading relationship the colonies had enjoyed with the British metropole under the empire would be replicated with France taking Britain's role. Indeed, the most radical aspect of the Plan of Treaties was the hope that Adams (and other delegates) entertained that somehow this transformation could be effected without the United States joining in a full, formal political alliance with France or another European power. Despite this hope, the Plan of Treaties is of a piece with the Declaration of Independence—they were mutually interlocking foreign policy documents. What the Declaration proclaimed, the Plan of Treaties promised to make real—the United States' entry into the Westphalian system of sovereign states as a "separate and equal" member of that community. As conventional as both the Plan of Treaties and Declaration of Independence (at least when considered as foreign policy papers) were, it was the Articles of Confederation that would foreshadow, if not in part confirm, the tremendous changes to the established political system of North America that the American Revolution would bring.[52]

Of the three documents that came out of Richard Henry Lee's 7 June resolution, the Articles of Confederation were the most difficult and problematic to draft. Within the large committee chosen to draft articles of confederation, the lead was taken by Pennsylvanian John Dickinson. He had drafted a set of twenty-two articles, the bulk of which remained intact when they were presented to Congress in July. Open discussion and debate of the draft articles defined Congress's business from mid-July to mid-August 1776, ultimately coming to frustration. Many delegates balked at the powers Dickinson and the committee wished to grant to Congress, especially in regard to western lands, but also respecting the sovereign power of the states generally. The final Articles of Confederation (numbering thirteen) were not agreed to until 15 November 1777. Historians of the Articles and of the Continental Congress have stressed the centrality that interrelated questions of state sovereignty and the sovereign powers of the central government played in shaping the debates surrounding the Articles of Confederation and the form they ultimately took.[53] As we will explore in chapter 4, the Articles ultimately were a failure as a foreign policy paper, at least in terms of facilitating the relations of the United States with the sovereign powers of Europe once the crisis of the American Revolutionary War had passed. The Articles did, however, provide a set of workable answers for the time being about how polity relations within North America would proceed. The states' internal ability to define themselves as republics and their ability to organize and deploy internal police powers—authority the states had claimed as colonial provinces during the Imperial Crisis—were not severely limited.[54] The Continental Congress would arbitrate between the states and coordinate their external relations—both in making diplomacy with the European powers and making war on Great Britain in order to preserve independence.[55] What was most radical, however, was the relationship the Articles of Confederation articulated between the United States and its American Indian neighbors. Where the colonial provinces and the Indian nations had been congruent polities under the aegis of the British Empire, and Congress had seemed initially to have sought to perpetuate the existing imperial system when it created Indian departments and commissioners in June 1775, a close reading of the manner in which the Articles were revised in 1776 and 1777 reveals the drastic transformation the American Revolution would bring to the negotiations between settler and indigenous polities in North America. The Philadelphian system would not include the American Indian nations.

It is inconceivable that American Indians disappeared from the minds of the delegates to the Continental Congress as they drafted the three key state papers of the summer of 1776. Although it frequently is ignored by historians, the Continental Congress and the city of Philadelphia played host to a delegation from four of the Iroquois Six Nations in the weeks before and after Richard Henry Lee's resolution for independence.[56] Concern about the disposition of the Six Nations had been on the minds of many in Congress, especially since the arrival of Philip Schuyler's infamous "drink a Bostonian's blood" letter of December 1775. The early months of 1776 had seen increased efforts on the part of British agents to get at least some of the Iroquois communities to abandon neutrality, and discussions at the Iroquois Grand Council at Onondaga in late March 1776 were contentious. When the invitation to a conference at Albany and a follow-up visit to the American capital arrived in Iroquoia, representatives of only four of the Six Nations opted to participate. By this time, the congressional military leadership—most notably George Washington—doubted that Iroquois neutrality would continue much longer and sought to recruit as many of the Six Nations to the American side as possible. Congressional agents sought to impress the Iroquois negotiators with American martial prowess—parades of American troops were conducted at Albany and then at Philadelphia.[57] Caesar Rodney observed on 28 May in Philadelphia the parade of five battalions of soldiers, "three companies of Artillery," "the Light-horse of the Militia," as well as three battalions of Continental troops, who were "all Reviewed . . . on the Common, by the Congress, Generals Washington, Gates and Mifflin," as well as other officers, a group of Presbyterian clergy, and the state assembly. Also in attendance were "21 Indians of the Six Nations who gave the Congress a War-dance."[58] The Congress's martial display was thus likely returned in spirit, if not in magnitude, by the Iroquois. However, such displays were only a part of the Iroquois visit. Although no formal treaty came from the delegation's time in Philadelphia, on 11 June 1776 the Iroquois visited the Congress in session, where gifts were exchanged, speeches were given, and the Iroquois gave the president of Congress, John Hancock, the name of Karanduawn (Kerantawa:neh), or the Great Tree. Shortly after the exchanges were made and the Iroquois delegation escorted out of the hall, Congress appointed Thomas Jefferson and the remainder of the committee to draft the Declaration of Independence.[59]

As Congress's committees began drafting the documents that made the United States, the Iroquois were not forgotten—at first. Like Benjamin Franklin's draft articles of confederation from the previous summer, the plan of confederation John Dickinson composed in June 1776 explicitly mentioned the Six Nations. More generally, Dickinson's articles sought to accord American Indian nations a relationship with the American states similar to that which had existed under the British Empire. Dickinson's fourteenth article began, "No Colony or Colonies shall engage in any War with any Nation of Indians without the Consent of the Union, unless such Colony or Colonies be actually invaded by Enemies." The article then enumerated the cases wherein a state could unilaterally go to war, that is, if "[they] shall have received certain Advice of a Resolution being formed by some Nation of Indians to invade such Colony or Colonies, and the Danger is so imminent as not to admit of a Delay, till the other Colonies can be consulted." The principle here was clear. In deciding matters of war and peace between the United States and the Indian nations, Congress, not the states, would be the arbiter. The committee, interestingly, deleted the first phrase "with any Nation of Indians," leaving the wording "No Colony or Colonies shall engage in any War without the Consent of the Union." This identical language was carried over into the war powers clauses of Article VI of the ratified Articles of Confederation. While seemingly expanding Congress's powers over war and peace to all enemy invasions, the effect was actually more complicated. By creating a silence on Indian nations in the clause in which the union's war powers were delineated, but leaving an explicit mention of enemy Indians in the state war powers clause, the overall effect was to preserve state-level agency in determining questions of war and peace vis-à-vis Indians, as opposed to war powers more generally. Furthermore, the revised article distinguishes between a state being "actually invaded by Enemies" on the one hand and simply a rumor ("Advice of a Resolution") of an Indian attack, and yet makes both equivalent justifications for a state to make war without the consent of Congress. In deleting one of Dickinson's phrases, the committee on the Articles drew a small, but invidious, distinction between European and American Indian polities who might make war on the United States. This is especially striking given that the Declaration of Independence itself had characterized Indian attacks on American settlements as extensions of the British ministry's war making ("He has excited . . . the merciless Indian Savages"). Where Indians were extensions of European power in the Declaration, they were being disaggregated and distinguished from European powers in the Articles.[60]

Dickinson's other attempt to preserve the fluidity in polity relations that characterized the British imperial system in North America was similarly thwarted. His fifteenth article began, "A perpetual Alliance offensive and defensive, is to be entered into by the Union as soon as may be with the Six Nations and all other Nations of Indians." The article further offered that boundaries of the Indian nations would "be ascertained; their Lands to be secured to them, and not encroached on." Furthermore, land sales and transfers between the Indian nations on the one hand and private parties or individual states on the other would be embargoed until the Congress and the union as a whole could ascertain boundaries and decide on a course for Indian policy—"for the general Benefit and Advantage of all the united

Colonies." An additional proposal of Dickinson's did not make it past the committee. The Congress had appointed Indian commissioners the previous year; Dickinson's article proposed to regulate their conduct and provide for their support. "Persons to be appointed by the Union to reside among the Indians in the proper Districts," Dickinson wrote, "who shall take Care to prevent Injustice in the Trade with them and shall be enabled at the Common Expence of the united Colonies by occasional Supplies to relieve their personal Wants and Distresses."[61] Taken together, Dickinson's complete draft of his fifteenth article put forward what appears in retrospect to be a remarkable vision of how the United States would conduct their relations with their American Indian neighbors. Congress would enter into alliances with the Iroquois and other neighboring Indian nations as soon as possible, collectively survey and adjudicate the boundaries between the colonies and the Indian nations, and then appoint Indian agents who would serve as honest brokers between Indian and settler populations on the frontier. While this vision is remarkable in that it did not come to pass and differs markedly from the system that did evolve in the North American interior during the Revolutionary War and its aftermath, it is less remarkable when compared to its predecessor regime. What Dickinson sought to do, like Franklin in his draft articles of the year before, was recreate the complicated borderlands diplomatic regime that had existed in North America at midcentury under the British Crown. American Indian commissioners would play the same roles that British Indian superintendents had—preventing settler-Native violence, extending Atlantic commercial networks into the Indian country, and laying the groundwork for regular, orderly, and peaceful land transfers from Natives to settlers when the metropolitan authority deemed such arrangements were necessary. Congress would play the overarching, legitimating role that the British monarch and ministry once had done.[62]

The vision that informed Dickinson's and Franklin's proposals moved deeper into eclipse after the Declaration of Independence. As the committee's excisions on Dickinson's fourteenth and fifteenth draft articles reveal, the dominant mood among delegates—let alone political elites operating at the state level—was to preserve state sovereignty and the ambit of action for state-level actors. While Indian treaties and alliances were still seen as useful and desirable, in July 1776 the Congress was unwilling to treat warfare between European and Indian enemies in the same fashion, nor was

Congress willing to allow its Indian commissioners to be defined as honest brokers who might seek to prevent injustices against Indians. A year later, when Congress took up the question of the Articles of Confederation once more, the system of congruent polity relations that defined the late imperial regime recedes even further into the background. Dickinson's fourteenth article was incorporated in Article VI with the committee's amendments; his fifteenth article, for all intents and purposes, disappeared. Article IX gave Congress "the exclusive right and power" of "regulating the trade and managing all affairs with the Indians," and "not members of any of the states, provided that the legislative right or any state within it own limits be not infringed or violated." Just as in the war powers clause, state-level initiative was preserved. No word of the necessity or even desirability of Indian alliances was mentioned. In an interesting point of contrast, Article XI allowed for the incorporation of Canada into the United States, should Canada ratify the Articles. (Other colonies' incorporation required nine of thirteen votes of the current states.)[63]

In June 1775, John Adams had wondered to James Warren "what we ought to do, with the Canadians and Indians?" By November 1777, with the completion of the Articles of Confederation, and the American victory at Saratoga raising hopes of a treaty with France, two different answers to the question had emerged. With the United States well on its way to joining the European-centered Westphalian states system, a place for European settler polities like Canada could still be found in the American confederation. For the Indian nations, the answer was different. The borderlands diplomatic system of negotiation and exchange that had seen settler and Native polities as congruent and that had sustained the British Empire was now being undone by the United States of America.

3

"Are We Not ... Independant States?"

Imagining and Realizing an Independent America

> The King I think may treat with us by virtue of his prerogative, as Independant States. For are we not in fact such? Hath not our Independance been acknowledged by France? Did she not ground her connection with us upon our having been in full possession of Independance ever since July 1776? Have we not reason to expect other Nations will follow the example of France?
>
> —Francis Dana, June 1778

In early 1779, the American Continental Congress proclaimed to the world that the independence of the thirteen former British colonies in North America could no longer be denied. With the publication of a 122-page pamphlet, *Observations on the American Revolution*, Congress made it clear, once and for all, that American independence was a reality and that reconciliation with the British metropolis was now an impossibility. "All negotiation for dependence," they told their fellow Americans, was "at an end." The rulers of Great Britain, if they were "under the guidance of reason," now had only one option: they would call off their war and "would desist from those efforts which threaten us." However, Congress did not truly expect such a course of action: "On the part of Great-Britain it is declared, that as we *will not* submit, and she *cannot* subdue, she will attempt to ruin and destroy."[1]

The specter now loomed that the American Revolutionary War would escalate and metastasize into something more total and more deadly. Yet the

Americans were undaunted. Congress proclaimed that it would respond to any provocations in kind: "On the part of America it is declared, that if war is prosecuted in a manner not conformable to the law of nations, the conduct of her enemies shall be retaliated." In such a case, Congress observed, no course of action was too extreme: "[T]he determination of America to retaliate . . . must terminate to the great prejudice of Britain." The means were readily at hand, as "the towns on her coast are at least as defenceless as ours; and their citizens, unused to arms, are utterly incapable of repelling an assault." Congress noted that a "small sum of money would wrap their metropolis in flames" and warned that British "subjects and adherents may easily be found in any part of the earth; and the dreaded scalping-knife itself may, in the hands of our riflemen, spread horror through their island." The message was clear. In order to defend America, total war was now, seemingly, the only option.[2]

The author of this pamphlet was New York delegate Gouverneur Morris. Readers may be shocked and surprised to find the man regarded as one of the most conservative of the American Revolutionaries authoring a tract advocating extraordinary acts of violence.[3] While overheated rhetoric was often part and parcel of Revolutionary pamphleteering, Morris deployed such vehement invective at this particular moment to serve a calculated political purpose. His threats of extreme violence are indicative of the height to which political tensions were raised during the course of 1778. *Observations on the American Revolution* appeared at the conclusion of a crucial set of episodes in the history of the movement for American independence, in which Americans faced a fundamental choice about the direction their revolution was to take.

In February 1778, the United States of America had concluded their first substantial treaties with a sovereign European power, the Kingdom of France. With recognition by a European power, the United States had cleared a major hurdle to enter the Westphalian states system. This American diplomatic achievement prompted the ministry of Lord North in Great Britain to offer the heretofore most generous terms of reconciliation and reunion to the American colonies. A commission headed by Frederick Howard, Earl of Carlisle, carried these peace terms to America, arriving in June 1778. With the arrival of the treaties with France and the offers of reconciliation with Britain in succession (the first in early May, the second in mid-June), the leaders of the American Congress seemingly faced a choice—

alliance with France and a continued war for independence or reunion with Britain and the reintegration of the colonies into the British Empire.[4]

The Continental Congress confronted this choice in a curious way. Rather than openly discuss and deliberate on the options at hand, Congress quickly ratified the treaties with France, and from the moment the Carlisle Commission arrived in North America, the leadership in Congress sought to curtail and limit discussion of reunion with Britain. Congress refused to receive representatives from the Carlisle Commission, cut off formal discussions of the commission's proposals, and sought to limit the ability of its delegates to communicate, both officially and unofficially, with members of the commission. Key delegates also authored extended newspaper essays attacking the commission and its proposals. The leaders of Congress did all they could in order to ensure the failure of the Carlisle Commission—shutting down official avenues of communication, flooding the public sphere with hostile rhetoric and imagery, and attempting, through restriction and intimidation, to choke off the semi-public space of private letter-writing and communication.

The events surrounding the Carlisle Commission's reception in America stand in contrast with the proceedings that, months before, had led to negotiation of the Treaty of Alliance in France and then to its reception and ratification in America. Between mid-1776 and 1778, the American ministers in France—Silas Deane, Arthur Lee, and Benjamin Franklin—utilized every method of communication available in their attempts to win recognition of the American cause. They paid official visits to the French foreign minister, Charles Gravier, Comte de Vergennes; they lobbied his subordinates; they peppered the ministry with letters and essays; they established relationships with private commercial interests; and they wrote essays extolling the American cause, which were printed in various European newspapers. All the avenues of engagement that the American Congress closed to the British commissioners in America had been left open for the American ministers in France. Additionally, the diplomacy of 1778 marked the final, unequivocal step in the passage of the thirteen United States from provinces in the British Empire to self-governing and sovereign political entities that were members of the Westphalian system of states. It was in 1778 that the vision the Declaration of Independence had articulated in July 1776—that the United States should "assume among the powers of the earth, the separate & equal station to which the laws of nature and nature's

God entitle them"—came to pass. The "candid world" had read the Americans' pleas, and it had answered. Ironically, the reality emerging from this answer was not an unalloyed good.[5]

Like the child who is admonished to be careful what she wishes for, the leaders of the United States did not foresee the unintended consequences that sprung from the European world's acceptance of their sovereignty. Beginning in 1779, with hopes of a British-American reconciliation gone, the Revolutionary War entered its most vicious phase. A close reader of Morris's pamphlet might have guessed at this eventually—as he wrote of English towns in flames, the tone conveyed was one of stridency, not compromise. British pamphleteers responded in kind. And battlefield commanders, on both the British and American sides, obliged their partisans in the public sphere; as the focus of major operations in America moved into the southern theater, the mode of warfare took on a much nastier cast. With the French-American victory at Yorktown in October 1781, the subsequent collapse of the North ministry, and the emergence of a new British ministry under the leadership William Petty-Fitzmaurice, Earl of Shelburne, many American political leaders adopted an optimistic outlook. They believed that a quick and generous peace treaty would be forthcoming, Great Britain and the United States would conclude a beneficial commercial arrangement, and the postwar period would be one of rising prosperity for the new United States. The contentious and difficult nature of the United States' peace negotiations with Great Britain and its diplomatic difficulties with other European sovereigns were signs that the road ahead of independent America would be rockier than most had imagined.

The Selling of an Alliance

When Silas Deane, the former congressional delegate from Connecticut, disembarked in Bordeaux in May 1776, he entered a European world beginning to experience the disarray that had affected America for over a year. European statesmen in Britain, France, and throughout the continent anxiously awaited any news from the American colonies, and arriving Americans were kept under a watchful eye by both French and British agents. Under such scrutiny, Deane had to be covert in his initial attempts to get the attention of the French court. He relied on mercantile contacts—first a Bordeaux banker named Jacques Barbeu-Duborg and then, more famously,

Pierre-Augustin Caron de Beaumarchais—to establish his fledgling and unrecognized ministry and to make contact with the Court of Versailles. At this initial stage, with the American colonies still not having declared independence, Beaumarchais urged Deane to handle his affairs with discretion. "I ask that you will employ all the discretion of which you realize that you have need, to avoid the attention of the English Ambassador, and not to make our Ministers apprehensive in consequence of his complaints, thus involving us in peculiar embarrassments," Beaumarchais told Deane. "Our only endeavor should be to escape all observation and not to excite remark in attaining our ends." With the American states not yet even claiming sovereignty, negotiations had to be kept as secret as possible. The normal protocols of official visits and receptions could not be adhered to; Deane adopted the pose of a Bermudian merchant in a futile attempt to disguise what he was doing from British agents.[6] While Deane could not officially represent the American states as sovereigns until they had declared their independence, keeping French support for the American colonies clandestine as long as possible was also the design of the Comte de Vergennes. Although certainly willing to consider an alliance with America in order to challenge Great Britain, Vergennes was waiting both to see how serious the American effort would be and for the completion of an ongoing French naval buildup to support whatever course of action Louis XVI's ministers might decide to take.[7]

The difficulties Deane faced during his initial months in France, as he struggled to master the complex procedural norms of eighteenth-century European diplomacy, were symbolic of the challenge inherent in negotiating on behalf of states that were, at best, only partially sovereign. Perhaps Deane's most basic difficulty in conducting negotiation was an inability to speak French (his written French was rudimentary at best, as well). During his first meeting with Vergennes, the minister's first secretary, Conrad-Alexandre Gérard was required to translate for him. This inability to speak French constantly put Deane in the position of relying on others, such as Beaumarchais or Duborg, to contract much of his business for him.[8] But even had he been more fluent, there was little room for him to participate in the polite world outside of, but adjunct to, the formal world of the court. Simply put, spies were everywhere. "The city swarms with Englishmen," Deane complained, noting that "I have had, and still have, a most difficult task to avoid their machinations." He described how, "not a coffee-house or theatre, or other place of publick diversion, but swarms with [British] emissaries." Constantly under surveillance, "but knowing the [French] Ministry are my friends," Deane allowed that "I attended these places as others, but cautiously avoid saying a word on American affairs anywhere except in my own hotel, or those of my intimate friends."[9]

Despite all these handicaps, Deane did the best he could. Even with the lack of formal and public diplomatic recognition for the United States, Deane realized quickly that Vergennes already supported the American cause in private, via Beaumarchais. In what was likely one of the least difficult acts of political intuition in American history, Deane deduced within a month that the private acts of enterprise on the part of the author of *The Barber of Seville* were really a front for the French government. The giveaway was "that a man should but a few months since confine himself from his creditors, and now on this occasion be able to advance half a million, is so extraordinary that it ceases to be a mystery." Deane surmised that "everything he says, writes, or does, is in reality the action of the Ministry." Deane still made every effort to have France publicly recognize the independence of the United States, and subsequent to that, engage them in treaties of commerce and alliance.[10]

Deane's diplomatic activities through most of 1776 consisted of writing letters and essays and sending them to Vergennes, while at the same time he coordinated shipments of war materiel to America with Beaumarchais. It is Deane's writing that concerns us here. Written communication was a vital pillar in the edifice of the political culture of diplomacy. In the eighteenth-century European world, there were several modes of written diplomatic communication, each of which served a particular purpose. Uncodified, but generally understood, distinctions in written diplomatic matter mirrored distinctions elsewhere in the eighteenth-century political culture of print.[11]

The most frequently utilized type of diplomatic writing was, of course, the letter. Letters were the briefest, and thus, the most utilized forms of diplomatic communication. Letters allowed a minister to communicate with his sovereign, with his subordinates, with family and friends, and most importantly, with the other ministers with whom he sought negotiations. Taken as a whole, letter writing constituted a form of communication that was alternatively public and private in nature. Letters could take on a personal or an official character, or sometimes both. An ongoing series of letters between two correspondents could become somewhat personal over time, although letters between the highest-ranking ministers from sovereigns at court usually maintained an official and formal character. Official dispatches between a minister and his sovereign were usually marked as such (often numbered); private communication was almost always labeled as "private." For a minister such as Silas Deane, who had diplomatic, financial, and personal business to attend to, keeping the two areas of business separate was a necessity. Early on in his mission, Robert Morris castigated Deane: "You have mixed business and Politics in your letter which is a bad example and I must try to avoid it."[12] Nonetheless, the contents and character of diplomatic correspondence—especially the often intercepted or lost transoceanic American diplomatic correspondence—of necessity remained fluid. Letters could be public or private documents, but their fluid character rendered letter writing, in toto, a "semi-public" space—even the most private correspondence could be marshaled to serve a public function. To take away a diplomat's ability to correspond was to take away his ability to function as a minister.[13]

Less frequently utilized, but as important as letters in the collection of written diplomatic tools, were longer formats. Diplomats often composed essays or memoranda (in French, *memoires*). Such longer written works were intended, not for a single correspondent, but to be seen by more than one person. Generally, they were meant for a group at court or in the ministry; sometimes *memoires* were designed to be circulated among a series of different European courts. Still, *memoires* were directed to a limited audience. A *memoir* was an addendum enclosed with a regular letter, in which the diplomat could outline at length the reasons and rationale behind the course of action he proposed in his shorter letter. Deane authored several such essays during the summer and autumn of 1776, the initial months of his mission to France. He addressed many of these *memoires* to the entire ministry, rather than specifically to Vergennes.[14] Such writings were necessary when a minister had limited access to court, as in Deane's case, but were also useful when a diplomat wanted to outline a new course of action concerning a complex issue.[15]

Finally, diplomats could take diplomatic communication to the largest audience of all—the entire European (and Atlantic) reading public. Diplomats could, and did, author essays to be printed in newspapers or printed in pamphlets as stand-alone publications. Deane, Franklin, and Lee planted essays in newspapers in many parts of Europe, and oversaw publication of the periodical *Affaires de l'Angleterre et de l'Amerique*.[16] John Adams in his *Letters from a Distinguished American* essays did the same.[17] Such published essays were designed to circulate throughout Europe, influencing both public opinion as well as opinion at courts where the Americans were unable to dispatch ministers. At the end of the Revolutionary War, Franklin reflected on the power of the press to British oppositionist Richard Price. "The ancient Greek and Roman orators could only speak to the number of citizens capable of being assembled within the reach of their voice," Franklin began. "Their *writings* had little effect," he continued, "because the bulk of the people could not read." Matters were different now in the eighteenth century. "Now by the press we can speak to nations; and good books and well written pamphlets have great and general influence. The facility, with which the same truths may be repeatedly enforced by placing them daily in different lights in *newspapers*, which are everywhere read, gives a great chance of establishing them." Finally, not only was communicating on point important, but communicating frequently helped to reinforce one's message. As Franklin put it, "And we now find, that it is not only right to strike while the iron is hot, but that it is very practicable to heat it by continually striking."[18] There were thus three potential audiences for the diplomat's written word—the one, the few, and the many.

The American commissioners in Paris understood the power of the written word as they attempted to shepherd the United States from dependent provinces in the extended polity of the British Empire to independent sovereigns in the Westphalian system. As they operated within the bounds of established European diplomatic culture, Franklin and Deane sought to transform the European political mind. Their writings endeavored to excite and stimulate the European geopolitical imagination, to get Vergennes and his ministry, as well as ministers at other European courts, to imagine a functioning states system that included the independent United States. Deane and Franklin offered arguments in the realm of political economy and the realm of geopolitics. They continually outlined the conventional wisdom of the need of the European states for the commercial engagement with American markets. Simultaneously, they imagined and described an expanded European-centered states system that included the United States. Integrating America into European political and commercial networks would serve to curtail growing British hegemony and thus further Continental Europe's interests.

In his *memoires* of summer and autumn 1776, Deane created two contrasting images within the geopolitical imagination in order to win French support for the American cause. He first painted a horrifying image of the result of a British victory in North America, where Britain reduced her American colonies to subjection and reduced the sovereigns of Europe to an equally subordinate status. Simultaneously, Deane held out a vision of an independent America tied to France via commercial alliance, in which France and the United States reaped untold benefits from access to each other's markets.

Deane conjured an image of a future Atlantic world where Britannia ruled absolutely—an inevitability if George III's forcible reconstitution of Britain's American empire was allowed to stand. Deane repeated the conventional wisdom among the American Revolutionaries that Great Britain's conduct during the Imperial Crisis was evidence of "her own favorite ambitious Views of fixing an Absolute & boundless Empire in the Western World." This goal led the British Crown to pursue "a Series of the most oppressive & cruel, as well as injurious Acts, both public & private," and as a result, the colonies were "Driven to the last resource, To Arms." But in laying out standard Revolutionary boilerplate, Deane was quite careful to illustrate that Britain's aggression in America was perilous for all other powers in the European world, with "Great Britain stiling herself the Mistress of the Ocean & Arbitress of Europe." Deane opined that in "applying to the Court of France," the American colonies were "confident" the court "will not suffer Countenance or aid to be given to the Oppressor." The specter Deane raised was that a government capable of asserting unmitigated dominion within its own constitutional system would likely attempt to achieve the same ends in the larger European-centered states system. Britain's imperial reorganization, the creation of a "System pregnant with" the American colonists' "immediate ruin," which "must ultimately affect every Power in Europe, interested in America," began "as early as 1764," immediately following the Seven Years' War. The current state of the American colonies was evidence that the "original design" of the "Ministry of Great Brittain," was the establishment of "an exclusive & absolute Dominion in America." With subtlety, Deane linked the present sad fate of the Thirteen Colonies with France's humiliating expulsion from North America in 1763, while also arguing that future prospects for the rest of Europe grew cloudier the tighter Britain's hold on America became. The

"Powers in Europe" would find it in their interest to intervene "in America" to "preserve their own Settlements in that Quarter of the Globe from falling under the power of Great Brittain." The weight of "the Oppressor" would be experienced by all Europeans as surely as it was currently being felt by heretofore loyal British American subjects.[19]

If a Westphalian system deranged by British hegemony was a stick with which Deane attempted to prod the French ministry, the prospect of a free and open commerce with the American colonies served as an irresistible carrot. Deane's lengthy August 1776 "Memoir on the Commerce of America, and Its Importance to Europe" relies on much of the logic that underlay John Adams's contemporaneous Model Treaty, namely that North American communities produced raw materials that European states needed, and therefore European governments would irresistibly lower their import duties and open their ports to American exporters. "This large exportation of the real necessaries of Life and simple materials, which has ultimately centered on Great Brittain . . . must always center in some part of Europe," Deane offered. The image was one of a growing and expanding American population committed primarily to agricultural production, as well as to production of other raw materials, such as timber and naval stores, in which a perpetual American periphery would feed the European metropolis that offered the best deal. And offer they would, wrote Deane: "Is not a Commerce of Four Millions annually in raw, or simple materials, paid for in Manufactures of the coarser, & cheaper kind, an Object worth attending to?" America's newfound commercial free agency could serve France in a twofold manner. French merchants and importers could take the place of their British counterparts. This would enrich France and impoverish Britain.[20]

The resources and endowments of America were a staple for Franklin when he began writing in Europe as part of the American lobbying effort in 1777. By early September 1777, Franklin had drafted a memorandum that was published in English and French, as well as privately circulated. In "Comparison of Great Britain and America as to Credit, 1777," Franklin, like Deane before him, focused on America's "natural advantages": its productive agricultural economy, its rising population, and the understanding that such agrarian republics produced a simple and virtuous people, trustworthy allies, to be sure. Where Deane had turned to geography, Franklin invoked demography. Attempting to prove to Continental interests that the American states were a safe credit risk, Franklin turned to the image of a rising and expanding population he had first articulated in his 1751 essay "Observations Concerning the Increase of Mankind." America trumped Britain when it came to the "Prospects of great future Ability" to pay off loans. With "a vast territory yet to be cultivated" and a population "who double themselves by a natural Propagation in 25 years" (as well as welcoming immigrants), the result would be that in America "every 20 years there will be a double Number of Inhabitants obliged to discharge publick Debts." A land of abundance deserved credit, and to grant credit generously was really in Europe's interest. A growing and expanding American population committed primarily to agricultural production in which a perpetual American periphery could feed the European metropolis was a vision that should have proved irresistible to Old World sovereigns. American independence thus served two ends: it maintained French security by weakening British dominion in North America, while also transforming the North Atlantic from a British commercial conduit into a European emporium.[21]

As appealing as this vision might have been, the Americans' calls for a new world order fell generally on deaf ears, and were heard least in the place they were proclaimed the loudest. The Americans' best friend, Charles Gravier, Comte de Vergennes, Louis XVI's foreign minister, did not attempt to reimagine the Westphalian states system. Vergennes did not need a new world order—the American states fit just fine (and most usefully) into the old one. Vergennes had little interest in commercial affairs, which lay beyond the purview of his ministry, and was generally unmoved by arguments focused on political economy. Geopolitics, not geoeconomics, moved Vergennes to action. And he did not see the need to remake the world in order to aggrandize French power and further French interests. Vergennes had only to imagine the Atlantic world prior to the Peace of Paris of 1763 to see the outlines of the world he wished to create. Students of Vergennes' policy have emphasized the relatively unimaginative nature of his political calculus. The overarching goal of Vergennes's policy was to weaken Britain—ideally to put France in the preeminent position in the European system, but at the minimum to restore the relative "balance" that existed before the settlements of 1763. He continued to operate under the paradigm of his predecessor, the Duc de Choiseul, who believed that the best way to weaken Britain was through increasing French naval strength and challenging Britain on the seas and in its colonial possessions. Vergennes wished to weaken Britain, knew the American war was a means to that end, and acted accordingly. With American independence, Vergennes did see a new Atlantic world, to be sure, but the new Atlantic he imagined was nowhere near as revolutionary as that envisioned by the American commissioners. To abuse a classic geopolitical metaphor, Vergennes simply saw a new piece at play on an old chessboard, while Franklin and Deane thought the chessboard had been resized and repainted.[22]

Or so they hoped. The old world order proved to have a great deal of staying power. In November 1777, military reality outpaced geopolitical imagination as word of British General John Burgoyne's surrender at Saratoga reached the British Isles and the European continent. The cascade of political calculations undertaken at both St. James and Versailles fell, for the most part, within the bounds of the old political calculus. The Vergennes ministry, already preparing for war, worried that Britain might approach the Americans with favorable terms for reunion. Many in the North ministry were very worried about the prospects of a French-American alliance and that Britain's American war could become one front in a wider war against the Bourbon monarchies. Several uncoordinated British attempts to secretly negotiate with Franklin, Deane, and Lee during December 1777 came to nothing. At the same time, Vergennes moved to make a French-American alliance a reality. And so it was on 6 February 1778. It is interesting to note that as the Americans and French entered into their alliance, they did so with very different conceptions of the shape of the larger system they now moved within together. What for the Americans was a transformation of the established Atlantic geopolitical order was simply business as usual for the French. The significance of the Americans' two-year-long project of stretching the geopolitical imagination is more significant for its effect on American, not French, minds. The American ministers now saw their independent states as indispensable cogs in a transatlantic political and commercial machine. Did they really need Great Britain anymore?

William Eden and the Vision of a Federalized British Empire

Regardless of what the Americans believed, the British government knew that it still needed America. Throughout the latter part of 1777, and especially following Burgoyne's defeat at the Battle of Saratoga, the North ministry was sensitive to any sign that France's support for the American cause might become open and official. Among the most concerned and connected to the problem was a member of the Board of Trade and a rising star in the North ministry, a Durham jurist named William Eden.[23] From late 1777 through the end of 1778, Eden would be one of the most prominent forces shaping the North ministry's approach to the American war, as he became the guiding hand behind the peace initiative, ultimately carried to America by the Carlisle Commission. Formulated in an attempt to stabilize the teetering North ministry in the wake of Saratoga, Eden's plans for the Carlisle Commission expanded the limits of the possible within the British Empire. In order to prevent the final and irrevocable ascension of the thirteen American colonies into the realm of sovereign states, Eden was willing to redistribute power within the British imperial system to a degree not contemplated even two years before. Eden envisioned a new Atlantic world, with the American states functioning economically much as Deane and Franklin had imagined, but existing politically as self-governing provinces within a federated British Empire, still subject, nominally, to the king and Parliament.

Eden's new imperial vision coalesced quickly, but not instantaneously. The victories of Horatio Gates over John Burgoyne in the Saratoga campaign in September and October 1777, and Burgoyne's surrender of 17 October accelerated British thought and action. While Lord North had contemplated opening serious negotiations with the American governments even before news of Saratoga reached Great Britain, the word of Burgoyne's defeat prompted him not only to think further about diplomacy, but also to consider his own resignation. In December 1777, Eden counseled North against this, as if he resigned now, his "successors would acquire the whole Credit of carrying the shatter'd Vessel into Port." Eden believed it was entirely within North's power to save the listing ship that was the British Empire. Of course, in order to do so, it was necessary to put to paper the heretofore nearly unthinkable, "Whether it will not be a wise Measure to desist from the Attempt to force internal operations in America?" Eden's logic was straightforward. As British troops could hold only a portion of the North American countryside, it would be better to withdraw and fortify them in key posts: Canada, New York City, Long Island, St. Augustine. The war could be prosecuted as a naval war, with the Royal Navy interdicting American commerce and destroying American port facilities, but this promised only to exhaust British resources and frustrate the public. It would be better to revive a peace commission, "take some Parliamentary measure," and "bring before the Public some Plan of Pacification." Eden began to outline all of the issues required by a settlement of the American rebellion, including the future situation of the Continental Congress, the Continental Army, and what to do about the legislation that had driven the colonies to revolt in the first place. North ultimately decided that Eden's proposal had merit, and Eden spent the remainder of the winter of 1777–78 formulating the outline of instructions and guidelines for a new peace commission.[24]

Negotiations with the Americans over the possibility of reshaping the Atlantic world and reconstituting the British Empire began almost immediately. In addition to his service to the Board of Trade, Eden maintained a network of spies and informants in France, the Low Countries, and the German states, which kept him apprized of the evolving American relationship with the European powers, especially France.[25] Foremost among Eden's secret agents was a Loyalist (with ties to New Hampshire) named Paul Wentworth, who shuttled between London, Paris, and Amsterdam throughout 1776 and 1777. Wentworth was apparently fluent in French, could mingle in all quarters of Parisian society, and his ability to gather information was unsurpassed.[26] Traveling to Paris in mid-December 1777, Wentworth sought and obtained a secret meeting with Silas Deane.[27] Meeting at Deane's Passy apartment for dinner, Wentworth and Deane talked into the evening. They rendezvoused the next day at a Parisian coffeehouse and commenced further talks. Wentworth recorded every detail of both conversations and transmitted them to Eden. The scene of the two sons of New England engaged in conversation offered a marked study in contrasts. Wentworth was an unapologetic Loyalist, whereas Deane tried very hard to play the good Revolutionary. According to Wentworth, Deane's "manner and Language" displayed "a great deal of Republican Pride, which He affects to imitate in the Character of Gov. Winthrop of the last Century, an Arch Republican, whose Maxims & Correspondence, He is always quoting from His Diary." The two began their first conversation over dinner, and debated at length the origins of the American Revolution. Deane went into great detail describing the abuses the Americans had suffered and the energy and ingenuity they had demonstrated in coming together to resist Britain. Deane "took Pains to show the part he had acted" in the first year of the Revolution, Wentworth dryly noted. Wentworth then parried Deane's arguments for a time, arguing that the liberties granted to the colonies in the seventeenth century were always meant to be temporary, that James I and Charles I had "encouraged Colonies for future Benefit, like planting woods; Nurse them well when young & don't take the profitt till late &c." The Americans had no right to complain now. The debate went on for a while, and could have gone on longer, but Wentworth had been sent by Eden to negotiate. At the conclusion of the first day, Wentworth presented Eden with a list of proposals for ending the war and reuniting the empire. Deane promised to look them over and report back the next day. When Wentworth called on Deane the next evening, Deane was meeting with Franklin and Lee, and Deane's servant requested that Wentworth wait for Deane at a local coffeehouse. Although Deane introduced Wentworth to Franklin, serious negotiations never occurred. Contact between Wentworth and the American commissioners never proceeded beyond preliminary discussions.[28]

Wentworth's December meetings with the commissioners were a culmination of sorts of over a year and a half of spying, surveillance, and information gathering in the French metropolis. For this whole period, Wentworth had peppered Eden with lengthy letters and memoranda on the Americans. As he gathered information on the American diplomats and their prospects, Wentworth also compiled a body of data on the identities and goals of the American Revolutionaries generally. Taken together, his reports thus constituted one of Eden's greatest sources of information on the American question. A prime example was a thirty-page report, composed at some point in 1777, in which Wentworth reported and opined on the progress and leadership of the American Revolution, identifying the leaders of the independence movement by state, and delineating their character and goals. The image Wentworth presented to Eden was that of a fractious union of colonies with a good deal of regional variation, holding little in common, and led by a cadre of committed, grasping provincials determined to maintain the wealth and status the Revolution had brought or promised them. Wentworth's memo conveys a picture of Revolutionary America as a diverse system of states in a complex and contested transition from membership in a polyglot British Empire to something different and unknown.

Wentworth first described to Eden the shape of the emerging American states system. The union created by the Confederation was anything but a united republic; in fact, Wentworth saw in the emergent Philadelphian system a Westphalian system in miniature. For purposes of analysis, he divided the colonies in three districts—New England, the Middle Colonies, and the Southern Colonies—and noted that "there are perhaps Stronger lines of distinct Character in these three districts, than in the three districts of the Realm in Europe." New England, along with Long Island, Vermont, and part of New York, a region "chiefly settled by Rigid Dissenters," Wentworth labeled "the Eastern Republick of Independants in Church & State: & they may follow the Confederacy of the Swiss Cantons." The second region, "from Hudsons River to Potowmack River, embracing the Proprietary Governments," was "called the Middle Republick of Toleration in Church & State, imitating the Union of the Seven Provinces." Finally, below the Potomac, lay "the Southern Republick," with a "Mixed Government Copyed nearly from Great Britain." Each district had one province at its head, Massachusetts, Pennsylvania, and Virginia, respectively, which had directed the others and spearheaded the rebellion.[29]

Turning back to the situation in the colonies in 1774 and 1775, Wentworth did not remember a majority, in any region, supporting independence. He identified four options entertained among British Americans at the time. They were: complete submission to Parliament; a return to the system of 1763; a return to 1763 with Parliamentary guarantees exempting the colonies from taxation; and complete "Independency." Wentworth wrote that many believed in complete submission to Parliament, while a majority simply wished a return to the system of 1763. But mismanagement from London, combined with "the Perseverance of a few Zealots," opened the floodgates. The Zealots' "dexterity & policy applyed to let in the thin, distant, & Needy Counties of each Province, to Vote equally with the Populous, Trading & Rich Counties," and thus "soon induced a Majority for" restraints on Parliament's power to tax and this "opened Roads to the Minds of the people little fitt to discuss weighty subjects, or easily misled by the variety of Interest & inducements which much disorders only could afford them."[30]

It was this set of resources, among others, that lay in intellectual tool kit of William Eden as he confronted a crisis in late 1777. Based on his own experience, as well as his espionage activities and subsequent meetings with the commissioners, Wentworth saw America as divided and amenable to reunion. He believed it was a vocal minority in key provinces, such as that led by Adams in Massachusetts, that pushed the American Revolution forward. Wentworth presented an image of Revolutionary America to Eden that emphasized the tenuous nature of the union, as well as the fractious politics that prevailed within each state. This was a diffuse system of diverse states that had seemingly little long-term prospect of remaining united as a single, coherent entity. Riven by internal faction as well, it would not be difficult to imagine a majority of Americans seizing the opportunity to rejoin the British Empire, given the right conditions.

A belief in internal factionalism within the colonies was the starting point for Eden's work in February and March 1778. Even once the French and American ministers had concluded the Treaty of Alliance and the Treaty of Amity and Commerce in early February, the North ministry believed that if they could present a plan for reunion and reconciliation to the Congress, ratification of the French treaties could be prevented and the empire saved. Eden knew the plan he devised had to be irresistible. His plan for conciliation would be constructed on the broadest base possible. This required turning back the clock on the Imperial Crisis, and reducing the evolved imperial constitution into something of a tabula rasa. The foundation of the new peace commission would be the repeal of most of the legislation that had offended the colonials. "The Tea Duty & Massachusetts Charter Bill" would go first, as "a proof of [the Ministry's] willingness to give satisfaction on those points," and would be followed by an "immediate Repeal of all the Acts" regulating the colonial trade "since 1763."[31] But rather than simply removing grievances rooted in inconvenient revenue legislation, Eden also wanted to speak to the Americans' constitutional concerns, and offer security for their homegrown governmental institutions.

The notes exchanged by Eden, North, George Germain, Alexander Wedderburn, Richard Jackson, and others involved in forming the peace commission reveal just how much was on the table at this moment, how North permitted Eden to essentially brainstorm a whole new imperial constitution. Much of the correspondence between the parties relative to the formation of the peace commission related to drafting the bill to appoint the commissioners, who the commissioners would be, the contents of their instructions, and how the bills would secure passage through Parliament. Ultimately, Eden secured his longtime friend Frederick Howard, Earl of Carlisle, to head the commission, and got himself on the commission as well. The third member was George Johnstone, a member of Parliament who had had a history of supporting the American cause during the Imperial Crisis. Both of the Howes, already in America making war, were also named in the Royal Commission, but they both ultimately declined to serve. Fascinatingly, the commission's official secretary was the Scottish philosopher Adam Ferguson, author of *An Essay on the History of Civil Society*. As Ferguson's writings proved most influential in eighteenth-century American political thinking, the junior member of the Carlisle Commission ironically likely did more to shape American political institutions than all his superiors combined.[32]

That, of course, is a different story. More important to the study here are the exchanges about the commission's goals and instructions. Solicitor General Alexander Wedderburn was charged with the drafting of instructions, but it was Eden who made his voice heard at many key moments. It was in this formulation that a new vision of the British imperial constitution took shape. One of the key documents among Eden's papers is a large working copy that was begun by Eden in March 1778 labeled "Hints." This document was obviously worked on in several hands, mostly those of Eden and Wedderburn. These working notes contain a number of remarkable concessions, foremost among them the stance Eden wanted to adopt in negotiating with Congress. "Their Confederacy is certainly a State *for the purpose of Treaty*—& if they call themselves the Representatives of the free & independent States appointed to treat with Commissioners from the Crown of Great Britain, or take any Synonimous Appellation, it does not seem necessary to make any Objections or even to make any indirect or implied protest." This was a concession of enormous significance. Accepting, or even conceding, the United States the status of "free & independent States" would for all intents and purposes mark Great Britain's acceptance of the Declaration of Independence and transform the character of the proposed negotiations. It did not make the final instructions, but it revealed how far many in the North ministry were prepared to go in order to end the war and undo the Franco-American Alliance.[33]

What the commissioners were able to offer, under terms of their final instructions, was no less startling. The final form of the commissioners' instructions gave them leeway to offer almost anything short of full independence. The commissioners would propose a cease-fire while negotiations ensued, and would allow the Continental Army to remain in the field. There was even talk that it could remain intact after the colonies were reunified with the empire, as the Continental Army officers could keep their commissions, and it would serve as the force designated to defend the colonies. The Continental Congress could remain intact as long as it did not infringe upon

British sovereignty. The colonies could send representatives to Parliament, and the colonies would have discretion of their own internal taxation, although commercial regulation would still fall primarily under metropolitan control. Importantly, all those involved in the rebellion could receive full pardons and amnesty, and the British government would gladly assume all the debts contracted by Congress in the prosecution of the war.[34]

The Carlisle Commission may have been tragically doomed from the start. Eden's continued micromanagement of the commission rubbed many the wrong way. Eden fretted about the titles of commissioners and whether they would be accorded full ambassadorial rank. He corresponded with the captain of their flagship to America, the *Trident*, wondering about the dimensions of state rooms, and whether the ship could fly a commodore's pennant, since it was carrying ambassadors. Eden's obsession with style even prompted sarcasm from George III himself. More damaging was the fact that, unknown to Eden, George Germain had secretly undercut much of the commission's bargaining power when he ordered the Howes to redeploy forces from the northern theater to East Florida. The *Trident* would divert from New York City to Philadelphia in order to rendezvous with Lord Howe's army. The commissioners arrived just days before Howe was planning to evacuate Philadelphia, delaying the evacuation until the commission could complete its work. As the army and its officers were packed and ready to leave Philadelphia, the Carlisle Commission managed to either offend or inconvenience the British army, most Philadelphians, and the Continental Congress all within a week's time.[35]

The significance of the Carlisle Commission was not so much that it stood a good chance of success, but in the intellectual effort that went into shaping it. In reimagining the structures of the extended polity of the British Empire, Eden and his cohort were forced to rethink their conception of how the political and commercial system of the Atlantic world could work. The Eden plan promised the North American states all the advantages of membership in the British Empire, with legislative guarantees of the internal freedom they had once enjoyed under the long century of "salutary neglect." But Eden, Johnstone, and Carlisle were handicapped: they could not grant the Americans their sine qua non—the status of "free & independent States." For the American Congress, independence and sovereignty had been but hopes and promises for two years, but now, with the ratification of the treaties from France, they were realities. And the leaders of Congress would not cede a hard-won geopolitical reality back to the misty realm of the geopolitical imagination. What they had pledged their lives, fortunes, and sacred honor to secure they would now hold onto by any means necessary.

Defeating the Carlisle Commission; Securing American Independence

The Carlisle Commission's flagship, the *Trident*, arrived at Philadelphia on 6 June 1778. A little over a week later, William Eden, like so many travelers before, conveyed his impressions of the New World to a family member back home: "It is impossible to give you an adequate Idea of the Vast Scale of this Country; I know little more of it than I saw in coming 150 miles up the Delaware, but I know enough to regret heartily that our own Rulers instead of making the Tour of Europe did not finish their Educations by a Voyage round the Coasts & Rivers of the Western Side of the Atlantic." Eden did not write that he now saw the futility of attempting to secure such a vast country by the force of arms. However, he was nonplussed by George Germain's change in American military strategy: "If some steps had not been taken at Home which we never learnt till we arrived here I have little Doubt that the Commission for Peace might in two or three Months have made a great impression—at present I am not sanguine."[36] Yet, by the time Eden put pen to paper to write these lines, the fate of the Carlisle Commission had been sealed—as much by what a few Americans had done in Congress as by what Germain and North had done back in London.

In the spring of 1778, Philadelphia and its environs were the main seat of the Revolutionary War. Sir William Howe's British regulars held Philadelphia. Sixteen miles to the west, having survived its brutal winter encampment at Valley Forge, was George Washington's Continental Army. Farther west, the town of York played host to the Continental Congress itself. The geography of war kept the Carlisle Commission and the Continental Congress separate from one another. But ultimately, it was far more than miles of Pennsylvania countryside that kept the two parties apart.

Upon their arrival in Philadelphia, the Carlisle Commission attempted to make contact with Congress in order to begin negotiations. Sealed documents were given to secretary Adam Ferguson to deliver to Congress. In order to pass from Philadelphia through Continental lines to York, Ferguson would need a passport from General George Washington. When he approached the American commander in chief, Washington was not sure how to respond. So, Washington dispatched a quick note to the president of Congress, Henry Laurens of South Carolina, asking for advice.[37] The receipt of Washington's letter prompted the first of a series of debates about how to respond to the Carlisle Commission. Even before Ferguson approached Washington, word had already reached Congress that the commissioners were in Philadelphia.[38] As far as can be known, the question of whether to grant Ferguson a passport was a contentious one. Congress appointed a committee, composed of Samuel Adams, Richard Henry Lee, and Henry Marchant to study the question. A draft report, now in Henry Laurens's papers, indicated that Congress was prepared to leave the question of whether to grant the passport to Washington's discretion. Yet the debate remained unresolved until Washington had solved the matter for them. Ferguson had given the triple-sealed documents to Washington, and Washington had then had his personal courier carry them to Congress on 13 June. Clearly, many in Congress had no desire to communicate with the Carlisle Commission at all. The Ferguson debate was but a precursor of things to come: "[T]he Scene begins to open," Samuel Adams noted.[39]

Eden, Carlisle, and Johnstone made various and immediate attempts to bolster the success of the commission's mission. Engaged in official correspondence with the Congress, the commissioners also attempted unofficial, semi-public communication. In early April, Johnstone, known to many as a friend of America in Parliament, dispatched letters to many of the American leaders with whom he had an acquaintance. Johnstone hoped that the Americans would ultimately choose reunion with Britain over alliance with France: "If it be (as I hope it is) the disposition of Good Men in the Provinces to Prefer freedom in Conjunction with Great Britain to an Union with the ancient Enemy of both, If it is their generous inclination to forget recent Injurys & recall to their remembrance former Benefits I am in hopes we may Yet be greatly Happy."[40] President Henry Laurens thought his letter from Johnstone was "much too polite to be sincere." Johnstone had also forwarded letters from many of Laurens's other British friends. This spate of correspondence from Britain troubled Laurens. As he wrote Horatio Gates, "[H]e has sent me Letters from my old & best friends in London all tending to the same point to wheedle us into resubjection, but if I do not misinterpret the intimations of one, a Man of as good sense as any in G Britain, & high in Esteem with the first Men on both sides at Court, these same Commissioners now are, or very soon will be, possessed of such Powers as will be acceptable at the Court House of York Town." This fusillade of correspondence to the congressional delegates and other American leaders was accompanied by an attempt to make a direct connection to the American people. On 10 June, the commissioners, with a guard of light troops, rode from Philadelphia to Germantown. Laurens saw the move as "certainly calculated for shewing themselves to the people."[41] This seems to be an accurate assessment. Addressing various audiences was, as Deane and Franklin had done in France, part and parcel of the process of making diplomacy. It was a process that the leaders of Congress would seek to derail.

On 13 June 1778, President Laurens opened the seals on the proclamation and letters the Carlisle Commission had sent to the Congress and began reading aloud. The delegates listened until Laurens got to the following passage:

> In our anxiety for preserving those sacred and essential interests we cannot help taking notice of the insidious interposition of a power which has from the first settlement of these colonies been actuated with enmity to us both. And notwithstanding the pretended date or present form of the French offers to North America, yet it is notorious that these were made in consequence of the plans of accommodation previously concerted in Great Britain and with a view to prevent our reconciliation and to prolong this destructive war.[42]

This outwardly expressed hostility toward France evoked immediate response. Gouverneur Morris rose and demanded that the president should stop reading the proclamation. Laurens did so. "Their letter is a combination of fraud, falsehood, insidious offers, and abuse of France, Concluding with a denial of Independence," Richard Henry Lee explained to Thomas Jefferson. "The sine qua non being withheld, you may judge what will be the fate of the rest."[43] In his notes, Charles Thomson recorded that "Some think the insulting way that the whole letter so far as read is an insult." This conclusion was held, Thomson believed, because the letter seemed "grounded on a supposition that we are so devoid of understanding and every sense of honor as to violate the treaties we have just entered into & give ourselves up to the mercy of" leaders who had "demonstrated that they have the will if they had but the power to reduce us to abject slavery and that they would exterminate rather than not subject us." But how would Congress respond to the Carlisle Commission? Thomson noted there were three options. First, Congress could write back to the commissioners and tell them that no terms would be listened to unless the United States' independence was officially recognized. Second, Congress could reject the letter based on the insult. Or, third, Congress could offer a rejection based on both grounds. There was no discussion of actually opening a dialogue with the commissioners, at least according to Thomson.[44]

Yet, apparently, some in Congress suspected that an unofficial dialogue could be taking place. On 16 June, Congress appointed Richard Henry Lee, Samuel Adams, and William Henry Drayton to a committee commissioned with the task of preparing "a resolution for preventing any correspondence with the enemy." The letters sent in a private capacity by Johnstone and others apparently troubled some delegates. On 17 June, the newly created committee reported back to Congress. Noting that "many letters, addressed to individuals of these United States, have been lately received from England, through the conveyance of the enemy, and some of them, which have been under the inspection of members of Congress, are found to contain ideas insidiously calculated to divide and delude the good people of these states," the committee proposed a resolution. The resolution "earnestly recommended to the legislative and executive authorities of the several states, to exercise the utmost care and vigilance, and take the most effectual measures to put a stop to so dangerous and criminal a correspondence." The proposed resolution also directed that "the Commander in Chief and the commanders in each and every military department" be "directed to carry the measures recommended in the above resolution into the most effectual execution."[45] The report was entirely in William Henry Drayton's handwriting. Essentially, Drayton wanted Congress to authorize the state governments and the Continental Army to take any and all measures to prevent the Carlisle Commission, or any other British subject, from discussing the prospect of reconciliation and reunion.

Drayton's proposals for restricting written communication within the United States knew no limits. At the same time Drayton's committee presented their resolution for intercepting British mail, "there was," in Henry Laurens's words, "an extraordinary Motion on our floor for calling upon Members to lay before Congress such Letters as they had received from the Commissioners or other persons, meaning persons in Great Britain on Political subjects."[46] Laurens led the objections to the motion and saw to its defeat.[47] The prospect of examining the mail of every American citizen was one thing, but asking the delegates to present their correspondence for each other to examine was a request of another order. As Laurens explained to Washington, "My Letters had been read by many Members & were at the service of every Gentleman who should request a perusal, but I could never consent to have my property taken from me by an Order from my fellow Citizens destitute of authority for the purpose."[48] The majority of delegates fell in line with Drayton's wishes, and soon spread the word beyond the halls of Congress that the Carlisle Commission, unless they recognized American independence, needed to be ignored. Thomas McKean told Caesar Rodney to "Be upon your guard with regard to Letters from the Enemy; they intend to seduce, corrupt & bribe by every method possible. Keep the whole militia under marching orders, if you have the power. Warn the people to double their vigilance, and not be lulled with these pleasing prospects, lest they meet with some terrible stroke, when they do not expect it."[49]

Eliminating the Carlisle Commission's communicative links with those beyond their immediate reach was seen as perfectly legitimate. The delegates understood that the making of diplomacy, which was ultimately what the Carlisle Commission was attempting, began with written communication. In closing off the ability to communicate using the written word, Congress impeded the commission's ability to alter public opinion. In the course of their debates over how to respond to the commissioners, the delegates grasped that simply opening negotiations and beginning the diplomatic process could be an immediate end. In his notes on debates, Francis Dana recorded some of the delegates' speculations: "The great point may be to draw us into a conference. For this purpose they offer to negotiate upon many matters beyond their powers under the Act of Parliamt." Since the act of Parliament made no provisions for recognizing American independence or withdrawing British regulars and naval forces from America, there was no way the Congress could negotiate without the commissioners violating their instructions. "Our refusal therefore brings the real matters of negotiation within the Act," Dana noted. Some in Congress wondered if they would be better off treating directly with the king, rather than Parliament: "The King I think may treat with us by virtue of his prerogative, as Independant States. For are we not in fact such? Hath not our Independance been acknowledged by France? Did she not ground her connection with us upon our having been in full possession of Independance ever since July 1776? Have we not reason to expect other Nations will follow the example of France?" Dana spelled out the realization the American Congress had. Their states had made the transition from provinces in an extended polity of the transatlantic British Empire to fully sovereign members of the European-centered states system. As Drayton wrote in an essay in the *Pennsylvania Gazette* of 20 June 1778, "America is independent *de facto et de jure*."[50] All that Deane and Franklin had imagined in Paris had been achieved on the east coast of North America.[51]

By the end of June, the commissioners realized that the changed geopolitical dynamics had doomed their negotiations. They reported to George Germain that the Treaty of Alliance was one of many factors that made their success difficult. "The treaty of alliance with France, the evacuation of Philadelphia, the leaving open of the whole coast of America to foreign supplies, the free entrance of prizes" all worked together and "elated the persons in authority through the revolted colonies that we could not expect an answer more decent than [the rejection they had received] at present."[52] Days later, the commissioners reported that "the decided rejection given by Congress to all terms of accommodation short of independence leaves no room to hope that any success will attend that commission with which we are honoured, except through the exertions of His Majesty's arms or by an appeal to the people at large or by negotiations with separate bodies of men and individuals." This projected course of action was anticipated by Congress, and in this light, its foreclosure of nonofficial avenues of communication doomed the commissioners' efforts for the remainder of the year in New York. No matter what the commissioners tried, the changed geopolitical dynamic was the bottom line. As the Earl of Carlisle told Eden, "The French interference gives a new colour to everything that relates to the American contest."[53]

The exchanges between the Carlisle commissioners and the more vocal delegates to Congress grew increasingly strident. William Henry Drayton and Gouverneur Morris authored several letters to the commission that were reprinted in the *Pennsylvania Gazette* and other newspapers. On 3 October 1778, after George Johnstone departed New York City for Great

Britain, the commissioners issued a "Manifesto and Proclamation" giving their final offer for the colonists to accept the king and Parliament's offer to reunite with the empire. But by this point the commissioners were simply going through the motions. Carlisle had already communicated to Eden that he felt America was irrevocably allied with France and that certain conclusions must now be drawn: "America has not only had recourse to a foreign power for Assistance, but with equal malice and perfidy has leagued herself with that, whose interests, and inclination have & always will dispose her by the convulsions of other states to attempt our destruction." In a sense, this was everything that the Americans wanted. The British had recognized the American states' passage from dependency to independence, but this recognition would lead to the conclusion that the United States, in alliance with Britain's Bourbon enemy, now needed to be soundly defeated on the field of battle.[54]

This was the context into which Gouverneur Morris's strident and caustic pamphlet *Observations on the American Revolution* appeared. Morris—and Congress—felt the need to explain what had transpired between Congress and the Carlisle Commission since June 1778, and to gird the American body politic for the war to come. Morris also had to justify the conduct of Congress. American independence was accepted as given and the commissioners' proposals were simply an attempt to reduce the Americans to a former state of subjection, dependence, and slavery. In reality, though, American independence was an uncertainty until the Treaties with France were ratified and then Britain responded to that development. With the acceptance, de facto and de jure, of American sovereignty by the great European powers, a threshold was crossed. At least, this was what the Americans hoped.

Acceptance on paper of American sovereignty by one European power did not guarantee that other states would follow suit, nor did it guarantee American victory over Great Britain. The French-American Alliance did help to bring both of these events to fruition, however. Official French acknowledgment of American independence came with increased financial support by the French government, and the engagement of British forces first by the French navy, and then the augmenting of the Continental Army by the French Expeditionary Force under the Comte de Rochambeau in 1780. Direct military aid by France was aided greatly by Vergennes's continued diplomacy. On 12 April 1779, France and Spain signed the Treaty of

Aranjuez, which pledged Spain to assist France in its war against Great Britain (but not to recognize American independence). The British navy's attempt to curtail commerce with the multiple belligerent powers led to a rupture with the Dutch, and the British declared war on the Netherlands in December 1780. The Dutch joined Vergennes's alliance, and by the summer months of 1781, Britain found itself fighting the combined navies of three powers (France, Spain, and the Netherlands) in the Atlantic, Caribbean, and the waters around Europe. Stretched to the limit, a fleet of British ships under Thomas Graves was defeated off the Capes of Virginia by French Admiral Comte de Grasse in early September 1781. De Grasse's victory trapped the army of British General Charles Cornwallis at Yorktown, Virginia, and the small American army that had pursued Cornwallis was augmented by the larger armies of George Washington and the Comte de Rochambeau, both of whom had been engaged in joint operations around New York City. With de Grasse closing off Chesapeake Bay, the allied forces laid siege to Cornwallis's army and forced his capitulation on 19 October 1781.[55]

Word reached Great Britain of Cornwallis's defeat in late February 1782 and set off a domestic political crisis. Parliament voted to discontinue offensive military operations in North America, and on 20 March the North ministry came crashing down. The Marquess of Rockingham replaced Lord North, but his death just four months later left William Petty-Fitzmaurice, Earl of Shelburne, at the head of the ministry. Serving as secretary of state for the colonies under Rockingham, Shelburne had appointed as his chief minister Richard Oswald, a Scots merchant with numerous American contacts. The news of Yorktown buoyed American fortunes elsewhere on the continent. The seven United Provinces of the Netherlands began to vote individually to recognize the independence of the United States of America. The States General of the Netherlands confirmed this collective judgment, and on 19 April 1782 officially recognized American independence. Minister John Adams left Amsterdam for Paris after this success, and John Jay (who had been involved in unsuccessful negotiations at the Spanish court) soon joined Franklin in Paris. Congress had commissioned all three men (as well as Henry Laurens, who had been taken prisoner by the British when his ship was captured at sea) to negotiate peace with Great Britain. Oswald met with the Americans in Paris in April 1782, and negotiations were on in earnest by the summer.[56]

The Preliminary Articles of Peace were concluded between Great Britain and the United States on 30 November 1782. Both Shelburne and Oswald hoped for a quick rapprochement between Britain and America, and this became evident in the terms of the preliminary treaty. The boundary of the United States was set at the Mississippi River in the West, the Floridas in the South, and the Great Lakes in the North—very generous terms given that the settled area of the Thirteen Colonies embraced only the eastern slope of the Appalachians, with a few exceptions. American fisherman had access to the Grand Banks fishery, while Britain retained the right to navigate the Mississippi River. And both Britain and America exchanged promises to recommend the restitution of property seized during the war, clauses that would be the most controversial and adhered to only in part. More controversial than the terms of the treaty was how the Americans had made it. After almost six years of placating the Comte de Vergennes, Benjamin Franklin made the bold decision to join with his fellow negotiators in negotiating a peace treaty with Great Britain independent of the French ministry—technically a violation of the terms of the Treaty of Alliance. When Vergennes learned of the Preliminary Articles of Peace, just the day before they were signed, he was nonplussed. The terms of peace "exceeded all that I thought possible," Vergennes mused; it seemed "that the English are purchasing peace rather than making it."[57] Vergennes's acquiescence in the American deal with Britain, and his determination to conclude a peace of his own were rooted in a variety of factors independent of the quality of the deal the Americans received. French forces had suffered setbacks in battles with the British in the Caribbean, and the removal of the Americans from the war weakened France's hand slightly. Vergennes was also concerned about affairs in Eastern Europe—Russia and Austria had concluded a secret treaty in 1781, and in autumn 1782, Empress Catherine of Russia had sent her armies into the Crimea to ensure the existence of a pro-Russian regime. Vergennes worried that a wider war between Russia and the Ottoman Empire (a longtime French ally) could break out. By late 1782, the Shelburne ministry was obviously weakening, and the time was right to cut a deal before a new ministry took power.[58]

American success at the Paris peace table had both confirmed the United States' full entry into the Westphalian states system and was also a product of that system. Unwittingly, the American ministers had exploited a weak British ministry and an overextended French ministry to secure favorable terms for American independence in the postwar period. It was almost too easy. The successes of the French-American Alliance and the Treaty of Paris gave American diplomats an inflated set of expectations about what the United States could achieve in the realm of the European diplomatic system. American diplomats had imagined the United States as vital cogs in the political machinery of the Westphalian states system and the commercial and political structures of the larger Atlantic world. Success in 1778 and 1782 raised American hopes that new commercial treaties with the European powers, even including Great Britain, and the resultant prosperity from these commercial arrangements, would come with ease. The United States' European negotiating partners saw a different reality. Immediately after the Articles of Confederation were formally ratified on 1 March 1781, the French minister to America, the Chevalier de la Luzerne, reported to Vergennes quite frankly that they "are by everyone's consent an incomplete and irregular System of government."[59] Even as peace was negotiated, British politicians, political thinkers, and writers (even those, such as Shelburne, who wished for a speedy reconciliation with the United States) were not sanguine about the Confederation's future.[60] While the European powers welcomed the United States into the Westphalian states system, they imagined America would play a limited role, at best, in European affairs. Few took the United States seriously. Recognition of this reality would prove to be one of the greatest spurs to transforming the United States' frame of government.

4

"Rendering Us Great and Respectable in the Eyes of the World"

The Diplomatic Imperative for the Federal Constitution

> [T]he new federal government offers the most flattering prospect to your petitioners of restoring system, firmness, and energy, to the present embarrassed and relaxed Union; of reviving our declining commerce, of supporting our tottering credit, of relieving us from the pressure of an unequal and inefficacious taxation, of giving us concord at home, and rendering us great and respectable in the eyes of the world.
> —PETITION TO THE PENNSYLVANIA RATIFYING CONVENTION, November 1787

On 17 September 1787, the Philadelphia Convention concluded the work that it had been involved in for almost four months—debating and drafting a new frame of government for the United States of America. In the years that followed the conclusion of peace with Great Britain, a significant number of Americans had come to agree with the Chevalier de la Luzerne that the Articles of Confederation "were an incomplete and irregular System of government."¹ While the violent Shays' Rebellion in Massachusetts during the winter of 1786–87 and the ongoing crisis of a shrinking money supply and rising taxes in many states gave the general unease Americans felt a greater sense of urgency in 1787, some of the most fundamental problems that confronted Americans and their governments had been present for years, and were visible as soon as the Revolutionary War came to a close. Particularly obvious was the inability of the diplomats of the United States to achieve what its national leaders wanted in the realms of the Westphalian and borderlands diplomatic systems. While the Articles of Confederation had given the Continental Congress the power to appoint diplomats and make treaties, individual states retained the powers to enact commercial regulations, which complicated the negotiation of commercial treaties with the European powers. Individual states also continued to engage American Indian nations in diplomacy, which frustrated congressional efforts to bring peace to the western borderlands and consolidate the national domain. The diplomatic weakness of the Confederation was apparent to almost every American, even those who did not approve of the Constitution that the Philadelphia Convention produced.[2]

The desire to give the United States' central government a stronger hand in making diplomacy was a key argument marshaled by the supporters of the new Constitution, the Federalists of 1787–88. For example, as the Pennsylvania Ratifying Convention began its deliberations in November 1787, newspaper essayists lobbying in support of ratification of the new Constitution constantly invoked the American Confederation's lack of power on the world stage. "A Plain Citizen" complained that "the American name" was "insulted and despised by all the world!" and implored his fellow citizens to support ratification in order to "guide [the] tottering footsteps" of "your bleeding country" from "the brink of ruin."[3] Using slightly less hyperbole was a group of petitioners from Carlisle, Pennsylvania. With "the strongest conviction," they suggested that "the new Federal Government offers the most flattering prospect" of "restoring firmness and energy, to the present embarrassed and relaxed Union." The petitioners asserted that a strong federal government would have the effect of "reviving our declining commerce, of supporting our tottering credit," and of "giving us concord at home, and rendering us great and respectable in the eye of the world."[4] The inability of the Confederation to engage with polities external to it, either in North America or in Europe, in a meaningful, orderly, and sustained fashion was one of the most potent arguments in favor of first revising the Articles of Confederation and then abandoning them for the federal Constitution.[5]

Americans quickly learned that their acceptance into the Westphalian states system—signaled first by the Treaty of Alliance with France, then by the recognition of the Netherlands, and finally by the Treaty of Paris with Great Britain itself—was a starting point rather than an ending point in their desire to sustain the United States as independent sovereignties. While European powers easily recognized the United States, especially after Great Britain had done so, getting these same European states to open their doors to American trade based on principles of reciprocity, or most-favored-nation status, was a far more difficult task. First, many European states doubted the ability of the weak Confederation government to enforce any treaty it might sign with the United States. Second, the larger European powers, especially Great Britain, soon realized that they would derive the benefits of trade with the Americans without having to concede most-favored-nation status via a treaty. Again, the Confederation was too weak to compel or demand changes that would even begin to approach something resembling fairness.

Related challenges presented themselves to the West, as the United States still engaged multiple American Indian nations via the remaining structures of the borderlands diplomatic regime. Beginning with the 1784 Treaty of Fort Stanwix, diplomats of the United States would attempt to impose a new set of norms on the political relationships between American settler polities and American Indian nations, replacing the customary, negotiated relationships of the "middle ground" with an assertion of the total, undivided sovereignty of the United States. Claiming that the Indian peoples of trans-Appalachia had suffered the same defeat as Great Britain in the Revolutionary War and were now conquered peoples, American negotiators would attempt to treat these Indian communities as subjects, rather than sovereign equals. Having not actually been conquered in any meaningful way by American arms, Indian leaders pushed back against these assertions in a variety of ways. Just as in the European diplomatic system, the American victory in the Revolutionary War had allowed American political leaders to imagine and attempt to act on a new set of norms in the North American interior, but the old structures were not gone yet, and America's negotiating partners demanded adherence to the old norms. For American political elites, the imperative for reforming the structure of the Confederation had been made manifest.

American political leaders soon realized that in order to solve the difficulties the United States was having relating to other sovereignties in both the European-centered Westphalian states system and the remnants of the borderlands system that still governed polity relations in the middle ground, their own states system—the Philadelphian system—needed to be reordered and reorganized. Sovereign power jealously held at the state level needed to be transferred to the federal government if diplomatic outcomes helpful to all the United States were to be accomplished.

The Irrelevance of John Adams
The Failure of Confederation Diplomacy in Europe

In the months following the conclusion of the Preliminary Articles of Peace, one of the American peace commissioners, John Adams, was brimming over with optimism. America's prospects looked bright. Adams believed that the innate value of American commerce would prove to be an irresistible inducement to all the European powers to open their doors to American produce.[6] He had already been imagining a rapprochement between the United States and Great Britain. Continuing to reside in Paris as he waited for the American and British governments to approve the Preliminary Articles, Adams found himself enmeshed in a small group of kindred spirits with whom he shared countless hours of private conversation, a group that included John Jay and British minister Richard Oswald. One evening in December 1782 at Jay's apartment at the Hôtel d'Orleans, the three men engaged in what Adams called a "very lively Conversation upon Politicks." Oswald had queried the other men as to what Britain's proper course in relating to the United States should now be. Adams stated that "[t]he Alpha and Omega of British Policy, towards America, was summed up in this one Maxim—See that American Independence is independent, independant of all the World, of [Britain] as well as of France." A fully independent United States—meaning an America not allied to one European power in particular—would be free to produce, truck, and exchange at will, and thus offer British consumers competitive prices and British manufacturers an ever-expanding market. A situation in which America was fully engaged with Europe, but unallied with any one power, would thus (somewhat counterintuitively) be the bedrock of a mutually beneficial commercial partnership between the United States and Great Britain.[7]

However, the unraveling of the hoped-for British-American rapprochement began almost immediately. Since his ascension in July 1782, the Earl of Shelburne's position at the head of the British ministry was increasingly tenuous. When word of the Preliminary Articles of Peace reached Britain, discontent was voiced in and out of Parliament. Those who never supported the American cause, Lord North foremost among them, were decidedly against the treaty. The generous boundary terms and the concessions on the fisheries rankled even those who had favored the American cause, such as Edmund Burke and Charles James Fox. American Loyalists in Britain lobbied hard for its rejection on all points. Together, both Fox and North saw an opportunity to bring down Shelburne and thus advance their own interests. Shelburne's ministry collapsed in February 1783, and in April, Fox and North engineered an unlikely coalition government. A blueprint for dealing with the Americans entered the public sphere when ministerial ally John Holroyd, Lord Sheffield, laid out compelling arguments against Shelburne's plans to reopen relatively free trade with the United States in his pamphlet *Observations on the Commerce of the American States*. Sheffield's indictment of treating the Americans as anything but a foreign power with no special status influenced many British statesmen. Parliament rejected Shelburne's American Intercourse Bill, and soon supported the Orders in Council of 2 July 1783. These decrees limited commerce between the United States and British colonies. They allowed the export of American produce into Great Britain and its colonies, but limited the trade between the United States and the remaining British colonies (especially the lucrative West Indies markets) to British-owned ships. The Americans' dream of an Anglo-American commercial treaty that would guarantee free trade, or at least reciprocity, seemed to be dead.[8]

On the continent, John Adams monitored these developments with increasing dread. In June, Adams could only observe that the "British nation and Ministry are in a very unsettled state."[9] On the eve of hearing of the 2 July Orders in Council, Adams could almost sense what was coming. "The West India commerce now gives us the most anxiety," he reported to the Congress's secretary for foreign affairs. "If the former British ministry had stood, we might have secured it from England," Adams noted, continuing that had that been the case, "France would have been obliged to admit us to their islands." Adams still had difficulty imagining why Britain would deny the United States access to the West Indies, which fell "into the natural system of the commerce of the United States." Ultimately, "there will be a commerce between us," Adams declared. He could not imagine why the British would want to push this into illegal channels where they could not extract revenue from it.[10] Thus, Adams was dumbfounded when he got word of the July Orders in Council. He thought the proclamation would "contribute effectually to make America afraid of England, and attach herself more closely to France." But Adams sensed there was more at work here than British short-sightedness:

> This proclamation is issued in full confidence that the United States have no confidence in one another; that they cannot agree to act in a body as one nation; that they cannot agree upon any navigation act, which may be common to the Thirteen States. Our proper remedy would be to confine our exports to American ships, to make a law that no article should be exported from any of the States in British ships, nor in the ships of any nation, which will not allow us reciprocally to import their productions in our ships. I am much afraid there is too good an understanding upon this subject between Versailles and St. James.

In one paragraph, Adams remarkably prefigured several key issues that would dominate American foreign policy discussion for decades to come—that the diffuse nature of American union could be exploited by foreign powers, that commercial retaliation was a viable American policy option, and that inherent tensions existed between the interests of the United States and those of the great Atlantic colonial powers, France and Britain. Most prescient in the short term was Adams's awareness that the nature of the American union under the Confederation was a liability.[11]

As Adams's dispatches crossed the Atlantic and were considered by Congress, his conclusions began to be shared by many. Congress saw that Britain was restricting commerce between the United States and the British colonies and that France would likely enact similar restrictions. Perceiving these developments as "injurious to the United States," Congress concluded that the challenges could only be met by "delegating a general power regulating their [the states'] commercial interests." The committee appointed to report on the problem—composed of Thomas Fitzsimmons, James Duane, and Arthur Lee—drew heavily on John Adams's letter of 18 July 1783. They concluded that it was "obvious" that the "union requires additional support from its members" and "that if the United States" are to "become more respectable it must be by the means of more energy in government." While Congress could see this reality, there was little they could do to improve it. They resolved to encourage the commissioners in Europe to make overtures to any and all European powers, in order to begin the process of making commercial treaties. But as far as making uniform commercial regulations or effecting "more energy" in the government of the union, Congress could only compose addresses to the thirteen states. The delegates could diagnose the problem, but could not administer the cure.[12]

John Adams became further aware of the limitations on American diplomats imposed by the Articles of Confederation during his tenure as American minister to Great Britain, which lasted from May 1785 through March 1788. In the wake of the 2 July 1783 Orders in Council, Adams's first desire was to negotiate and conclude a treaty of commerce with Great Britain. Adams preferred a treaty based on the principal of reciprocity, which meant that Americans would subject British importers to "no higher duties than our own citizens" and the British would do the same. The fact that the Articles of Confederation gave the power to negotiate treaties to Congress but left commercial regulations (duties and other taxes) in the hands of the state governments made the American situation impossible. To conclude a commercial treaty based on the principle of reciprocity or even most-favored-nation status (in which America and Britain would simply treat each other's commerce as they treated any other foreign power —no better, no worse) would require "equalizing duties" between the thirteen states. For Adams, it seemed a dubious prospect: "this cannot be done, but by a concert of all the States; if such a concert can be effected by recommendations of congress, so much the better; if it cannot, I see no other remedy but to give congress the power." The United States needed to speak with one voice if they had any hope of getting what they wanted from Great Britain.[13]

The nature of the American Confederation was made an issue immediately preceding John Adams's arrival in Great Britain in May 1785. Adams wrote to John Jay, who was now the Confederation's secretary for foreign affairs, "that the British cabinet have conceived doubts, whether congress have power to treat of commercial matters, and whether our States should not separately grant their full powers to a minister." Adams balked at such a notion; the concept of each state conducting its own diplomacy was untenable: "The idea of thirteen plenipotentiaries meeting together in a congress at every court in Europe, each with a full power and distinct instructions from his State, presents to view such a picture of confusion, altercation, expense, and endless delay, as must convince every man of its impracticability." The list of difficulties potentially created by such an arrangement went on:

> Neither is there less absurdity in supposing that all the States should unite in the separate election of the same man, since there is not, never was, and never will be, a citizen whom each State would separately prefer for conducting the negotiation. It is equally inconceivable that each State should separately send a full power and separate instructions to the ministers appointed by congress. What a heterogeneous mass of papers, full of different objects, various views, and inconsistent and contradictory orders, must such a man pull out of *portefeuille*, from time to time, to regulate his judgment and conduct! He must be accountable, too, to thirteen different tribunals for his conduct; a situation in which no man would ever consent to stand, if it is possible, which I do not believe, that any State should ever wish for such a system.

Yet this was the situation that the British cabinet alleged existed, given the nature of the Articles of Confederation, and that required a response from Minister Adams. "If the British ministry wish and seek for delays, this will be their pretext," Adams glumly conceded. "It is very possible the cabinet of St. James may decline entering into any conferences at all upon the subject of a treaty of commerce, until the powers of congress are enlarged." Adams believed that the "people of America" needed to "turn the deliberations in their assemblies to this object" with dispatch. "It behoves the United States," Adams pleaded, "to knit themselves together in the bands of affection and mutual confidence, search their own resources to the bottom, form their foreign commerce into a system, and encourage their own navigation and seamen, and to these ends their carrying trade." At the moment, Adams allowed that such a measure could technically be done with the "concurrence of nine States," but his language certainly pointed to a more permanent arrangement. The making of diplomacy starkly revealed the inadequacies of the Articles of Confederation.[14]

The ministry of William Pitt the Younger could toy with Adams because its ministers perceived that the United States was weak and the British Empire was strong. Adams bluntly conveyed the state of the situation to Jay. The "British ministers and merchants are certain that they shall enjoy all the profits of our commerce under their own partial regulations." This was due in large part, in the British view, to "the superior abilities of British manufacturers, and the greater capitals of their merchants," which "enabled them to give our traders better bargains and longer credit than any others in Europe." British opinion was that the Americans "must come to them who can furnish us with goods of the best qualities, at the cheapest rates, and allow us the longest time to pay." Adams despised this overconfidence, but he had to admit that "there is too much truth" in it.[15] The hopes of the United States concluding a favorable commercial treaty with Britain were slim. Adams's counterpart in France, Thomas Jefferson, was facing similar difficulties in getting French markets opened to American agricultural goods and raw materials.[16] And within a year, the weakness of the American Confederation was apparent in another European theater as well. Seizures of American ships and sailors by the North African regency of Algiers exposed American feebleness. Not having the unlimited funds with which to ransom captive sailors and buy a peace treaty (as most of the European powers did), Adams and Jefferson debated going to war against Algiers and the other Barbary States. John Adams saw that a war would require a naval buildup, which was just not going to happen. "I perceive that neither Force nor Money will be applied," he told Jefferson. "Our States are so backward that they will do nothing for some years," he pessimistically concluded. Jefferson also wished to take a proactive stance, but proposed an alliance with other small European states as a counterweight against the Barbary States. It was another solution that went nowhere. With no central organizing principle or power, the individual United States were at the mercy of others, everywhere their diplomats looked.[17]

The Strange Diplomacy of Fort Stanwix
The Confederation's Failure on the Borderlands

Just as American statesmen like John Adams and Thomas Jefferson hoped that the Treaty of Paris would signal the acceptance of the United States into the European-centered states system and open the doors to commercial treaties and prosperity, American statesmen also imagined that a similar revolution of diplomatic affairs would unfold to the west, and that American independence would simplify the complicated business of treaty making in the Indian country. Concluding treaties with the American

Indian nations within the new borders of the United States was of vital interest to both the Continental Congress and the individual states—the western lands (meaning Indian lands) were understood to be the most valuable resource possessed by the newly independent nation. White American elites desired treaties with the relevant Indian nations that would provide for land transfers to either the central or state governments, to be followed by land surveys and land sales. The looming question was how the United States should go about convincing the various Indian nations to negotiate treaties and sell their lands.

Two answers presented themselves. The first was to claim that the American victory in the Revolutionary War had ushered in a new state of affairs in North America and promulgate a new set of norms upon which to base diplomacy between the Indian nations and the settler polities. The second option was to continue to operate within the established normative framework of the old borderlands diplomatic regime that had governed settler-Indian relations under the British Empire; in other words, utilize the diplomatic frameworks of the "middle ground" and expand white settlements slowly. Studying the question as the Revolutionary War was ending, the Continental Congress recommended the second course of action.

In the late summer of 1783, even before Congress had received the official copies of the Definitive Treaty of Peace, they had received a report from their Committee on Indian Affairs recommending a postwar Indian policy of engagement and moderation. The committee, led by delegate James Duane of New York, acknowledged that the Indians in the Great Lakes and Ohio Valley regions were "not in a temper to relinquish their territorial claims," and that intense pressure could drive them to seek alliance with the British in Canada, where, it was speculated, "they would find a welcome reception." Furthermore, an aggressive Indian policy could lead to a renewal of war, which would likely lead to the necessity of "numerous garrisons and an expensive peace establishment." The necessity of not provoking the various Algonkian and Iroquoian nations was obvious. Yet the United States openly and unapologetically coveted the land. "[I]t is just and necessary that lines of property should be ascertained and established between the United States and [the Indians], which will be convenient to the respective tribes and, and commensurate to the public wants," the committee reasoned, "because the faith of the United States stands pledged to grant portions of the uncultivated lands as a bounty to the army,

... and the public finances do not admit of any considerable expenditure to extinguish Indian claims upon such lands." The American weaknesses that were becoming apparent in Europe were also evident in North America—Congress could not afford to buy Indian land, nor could it afford an army to conquer it, so it would have to acquire title through negotiation.[18]

The Continental Congress appointed Arthur Lee, Richard Butler, and Oliver Wolcott as its first Indian commissioners in October 1783. Their initial task was to negotiate with the Iroquois Six Nations. The treaty they would produce a year later would be among the most controversial pieces of Indian diplomacy in American history. As they embarked on their work, the congressional commissioners betrayed little knowledge of just how delicate the situation for those on Iroquois side had become. The Iroquois Confederacy had been torn apart by the American Revolution. Two nations, the Oneida and the Tuscarora, sided with the United States, while the Mohawk, Onondaga, Seneca, and Cayuga fought with Great Britain.[19] The communities of each nation fought not only the European armies, but also the opposing Iroquois forces as well. With the conclusion of fighting, healing the breech between the Six Nations and reconstituting the Iroquois League and Confederacy was not an easy task. Although they had suffered at the hands of British and Iroquois forces during the war, the Oneida and Tuscarora continued to subsist on their lands in what is today central upstate New York. Many Onondaga, Cayuga, Seneca, and some Mohawk had relocated to far western New York, with the council fire that signified the unity of the Iroquois Confederacy lit at an Onondaga settlement on Buffalo Creek.[20] These communities counted among them factions led by the Seneca leaders Cornplanter and Red Jacket. Further complicating matters was a growing Iroquois center in Canada. Shortly after the Treaty of Paris, the governor of Canada, Frederick Haldimand, had granted the Loyalist Mohawk leader Joseph Brant (Thayendanegea) a tract of land in Canada on which to settle. Communities representing all of the Six Nations flocked to Brant's land along the Grand River. A band of Onondagas here had also lit a separate council fire, and the emergent Grand River league also identified itself as the Six Nations. The Iroquois were far from united as they contemplated the prospect of negotiating with Congress in the coming year.[21]

The Iroquois were not the only people divided. As Congress had dispatched commissioners to Iroquoia, it was concerned about the intensifying rivalries between the individual states and between the states and Congress, especially in regard to issues concerning land. James Duane's Committee on Indian Affairs recognized that interstate rivalry was driving Congress's desire to act quickly. In a passage that was crossed out of the official journals, the committee noted in October 1783 that "some of the states have already assigned to the officers and privates of their respective lines lands claimed to be within their jurisdictions and from which the Indians have been expelled during the course of the war." The omnipresent fear was that "unless some agreement is seasonably made under the authority of Congress," there would be "fresh discontent and hostilities." States could conclude conflicting treaties, spurring interstate rivalry, or simply expropriate Indian land, potentially inciting more violence. This prospect of individual state initiative outside of the supervision of Congress loomed in the state of New York in 1784, as Lee, Butler, and Wolcott made their way to that state to negotiate with the Six Nations.[22]

Rumors had been spreading through Iroquoia since the summer of 1783 that the United States planned to expropriate all of the lands of those nations that had fought on the British side.[23] Although this was the thrust of what the congressional commissioners would eventually propose, this was not the initial design of the Continental Congress, at least officially. According to the instructions to the commissioners drawn up in congressional committee, it was asserted that the northern Indians, including the Iroquois, needed to "be informed that after a contest of eight years for the sovereignty of this country Great Britain has relinquished to the United States all claim to the country within the limits" spelled out in the Treaty of Paris. Initially, the committee had written that Great Britain had "ceded all the lands" within the said boundaries, but this phrase was crossed out of the official journals. Apparently, Congress understood that the sovereignty they had won was not an outright cession of lands, but only a claim to land, and the privilege to negotiate with the inhabitants.[24] Congress also went on the record as supporting the establishment of a "boundary line" between Anglo-American and Indian settlements as well as principles to regulate the trade between Anglo-American and Indian communities. Calls for strict federal regulation of the middle ground, in concert with claims to desire "friendship" with all Indians and assurances that "the country is large enough to contain and support us all," prefigured the policies of "benevolence" and "civilization" that would gain currency in the 1790s.[25]

The Treaty of Paris was officially ratified in January 1784, and by the summer of that same year, elements of the report of Congress's Committee on Indian Affairs had proven quite prescient. After Congress had commissioned Lee, Butler, and Wolcott in October 1783 with the power to negotiate with all of the Indians in the Northern Department, Pennsylvania readily acquiesced to the congressional prerogative. The state of New York was not as forthcoming. Among the New Yorkers who understood the danger to state power posed by the work of congressional Indian commissioners was the very same James Duane who had headed the Committee on Indian Affairs the previous year. By the spring of 1784, Duane was now the mayor of New York City, and, like many subsequent New York mayors, he had few qualms about speaking his mind on issues beyond the city limits.[26] In a letter written in July or early August 1784 to New York governor George Clinton, Duane spelled out the dangers posed by the proposed work of the congressional commissioners. As the majority of the Six Nations of Iroquois had been at "open War with the United States" and the Treaty of Paris ignored them totally, Congress claimed, under Article IX of the Confederation, "the exclusive Right to make this peace" with the Iroquois. "If the Tribes are to be considered as independant nations, detached from the State, and absolutely unconnected with it, the Claim of Congress" would be impossible to contest, Duane explained. In order to prevent this congressional usurpation of New York's power to negotiate, he asserted, "There is then an indispensable Necessity that these Tribes should be treated as antient Dependants on this State, placed under its protection, with all their territorial Rights, by their own consent publickly manifested in solemn and repeated Treaties." If the "Tribes in question" fell "under the character of Members of the State," then "Congress would have no concern" with them. Duane saw that for New York to preserve its prerogative to negotiate with the Six Nations (and maintain unfettered access to Iroquois lands), it had to do whatever was necessary in order to frustrate and head off the congressionally commissioned negotiators' attempts to treat with the Six Nations.[27]

In Duane's mind, the best way for the state of New York to preserve its privileged negotiating position with the Iroquois was to unilaterally obliterate the structures of negotiation. Eliminating the diplomatic arena in which they operated would strip the Iroquois of their sovereign status and their standing to contract treaties. Duane imagined that it would then be necessary for the Iroquois nations to "be reconciled to the Idea of being Members of the State, dependant upon its government and resting upon its Protection." The only way to accomplish this would be to utterly and totally transform the manner in which the government of the state of New York interacted with the leadership of the various Iroquois nations. "[T]he Stile, as well as the substance, of the Communications on the part of the Government are very material," Duane observed. "[I]nstead of conforming to the ceremonies practiced in Negociations among the Indians it woud be wise to bring them to adopt, gradually our forms." Duane wanted New York to abandon the rhetoric and ceremony of the Covenant Chain, which had been the glue of Iroquois–New York relations since the seventeenth century. He suggested to Clinton that "neither Belts nor strings" should be used "in any Communication" and that the words "nations, or Six Nations, or Confederates, or Council Fire at Onondaga" or other terms that carried connotations of sovereignty had to be abandoned. Duane's reasoning for abandoning the long-established modes of treaty making were twofold. First, he understood that the Iroquois had used diplomacy in general, and their own diplomatic culture in particular, to preserve their fragile geopolitical position between New York and Canada, and for New York to now play along was ridiculous. Duane saw this "disgraceful system of pensioning, courting and flattering them as great and mighty nations" only resulted in those who treated becoming the "Fools and Slaves" of the Iroquois. Second, Duane understood that, under the Articles of Confederation, treating with any distinct and "independant" Indian nation would place those negotiations under congressional jurisdiction. To maintain the forms of the Covenant Chain would de facto recognize the continued "independence" of the Iroquois nations and thus be "offensive to Congress." Thus, Duane believed eliminating the established forms of Iroquois diplomatic negotiation and treaty making was the only sure way to guarantee New York's interests.[28]

While Governor Clinton did not follow Duane's prescriptions to the letter, he understood that New York's interests and those of Congress were at odds with one another. Clinton knew he could not, as Duane wished, abandon the established forms of the Covenant Chain. The Iroquois nations, even in their weakened condition, would simply ignore him. He did, however, assert the Indians' dependant status in order to keep the congressional negotiators at bay, noting that the Iroquois resided "within the

"*Rendering Us Great and Respectable*" 133

Jurisdiction of this State."²⁹ Clinton's assertions held little weight in the minds of Lee, Butler, and Wolcott. In their response to Clinton's recommendation that they leave treaty making with the Iroquois to the state of New York, they noted that Pennsylvania had already acknowledged congressional primacy in the process. They further assured the governor that New York would still be allowed to enter into agreements with the Iroquois, but that this "business" would "be more properly transacted at the same time with, and in subordination to the General Treaty," which they had been commissioned to negotiate.³⁰ Clinton disagreed. Ultimately, two treaty conferences were held at Fort Stanwix. In September, Clinton led a state delegation to treat with a number of Iroquois leaders, and in October, Wolcott, Butler, and Lee arrived at the same locale to negotiate a treaty with the Iroquois on behalf of Congress. The question over which government, Congress or New York, would be the primary negotiator with the Iroquois nations was not merely semantic. The stakes were high, both in terms of power and precedent. The Six Nations still technically held title to much of upstate New York, and were seen as having valuable diplomatic connections with the Algonkians and Iroquoians of the Great Lakes and Ohio Valley, as well as the Iroquois settling in Canada. New York did not want to lose its exclusive access to this land and power. Similarly, if Congress did not assert its role as first negotiator with these Indian nations, its subsequent assertions would also likely fall on deaf ears.³¹

The Iroquois negotiators also came to Fort Stanwix in autumn 1784 with sophisticated, and sometimes divergent, agendas. As rumors spread that the United States or New York would claim the right of conquest over all of their lands, the Iroquois who remained within the borders of the United States sought to preserve their sovereignty. A large delegation—including the Seneca leaders Joseph Brant and Cornplanter—attended the September Fort Stanwix conference with Clinton and the New Yorkers, while a slightly smaller delegation attended the October federal conference. Brant's Mohawks and the other Iroquois who settled with him in Canada ultimately opted to ignore both New York and Congress, treat with the British, and settle beyond the borders of the United States. They did not make this decision without assessing the changed legal and geopolitical dynamic wrought by the Peace of Paris. Four days into the negotiations with the state of New York at Fort Stanwix, Brant spelled out the difficulties the Iroquois perceived with sovereign power being divided between Congress and New

York. Addressing Clinton and the other New York commissioners, Brant proclaimed, "You again spoke and made Us acquainted that the powers of managing Indian Affairs at large belonged to Congress, and that they had appointed Commissioners for this purpose, and that You were appointed by this particular State, to manage Indian Affairs with Indians residing within the Bounds thereof, in Consequence of which you appear here at this Place." Brant and the Iroquois communities for which he spoke understood that it made no sense for them to negotiate with two distinct entities claiming the same sovereign power. "Here lies some Difficulty in our Minds," Brant continued, "that there should be two separate bodies to manage these Affairs, for this does not agree with our ancient Customs." The Covenant Chain had always extended *through* the colony of New York to the king of England; now the Iroquois were seemingly being asked to choose between New York or the Continental Congress, both claiming the sovereignty the king once held. Three days later, the New York commissioners laid copies of the Articles of Confederation, the New York state constitution, and the New York state laws authorizing the negotiations before the Iroquois leaders. These documents, in addition to the Treaty of Paris itself, had an effect on Brant and the other Iroquois negotiators.[32]

In his speech on the closing day of the conference, Brant acknowledged the right of the state of New York's commissioners to treat "with Us the six Nations who live and reside within its limits," but he ultimately refused to sell more land, claiming, "We are not authorized to stipulate any particular Cession of Lands." Shrewdly, he also noted that some small tracts of land near the forts at Niagara and Oswego, already ceded to the colony of New York in the name of the king, now did belong to New York under the terms of the Treaty of Paris. Brant acknowledged that the state of New York had the right to consent to any cession of lands within its borders, but he also noted that it was the wish of the Iroquois communities for which he spoke to negotiate with the congressional commissioners first. The delegations of the various Iroquois nations present at the first meeting demonstrated an acute awareness of what the Treaty of Paris actually said, what powers to negotiate New York retained, as well as the fact that under the Articles of Confederation, the bulk of the power over Indian affairs was placed in the hands of the Congress.[33]

Establishing the preeminence of the Congress in diplomatic relations with the Iroquois was the primary task facing the congressional commissioners during negotiations the next month at Fort Stanwix. As Lee, Butler, and Wolcott introduced themselves to the assembled negotiators, among the first statements they offered was their assurance that "we have full authority to transact all business between the United States, and you." They combined this with a pointed disavowal of the business conducted at the same site the previous month, stating that "without the authority of Congress no business can be valid that may be attempted by particular people or States." This introductory speech by the commissioners occurred on 3 October 1784. Preliminaries continued the next day, with an oration by the Marquis de Lafayette, who was then touring New York State with the Virginian legislator James Madison. Serious negotiations between the commissioners and the Iroquois leaders did not begin for over a week. One reason for the delay was New York's attempt to disrupt the treaty negotiations. At Governor Clinton's request, the state militia officer Peter Schuyler had remained at Fort Stanwix, where he continued to distribute liquor and dissuade the Iroquois from dealing with the congressional agents. The commissioners communicated their displeasure to Schuyler and ordered guards to keep him and his agents out of the official treaty grounds.[34]

When official negotiations resumed on 12 October, Lee, Butler, and Wolcott dropped a proverbial bomb on their counterpart negotiators. Invoking the Treaty of Paris, the commissioners noted "that in this treaty, no mention is made by the King of Great Britain of any Indian Nation or tribe whatever, but that he left those tribes to seek for peace with the United States, upon such terms as the United States shall think just and reasonable." For any American Indian community within the boundaries of the United States, there would be no dealing with Great Britain, as "you may be satisfied that the United States are the sole sovereigns within the limits now described to you in the treaty with the King of Great Britain, and therefore the sole power to whom the nations living within those limits are hereafter to look up for protection." The meaning was clear; the United States now held the right of preemption to Iroquoia. (Preemption was the legal principle developed by European settlers in America by which only one European sovereign had the right to negotiate with an Indian nation; that Indian nation was seen to reside solely within a European sovereign's claimed borders.) In the vision the commissioners put forward, the only way to peace (or any diplomatic relations) for the Six Nations was under the aegis of the United States.[35]

The main goal of most of the Iroquois negotiators at both the September and October negotiations at Fort Stanwix was to preserve as much as of their sovereignty as possible. The Iroquois leaders wanted to maintain the long-standing structures and norms of the borderlands diplomatic system that had sustained them for nearly a century and a half. This required that they be able to negotiate agreements and contract alliances with any Westphalian system sovereign at their borders—in this case, they wished to be able to negotiate with both the United States and Great Britain. The Mohawk leader Aaron Hill spelled out this logic in a speech on 17 October, unequivocally stating, "We are free, and independent, and at present under no influence." Hill acknowledged that most of the Iroquois had "hitherto been bound by the Great King [of Great Britain], but he having broken the chain, and left us to ourselves, we are again free and independent." Hill had previously explained the knowledge and the logic that had drawn the Iroquois negotiators present into their current negotiation with the congressional commissioners. The Iroquois maintained they had "written to the Governor of New York, requesting" that he hold a conference that could produce "a continental treaty," rather than a "particular one" with only the state of New York. With New York holding a conference in September, and Pennsylvanian commissioners attending with the congressional commissioners in October, the Iroquois leadership for which Aaron Hill spoke could see firsthand that there was division among the states. In decades past, when Corlaer (New York) and Onas (Pennsylvania) had been at odds with one another, appeals to reconciliation were always addressed to the figure at the far end of the Covenant Chain, the father-figure of the "Great King." The Iroquois understood that Congress, speaking for all the states, and offering a "continental treaty," now stood in place of the "Great King." Hill's speech was a call to the congressional commissioner to forge a new chain, under the same principles of relative independence that had attached the Iroquois to the extended, composite polity of the British Empire before the Revolution, while he also retained the right to continue to negotiate with the British. Not wanting to be contained wholly within the borders of the state of New York nor even the United States as a whole, Hill's people sought to maintain as much of their sovereign power and freedom of diplomatic action as possible.[36]

The congressional commissioners abandoned the reciprocity of sovereignty of the Covenant Chain. On 20 October, Arthur Lee addressed the

Iroquois and made the most controversial statement of the Fort Stanwix conference. He asserted that the Iroquois were not a "free and independent nation," but rather a "subdued people." Lee continued with his indictment, "[Y]ou have been overcome in a war which you entered into with us, not only without provocation, but in violation of most sacred obligations." The commissioners seemed to say that the United States could lay to claim to all of the lands granted by the Treaty of Paris: "The King of Great Britain ceded to the United States *the whole*, by the right of conquest they might *claim the whole.*" This was rhetorical excess and wishful thinking on several counts. In the territory west of the Appalachians, Congress had received only Virginia's cession of its western lands that March, and many states still claimed lands in the West. Additionally, the commissioners knew they still had to proceed to the Ohio Valley to treat in person with the Indian communities there. Finally, the bulk of the Iroquois lands lay within the bounds of the states of New York and Pennsylvania, and Congress had no say at all over the disposition of these lands. But still the commissioners wanted captives returned and a new boundary line drawn between the United States and the Six Nations. But the inflated rhetoric served a purpose. By claiming the United States had conquered the Iroquois under the Treaty of Paris, they overcame the jurisdictional difficulties inherent in a negotiation with an Indian nation that resided almost entirely within the sovereign state of New York.[37]

The Iroquois leadership balked at the implications of "conquest theory," but in the end they had little choice but to accept the commissioners' treaty terms, as the United States offered the Iroquois a new dispensation in polity relations that was more palatable than the available alternative. Subsequently, Hill and other Iroquois would claim they were coerced into the disagreeable Treaty of Fort Stanwix. Certainly, the American commissioners had grown increasingly impatient as the negotiations dragged on. The Iroquois had roughly four alternatives available at Fort Stanwix. First, they could resume warfare against the United States. This was not a real option, as Iroquoia remained devastated from the War for Independence, and the Six Nations were still divided. Second, they could remain under the protection of the old father, the "Great King," and relocate inside British Canada. This was the option chosen by the Mohawk community of Joseph Brant and the other Grand River Iroquois. For the Iroquois who remained inside the borders of the United States, the two final options were to treat with the United States Congress or treat directly with the state of New York. By rejecting George Clinton's offers at the September Fort Stanwix conference and attending the October congressional conference, Aaron Hill, Cornplanter, and the other New York Iroquois had made an important decision that started them down that fourth path. In the final Treaty of Fort Stanwix in October, the United States asked only for a cession of land claims in far-western New York State and beyond, the bulk of which the Iroquois had already ceded in 1768. Furthermore, to treat only with New York, as Clinton had explained it (and as the Articles of Confederation stated), the Iroquois would have conceded their complete and total subordination and subjection to the state of New York. Turning away from Congress at Fort Stanwix meant turning away from Congress forever. A congressional treaty that was rooted in bad principles but that asked for few sacrifices was a far better alternative than a state treaty that immediately opened the floodgates to a massive loss of land. Of course, the floodgates were soon opened anyway, as the state of New York began to make inroads into Iroquoia throughout the 1780s.[38]

Congress's Indian commissioners made their way into the Ohio Valley the next year and sought negotiations with the Indian nations there under the same principles of "conquest theory." While a small number of representatives of the Delaware, Wyandot, Ottawa, and Chippewa Indians signed the 1785 Treaty of Fort McIntosh, and a number of Shawnee leaders signed a treaty concluded at the mouth of the Great Miami River the next year, the vast majority of the Indian peoples of what was soon to be the Northwest Territory rejected the notions proposed by the congressional commissioners of the sovereignty of the United States over them. Nonetheless, white settlers began to traverse the Appalachian Mountains and move down the Ohio Valley, settling in the Forks of the Ohio region as well as in Virginia's Kentucky District. Low-intensity warfare between many of the northwestern Indians and the various settler communities continued throughout the 1780s.[39]

By the middle of the summer of 1787, the disorder on the frontier between the United States and the Indian country was a reality that rendered a stronger Confederation an absolute imperative. This was the view from Vincennes, a strategically important village and trading center on the Wabash River (a northern tributary of the Ohio), where, in August 1787, Lieutenant Colonel Josiah Harmar had led a detachment of what remained of the U.S. Army after the Continental Army had been disbanded. Harmar had found a community that evinced the need for a power, any power, to interpose and provide order—at least this was the view of one of Vincennes most politically astute residents, a French-born merchant and trader named Barthélemi Tardiveau. Surveying the situation for Harmar shortly after his arrival, Tardiveau believed that the Revolutionary Era Ohio Valley had been progressively "marked by all the excesses that can be the result of self-created authority, wanton aggression, and boundless tyranny," and that it was "high time to wash off the stain that the conduct of a lawless mob . . . [had] impress'd on the American character." He perceived that the diffuse nature of the American union under the Articles of Confederation was at the root of the problems faced in the Ohio Valley. "Republicks such as the American States, where extensive & far distant frontiers are generally inhabited by a sort of people who are yet to mistake the idea of licentiousness for that of liberty," and "where the reins of government are slacken'd before they reach the circumference," ultimately were places "where administration cannot interfere in the dealings between white & red men." The British and, especially, the French before them had not had such difficulties, at least in Tardiveau's mind. "Under a more absolute government, the hand of power holds everywhere the helm with equal steadiness," and thus the "Indian trade is reduced into a system; it has its regulations & laws." He believed that the Americans needed, somehow, to mimic such an arrangement, if order was to come to the Ohio Valley. "I am decidedly of the opinion," Tardiveau wrote, "that no treaty of peace, likely to be lasting, can be made with the Indians except [if] you are invested with powers energetick enough to keep the whites under subjection & call them to a severe account if, by any misconduct of theirs, differences shou'd arise with the savages; and I think you ought to lay this matter before Congress."[40]

While Harmar and his immediate superior, Secretary at War Henry Knox, would come to agree with most of Tardiveau's prescriptions in the coming months and years (eventual Republicans would likely accuse Knox of agreeing a little too much), they knew that laying the matter "before Congress" in 1787 would have little effect. Indeed, the weakness of governmental power, so obvious to Tardiveau, was the reason for the deliberations at the convention in Philadelphia, occurring at the very moment he penned his letter. Securing order in the West and bringing some force to Indian diplomacy—and diplomacy with the European powers as well—were key imperatives behind the movement to rework and revise the Articles of Confederation that culminated in the Annapolis and Philadelphia conventions.

THE PHILADELPHIAN SOLUTION
Reorganizing Diplomatic Power under the Federal Constitution

Leading the charge to reform and revise the Articles of Confederation was Virginian James Madison—arguably the most thorough American student of the ways of diplomacy, the law of nations, and the science of how polities related to one another. Although he spent his entire life in North America, it was through his correspondence with his friend Thomas Jefferson that Madison learned about the frustrations of the American diplomats in Europe and from correspondents in Kentucky that he grew worried about disorder in the trans-Appalachian region. He perceived the diplomatic imperative as well as any American. Serving as a delegate to Congress and in the Virginia legislature, Madison experienced equally the frustrations inherent in the weak form of national government provided for in the Articles of Confederation. He thus came to be one of the United States' leading exponents of constitutional reform in the mid-1780s.[41]

Madison's intellectual endeavors of the summer of 1786 constituted a key milestone on his path to becoming one of the leading architects of the federal Constitution and the new theories of federalism that underpinned it. At the end of 1783, Madison's tenure as a Virginia delegate to Congress ended, and in the spring of 1784 Madison took a seat in Virginia's lower legislative house, the House of Delegates. Madison's tenure as a Virginia legislator during these years turned him from general suspicion toward plans for a stronger union of the states, to a belief in its necessity. Madison witnessed how British mercantile interests were aggrandizing control of Virginia's commerce. Virginian planters had increasingly little say in how their produce was transported to other Atlantic ports. A stronger economic alliance with shipping interests in the Mid-Atlantic and New England states would give Virginia more control over its economic destiny. And given that it shared the vital waterways of the Potomac River and the Chesapeake Bay with neighboring Maryland, some form of interstate accommodation regarding commerce was desperately needed. The imperatives felt by Adams and Jefferson on one side of the Atlantic were felt by Madison on the other. Madison saw that strengthening the bonds of the

Confederation was the only way to achieve respect on the Atlantic and, in doing so, preserve prosperity in North America. After serving in the state legislature since 1784 and then witnessing the failure of the Mount Vernon Conference between Maryland and Virginia, Madison anxiously anticipated the September 1786 Annapolis Convention.[42]

In preparation for the Annapolis Convention, Madison ensconced himself on his plantation in the rolling foothills of Virginia's Orange County, where he embarked on an exercise in the study of history and comparative government. The fruit of Madison's labors during the summer of 1786 was a lengthy working document, generally referred to as "Notes on Ancient and Modern Confederacies." It made use of ancient and modern political history, compiling descriptive lists of polities and their modes of governance. Madison compiled his "Notes" in order to understand how polities that were composites of different republics had actually functioned. He wanted to understand how confederated republics worked, why they failed, and what political structures might be made use of by Revolutionary Americans.[43]

A reading of Madison's "Notes on Confederacies" reveals that the institutions and modes of diplomacy were an important concern, although they were not his only one—how the instruments involved in making diplomacy connected with the other structures of a confederacy's governance was also vitally important. In the "Notes," Madison examined three confederations from antiquity (the Lycian, the Amphyctionic, and the Achaean), and three from modern history—the Helvitic (or Swiss), the Belgic (meaning the Netherlands), and the Germanic (meaning the Holy Roman Empire). Madison made general notes as to each confederacy's characteristics, and specifically noted the nature of the "Foedral Authority" in each, as well as the "Vices of the Constitution" in each case. Madison noted that each confederacy contained some element of diplomatic power and military power under the head of federal authority. In the Achaean Confederacy, for example, the authority to send and receive ambassadors, as well as the authority to contract foreign alliances, were federal powers.[44] In the modern confederacies, federal authority was variegated and delineated to a much greater degree. Madison found one of the "Vices of the Constitution" of the loose confederation of the Swiss to be the "weakness of the Union." There were different classes of cantons in the Swiss Confederation, and the senior members of the confederacy had a greater say in the matter of declaring war. Additionally, Madison noted that "Foreign Ministers from different

Nations reside in different Cantons," although ministers with "letters of Credence for the whole Confederacy address them to Zurich the chief Canton." This was a loose confederation indeed—almost replicating the nightmare scenario John Adams had imagined of needing thirteen American plenipotentiaries for every European court.[45]

It was the Dutch Republic that offered Madison the most developed example of a confederation and the most complex construction of a federal union. It had a legislative body (the States General) wherein each province was represented, as well as separate executive authority (subordinate to the States General), which was placed in a Council of State, which in turn both included the singular office of Stadtholder and oversaw the Chamber of Accounts, which managed the treasury. Each province retained its own sovereignty within its borders, and no treaty could be accepted without the consent of every province. Interestingly, it was the Stadtholder who managed the day-to-day conduct of diplomacy, receiving ambassadors and assisting in their appointment; the Stadtholder also served as the head of the military as captain general of the army and admiral general of the navy. However, Madison found that this confederate structure, too, had its vices in the realm of diplomacy. Since each province had what was essentially a veto power, foreign governments could hamstring any treaty with the Dutch by "gaining a single province or City." This weakness in their confederation had caused the Dutch to abandon their most republican government and place most of the executive and legislative prerogatives in the hands of the Stadtholder.[46]

History thus offered Madison many raw materials for reimagining the American Confederation, but no concrete model in and of itself, and no sure formula for success. History did reveal that the diplomatic imperative for a stronger union, which Americans felt obliquely in the 1780s, was not unique. Weak, decentralized confederate republics were often preyed upon by their neighbors. Yet, to concentrate all federal power (including authority over all aspects of foreign relations) in a single set of hands could spell doom for republican government. During the course of a summer of research, and a few pages of notes, Madison began to perceive many of the axioms that would guide his approach for years to come in thinking about how a confederate republic could and should make diplomacy. First, he saw that preserving republican government in a composite polity would require the balancing of power between the constituent polities and the central authority as much, if not more, than it required balancing power between the social orders. Second, Madison saw that the management of diplomacy could make or break such a confederated polity. Third, diplomatic power had several elements—the appointment of ambassadors, the reception of foreign ambassadors, the management of negotiations, and the final ratification of treaties (and, it should not be forgotten, the making of war). As a confederate structure could (and had to) divide governmental power between the federal center and the constituent republics, the management of relations between these constituent polities and foreign powers could likewise be divided. Surely, the imperatives of diplomacy pulled the union to the center, yet Madison's studies gave him an understanding of how the diplomatic power itself could be subdivided and parceled in order to preserve republicanism.

These insights informed Madison's work during the Philadelphia Convention of 1787, and his advocacy for the ratification of the Constitution in 1787–88. The imperative to rationalize diplomacy was almost a universal given among those who supported and participated in the federal project during the summer of 1787. As the historians Jack Rakove and Frederick Marks have both noted, the treaty-making power was the subject of minimal discussion during the Philadelphia Convention. Considered on only a few occasions in passing during the first two and half months of the convention, through mid- to late August, when the convention had discussed the treaty-making power at all, they had debated between locating the power in Senate or in the House of Representatives. It was not until 4 September that the convention agreed to divide both the treaty-making power and the power to appoint ambassadors between the president and the Senate. A similar plan had been proposed by Alexander Hamilton in June, but it had gone nowhere. The new proposal generated only a little debate, and the bulk of the delegates supported keeping the Senate's two-thirds vote to advise and consent on a treaty, in order to give the states a major voice in the diplomatic process and to provide a negative, should a treaty inconvenience one section in particular. But despite the Senate's important role, the bulk of the task of managing and making diplomacy was placed in the hands of the president and the executive branch. While some convention delegates would later lament that so much of the construction of the executive's powers had transpired in the rush of the final two weeks of the convention, the obvious need for a strong, firm hand in managing the foreign relations of the United States informed most of the delegates' assent in the matter. The need for a strong hand in managing the diplomacy of the United States would also be a constant refrain of the supporters of the Constitution during the ratification debates.[47]

Concerns over international relations were foremost on the minds of the most famous proponents of ratification, the "Publius" essayists, who began writing in New York about a month after the promulgation of the federal Constitution. The bulk of John Jay's initial contributions to the *Federalist* focused on the sharp line that, theoretically, had been drawn between the Philadelphian states system and the larger Westphalian system—keeping the American states free from the conflicts that constantly disrupted the peace of Europe. As Jay described it, the multitude of connections between the United States and the wider worlds of sovereigns under the Articles of Confederation were inherently dangerous. A single superintending diplomatic authority would help to keep peace. In a territory so vast as the American confederation, conflicts detrimental to the whole could arise from "local circumstances." Although such events often arose in response to "direct and unlawful violence," conflict tended to be "more frequently caused by the passions and the interests of a part than of the whole, of one or two States than of the Union." A more centralized union would serve to dilute the passions of local communities that were in direct contact with foreign powers, while also providing a more credible deterrent to foreign powers in the first instance. In the realm of the great powers, diplomatic measures that were "accepted as satisfactory from a strong united nation" tended to be "rejected as unsatisfactory if offered by a State or Confederacy of little consideration or power."[48] A modicum of centralization was the key to rationalizing the juncture between the American states and the wider European-centered system of sovereigns and empires. "The safety of the whole is the interest of the whole," Jay asserted. Small states and large states, southern states and northern states, all would be equally regarded under the new government: "In the formation of treaties it will regard the interest of the whole, and the particular interests of the parts as connected with that of the whole." Although the individual states acceded a portion of their liberties as sovereignties, it was actually in their interests to do so, as the federal union would be able to "apply the resources and power of the whole to the defence of any particular part," and it could do so "more easily and expeditiously than State Governments, or separate confederacies can possibly do."[49]

Yet "Publius" only hinted at the magnitude of change for the American states that could be effected by the new federal union. In erecting a cordon between the individual thirteen states and the European powers, the relations between the thirteen sovereigns would be transformed. The potential, as well as the reality, of conflict between the thirteen states was a constant theme of the early numbers of the *Federalist*, whether in Jay's descriptions of individual states painlessly ceding points of local interest to serve a greater whole in foreign affairs, or in Hamilton's nightmare vision in *Federalist* No. 9 of thirteen disunited states, girdled with standing armies and restrictive commercial regulations, engaged in a perpetual war of each against all.[50] What the "Publius" collaborators understood was that even under the plan drafted by the Philadelphia Convention, the thirteen states retained more than a bare residuum of sovereignty. The Constitution did not transform the United States into a single, unified state, rather it amalgamated them into, as Hamilton described it, a *"Confederate Republic."* In this arrangement, the "State Governments" were "constituent parts of the national sovereignty" through their "direct representation in the Senate," while they simultaneously retained in "their possession certain exclusive and very important portions of sovereign power."[51] Writing outside the confines of "Publius," James Madison more famously christened the arrangement an "extended Republic."[52] While the Constitution's defenders understood that the document's wiser arrangement of diplomatic powers necessitated a rearrangement of sovereignty within the American union, few were willing to publicly contemplate how the exercise of diplomacy might shift the delicate balances between the center and the states. Yet, this issue surfaced time and again during the state ratification debates in 1787 and 1788. Madison's Virginia was the site of one of the more telling exchanges.

It was on 4 June 1788, the third day of the Virginia Ratifying Convention, when the convention resolved itself into the Committee of the Whole, and began Virginia's official debate over the new Constitution. The second delegate to speak was Patrick Henry, who was adamantly opposed to the new Constitution. After an initial attempt during procedural business to get the Virginia Convention to censure the Philadelphia Convention for exceeding its mandate, Henry turned his energies to attacking the new Constitution's substance. "I conceive the republic to be in extreme danger," he observed, claiming this danger came from the new Constitution's "fatal system" that provided for "the utter annihilation of the most solemn engagements of the States." Henry was disturbed that the new federal government could begin operation with only nine of the thirteen states; it was thus, in his thinking, a totally new confederacy in the place of the old one. And changing the shape of the Confederation changed everything, Henry warned. "It goes to the annihilation of those solemn treaties we have formed with foreign nations." What would become of the Treaty of Alliance with France? "We are in alliance with the Spaniards, the Dutch, the Prussians," Henry exclaimed, "Those treaties bound us as thirteen States, confederated together—Yet, here is a proposal to sever that confederacy." Henry then put the question before his fellow Virginians in the starkest form: "Is it possible that we shall abandon all our treaties and national engagements?—And for what?" Henry thus attempted to turn one of the strongest arguments for ratifying the Constitution—that it would strengthen the diplomatic prospects of the United States—on its head.[53]

The Constitution's defenders quickly shot back. Edmund Randolph, who rose immediately to counter Henry, was blunt: "The Honorable Gentleman [Henry] asks, why should we adopt a system, that shall annihilate and destroy our treaties with France, and other nations?" The answer was obvious. "I think," Randolph stated, "that these treaties are violated already, under the Honorable Gentleman's favorite system."[54] Yet, Henry saw something that the majority of his fellow delegates either missed or ignored. The framework that held the thirteen states together—the Articles of Confederation—was a treaty like any other. In changing the "treaty" that was the Articles of Confederation, the Philadelphia Convention had reorganized an entire system of states, giving the American union a structure it had not had before. Greater agency in the larger Westphalian system and in the borderlands diplomatic regime would come only through changing the dynamics of the Philadelphian system of which the thirteen states were all a part. Indeed, Henry's partner in opposition, George Mason, later fixated on the new federal government's expanded treaty-making powers ("a most dangerous clause"), where he contemplated the possibility of a small number of scheming states using the treaty power to force a new "supreme law of the land" on the other states.[55] Henry worried that since, as he saw it, the Constitution created "one great consolidated National Government," it destroyed the sovereignties that had contracted the treaties of the 1780s and thus abrogated the said treaties.[56] Although this did not come to pass, the new reality was no less problematic. Henry's larger message rang true—those who blindly followed the imperative of diplomacy to strengthen and centralize the government of the United States had to be wary of the unintended consequences of any recalibration of sovereign power. It was a lesson that Henry's main opponent in the Virginia Convention—James Madison—would learn the hard way in the years to come.

"To Be Considered as Foreign Nations"

The Ambiguous Triumph of Federalist Statecraft

> The independent nations and tribes of indians ought to be considered as foreign nations, not as the subjects of any particular state—each individual State indeed will retain the right of pre-emption of all lands within its limits, which will not be abridged. But the general Sovereignty must possess the right of making all treaties on the execution or violation of which depend peace or war.
> —Henry Knox to George Washington, July 1789

A little over a month after taking the oath of office, the new president of the United States, George Washington, made use of a brief lull in the business of his office to ascertain the nature of the issues that would confront him and the United States during his first term as president. In early June 1789, Washington dispatched brief notes to the secretaries of war (Henry Knox) and treasury (Alexander Hamilton), and to the acting secretary of foreign affairs (John Jay), asking for a "clear account" of each department's business, that would contain "a full, precise and distinct *general idea* of the United States, so far as they are comprehended in, or connected with" each secretary's department. At about the time Washington sent these requests to Knox, Hamilton, and Jay, he had spent several days going over the previous year's correspondence between the American minister to France (Thomas Jefferson) and Jay. Within a month, Washington had received a detailed series of memoranda on the state of relations between the United States and its American Indian neighbors from Secretary of

War Knox. These memoranda, in concert with Washington's own notes of Jay's correspondence, painted a clear, if sobering, picture of the situation of the United States in the wider world. The United States faced challenges toward both the East and the West. From the letterbooks of the secretary of foreign affairs, Washington read of the 1788 Consular Convention between France and the United States, as well as the events unfolding within France itself that would lead to the beginning of the French Revolution at almost the same time he was engaged in note taking. From Knox, Washington received detailed descriptions of the internal state and external relations of the important southern Indian nations—the Creek, the Cherokee, the Choctaw, and the Chickasaw—as well as a general view of the state of relations between the United States and the Indian nations of eastern North America. This information was forwarded with Knox's prescriptions on how the federal government's policy on the United States' Indian neighbors should unfold in the months and years to come.[1]

Perusing the files and memoranda of his secretaries, Washington would have perceived the variety of the United States' external relationships—with European sovereigns and with the Indian nations. He also would have quickly understood that the decision made at Philadelphia (which he had presided over) and ratified by the states for a stronger union that could allow American diplomats to effect meaningful and desirable outcomes in the larger states system was a needed one. Yet, as the 1790s unfolded and Washington and his cabinet began engaging in diplomatic activity, their actions revealed the fragility of that consensus. The extent to which the new federal union reapportioned sovereignty among the United States had never been firmly agreed upon. In fact, the very ambiguity of the new union's structure had been one of its selling points during the ratification debates. While the emergent Federalist Party tied the diplomatic imperative to a larger, centralizing imperative, the emergent Jeffersonian Republican Party had felt that following the dictates of the diplomatic imperative went hand in hand with an imperative to preserve sovereignty (and with it, republicanism) at the state level. Battles over how to craft and then deploy the federal government's new diplomatic machinery soon became battles over the meaning of the new Constitution itself.

Aggravating latent divisions over the proper balance of power within the American union were events beyond the borders of the United States. While the Washington administration opened up diplomatic relations with the large southern Creek and Cherokee Indian nations soon after taking office, the various smaller Indian nations of the Ohio Valley resisted American attempts to treat (and thus acquire their land), touching off a war that would last from 1790 until 1795. In Europe, the French Revolution, begun in the late spring of 1789, initially unfolded to the applause of nearly every American. But in the summer of 1792, with radical voices gaining more power and deposing the National Assembly in favor of the National Convention and the infamous Committee of Public Safety, Europe was soon wracked by war. Austria and Prussia declared war against France in support of Louis XVI and Marie Antoinette, and after Louis' trial and January 1793 execution, France was also at war with the Netherlands, Spain, and Great Britain. Americans were divided as to whether to support or denounce the revolutionary regime in France, and Washington's cabinet was divided as to whether the United States was bound to recognize the new regime and whether the 1778 Treaty of Alliance was still in effect. Washington's decision to remain neutral in the European war and also to continue to trade equally with all belligerents led to an increase in British seizures of American merchant shipping, which in turn prompted the dispatch of John Jay to negotiate a formal commercial treaty between the United States and Great Britain. The resulting "Jay Treaty" became a lightning rod for domestic criticism, although simultaneous treaties the Washington administration concluded with Spain, Algiers, and the various Indian nations of the Northwest were approved by the Senate without controversy. After the ratification of the Jay Treaty in 1795, revolutionary France interpreted the treaty as a de facto American alliance with Britain and began to prey on American merchant shipping, much as the British had done. A failed bout of diplomacy in 1797 under President John Adams was followed by the undeclared Quasi-War with France, which terminated in 1800 with the accession of Napoleon Bonaparte to power in France. Bonaparte concluded peace (briefly) with Britain, which allowed America's Atlantic commerce to expand enormously, and then, with the collapse of Bonaparte's project to build an empire in the Americas after his army's defeat in Saint-Domingue, he offered to sell the Louisiana territory to the United States.

While the Federalists and Jeffersonian Republicans both were committed to ensuring the United States utilized the strengthened diplomatic apparatus provided for by the federal Constitution, they differed over two key issues—the extent to which balances of sovereign power needed to recalibrated within the union, and the goals toward which the newly empowered American diplomats should be directed. The Federalists sought to centralize sovereign power within the Philadelphian system in order to win commercial concessions for American producers, merchants, and carriers in the realm of Westphalian diplomacy, but particularly in negotiations with Great Britain. In order to achieve these ends in the short term, they were also willing to maintain the diplomatic norms of the borderlands in conducting Indian diplomacy. The Jefferson Republicans were uncomfortable with the extreme centralizing tendencies of the Federalist program within the American union; they wished for openings in all European markets, not simply British ones; and they wanted the federal government to play an active role in acquiring Indian land and opening the West for the expansion of settlement within existing state borders and also for the settlement and creation of new states. These differences constituted two distinct normative visions for how sovereign power should be structured across the three states systems. Ironically, while disagreements over norms fueled the partisan conflict that ultimately propelled the Jeffersonian Republican Party to victory in the congressional and presidential Elections of 1800, once in power, the Jeffersonians would utilize the new diplomatic apparatus the Federalists had built to achieve their own ends.

Executive Decisions
The Early Consensus in Organizing Diplomatic Powers

At the beginning, all were in agreement over the question of constructing the diplomatic powers of the new federal government. One of the first tasks that the Congress and the executive branch undertook in New York City during the spring of 1789 was the creation of a diplomatic establishment. Memories of the Confederation Congress's ineffective diplomacy remained fresh well into 1790. Representative James Madison led proponents of an energetic foreign policy, arguing that control over the diplomatic process should be given to the president, aside from the few exceptions prescribed by the Constitution. Few contemplated the baneful effects such a concentration of power could have upon relations between the federal government and the states. The near unanimity that accompanied the creation of what would become the State Department reveals the continuing force of the spirit of consensus from the Philadelphia Convention into the First Congress.

During debates over the bill authorizing the organization of a Department of Foreign Affairs, members of the House of Representatives discussed the efficacy of a proposed clause that would allow the president unlimited power to remove the officers he had only a share of the power to appoint. Some were opposed to this measure, believing that as the Senate had the responsibility to advise and consent to appointments, it should not be excluded from the related power of removal. With the threat of removal constantly hanging over the heads of all of the executive officers, the president would hold "their thread of life," and "his power will be sovereign over them." This was too much authority. The Senate's power to check the president would be rendered meaningless, and some congressmen raised the specter of an aggrandizing "Supreme Executive."[2] Many feared unrestrained executive power, especially considering that a future president might be less scrupulous and restrained than the current occupant of the executive office, the revered Washington. Despite such concerns, the desire to give the executive as much authority as possible in fashioning a diplomatic establishment carried the day.[3]

Proponents of a strong, central diplomatic establishment argued that their construction of executive power was both constitutional and necessary. Madison, who had initially proposed the creation of a department of foreign affairs in a resolution of 19 May 1789, led the charge, arguing for the Foreign Affairs Bill's constitutionality. His argument was a straightforward one, as he noted that the Constitution divided the legislative, executive, and judicial powers among the three branches of government. Although *all* of the executive's powers were not granted exclusively to the president, the exceptions were clearly specified by the Constitution. So Madison asserted that the question before the House was simply, "Is the power of displacing [an appointee], an executive power?" He answered in the affirmative, noting "that if any power whatsoever is in its nature executive, it is the power of appointing, overseeing, and controlling those who execute the laws."[4] Since the power of removal was not specifically granted to Congress, it would be improper for the legislature to assume it. Buttressed by Madison's constitutional interpretation, other Congressmen attacked the opponents' efforts to interpose the Congress into the diplomatic process. Egbert Benson of New York reminded his colleagues that the secretary of state would be "committed to negotiations with the ministers of foreign courts," which was "a very delicate trust." Benson imagined a scenario in which a president discovered misconduct on the part of a diplomat, but for whatever reason, the Senate refused to remove him. In such a case, "the President would then have a man forced on him whom he considered unfaithful." In diplomatic negotiations, the president needed to have the final word; the executive had to speak with one voice, or diplomacy would be impossible. Benson warned, "Without a confidence in the Executive Department, its operations would be subject to perpetual discord, and the administration of the Government become impracticable."[5] With the need for an executive department to handle foreign affairs agreed upon, and a majority convinced of the need for the president's prerogatives to predominate in that department, the Foreign Affairs Bill passed both the House and the Senate and was signed into law in July 1789. A majority of the First Congress were convinced of the necessity of the federal executive having a strong hand and taking the lead in the process of diplomacy. The concentration of diplomatic power in the hands of the executive continued when the new State Department finally had a secretary at its head.

Upon becoming secretary of state, Thomas Jefferson took the lead from the Congress in constructing the new federal diplomatic establishment. In 1790, Jefferson acted in accordance with a belief that the executive should have as unfettered a hand as possible in shaping American foreign policy. It must be acknowledged that no one in the federal government argued for absolute executive power over diplomacy. Jefferson, Washington, and the remainder of the administration, as well as the Congress, were all aware that diplomacy was not purely the prerogative of the president. The Constitution gave Congress the power to declare war, and it also gave the Senate the duty to "advise and consent" regarding any diplomatic officer the president appointed, as well as any treaty his diplomats concluded. But it remained unclear as to the extent to which this advisory power could be construed. Members of the administration, Jefferson included, argued for a maximal construction of executive power and a minimal construction of congressional power. In April 1790, Washington asked Jefferson about the limits of the Senate's power over diplomatic officers, wondering specifically if the Senate's power to advise and consent on appointments extended to a power over the determination of a minister's grade. What seemed to be a minor point of protocol quickly took on a greater significance.

Jefferson's five years as the United States' minister to France had taught him firsthand the importance that issues of protocol had in foreign courts. In all manners of diplomatic ceremony, European courts still embraced the principle of "precedence"—that is, each diplomat from a foreign sovereign had a rank, which was dictated both by his country of origin, as well as the grade of his office. Ambassadors were of a higher rank than ministers, a minister was of a higher rank than a chargé d'affaires, and so on. Higher-ranking ministers had more privileges, but also had more responsibilities in formal negotiations, as well as in the world of entertainments that was part and parcel of the culture of diplomacy. Put bluntly, the higher the minister's rank, the more money he would need to entertain, to see and be seen, to participate in the life of the court, and in short, to perform his functions adequately. Time and again in France, Jefferson had experienced firsthand the embarrassments that could befall a cash-strapped minister at a foreign court. Understanding how crucial questions of diplomatic protocol were to the making of foreign policy, Jefferson was not going to let their control slip from the executive's hand.[6]

Jefferson, drawing on his diplomatic experience, explained to Washington the significance of protocol and the importance of the executive branch retaining control over it. In a memorandum to the president, Jefferson noted that in considering the question of "Whether the Senate has a right to negative the *grade*" of an appointee, he thought it did not. "The transaction of business with foreign nations is Executive altogether," Jefferson asserted. Therefore, he argued, the making of diplomacy "belongs then to the head of that department, *except* as to such portions of it as are specifically submitted to the Senate," and, echoing Madison's defense of the Foreign Affairs Bill, Jefferson further cautioned that these "*Exceptions* are to be construed strictly." In Jefferson's understanding, the commissioning of a diplomat was a complicated process, ordained by the law of nations, and one whose complexity the Constitution both explicitly and implicitly recognized. He noted that the "Constitution itself" specified that the president *nominated* the diplomat, the president and the Senate together *appointed* him, and the president himself finally *commissioned* the diplomat. Jefferson also noted that the Constitution omitted discussion of the other actions necessary in naming a diplomat, the choice of his destination and the choice of his grade. As both a diplomat and a student of the law of nations, Jefferson saw the appointment of a diplomat as an intensely formalized and legalistic process, the "natural order" of which proceeded through "destination," "grade," "nomination," "appointment," and "commission." The Constitution gave the Senate a hand in only one step of this process.[7]

Jefferson's understanding of the law of nations and the art of diplomacy led him to a strict construction of the Constitution that gave the executive extraordinarily broad powers over diplomacy. There was no other way for Jefferson to interpret the document. The Constitution gave the Senate no negative as to where a minister was to be sent, or what grade of minister was to be commissioned, only on his competence to serve. Jefferson offered that the "Senate is not supposed by the Constitution to be acquainted with the concerns of the Executive department." They had no voice in the particulars of diplomatic appointments because "it was not intended that these should be communicated to them." Therefore, the Senate simply could not be "qualified to judge of the necessity which calls for a mission to any particular place, or of the particular grade, more or less marked, which special and secret circumstances may call for." Jefferson left no doubt that "all this is left to the President," for "if the Constitution had meant to give the Senate a negative" on any of these questions, "it would have said so in direct terms."[8]

Although Madison's and Jefferson's consolidationist measures might, in retrospect, surprise us, considered in historical context, they should not. Even as he parsed the minutiae of the Foreign Affairs Bill, Madison had already foreseen the potential baneful effects of the consolidation of diplomatic power, and he had worked through the manner in which powers over diplomacy could be divided and checked. Two points deserve mention in this context. First, in the debates on the Foreign Affairs Bill, Madison acknowledged that the Senate retained some important checks on the president's diplomatic prerogatives. Jefferson likewise acknowledged the Senate's share of diplomatic power. Second, it can be argued that Madison and Jefferson understood, but underestimated, the dangers inherent in placing the bulk of diplomatic power in the hands of the executive. A decade of having no executive control over American diplomacy had nearly led to disaster; the new system, any system, was better than the Confederation. But as the years of the first Washington administration unfolded, Jefferson and Madison began to sense the danger in a set of institutions and a constitutional construction they had initially argued for so vociferously.

Knoxian Indian Policy and the Apogee of Federalist Statecraft

A majority of the men involved in the shaping of the new federal government felt the imperative toward centralization that diplomatic negotiation impelled. The leading architects of the emerging Federalist modes of statecraft were George Washington's secretary of the treasury, Alexander Hamilton, and secretary of war, Henry Knox. Although Thomas Jefferson, as secretary of state, ostensibly oversaw the relationship between the United States and foreign powers, the indeterminacy inherent in a new frame of government gave Knox and Hamilton plenty of space to expand their power. Through aggressive promotion of their commercial, military, and Indian policies, Hamilton and Knox limited the ability of Jefferson's smaller and more moribund State Department to affect American state relations in the manner in which he desired. In order to bring their policies to fruition, Hamilton and Knox needed to expand existing institutions (the army, the Indian agencies, the revenue service) or create new ones (the Bank of the United States, the Indian factory system), while Jefferson wanted to keep the "diplomatic corps" (such as it was) small and inexpensive. Hamilton's and Knox's breadth of vision and political philosophy worked to their advantage in manifold and reinforcing ways. They effectively took the real political power to make diplomacy out of Jefferson's hands. Simultaneously, Hamilton's and Knox's policy initiatives had to actively take power and sovereignty directly from the hands of the states and from the Congress.[9]

The emerging Federalist leadership did not see the federal government acting as the Continental Congress had done—as a gatekeeper between the individual sovereign states and the larger and more powerful European sovereigns beyond its borders. Rather, Knox and Hamilton saw the federal government serving as the focus of American sovereignty and the only legitimate nexus between the citizens of the United States and the Westphalian and the borderlands diplomatic systems. The sovereignty of the states would increasingly be residual, rather than vital. This was not just a vision of how to get diplomacy done, but a new schema for national identity and national loyalty. As the federal center became the locus of American sovereignty, each individual would soon see it, and not their state government, as the most likely and effective promoter of his self-interest. This would be true of New England merchants, southern planters, and western farmers, all of whom would turn to the federal center for protection from hostile foreigners as well as each other. Knox let the universality of these political principles revealingly slip in a letter to William Blount about relations with the southern Indians. "The great object in managing Indians, or indeed any other men, however enlightened, is to obtain their confidence," the Secretary of War wrote. "This cannot be done but by convincing them of an attention to their interests." Ultimately, "[d]eeply convinced of this general disposition of their protectors, they will be yielding in small matters." Never was the governing ethos of the Federalists laid so bare: reasonable men (and by extension, reasonable sovereign communities of men) took stock of the world around them, and then they reasonably submitted to the judgment of their betters. This belief in the innate venality of mankind undergirded the twin pillars of Federalist state relations—Knoxian Indian policy and Hamiltonian commercial policy. Human selfishness, first channeled into networks of commerce, and then shackled by the complexity of the new financial apparatus, would bind sovereign state and Indian nation, Anglo-American and American Indian alike, to the federal center.[10]

Acknowledging the difficulties of the Confederation era, Knox consciously charted a new course for the United States' diplomacy with American Indians. In Knox's plans, articulated in several memoranda sent to George Washington in the months following his inauguration, the federal government would constructively engage the various Indian communities along the borderlands of the United States, facilitating regularized commercial interaction between the federal government and the Indians, while preventing destructive and expensive warfare. With agents residing among the various Indian communities and facilitating (some would say forcing) their adoption of Anglo-American modes of agriculture, household industry, and commerce, the gradual "civilization" of the American Indians could proceed apace.[11] However, Knox downplayed the difficulties inherent in managing the nexus between the Philadelphian and Westphalian states systems. Knox wanted to end the inconsistency and conflict that had persisted between Americans and their Indian neighbors under the Confederation by eliminating the individual states from the equation as much as possible. The "great source of all Indian wars are disputes about their boundaries," Knox surmised. When the federal government asserted, "the Indian tribes possess the right of the soil of all lands within their limits and that they are not to be divested except by fair and bona fide purchases, made under the authority . . . of the United States" via the promulgation of a "declarative Law," a source of tension would be eliminated. "No individual State could with propriety complain of invasion of its territorial rights," Knox claimed. "The independent nations and tribes of Indians ought to be considered as foreign nations, not as the subjects of any particular state," he continued. While "each individual State indeed will retain the right of preemption of all lands within its limits, which will not be abridged," Knox made it clear who was to be the final arbiter. "But the general Sovereignty [meaning the federal government] must possess the right of making all treaties on the execution or violation of which depend peace or war."[12]

Knoxian Indian policy did not mean that the United States stopped coveting Indian land. Far from it. The timetable for land acquisition had simply been delayed, while the modus operandi had been changed. Strong leadership from the federal government would mitigate conflict between settlers and Indians, begin the "civilization" of Indian peoples within American borders, setting the stage for land transfers at some future date. While most American Indians would have disagreed, Knox and other Federalists saw this policy as the height of humanitarianism. The old injustices were at an end, he believed: "Whatever may have been the conduct some of the late British Colonies in their separate capacities toward the Indians, yet the same cannot be charged against the national character of the United States." The new order would be one where the "obligations of Policy, humanity, and Justice" were respected, and this required a "noble liberal and disinterested administration of indian affairs [sic]." Constraining the individual states and their enterprising republican citizens was vital: "Although the disposition of the people of the States to emigrate into the Indian country cannot be effectually prevented, it may be restrained and regulated." Prevention could be effected through "the postponing of new purchases [sic] of Indian territory, and by prohibiting the Citizens from intruding on Indian Lands," and by "forming Colonies under the direction of Government and by posting a body of troops to execute their orders." Knox thought, as did many of his contemporaries, that by slowing the westward movement, and engaging in policies of philanthropy toward American Indians, their eventual "civilization" would result, and these "civilized" Indians would happily sell the "excess" lands. The way for white settlement of the trans-Appalachian West would be cleared peacefully. Knox also acknowledged that many white

Americans were impatient to move west, and that the desires of some American citizens and possibly some American states would be at odds with the direction the Federalists wished to turn the central government.[13]

The Washington administration's first successful diplomatic negotiations of any kind were with the Creek Indians; they began in 1789 and culminated in the Treaty of New York of August 1790. While the success of these negotiations affirmed executive supremacy in the realm of diplomacy, they also prompted one of the earliest discussions of the potential of the Constitution's treaty-making power, as well as the reapportionment of sovereign power in the union.[14] Secretary of State Thomas Jefferson reacted to Knox's initiatives with the Creek nation with approval (although with a small amount of bewilderment about the appropriate protocols of Indian diplomacy.)[15] Months before the Treaty of New York, Jefferson had asserted that respecting Indian title to the land they occupied had "become a principle of the law of nations, fundamental with respect to America."[16] In the New York negotiations, the Creeks' chief, Alexander McGillivray, could thus claim the right to determine which Americans traded inside the Creek nation. Jefferson acknowledged that the Creeks were for all intents and purposes sovereign; they had the "right to give us their peace, and to withhold their commerce, to place it under what monopolies or regulations they please." Furthermore, an explicit agreement on this point would be in the interest of the United States, as "we gain some advantage in substituting citizens of the U.S." in places of "both British and Spaniards" as the principal agents of commerce with the Creek nation. Viewing the transatlantic geopolitical dynamic as a whole, Jefferson saw that a treaty clause that potentially compromised the rights and interests of particular states might nonetheless serve a more inclusive national interest.[17]

While Jefferson supported Knox's Indian policy, he did express minor doubts regarding the implications of Knox's policy for the structure of the American union. As early as 1783–84, during the debate over the ratification of Treaty of Paris, Jefferson had noted the potential of the treaty-making power to alter political relationships between the sovereign members of the union and even inside the states themselves. This awareness surfaced as he wondered in his July 1790 memorandum about the role the American government would play in maintaining the Creeks' monopolistic commercial practices. Any treaty clause that dealt with questions of commerce was fraught with danger, for a "treaty made by the President with the concurrence of two thirds of the Senate, is a law of the land, and a law of superior order, because it not only repeals past laws, but cannot itself be repealed by future ones." Any international agreement, including treaties with Indians, could thus make law within the American states system. A treaty might "expressly stipulate" that "no person be permitted to trade in the Creek country, without a licence [sic] from the President," giving the executive extraordinary discretion over the regulation of American commerce and preempting both federal and state legislatures. Despite such concerns, Jefferson wrote that, in fact, "no law will be violated" under the Creek treaty. A month later, Jefferson reaffirmed his respect for Indian sovereignty and the sanctity of American treaties with the Cherokee nation.[18]

Although his misgivings increased, Jefferson still held fast, a year later, to his belief in the need to respect Indian sovereignty. When the question of the validity of certain early Yazoo land sales came up again in August 1791, Jefferson reiterated his position about the inviolate nature of Indian sovereignty: "The Indians have a right to the occupation of their Lands independent of the States within whose chartered lines they happen to be." These rights persisted until the Indians "cede them by Treaty or other transaction equivalent to a Treaty." Furthermore, if the states persisted in allowing settlement on unceded lands, "the Government will think itself bound" to "remove them" by the use of "public force."[19] A strict reading of the Constitution, in light of Jefferson's understanding of the law of nations, thus gave the central government an enormous opening to affect political and legal relations *within* the states. Publicly, this was the law, but privately it would prove increasingly troublesome to Jefferson. His concerns about the changing balances of sovereign power within the federal union, raised by Knox's Indian diplomacy, were further piqued by Alexander Hamilton's emerging financial program. What Knox did to state prerogatives to negotiate with Indians and manage state land policies, Hamilton did to the states' ability to manage their own finances and thus direct economic development at the local level; the power to act was taken from the hands of the states and placed in the hands of the federal government, the executive in particular.[20]

The dangers that Federalist statecraft posed to the vision of the American union held dear by the Jeffersonian Republicans became clear as the crises surrounding the French Revolution unfolded. Matters came to a head in early 1793, after the execution of Louis XVI, when word reached North America that the French National Convention had appointed and dispatched a new minister to the United States.[21] Few were sure what the minister, Edmund Charles Genêt, would do when he arrived in America. The act of formally receiving him was perceived by some as an implicit recognition of the new regime. Many in the federal government, and especially in the Washington administration, felt that it was thus necessary to clarify the diplomatic position of the United States relative to France. The key questions were: whether the United States should formally receive Genêt; to what extent the 1778 Treaty of Alliance was still binding on the United States; and how the government should promulgate the decisions it reached regarding these issues. In a series of cabinet meetings in the late winter and early spring of 1793, a consensus emerged in the Washington administration: Genêt would be received.[22] Of greater import was the status of the Treaty of Alliance of 1778. The cabinet worried that Genêt would ask for American assistance against France's adversaries under the terms of the Treaty of Alliance. While no one expected the United States to dispatch an army to Europe, it was quite reasonable to expect that the French might ask for assistance in reconquering their Caribbean possessions, or ask the United States to either serve as a base for privateering against the navies of France's enemies or allow Americans to engage in privateering themselves. Any of these actions would have the effect of rendering the United States a belligerent, and would compromise American neutrality. Every member of the cabinet wished to avoid this, and, in Washington's words, "preserve a strict neutrality between the powers at war."[23] The decided method of clarification was to offer a proclamation that stated both to foreign powers and to American citizens that the United States was avowedly neutral in the current conflict. Despite this unanimity, the proper manner in which to offer this "Proclamation of Neutrality" was hotly contested.[24]

The fullest exposition of the issues involved occurred in an extended debate in newspaper essays between Alexander Hamilton, writing as "Pacificus," and James Madison, writing as "Helvidius." Hamilton issued seven "Pacificus" essays in the *Gazette of the United States* between 29 June and 27 July 1793. The first essay addressed the issue of whether the executive had the power to issue the proclamation, while the subsequent numbers discussed the status of the 1778 treaties with France, the proper disposition of the United States toward France, and the timing of the proclamation. Hamilton centered his discussion around the status of the making of diplomacy as an executive power. His argument was that the making of diplomacy—according to "general theory and practice"—*was* an executive function, and that unless a portion of those powers were expressly given to the legislature or judiciary, such powers remained in the hands of the executive.[25] Upon the urging of Jefferson, Madison drafted the five "Helvidius" essays between 24 August and 18 September.[26] Although Madison had utilized logic similar to Hamilton's in justifying the president's power of appointment in the debate over the Foreign Affairs Act, the argument he elaborated in the "Helvidius" essays made it clear that this reasoning did not apply in the current context. In challenging "Pacificus," Madison first took issue with Hamilton's broad construction of executive diplomatic powers. The treaty-making power was divided between the legislature and the executive, while the power to declare war was solely a legislative one. Any analogies one could make between the executive's unlimited removal power ("the power to displace a subaltern officer employed in the execution of the laws") and the "power to make treaties, and to declare war" were unfounded. These powers were not "of a kindred nature." Madison thus justified the position he had taken as a member of the First Congress, while he assailed Hamilton's extensive construction of executive power under the aegis of diplomacy.[27]

Challenging the Washington administration's concentration of diplomatic power in the hands of the executive was one of the most important thrusts in the Jeffersonian Republicans' opposition to the administration's diplomacy, be it Indian diplomacy, the Neutrality Proclamation, or the Jay Treaty. After Washington signed the Jay Treaty on 14 August 1795, a debate in the House of Representatives ensued the following March, as the House considered enabling legislation to enforce the treaty. The Jeffersonian Republicans requested that Washington send them copies of Jay's instructions and the official correspondence of the negotiations of the treaty. Washington turned down the request, but not before the House debated the same issues Madison and Hamilton had in the Pacificus-Helvidius debates of almost three years before.[28] Madison, Jefferson, and the Jeffersonian Republicans fixated on the constitutional issues surrounding the diplomatic powers because much of their critique of Federalist diplomacy was over the procedural norms under which it was being conducted, rather than the results. For example, the Republicans had approved of the Treaty of San Lorenzo with Spain, concluded in October 1795, which granted American shippers the duty-free right of deposit at the port of New Orleans, and acceded to American conceptions of neutral rights, most notably the idea that "free ships make free goods." It was a treaty that appealed to both Republican producers and Federalist merchants.[29] There was also bipartisan support for the August 1795 Treaty of Greenville, negotiated by General Anthony Wayne with the leaders of a confederation of American Indians in the Northwest Territory, in the wake of Wayne's victory at the Battle of Fallen Timbers the previous year. In addition to vindicating Knox's Indian and military policies, the treaty secured a large land cession that would provide security for settler populations in the territory that would become Ohio, as well as the new state of Kentucky. With these victories acknowledged, the Jeffersonian Republicans continued to worry that Federalist diplomacy had the potential to continue to undermine the sovereignty of the states, and derange the structures of the federal union, all in the name of winning a few extra concessions in the realm of European diplomacy.[30]

It was the subject and source of these concessions that the Federalists hoped to win that proved so troubling to Jefferson, Madison, and the remainder of the Jeffersonian Republicans. They believed that Federalist diplomacy, especially the Jay Treaty, tied the United States' commercial and economic fortunes too tightly to those of Great Britain, when the United States should be trying to play the role of a commercial "free-agent," seeking the best deals for its producers, consumers, merchants, and carriers, matching in-kind foreign offers to open their commerce to the United States, while discriminating against foreign powers that refused to ameliorate restrictions on American commerce. This was the thrust of the prescriptions Jefferson had put forward in his final state paper to Congress before his resignation from the office of secretary of state in December 1793.[31] Madison expanded the critique of Federalist policy in his April 1795 pamphlet *Political Observations*, which was, in large part, an attack on Federalist commercial policy toward Great Britain before the Jay Treaty. Madison specifically attacked the Federalists' unwillingness to support the Jeffersonian Republicans' plan of commercial retaliation against Great Britain for its continued high duties on American produce and their unwillingness to consider a commercial relationship that even began to approach a basis in reciprocity. The grievances were as old as the diplomatic imperative. Early in the essay, Madison revisited the history of the 1780s and reminded readers of the nature of the commercial relationship between Britain and the United States. The United States, weak and almost disunited under the Articles of Confederation, had been exploited by a callow British ministry's institution of a capricious commercial regime. In response, "the states labored by separate efforts, to counteract the unequal laws of Great Britain." Separately, they could not effect a change in British commercial regulations. This is what had been a major impetus behind the conventions at Annapolis and Philadelphia. The whole point of the new Constitution, and its concentration of diplomatic power at the federal center, Madison maintained, had been to challenge British commercial power to the benefit of the individual states. But not only were the Federalists refusing to deploy federal diplomatic power to challenge Great Britain for the benefit of the several states, they were simultaneously attempting to usurp further sovereign powers from the states themselves, as Madison argued, "from a gradual assumption or extension of discretionary powers in the executive departments; from successive augmentations of the standing army; and from the perpetuity and progression of public debts and taxes." In the Jeffersonian Republican view, bad policy and bad constitutional construction were going hand in hand.[32]

George Washington himself attempted to ameliorate these concerns by charting a national consensus for making diplomacy in his Farewell Address of September 1796. Although Washington's valedictory had initially been drafted by James Madison when Washington first contemplated retirement in 1792, the bulk of the address—concerned with diplomacy, union, and transatlantic geopolitics—was shaped by Alexander Hamilton, who had left his post as secretary of the treasury in January 1795 but still regularly advised Washington. Hamilton's suggestions as to the timing and content of the Farewell Address are often seen as an attempt to shape the outcome of the presidential election of 1796. Yet the overall message of the speech is ostensibly one of conciliation and unity.[33] Washington focused on both the nature of the American union and its position between the Westphalian and borderlands systems. A strong union would keep the United States from being consumed. Invoking the union, Washington referred to "the sacred ties which now link together the various parts," while he asserted that the bonds of union were "a main pillar in the edifice of your real independence, the support of your tranquility at home, your peace abroad; of your safety; of your prosperity; of that very liberty which you so highly prize." National identity had to trump local and sectional ties: "The name of American, which belongs to you in your national capacity, must always exalt the just pride of patriotism more than any appellation derived from local discriminations." Washington then went on to show how the points of contact between the American union and the sovereignties beyond its borders served as foci for distrust and discord within the United States. He pointed specifically to the recently concluded Treaty of San Lorenzo, the potential outcome of which had been a source of anxiety for westerners, as proof that the federal government kept every citizen's interests in view. "To the efficacy and permanency of your Union, a government for the whole is indispensable," Washington counseled. "No alliance, however strict, between the parts can be an adequate substitute." Interestingly, Washington's admonitions here reveal the extent to which state sovereignty had *not* diminished, but had continued relatively intact. The potential combinations of sovereigns (the definition of an "alliance") within the federal union remained within the realm of the possible. Because the American states retained sovereignty, reconciling the relationship between the individual states with the relationship between the United States and foreign sovereigns retained the sensitivity and difficulty that had characterized it under the Confederation. Events evolving alongside the Farewell Address bear out just how fragile the American union remained.[34]

The Treaty of Colerain and Origins of the Principles of '98

Even as George Washington contemplated the contents of his Farewell Address during the summer of 1796, the administration was already attempting to add another treaty to the Federalists' diplomatic edifice. In the spring of that year, Secretary of War James McHenry tapped North Carolina's Benjamin Hawkins, South Carolina's Andrew Pickens, and Pennsylvania's George Clymer to serve as commissioners for a treaty between the Creek nation and the government of the United States. By the end of May, all three commissioners, along with the superintendent for Indian affairs for the Southern Department, Georgia's James Seagrove, and a guard of Continental troops under the command of Colonel Henry Gaither, had arrived at the site of the treaty negotiations, the town of Colerain, Georgia. Colerain lay on the St. Marys River, at the edge of the great Okefenokee Swamp and on the extreme southern boundary of Georgia—geographically, the outpost was closer to the Spanish entrepôt of St. Augustine than it was to Georgia's chief port city, Savannah. Camped outside of Colerain were, according to the official count, 435 Creeks, including "twenty-two kings, seventy-five principal chiefs, and one hundred and fifty-two warriors."[35] Also at Colerain were three commissioners appointed by the state of Georgia, James Jackson, James Hendricks, and James Simms, along with a small entourage that included a small detachment of state militia. For a month, Hawkins, Clymer, and Pickens would be embroiled in negotiations with both of these parties, attempting to arbitrate the divergent interests of the Creek nation, the state of Georgia, and the federal government. The resulting Treaty of Colerain contained elements that certainly upset the Creek delegation (a small land cession), but it rankled the Georgia commissioners to an even greater degree. Examining the negotiation of the Treaty of Colerain, and the events leading to it and immediately following it, illustrates how Federalist agents continued to translate Knoxian Indian diplomacy into action and reality, while simultaneously revealing how these policies and practices alienated local elites and, in the process, state governments. The backlash against Federalist management of the Philadelphian system, which culminated in the Republican vision articulated in the Kentucky and Virginia Resolutions of 1798–99, began on the frontiers.

Initially, Creek diplomacy had been one of the great success stories of Washington's first secretary of war, Henry Knox. In the summer of 1790, Knox had invited the war chief of the Creek nation, Scots-Creek Alexander McGillivray, and other Creek leaders to New York City, where they concluded a treaty that opened the Creek nation to American commerce and secured Creek borders. Two treaties with the Cherokee, one at Holston River in 1791 and the other at Philadelphia in 1794, followed. Knox pushed for treaties with the larger, more powerful southern Indian confederacies, while pursuing warfare against the smaller, more diverse, and generally more violent Indian polities in the Northwest Territory. This policy had several important implications. In the federally managed Northwest Territory, Indian villages were pushed back under the Treaty of Greenville to make way for what would become the state of Ohio. Both in the Southwest Territory (what would become Tennessee) and in the state of Georgia, the powerful Creeks and Cherokees had been forced to give up relatively little land. This was seen as particularly onerous in Georgia, where the Treaty of New York had, for all intents and purposes, abrogated two treaties the state of Georgia had made with a minority faction of the Creek nation during the Confederation.[36] Many Georgians never accepted the new state of affairs, and low-intensity conflict between some Georgians and some Creek villages continued. As one incident of violence begat the next one, relations between American settlers and the Creek Indians had degenerated into almost open warfare by the summer of 1793. Based on reports from his agent James Seagrove and army officer Henry Gaither, Knox placed the bulk of the blame on the Georgians. The impression he received was that "the Creeks are generally disposed for peace, but there is too much reason to apprehend, that the conduct of certain lawless whites, on the frontiers of Georgia, will prevent that desirable event from being realized."[37]

The governor and legislature of Georgia raised the stakes of the situation in late 1794 and early 1795. Four separate pieces of state legislation chartered four new land companies, the Upper Mississippi Company, the Tennessee Company, the Georgia Company, and the Georgia Mississippi Company. To these four companies, the state of Georgia had deeded its claims to land that would eventually comprise nearly all of the state of Mississippi and half of the state of Alabama. This was the start of the infamous Yazoo land fraud, a scandal that would affect Georgian and American political life for years to come, ultimately culminating in the Supreme Court case of *Fletcher v. Peck* (1810).[38] But before the Yazoo companies entered the ongoing annals of America's collapsed speculative bubbles, they had an immediate effect on the geopolitical dynamics between Georgia and the Creek nation. The Yazoo charters claimed Georgia's rights to some of the lands it was selling under a 1785 treaty with the Creeks. The charter justified this treaty with a specific and direct quote of the Articles of Confederation. The Yazoo charter also mentioned the Treaty of New York, but did not discuss the fact that both Knox and the Creek leaders who negotiated it accepted that it superseded the Treaties of Galphinton and Shoulderbone Creek, which the Creeks regarded as illegitimate. Georgia clung to the continued legality of Confederation treaties neither the federal government nor the Creeks recognized. Even more suspect was Section 18 of the Yazoo companies' charters. It called on the "said grantees, and purchasers of land aforesaid," to "forebear all hostile and wanton attacks on any of the Indian tribes which may be found within the limits of this State, and keep this State free from all charges and expenses which may attend the preserving of peace between the said Indians and the grantees, and extinguishing the Indian claims to the territory included within their respective purchases." The state of Georgia essentially placed the responsibility for negotiating with the various Creek, Cherokee, Choctaw, and Chickasaw Indians in the hands of private parties, put all the cost for purchasing their lands on the private companies, and then politely asked these same companies to make sure no one went out and killed these same Indians. This was not only unwise, but also unconstitutional. Regardless, the Yazoo land sales committed the state of Georgia to preserving the integrity of the treaties it had made with the Creeks under the Confederation.[39]

These overlapping and mutually exclusive claims to sovereignty by Georgia, the Creeks, and the federal government were the main issue that fueled division and discontent during the negotiation of the Treaty of Colerain. In late May, the federal commissioners began to arrive at Colerain on the St. Marys River. Before negotiations opened, the first two commissioners present established regulations to limit military, Indian, and civilian interaction, in order that the conference would proceed smoothly and in accordance with the established protocols of Creek-American diplomacy. The regulations specified a campsite for the Indians, limited the carrying of weapons in the Indian camp, and restricted access to the camp to only those with the federal commissioners' permission. In short, by their orders of 26 May, Hawkins and Clymer created and cordoned off a federally controlled space wherein negotiations could proceed without corruption from local interests and actors.[40] The desired regularity was quickly threatened, however. On 30 May, the three commissioners from the state of Georgia, Hendricks, Jackson, and Simms, also arrived at Colerain, and disembarked from their schooner, the *Fair Play*. The Georgians were seeking further land cessions from the Creeks, and under the Constitution, any such cession had to proceed under the aegis of the federal government. The federal commissioners extended the Georgians an invitation to dine and encamp with them, but the Georgians demurred. They had brought a detachment of state militia with them, ostensibly in order to protect their supplies, and they were anxious to know what provisions could be made for them. The federal commissioners were "surprised" at the presence of state troops, since regulations sent from the War Department to the governor of Georgia apparently made it clear that "the [federal] troops at this place are in sufficient number to protect and give respectability to the negotiation." Hawkins, Pickens, and Clymer communicated this to the Georgians, but nonetheless ordered the ranking U.S. Army officer, Colonel Henry Gaither, to accommodate the party from Georgia.⁴¹ The federal commissioners' attempts at accommodation led to a disagreement that quickly gained intensity and threatened to spin out of control. The federal commissioners found themselves, for all intents and purposes, engaged in negotiation with the state of Georgia before they could even think about beginning their planned negotiation with the Creek Indians.

The Georgia commissioners refused to concede even the most minor point to the federal commissioners, lest it be interpreted as an abrogation of Georgia's sovereignty. James Hendricks dispatched a vitriolic letter to the federal commissioners the day after his arrival. The Georgians had not brought their small militia detachment to "give respectability to the negotiation," but to protect their property. Had they wanted to assert "respectability," their "State could have ordered four or five hundred men to attend the treaty," but this would have only complicated the treaty negotiations and induced "jealousies." But in light of these comments by the federal commissioners, the Georgians felt insulted by the subsequent offer to protect their goods with a federal guard. Hendricks further noted that President Washington had declared, both to the Senate and to the governor of Georgia, that "one half of the expense [of the treaty] shall be borne by the State of Georgia." The Georgians saw themselves as equal partners with the federal commissioners in the act of treaty making, but Hawkins, Clymer, and Pickens were not treating them with the proper respect. The federal commissioners' regulations of the treaty ground, which prohibited private citizens from visiting with the Creek Indians without express permission from the federal commissioners, were also insulting. The regulations, "stuck at the gates of the garrison," were "objectionable in many respects, and highly derogatory to the dignity of the State we represent." How could Benjamin Hawkins, Andrew Pickens, and George Clymer presume to tell Georgians where they could and could not go within the sovereign state of Georgia?: "We know of no power on earth, competent to hinder a citizen of Georgia, observing the laws of his country, from exercising the locomotive faculty, within the limits of the State, in the most liberal extent." Hendricks had practically thrown down the gauntlet: "We even consider ourselves to have been in a degree insulted, and consequently the State which we belong to." Clearly, the Georgians had more on their minds than food and shelter for twenty militiamen.⁴²

The federal commissioners responded by arguing that they had to deal with a larger set of interests than simply those of the state of Georgia and that, frankly, the Constitution and laws of the United States placed them in charge and that they would act accordingly. Hawkins, Clymer, and Pickens reminded the Georgia commissioners that "militia, when put into service, are subject to the articles of war," and as Colonel Gaither was the ranking officer and commander of a military post, any state militia had to obey his orders. To ignore the articles of war was a dangerous precedent. The federal commissioners then admitted to the Georgians that they saw their utilization of state militia as deliberately provocative. "You are aware of the jealousies of the Creeks in all things relating to your State," the commissioners wrote. "Alarms have gone forth that they were to encounter the Georgia militia at the intended treaty, and with some effect, too, in lessening the otherwise very numerous representation that might have been expected at it." The commissioners then noted that the regulations that they had promulgated to insulate the treaty ground from local pressures had given "satisfaction" and reassurance to the Creek chiefs already present. They also reminded the Georgians that their claim of having paid for half the treaty was somewhat disingenuous. Georgia was responsible for half of the costs of the Indians' support during the negotiations. This did not include support for the commissioners or the military, or any of the costs that would arise from the treaty itself. Given all this, the federal commissioners continued, "we cannot admit that the honor of the State has been in any wise derogated from, in our rule; but, if it must be so, in the eyes of the State, it is doubtless owing to the circumstances which it has itself produced." Hawkins, Clymer, and Pickens were blunt. Georgia's track record in the previous decade of relations with the Creeks was not encouraging—illegitimate treaties, low-intensity warfare, fraudulent land sales, and outright intimidation—and now the federal government had shown up to clean up the mess, for the sake of Georgia, for the Creeks, and for the United States of America as a whole. Here was the Federalist ethos in action—the federal government taking the interests of all into account, and putting local, particular, parochial interests in their place.[43]

In their exchanges over the next few days, the commissioners on both sides inched back from the rhetorical precipice onto which they had rushed headlong during their initial days together. Hendricks assured the federal commissioners that the violence perpetrated by white Georgians upon various Creek communities had not been done under the authority of the state. Hendricks confessed that he was at a loss over what to do; if he pulled the state militia from guarding the state stores, it would "make us censurable in the eyes of our country." Hendricks was as concerned about saving face—for the commissioners and for the state—as he was concerned about protecting state property. Perhaps the federal commissioners would consent "to a conference on the subjects of our disagreements"? The federal commissioners seized the olive branch, and they, too, backed away from the "warmth" of the earlier exchange. They assured the Georgians that there would be no talk of land cessions or sales without the Georgia commissioners being present. They claimed that when they laid the blame for the current situation at Georgia's feet—"the circumstances which it has itself produced"—they were really discussing only the militia dispute, nothing more. The federal commissioners then made the move to leave the federal garrison and meet the Georgia commissioners on their own ground. The dispute over the militia was dropped. Although the Georgia and federal Commissioners were able to defuse their dispute, the incident remains enormously revealing. Within hours of their coming into contact with one another, agents of the state of Georgia and the federal government were engaged in a vitriolic correspondence about Indian treaty protocols. But the issue was not simply about the presence of militiamen or access to the treaty ground—the key question was, "Who is in charge?" The Federalists believed that the Constitution gave one answer (the federal government), but Georgia could, and did, claim that they retained a role in the treaty-making process. Without subtlety, but to great effect, they made these concerns apparent to the federal commissioners.

On 16 June 1796, the formal negotiations between the Americans and the Creeks began. "[U]nder the flag of the United States," the "beloved men, chiefs and warriors of the Creek nation," the "beloved men chosen by the President of the United States," and the "beloved men of Georgia" sat in the center of the treaty ground, witnessing ceremonial dancing while the Creek leaders offered calumets to the Americans to smoke. The ceremonies unfolded and introductions were made. On the third day of the treaty conference, the Georgians prepared to address the whole. Before speaking, the Georgia commissioners showed their proposed talk to the federal commissioners. In their journal, the federal commissioners noted, "We had told the gentlemen, that one statement of theirs was inadmissible, as not being a fact.

They said, 'Georgia was not present at New York, when the treaty was made.'" This statement stunned the federal commissioners: "The contrary was manifest; they were always represented in the Senate, where there were a competent number for business, but, on the present occasion, their two senators were present, and voted against the ratification." This comment was stricken from the Georgians' talk, but the controversy had not ended. James Jackson addressed the Creeks for Georgia. He "dwelt with peculiar emphasis on the treaties of Augusta, Galphinton, and Shoulderbone, heretofore concluded between the Creeks and Georgia, the violation of these treaties, the claims arising out of them, and concluded with observing, that those claims, ... were still valid." The Georgians also presented the Creeks with a bill for $110,000 in lost property they wished restored. The Creek reaction to the Georgian talk was interesting. While they had voiced assent to most of the points offered by the federal commissioners, they fell silent as Jackson moved through his talk. The Creek leaders questioned the validity of the Treaty of Galphinton, and "[w]hen the commissioners exhibited the roll of claims against them, and the particulars were enumerated, they listened till the article hogs were numbered, when they all laughed." The conference then broke up momentarily. Creek chief Big Warrior approached the federal commissioners. With a bit of dry wit, he requested a roll of paper just a little longer and larger than the one the Georgians had presented, as he was sure he could fill it up with a greater number of articles of property that the Creeks had lost. Another unnamed Creek leader wondered aloud how the Georgians knew whether the hogs, which ranged freely in the forests, had been killed by bears or Indians. The Georgians were not coming off well; just as the federal commissioners saw the Georgians' claims as legally spurious, the Creek leadership saw their claims as practically ridiculous.[44]

Over the next several days, the federal commissioners outlined their requests and desires to the Creek leadership. Chief among these requests was the establishment of factories within the boundaries of the Creek nation, wherein the commerce between American citizens and the Creeks would now proceed, in accordance with the Indian Trade and Intercourse Act. This was agreed to. As the negotiations moved forward, the main sticking point of the negotiations between the federal commissioners and the Creeks was a disputed section of land on the Oconee River. The Georgians claimed it was theirs; the federal negotiators claimed that it had been ceded to the United States and Georgia by the terms of the 1790

Treaty of New York; and the Creek leadership maintained that the stretch of land in question had not been ceded at all. The Creeks claimed ignorance; their late chief Alexander McGillivray had been dishonest, they said, when describing the treaty's contents to the other leaders of the Creek nation. While no one would have praised the late McGillivray for his scruples, and the Creeks' claims of ignorance thus could have held some merit, the Georgian interest in the Oconee lands severely militated against the Creek leadership's claims. The federal commissioners agreed that they could agree to blame McGillivray for the Creeks' ignorance of the Treaty of New York, but there was a larger and more pressing reality. The "Georgians, who own this land, have paid taxes for it," and since the state of Georgia now depended on this income, some of which was likely devoted to supporting the state's and the federal government's trade and intercourse with the Creeks, the federal government could not consent to the Creeks retaining it. In exchange for a firm boundary between Georgia and the Creek nation and the establishment of a new federal trading house, the Creeks consented to the cession.[45]

Although the Treaty of Colerain brought peace to Creek-Georgian relations, won the Georgians clear title to a stretch of coveted land, and provided for the establishment of the new federally mandated trading factory, it starkly revealed a deep wound in the federal-state relationship. Hawkins, Clymer, and Pickens were astounded by the behavior of the Georgian commissioners and, by extension, the behavior of the state of Georgia itself. After the conference had concluded, the three federal commissioners dispatched letters to Secretary of War James McHenry and to Georgia governor Jared Irwin severely castigating the Georgia commissioners. The federal commissioners told McHenry that, in their considered opinion, none of the posts in the Indian country should be left in Georgian hands: "it is indispensably necessary, that the posts and garrisons should be out of the jurisdiction of the State, and solely under that of the United States." Tensions between the Creeks and the state of Georgia remained high.[46] In their letter to Governor Irwin, the commissioners were even more blunt. In response to a written reprimand from the Georgia commissioners deploring their maltreatment at the hands of the federal commissioners, Hawkins, Clymer, and Pickens were careful to note who was truly to blame: "Your commissioners, frequently speaking of our ruling and arbitrary conduct, forgot it is only applicable to themselves." The federal agents continued, "It may be necessary to observe, that they have altogether mistaken the nature of their authority, and have assumed a high diplomatic character." The Georgians simply did not know their place: "Such high self-created pretensions not being yielded to, on our part, is, no doubt, the real ground of the discontent apparent throughout the whole of their performance."[47]

While stinging even to modern ears, the language of the Federalist federal commissioners is deeply revealing. By dismissing the Georgian commissioners' asserted position of authority as a "self-created pretension," the federal commissioners (perhaps knowingly) used language that linked their actions with the suspect (in Federalists' minds) Democratic-Republican societies—societies President Washington himself had derisively and dismissively labeled as "self-created." The language the Federalists used indicated that they felt the Georgian commissioners had no standing, or, at the least, did not have the scope of authority they claimed. The epithet thus curtly dismissed Georgia's sovereignty, under which the Georgia commissioners claimed their authority to act. In one paragraph, the federal commissioners managed to insult both the sovereign state of Georgia and its appointed commissioners. Whether this was done intentionally or simply out of ignorance is unclear. It does with certainty speak to a profound level of misunderstanding between federal agents and state officials, and between the Federalists at the center and Republicans at the state-level periphery. The Federalists saw the actions of officials at the state level, especially those on the borders of the Indian country, as inimical to their larger plans of rationalizing American interaction with the wider world of the borderlands and Westphalian systems. Limiting state authority served the federal—and Federalist—interests. The Federalists easily, and almost unthinkingly, dismissed state officials. The states saw the situation in the opposite manner. The federal government existed to serve the interests of the several states. Pushy, over-refined, quasi-monarchical Federalist Indian agents were but the most obvious sign of a government that was proving increasingly hostile to the interests of the many—and many states. It was only natural for men in this position to now vote Republican and to assert their state's sovereignty boldly and proudly when they had the opportunity.[48]

In managing Indian diplomacy, Federalist policymakers could assert federal prerogatives and perhaps alienate one or, at most, two states at a time. A miscalculation or misunderstanding in the conduct of diplomacy with a European power had the potential to anger or alienate a much larger constituency. This was exactly what occurred in 1798, during the undeclared naval war, or Quasi-War, with France. Facing what some felt was an imminent war with the French Republic, the Federalist-dominated Fifth Congress passed, and President John Adams signed into law, some of the most constitutionally suspect legislation in American history: the Alien Friends Act, the Alien Enemies Act, and the Sedition Act. In the midst of a diplomatic crisis, the federal government undertook to curtail immigration, to place suspect immigrants under surveillance, and to limit the operation of the free press. For the Republicans, it was a step too far. Diplomatic crises, such as the Genêt mission or the Jay Treaty, had always seemed to provide the perfect rationale (or excuse) for consolidating power over diplomacy in the executive branch and, as a result, solidifying sovereign powers once in the hands of states in the hands of the federal government. The Alien and Sedition Acts emerged in the public mind as such blatant attempts to transform the constitutional dynamics of the American union that they demanded a response.[49] The challenge Federalist elites had experienced in microcosm at Colerain in 1796 was replicated on the national level between 1798 and 1800. The Republican response was much more cogent and resourceful than that offered on the Georgia borderlands by a few disgruntled Indian commissioners. The irony that would emerge from the subsequent Jefferson presidency, however, was that as the challenges the United States confronted on both the European and American frontiers did not disappear, and whether through the conclusion of the Georgia Compact with its promise of Indian dispossession or the purchase of Louisiana in contravention of Jefferson's own vision of what was constitutional, the Jeffersonian Republicans found themselves utilizing the Federalist-crafted diplomatic machinery rather than dismantling it.

6

Enlarging "Our Association"

The Triumph of the Diplomacy of Conquest

> But who can limit the extent to which the federative principle may operate effectively? The larger our association, the less it will be shaken by local passions; and in any view, is it not better that the opposite bank of the Mississippi should be settled by our own brethren and children, than by strangers of another family? With which shall we be most likely to live in harmony and friendly intercourse?
>
> —THOMAS JEFFERSON, second inaugural address, 1805

On 3 December 1804, Senator William Plumer prepared to dine with the president of the United States. That Plumer, a Federalist from New Hampshire, should receive an invitation from Republican President Thomas Jefferson was a little remarkable; Plumer noted in his journal that Jefferson had recently ceased to invite many of his more vociferous opponents to dinner. Like many opposition politicians through the years, Plumer surveyed the acts of his rival with a most critical eye. He noticed that Jefferson's invitation seemed peculiar: "It is Th: Jefferson not the President of the United States that invites." Plumer wryly noted, "yet were he not the President I presume I should not be invited." Virginia senator William Branch Giles had explained to Plumer that Jefferson adopted this form ("the invitation of a private gentleman") in order to avoid the requirements of a formal state dinner in which he would be compelled "to invite all the members of both Houses of Congress." Giles could not concede, and perhaps did not know, that throughout his presidency, Jefferson preferred to keep his dinners in Washington small, in order that he could converse with—and listen to—everyone at his table. Such dinners were an important venue in which Jefferson gathered political intelligence. Conversely, dinner at the President's House was a place in which Jefferson could send political messages to his allies and opponents, a reality to which William Plumer's record of his December 1804 dinner with Jefferson testifies.[1]

Plumer's journal reveals a President Jefferson who was a fastidious host. Jefferson, true to form, had invited only Federalists (two senators including Plumer and eight representatives), as well as "his two sons in law" to this particular dinner. According to Plumer, "He was well dressed—A new suit of black—silk hose—shoes—clean linen, & his hair highly powdered." Jefferson "performed the honors of the table with great facility," although he was not as talkative on this day as he had been at earlier dinners; Plumer felt he was a little "low spirited." Whatever his mood might have been, Jefferson was generous with his fare. "His dinner was elegant & rich—his wines were very good—there were eight different kinds of which there were rich Hungary, & still richer *Tokay*." Plumer also noted that Jefferson's "table furnished a great variety of pies, fruits & nuts." Beyond fine food and wine, two items that contained political messages also sat atop the president's table. The first was a remnant of the Mammoth Cheese, an enormous wheel of cheese that has been produced by New England dairy farmers and sent to Jefferson on the occasion of his first inauguration in March 1801. Plumer, again rather dryly, wrote that the nearly four-year-old cheese was "very far from being good." One can surmise that the Mammoth Cheese was brought out less for sustenance and more for political effect: Jefferson's reelection by the Electoral College was a pending formality, and New England, the last bastion of Federalism, was becoming more Republican each day. The other, perhaps more provocative, political prop Jefferson deployed on his dinner table were "two bottles of water brought from the river Mississippi." The water from the Mississippi River, placed alongside the European wines, evoked the Jefferson administration's great diplomatic triumph of the previous year, the acquisition of the vast Louisiana Territory. The entire Mississippi-Missouri river system, from its mouth near New Orleans to its source in modern-day Montana (then being searched for by Meriwether Lewis and William Clark), was now American territory. This was an outcome that William Plumer and his fellow Federalist dinner guests had worked to avoid, as they had struggled in vain to defeat the ratification of the Louisiana treaties in

October 1803. President Jefferson could not help but remind his political opponents of their string of failures during the previous year.[2]

Jefferson's placement of bottles of Mississippi River water on his dinner table next to bottles of European wine was, interestingly, more evocative than he likely realized. While, like the Mammoth Cheese, the Mississippi water would have been unpleasing to the palette, Jefferson's placement of the water bottles reminded his guests that the potential for consumption of this water was now manifest (given that the Mississippi was now, in theory at least, a wholly American river). The two great pillars of the Republican political program that Jefferson rode to the presidency and that sustained him in office, namely democratic politics and westward expansion, were symbolized, respectively, by the Mammoth Cheese and the Mississippi River water. That Jefferson's political program could be symbolized, even unconsciously, by foodstuffs meant to be consumed is suggestive. Acts of consumption—real or imagined, completed or foresworn—had hung over American politics since the era of the American Revolution and continued to do so into the early nineteenth century. The political economy that the United States' Revolutionary diplomats had sold to the European powers was premised on networks of commerce driven by reciprocal acts of production and consumption in America and Europe.[3] Affirming many aspects of the Revolutionary vision, the Jeffersonian political economy, which privileged Americans' role as agricultural producers, had triumphed at the polls in 1800 and supplanted the Hamiltonian political economy, which had privileged Americans' role as consumers of British manufactured goods and other European luxuries.[4] Yet, as Jefferson's dinner table testified, the realities of American life were far more complex. American producers were also consumers; production and consumption were interrelated rather than dichotomous. Jeffersonian political economy, and the diplomacy designed to facilitate it, acknowledged this.[5]

At the same time, the scale and scope of consumption in America underwent a process of expansion during Jefferson's years in power (as well as those of Jefferson's protégé and successor, James Madison). The consumption of European manufactures was a phenomenon not limited to the American seaports where these goods were off-loaded—increasingly from American-owned and manned ships—but extended away from the seaboard to the hinterlands of European settlement, and then into the communities of the American Indian nations beyond. In the years following

Jefferson's inauguration as president, consumption would move to the foreground of the negotiations between the United States and the American Indian peoples. Manufactured goods such as plows and spinning wheels would aid and abet the project of "civilization," as federal officers encouraged Indians to conform their lifeways to European norms. Less obviously, but more insidiously, the very scope of consumption itself was undergoing an expansion. The presence of a small piece of the Mississippi River on President Jefferson's dinner table testified to the prospect that the North American interior itself could be consumed—although it was not the water of the West, but its land that American policy would transform into a commodity during the first decades of the nineteenth century. The political negotiations of the United States would be devoted, more and more, to the facilitation of consumption—of American produce by Europeans, of European goods by American Indians, and of both European goods and of American Indian land by citizens of the United States. The assumption and recognition of the full sovereign power of the United States in the Westphalian states system, confirmed in the postwar settlements after 1815, ultimately set all aspects of this complex equation in balance with one another.

The story of this last chapter is the story of how the final set of negotiations of the Revolutionary Era set into place the calculus of sovereign power that would underlie the transition to modernity for the United States and its neighbors. As the Louisiana Purchase was being ratified by the United States of America and the Consulate of France, war was erupting in Europe. Between the collapse of the Peace of Amiens in 1803 and the final end of the Napoleonic adventure at Waterloo in 1815, war would engulf the European and Atlantic world. The Napoleonic Wars would find France and its satellites on one side and Great Britain and a rotating set of continental allies on the other. Attempting to remain neutral, the United States attempted to engage in commerce with each of Europe's great powers, to the chagrin of both. And while Britain and France attempted to shut down America's trade with the other, Americans also worried about the potential for any belligerent European power to influence the Indian nations on the United States' borderlands or engage in other courses of action that might alter the geopolitical balances in North America. American diplomats in Europe sought to defend the United States' rights as a neutral to trade with all the ports of Europe; American diplomats on the western borderlands sought to acquire title to strategically significant tracts of land (such as those along the main waterways), while keeping the several and various Indian nations allied with the United States. Both sets of diplomacy, in great part, failed. The United States declared war on Great Britain in June 1812 and at the same time it found itself at war with two Indian groups—the Creek "Red Sticks" in the South and the pan-Indian alliance of the Shawnee Prophet and his brother Tecumseh in the North. Although the United States failed in its main objective in the War of 1812 (the seizure of Canada), Great Britain was fought to a draw, Tecumseh killed, and both the Prophet's movement and that of the Red Sticks were defeated. With the Treaty of Ghent (1814–15), Great Britain and the United States concluded peace, and set the stage for the resolution of long-standing disagreements over commerce as well as the eventual demilitarization of the Canadian border. The United States was a full and unconditional member of the Westphalian states system. At the same time, Britain foreswore any contact with Indian peoples inside the United States' borders. Four years later, the Transcontinental Treaty and the Florida Cession effected a similar outcome with Spain (the Spanish Empire in the Americas entering into its twilight phase at this point). With the last European powers in the Americas turning their back on the Native peoples inside the United States, the American Indians' participation in the last remnants of the eighteenth-century borderlands diplomatic regime was now at an end. Although treaty making between the federal government and the Indian nations persisted, the rise and triumph of Andrew Jackson and his eponymous brand of American democracy confirmed this diplomacy to be something less than it once was.

THE PERILS OF CONSUMPTION
Jeffersonian Political Economy and Diplomacy

Four months after Thomas Jefferson entertained William Plumer, he made a one-mile journey from the President's House to the Capitol, where, inside the Senate chamber, he took the presidential oath of office for a second time and delivered his second inaugural address. While only a minority of the members of Congress actually attended Jefferson's 4 March 1805 inaugural, all would have been able to read the address, as it was printed before it was given in the *National Intelligencer*, and soon reprinted throughout the United States.[6] The nation that Jefferson described in his speech was by all accounts doing well, yet anxieties lurked on all horizons. Jefferson pledged his administration to "cultivate the friendship of all nations" in the course of "the transaction of your foreign affairs." He put forward that the United States favored no particular nation over another, and "cherished mutual interest and intercourse on fair and equal terms." In other words, the United States' diplomacy had been directed toward securing relationships with other sovereign nations that promoted free and fair trade and thus rooted trade regulations in principles of reciprocity.[7]

Jefferson's second inaugural address spent relatively little time and few words discussing diplomacy with Europe, however. The middle section of the address dwelt on the Louisiana Purchase (ratified seventeen months before) and the relationship between the United States government and the American Indian peoples. The second inaugural address made it clear that westward expansion and settlement on Indian lands would be an active part of American policy. Gone was any pessimism about the potential for a future secession of the western states from the Union. "I know that the acquisition of Louisiana has been disapproved by some, from a candid apprehension that the enlargement of our territory would endanger its union," he said. (Jefferson left unsaid that he was one of those who had contemplated such dangers in the summer of 1803.) Jefferson answered all critics without equivocation: "But who can limit the extent to which the federative principle may operate effectively?" Provided that these lands were settled by those capable of forming self-governing state-republics, the union that was the United States could extend westward and encompass all of the Louisiana Territory or even beyond it—theoretically there were no limits. Where once a large union was seen as a danger, it was now a blessing. Endorsing the notion put forward in 1787 by Madison in Number 10 of the *Federalist*, Jefferson then said, "The larger our association, the less it will be shaken by local passions." And the security wrought by settling Louisiana would come not only from the strengthening of the American federal republic, but from ensuring that an enemy nation would not take up residence on the union's western flank. Jefferson asked rhetorically: "[I]s it not better that the opposite bank of the Mississippi should be settled by our own brethren and children, than by strangers of another family? With which shall we be most likely to live in harmony and friendly intercourse?" Four years before, during his First Inaugural, Jefferson had described the United States as "possessing a chosen country, with room enough for our descendants to the thousandth and thousandth generation." Now that "chosen country" included the west bank of the Mississippi as well.[8]

Of course, the territory that the future sons and daughters of America were to inhabit in the West was not unoccupied; Thomas Jefferson knew and understood this. The future expansion of American union would come at the expense of the preexisting American Indian polities. This was, in the mind of the president, sad but unavoidable. "The aboriginal inhabitants of these countries I have regarded with the commiseration their history inspires," Jefferson said. American Indians were "Endowed with the faculties and rights of men" and "an ardent love of liberty and independence" but "had been overwhelmed by the current" of "the stream of overflowing population from other regions directed to these shores," and the ability of the American Indian population to continue to subsist was now in serious doubt. "Humanity enjoins us to teach them agriculture and the domestic arts," Jefferson pleaded, "to encourage them to that industry which alone can enable them to maintain their place in existence, and prepare them in time for that state of society, which to bodily comforts adds the improvement of the mind and morals." The "civilization" project put forward a decade and a half before by Secretary of War Henry Knox remained in effect; if anything, it would be accelerated. "We have therefore liberally furnished them with the implements of husbandry and household use; we have placed among them instructors in the arts of the first necessity; and they are covered with the aegis of the law against aggressors from among ourselves." The nexus of consumption reveals itself here as well. Through the adoption and use of European manufactured goods, such as plows, pots, and spinning wheels, the American Indian would be transformed into a consumer and a producer. The acquisition of Louisiana had thus changed the scale, but not the scope, of the American diplomatic project vis-à-vis the American Indian nations that Jefferson had articulated in January 1803 during the Mississippi Crisis (the diplomatic crisis touched off by the brief closure of the Mississippi River). The United States was committed to the three-part project of maintaining and strengthening its alliances with neighboring Indian polities, using commerce to promote "civilization," and acquiring Indian land through negotiated, legal transactions. But whereas there had been limits on the expansion of the United States' settler communities before the Louisiana Purchase, either by policy (the Federalists' desire for slow, measured expansion) or by geography (the Mississippi boundary imposed limits on all but the most imperial imaginations before 1803), the Indians now faced an American government less inclined to play the role of honest broker, and more inclined to play the role of real estate broker.[9]

Facilitating American commerce and the consumption of European goods and American Indian lands remained the modus vivendi of the diplomacy of the Jefferson administration following the Louisiana Purchase. Although the transformation of the Mississippi into an American river and New Orleans into an American entrepôt secured western farmers' access to Atlantic markets, this did not mean that American producers and consumers were going to be less affected by political changes in Europe. If anything, the Louisiana Purchase, by setting American engagement with transatlantic commerce on a firmer and more dependable footing, served to further enmesh the fates of American consumers, producers, and carriers with their European counterparts. The pressure on the Jefferson administration to keep commerce flowing freely between Europe, North America, and the Caribbean would be more keenly felt than ever.[10]

If, when he gave his second inaugural address, President Jefferson was aware that his first term as president had been exceptional, in that it was marked by relative quiescence in the Westphalian states system, his text did not betray it. And yet, as Jefferson spoke, the special circumstances that allowed the United States to prosper for four years were coming to an end. As we have already seen, the 1790s were defined by the war pitting the successive governments of revolutionary France against Great Britain and the continental powers of the Old Regime. With the 1799 coup d'état of the Eighteenth Brumaire and the emergence of First Consul Napoleon Bonaparte as the head of state, France began to slowly deescalate the still-ongoing French Revolutionary Wars. Bonaparte ended the undeclared war with the United States (Treaty of Mortefontaine, 1800); then Austria sued for peace (Treaty of Lunéville, 1801); and finally France made peace with Great Britain (Treaty of Amiens, 1802). When Bonaparte's attempt to establish an American empire foundered with Charles Leclerc's failure to defeat the revolution against French rule in Saint-Domingue (later Haiti), he offered Louisiana to the Americans and stepped up aggressive actions in Europe that led to the collapse of the peace. By the time of the ratification of the Louisiana Treaties in November 1803, Great Britain and France were once again at war.[11]

While the first few years of the nineteenth century were, to be sure, not without international tension, they were relatively quiet when compared with what was to come. And they were prosperous years for the United States. With both the Jay Treaty and the Treaty of Mortefontaine in place, the producers, consumers, and carriers of the United States had most-favored-nation access to both British and French markets. A liberal ruling by the British Admiralty Court in 1800, known as the *Polly* decision (after the name of the ship involved), allowed the American carrying trade to flourish. Under the *Polly* decision, the practice of the so-called "broken voyage" was legitimated. American ship captains could carry products from one nation's ports to another nation's, provided they made a stop in the United States and paid American import duties. With the payment of the duty, their cargoes now became American exports and as such were considered American and thus neutral. The so-called "reexport" trade flourished under the *Polly* precedent—between 1802 and 1805, the average annual value of American reexports grew from $32 million to over $60 million. American carriers were using this principle primarily to carry produce between the Caribbean islands of the British, French, Spanish, and Dutch empires and ports all over the European continent. With much of Europe's merchant marine involved in, or limited by, the wars between the Great Powers, the neutral American carrying trade rushed in to fill the gaps. The *Polly* decision was so important in allowing this to happen because it gave American carriers engaging in trade with belligerents immunity from seizure by the Royal Navy through a loophole in the British government's long-standing interpretation of the law of the nations. The British government's "Rule of 1756"—promulgated during the Seven Years' War—held that commerce that was illegal during peacetime could not be made legal during wartime. Although the United States' commercial treaties with the European powers had given Americans more open access to continental markets, colonial markets remained more restricted due to the persistence of mercantilism—thus, the Americans did benefit from opportunities caused by the European wars. At the same time, American officials believed neutral trade with belligerent powers to be legal and immune from seizure under the principle that "free ships made free goods." American diplomats simply read the law of nations differently than did British Admiralty courts, believing that belligerent or neutral status attached to the ship, not the cargo. The emergence of the reexport trade under the *Polly* precedent had made the argument mostly academic. This changed in 1805, when the Admiralty closed the reexport trade with the *Essex* case.[12]

The *Essex* decision was but the first step in a series of choices that were made by the governments of Britain and France that put the United States in a disadvantageous position commercially, and that ultimately drew the United States into war seven years later. The Peace of Amiens collapsed in late 1803, and the European powers embarked upon a course of war that would be more total than anything seen in the previous century. There would be little place for the vision of neutrality put forward by the leaders of the United States. With the resignation of Henry Addington in May 1804, William Pitt the Younger was elected head of the British ministry. Just as he had done during the French Revolutionary Wars of the previous decade, Pitt made Britain the linchpin of the coalition against France. A week after Pitt took charge of the British government, First Consul Bonaparte proclaimed the French Empire and himself, Emperor Napoleon. Imperial France would now make war to spread the blessings of the French Revolution across Europe. Initially, the allies (known as the Third Coalition) fared well against Napoleon, with the resounding defeat of French and Spanish naval forces at Trafalgar in October 1805 (which gave the Royal Navy mastery of the Atlantic and Mediterranean). However, with Napoleon's defeat of Austria (Austerliz, December 1805), Prussia (Jena and Auerstadt, October 1806), and Russia (Friedland, September 1807), Great Britain remained the only European power that had not been conquered or neutralized by the Grande Armée. Britain was the only nation remaining in active, armed resistance to Emperor Napoleon's attempt at the complete domination of the European continent and states system (although Austria would briefly rejoin the fight in 1809). Both Britain and France saw the conflict as a fight for survival, and following this logic, implicitly or explicitly cast aside most of the laws of nations, while attempting to force the other into submission. Both powers sought to deny each other the materiel required for making war; each sought to blockade or at least disrupt the other's seaborne commerce.[13]

Although the United States was formally neutral and attempted to maintain trade with both powers, neither Great Britain nor France saw American trade with its enemy as benign. In Britain, to the extent that the British political nation thought about commerce with the Americans, the attitude of suspicion and contempt that had been part of the program of Lord Sheffield and the neomercantilists in the 1780s remained strong. While Sheffield himself continued to publish pamphlets calling for restrictions against American commerce, most influential was an 1805 pamphlet by the lawyer James Stephen called *War in Disguise; Or, the Fraud of the Neutral Flags*. Stephen argued that the Addington ministry's lenient policy toward neutral commerce, embodied by the *Polly* decision, was a mistake. Neutral commerce served only to benefit Napoleon and his puppets; there was no benefit to Britain. Since the British advantage lay with seapower, Stephen believed, Britain needed to return to strict enforcement of the Rule of 1756 and use the Royal Navy to aggressively police the oceans and actively crush any illegal neutral commerce. Stephen's pamphlet had been unofficially approved by Pitt, and after its publication, he was rewarded with a seat in the House of Commons.[14] Conversely, the United States had only a few friends in Parliament and the British public sphere. By the autumn of 1807, the ministry and the Commons were led by Spencer Perceval, a strong adherent of the neomercantilist line that Stephen had vociferously put forward. Perceval would head the British government until his assassination in May 1812.[15]

The drift at the head of the British government was counterpoised by Napoleon's organization, domination, and triumph on the continent. Four different men led the British government during the months between Austerlitz and Friedland, during which time all of Britain's major continental allies had been defeated by Napoleon's armies. And while Great Britain remained the only major power opposing France militarily, Emperor Napoleon had also declared economic warfare against the British Empire. On 21 November 1806, Napoleon issued the Berlin Decree, which forbade the importation of British goods into France, any of the empire's satellite kingdoms, or any nation allied with France—effectively, the entire European continent was now officially closed to British imports. The "Continental System" had been born. The Berlin Decree also interdicted the postal service from Britain to the continent, and provided for the immediate imprisonment of British subjects found on French soil. Britain's response to these measures was equally totalizing. The ministry, over which Perceval was consolidating control, issued a series of Orders in Council during 1807. In January, the British government forbade trade between one French or French-occupied port and another, and subsequent orders in November closed the European continent to imports altogether, including those of neutral nations. Napoleon's retaliatory Milan Decrees of November and December 1807 closed European ports to neutral shipping as well. While both belligerents had imposed commercial restrictions on one another going back to the French Revolutionary Wars, the measures enacted in 1806 and 1807 were of an entirely different order. Both parties were engaged in total economic warfare; each attempted to eliminate the commerce of the other. The neutral nations that remained, including the United States, were caught in the middle.[16]

By the time word of the November Orders in Council and the Milan Decrees reached the United States, Americans were already aware that a new regime was descending over the Westphalian states system, one that would grant them few advantages. As the Jay Treaty was expiring in 1806, American ministers James Monroe and William Pinkney negotiated with William Eden, 1st Baron of Auckland, for a new commercial treaty between Britain and America. Although negotiating under the aegis of the Fox ministry, Auckland remained committed to the neomercantilist principles he had adopted in 1779 in the wake of the failure of the Carlisle Commission. The treaty that was finally agreed to (the so-called Monroe-Pinkney Treaty) renewed most-favored-nation status for American trade with Britain itself and returned the reexport trade to the rules of the *Polly* precedent, but this still theoretically limited America trade as the legality of the Rule of 1756 was not challenged. Britain gave no concessions on the issue of impressment (the British practice of forcibly removing seamen it identified as British subjects from American ships) or on the question of compensation for previous seizures of American shipping. After consultation with Madison, Jefferson ultimately decided not to send the treaty to the Senate for ratification. Shortly after the president made this decision, the infamous *Chesapeake–Leopard* incident occurred.[17]

On 22 June 1807 off Norfolk, Virginia, the HMS *Leopard*, searching for Royal Navy deserters, fired at the American naval frigate USS *Chesapeake*. The *Leopard* then sent a boarding party onto the American ship, and forcibly removed four men who were identified as deserters from the Royal Navy. American public opinion was outraged at the obvious violation of American sovereignty, and Jefferson contemplated declaring war on Britain throughout the remainder of the summer of 1807. With the American merchant fleet at sea during the summer, Jefferson held off on calling a special session of Congress and asking for a declaration of war, and when Congress finally convened for its winter session, the news of the Milan Decrees and the Orders in Council reached the United States. The situation that awaited American ships approaching the European continent would be a dire one indeed. Not wanting to risk the entire American carrying trade, Jefferson put thoughts of a war declaration aside and asked Congress to approve a complete closure of American foreign commerce. Congress quickly obliged with legislation, and on 22 December 1807 Jefferson signed the Embargo Act into law. It was now illegal for any American ship to sail to any foreign port. Although the embargo was initially seen as a temporary measure to protect American shipping, it dragged on deep into 1808, as neither Britain nor France showed any signs of changing their policies toward neutral shipping.[18]

Almost a year after agreeing to its passage, Congress took time to assess the impact of the embargo and the position of the United States in the larger Atlantic world. A stark assessment of the American situation was offered to the House of Representatives by Representative George Washington Campbell of Tennessee. Offering a report of a special committee chosen to respond to President Jefferson's annual message, Campbell began with alarm, stating that "the United States are, for the first time since the treaty which terminated the Revolutionary War, placed in a situation equally difficult, critical, and dangerous." The United States were at risk because the Westphalian states system had descended into what amounted to anarchy.

> Those principles, recognised by the civilized world under the name of law of nations, which heretofore controlled belligerent Powers, regulated the duties of neutrals and protected their rights, are now avowedly disregarded or forgotten by Great Britain and France. Each of those two nations captures and condemns all American vessels trading with her enemies or her enemy's allies; and every European Power having become a party in the contest, the whole of our commerce with Europe and European colonies, becomes liable to capture by one or the other. If there be any nominal exception, it is made on a condition of tribute, which only adds insult to injury.[19]

Campbell's report went on to recapitulate the history of the restrictions and counter-restrictions on neutral commerce issued by both Great Britain and France, and the depredations committed against the shipping of the United States as a result, while asserting that all of this amounted to manifest violations of the law of nations. "The Berlin Decree as expounded and executed subsequent to the 18th of September, 1807, and the British Orders in Council of the 11th November ensuing, are therefore," Campbell asserted, "as they respect the United States, contemporaneous aggressions of the belligerent Powers, equally unprovoked and equally indefensible on the presumed ground of acquiescence." Yet, it remained an open question what course of action was open to the United States to counter this aggression. "In that state of things, what course ought the United States to pursue?" Campbell asked. "Your committee can perceive no other alternative, but abject and degraded submission; war with both nations; or a continuance and enforcement of the present suspension of commerce." With no good alternatives at hand, the embargo would continue into 1809, lasting for the remainder of Thomas Jefferson's term as president, and continuing into the beginning of that of his successor, James Madison.[20]

The turnabout of the situation of the United States in the four years between Jefferson's 1805 inauguration and Madison's in March 1809 could not have been more stark. The negotiations with France that had ended the Quasi-War in 1800 and then made the Mississippi Valley American territory in 1803, in concert with the preexisting commercial treaty with Great Britain, had integrated the United States within European-centered commercial networks to a greater degree than had been the case under the Federalists in the 1790s. American commerce with Europe and its imperial peripheries was increasing over the course of Jefferson's first term, and American economic growth and prosperity was a product of Americans' triple role as producers, consumers, and carriers in the transatlantic marketplace. Yet this position was ultimately a perilous one, and Americans could only stand aside and reflect on their powerlessness. Although Americans like Representative George W. Campbell did realistically assess their plight, they also could not help but see French and British policies as insulting acts of aggression. And the desire for action to overturn the perceived injustices could only remain suppressed for so long.

Securing the "Western Boundary"
The Transformation of Borderlands Diplomacy

If his Nashville neighbors knew nothing else about him, they knew that local attorney Andrew Jackson was a man of action. As adept with the dueling pistol and the clenched fist as he was with the legal brief, by early

1809 Jackson had amassed a record of public service—serving as a United States senator and a justice of the Tennessee Supreme Court—as well as record of public violence: he had participated in many duels, killing at least one man, and had legally contested several charges of assault and battery. So, when Jackson rose to address a meeting of Nashville citizens on 16 January 1809, he commanded a measure of respect from all quarters and classes of the population. The subject that compelled Jackson's public address was the same subject that had vexed his fellow Tennessean George W. Campbell months before, namely "the tyrannic decrees of the French government and British orders in council, which at once prostrates the rights and sovereignty of our common country." Jackson reminded his listeners that they ("the people of this portion of the union") were "burning with indignation and resentment" against French and British policies as much as the people of the eastern, maritime states. The citizens' meeting and Jackson's address, printed in the *Carthage Gazette* newspaper, were public testimony of the desire to embrace the shared sacrifice called for by the embargo —sentiments quite commonly expressed by public figures as the embargo entered its second year, and grumblings against it and evasions of it became more common. That the people of Jackson's Nashville were feeling the effects of the embargo and listening to the calls for shared sacrifice for the good of the union is testimony to how universal the reach of transatlantic markets (and European political conflicts) had become in the North American interior. There was no escape from the troubles of the European-centered states system.[21]

In the background of the debates over how the United States should respond to the war between Britain and France was what Jackson had labeled "the peculiar situation in which this part of the union is placed," or, in other words, the reality that the Mississippi Valley and the American West remained a contested space. While the relatively few sons of New England and the Mid-Atlantic states who went to sea feared impressments in the Royal Navy, the vast majority of the sons of Tennessee feared a call to arms to defend their communities from invading European armies or their American Indian proxies. When the state of Tennessee's new governor, Willie Blount, took office in late 1809, he observed that his state's environs remained a seat of potential conflict and a hothouse of anxieties. Writing to Jackson just a few months after he took office, Blount noted the precarious situation posed by Tennessee's western frontier, the Mississippi River. The "time seems fast approaching when it will be indispensably necessary for the general government to have Nations of friends settled on that their frontier." Blount was primarily concerned with the ongoing war between Britain and France. "I mean by it," he continued, "that the conduct of European nations is such, that neutral rights have long been disregarded, and if the United States should in support of their rights have to contend with those nations, it would be sound policy in us to gain strength in that quarter of our territory, for it would not be unreasonable to suppose that a part of foreign policy would be to get possession of that part of the territory of the United States." Even in the middle of the North American continent, the potential repercussions of a war on the eastern side of the Atlantic could be imagined everywhere.[22]

The fears of the governor of Tennessee were multifold. While Blount's evocation of a potential French or British seizure of all or part of the Mississippi Valley seems fantastical in retrospect, it is important to remember that Louisiana had changed hands twice in the previous decade, and a permanent American hold on the trans-Mississippi was by no means assured. No matter where it might end, the conflict between Britain and France, and its effects on the United States, were all very real. As Blount's letter recounted, for over a year American ships, cargoes, and mariners were either being seized or being threatened with seizure by both belligerents. President Jefferson had attempted to insulate Americans from the depredations of both parties involved in the Napoleonic Wars by closing off the United States to all foreign commerce. But the embargo had been a failure —it was an economic disaster for the United States, and it failed to win concessions from either Britain or France. By the time Blount put pen to paper in December 1809, Jefferson's successor to the presidency, James Madison, had abandoned the embargo in favor of more limited restrictions on American trade with the belligerent powers. But the United States still suffered, and as the war between the two superpowers of the early nineteenth century continued, Willie Blount was only one of thousands of Americans who worried that their country might be drawn deeper into it.[23]

Of course, threats to Americans' security did not need to come directly from Europe. As Blount continued his letter to Jackson, he did not look overseas, but simply to the far banks of the Tennessee River to find a threat to his state's interests—the continued presence within its borders of the Cherokee and the Chickasaw Indian nations. In order to preserve peace and further prosperity, Tennessee had followed the Indian policy of the federal government since it was formulated by Secretary of War Henry Knox during the first year of the George Washington administration: the United States would respect the sovereignty of the Indian nations while they sought to acquire title to as much Indian land as they could. The only instrument for acquiring such land was a federally negotiated and constitutionally ratified treaty between the United States and a particular Indian nation. "Tennessee in aid of the policy of the United States towards Indians has as yet acquiesced in considering them as tenants at will," was how Blount described the practice. But he made it clear that he felt that "acquiescing" in this policy was always Tennessee's choice. "We really do own the lands claimed by those nations within our limits, the uncontrouled jurisdiction over it we must sooner or later have and exercise, to exchange with them is an act of liberality on our part." While Blount approved of the existing "liberal policy" of the United States toward the "nations of Indians" and wished "that it may preserve the friendship and secure the attachment of those nations to the United States for ever," his liberality had his limits. "For our benefit and accommodation as a State, I wish them [the Indians] to be led away from us," he stated. Thus Blount proposed "an exchange of territory" in which the Chickasaw and Cherokee would cede their lands within Tennessee for "vacant lands on the west of the Mississippi."[24]

Blount was certainly not the first American political leader to propose a program of voluntary Indian removal—Jefferson himself talked of such a program throughout his presidency—but what is interesting is how he adapted the idea of Indian removal to serve the foreign policy conundrum raised by the Napoleonic Wars. Hoping that the "general government" would see to having "Nations of friends" settled on the western bank of the Mississippi meant, at this particular moment, not communities of Anglo-Americans (as Jefferson had postulated in his second inaugural address), but nations of American Indians. The negotiated removal of the Cherokee and Chickasaw from inside Tennessee to the vast territory of Louisiana would help secure the Mississippi Valley for the interests of the United States. Such a policy would, of course, also open up vast stretches of land within Tennessee for sale and development—something quite dear to local Tennesseans like Blount and Jackson. But the Indians would benefit, too. Removal, at least in Blount's thinking, would be the best thing for the Cherokee and Chickasaw.[25]

[I]t would be promotive of their interests as Nations to settle over the mississippi—game is very abundant, the climate friendly to their constitutions, and much of the country is inhabited by people (Indians) whose manners and customs are more assimilated to their's than those of the people where they now live—at present they are surrounded by States thickly populated by people who have different interests[.]

Finally, Blount hoped that the resettlement of the Cherokee and Chickasaw west of the Mississippi would be an engine that would assist in the trans-Mississippi region's eventual incorporation into the United States. The Cherokee and Chickasaw, "their friendship for the United States being firm (bottomed on their interest) they could assist in protecting the citizens of the general government over them," while at the same time "by their intercourse with the neighbouring Indians could by precept and example civilize them faster and make favorable impressions on them of the friendship of the United States towards Indians in general." That displaced Indian nations might not be the most enthusiastic advocates for American benevolence did not seem to enter his mind. Nonetheless, like so many policymakers throughout history who have tried to see an opportunity in every crisis, Willie Blount's proposals promised to alleviate the risks to the United States' hold on the Mississippi Valley posed by the ongoing diplomatic crisis with Britain and France, while at same time securing Tennessee's title to the lands within its borders and furthering the Knoxian-Jeffersonian project of Indian "civilization."[26]

Willie Blount's letter to Andrew Jackson encapsulates how, even after Thomas Jefferson's two terms as president of the United States, the American union remained intermeshed in the larger European-centered states system. Even if they wanted to, Americans could not disentangle themselves from Europe. American agricultural producers depended on access to European markets (both in continental Europe and in the plantation colonies of the Caribbean basin) to sell their surpluses and earn a profit, while American consumers craved the manufactured goods being produced by European (read British) industry. This was why Tennesseans like Blount and Jackson, living hundreds of miles from the Atlantic Ocean, were so incensed about British and French depredations against American merchant vessels. The multinational (and multiracial) character of Mississippi Valley settlements like St. Louis and New Orleans testified to the fleeting nature of imperial control in the region as well as the reality that the American Indian peoples of the region remained free agents in the great game of interimperial rivalry. While we know now, with hindsight, that the Louisiana Purchase of 1803 marked a turning point in the geopolitical history of North America, men like Willie Blount, Andrew Jackson, and Thomas Jefferson still saw an American world with a most uncertain future. Looking west, they did not see an empty canvas on which America's manifest destiny would unfold, but a populated and contested ground.[27]

Blount's imagining of the removal of eastern American Indian populations to the western side of the Mississippi was only a more extreme version of a policy of dispossession and land acquisition that had been under way for most of the Jefferson administration. In 1802, with the conclusion of the Georgia Compact, the Jefferson administration had committed the federal government to, at some point in the future, extinguishing all the Indian title within the boundaries of the state of Georgia, in exchange for Georgia's cession of its claims to the land that would become the states of Alabama and Mississippi.[28] It was during the Mississippi Crisis of 1802–3—brought about when the Spanish intendant at New Orleans effectively closed the port to American commerce—that Jefferson explicitly put forward his policy regarding Indian diplomacy. The United States would make treaties with its American Indian neighbors that would both safeguard its borders and provide for the eventual accumulation of most of the lands of the Indian nations. "Our object being one of great importance," Jefferson wrote to Secretary of War Henry Dearborn, "is the establishment of a strong front on our Western boundary, the Mississippi, securing us on that side, as our front on the Atlantic does towards the East." He further elaborated that "our proceedings with the Indians should tend systematically to that object, leaving the extinguishment of title in the interior country to fall in as occasions may arise."[29] As rumors of the transfer of Louisiana from Spain to France spread from Europe to North America in early 1803, Jefferson warned his secretary of war that "a light French breeze has already reached most of the Indians" and ordered him to pick up the pace of the treaty-making process.[30] Of course, the sale of Louisiana from France to the United States rendered these specific concerns moot, but the specter of European interference in the American interior or the reestablishment of a presence of one of the European powers in the Mississippi Valley did not go away during Jefferson's presidency, as Blount's 1809 letter testifies, and they really did not disappear until after the War of 1812. Geostrategic considerations remained the paramount motive force in the United States' diplomacy with American Indian nations through the War of 1812.[31]

Yet as Jefferson's "Hints" to Dearborn in 1802, his second inaugural address in 1805, and many other letters written during his presidential administration make clear, Jefferson's Indian diplomacy, as well as his "humanitarian" desire to "civilize" the Indians, were also rooted in a desire to acquire title to as much Indian land as possible. Jefferson imagined to Dearborn that "the Indians once being closed in between strong settled countries on the Mississippi & Atlantic, will for want of game, be forced to agriculture, will find that small portions of land well improved, will be worth more to them than extensive forests unemployed." The upshot of this development for the United States was that not needing these extensive lands, the Indians "will be continually parting with portions of them, for money to buy stock, utensils, & necessaries for their farms & families."[32] This was the formulation, albeit in slightly more refined language, that Jefferson would present to the nation as a whole in his second inaugural address. The gradual "civilization" of the Indians, aided by their consumption of European manufactures, would turn them into good republican producers. This would free up thousands of acres of land that could in turn be commodified by the United States government, and consumed by white American farmers anxious to purchase new lands. The only problem inherent in this formulation was the contingency that the various American Indian communities might not want to sell their lands. To handle this, Jefferson was not above stacking the deck in the federal government's favor. As he famously wrote to the governor of the Indiana Territory, William Henry Harrison, in February 1803, in order "to promote this disposition to exchange lands, which they have to spare and we want, for necessaries, which we have to spare and they want, we shall push our trading uses, and be glad to see good and influential individuals among them run into debt, because we observe that when these debts get beyond what the individuals can pay, they become willing to lop them off by a cession of lands."[33] And of all the agents Jefferson would charge with executing his brand of Indian diplomacy—Benjamin Hawkins, Return Jonathan Meigs, James Wilkinson, William Clark—none would as persistent as Harrison in extracting land cessions from his American Indian counterparts. Fascinatingly, the cession (a large chunk of what would become central Indiana) that Harrison was able to extract from the Delaware, Potowatomi, and Miami Indians at the 1809 Treaty of Fort Wayne was furthered by Napoleon's and Perceval's closure of the European market. With nowhere for government factors to ship the furs the Indian hunters gathered (European furriers being the major consumers of furs), the various communities of Ohio Valley Indians had found their furs unsold and thus went deeper into debt despite their own acts of industry. The transatlantic commercial and diplomatic networks that had served North America's Native peoples so well for so long were now subtly turning against them. Disorder in the Atlantic world aided the Machiavellian diplomacy of federal agents like William Henry Harrison, while it simultaneously pushed local officials like Willie Blount to contemplate even more radical schemes of dispossession. Such visions could—and would—be realized when war began in the summer of 1812.[34]

The Jackson Doctrine

As March 1814 drew to close, Andrew Jackson found himself nearing the end of a perilous pursuit. The United States had been at war with Great Britain for almost two years. A general in the Tennessee militia, Jackson had answered the call to arms as soon as the Congress had approved President James Madison's request for a declaration of war on 18 June 1812. Although the fighting men of the Southwest had been mobilized, combat was infrequent in the southern theater until the summer of 1813. In August, a civil war within the Creek Indian nation had expanded into United States territory and affected American lives. Responding to the calls from Shawnee leaders Tecumseh and Tenskwatawa (the Shawnee Prophet), many Creeks embraced a nativist religious revival similar to the one that had been put forward by the Shawnee brothers in the Ohio Valley. The revivalists, known as the "Red Sticks" for the red-painted war clubs they wielded, rejected European trade goods and advocated aggressively pushing white settlers away from the Creek nation, if not getting them to leave North America altogether. As many Creeks had adapted to European lifeways for decades— with a small minority even maintaining plantations, holding African American slaves, and producing cash crops—the Red Stick movement divided the Creek nation and led to a civil war. In August 1813, a group of Red Stick warriors attacked a small stockade on the property of Samuel Mims (near modern Mobile, Alabama) holding hundreds of whites, African Americans, métis, and Creeks allied with the United States. The Red Sticks destroyed the stockade and killed more than two hundred of the settlers. The "Ft. Mims Massacre" spurred American intervention in the Creek civil war. The fact that the Red Sticks were trading for armaments and ammunition with British factors at the Spanish post of Pensacola provided an additional *causus belli*. If British forces ever invaded the Southwest, the Red Sticks would be potent allies to the British war effort. Jackson was given orders to neutralize the Red Sticks—battles between his forces and the Red Sticks would rage from autumn 1813 to the spring of 1814.[35]

The record of Jackson's incursion into the Creek nation in the aftermath of Fort Mims had been mixed. Beginning the campaign with two brigades of militia numbering about 2,500 men, in November 1813 Jackson scored two early victories along the Coosa River over the Red Sticks, at first at Tallushatchee and then at Talladega. However, the winter of 1813–14 was very difficult for Jackson. Like American arms in the northern theater of the War of 1812, Jackson's forces were plagued by lack of supplies and militia under short-term enlistments who attempted to leave the field before the campaign was complete. At the Battle of Emuckfaw in January 1814, Jackson was able to draw the Red Sticks into a fight that he won, although his victory depended upon Creek and Cherokee allies augmenting his depleted force of Tennessee militia. The Tennesseans and the Red Sticks were now involved in a war of attrition, one that Jackson's men were winning. The Red Sticks, under the command of a war leader named Menewa and the Prophet Monahee, gathered their remaining warriors, women, and children at the village of Tohopeka. The village was located on a wide, wooded bend in the Tallapoosa River; the whites called the site Horseshoe Bend. Guarded by moving water on three sides, the Red Sticks had constructed a fortification at the base of the peninsula. "It is difficult to conceive a situation more eligible for defence than one they had chosen," Jackson later recounted, "or one rendered more secure by the skill with which they had erected their breast work, it was from five to eight feet high, and extended across the point in such a direction, as that force approaching it, would be exposed to a double fire while they [the Red Sticks] lay in a perfect security behind." As he made plans to attack the Red Stick force at Tohopeka, Jackson probably imagined that while the American war against the Creek Red Sticks would likely come to an end at the Horseshoe Bend, it would certainly come at a high cost.[36]

The cost would be far higher for the Red Stick Creeks than it would be for the Americans and their Indian allies. "Determined to exterminate them," Jackson adopted tactics that would ensure decisive victory without the Red Sticks' escape. Jackson divided his forces, sending General John Coffee's horsemen and most of the Creek and Cherokee allies to opposite banks at the river bend. Jackson himself would launch a frontal assault on the Red Sticks' breastworks. From a distance, Jackson's infantry and artillery (two cannon) fired at the front of the breastworks while a detachment from Coffee's forces crossed the Tallapoosa by canoe, set fire to Tohopeka, and then attacked the Red Sticks defending the breastwork from behind. Jackson then let his men launch a frontal assault. "The enemy were compleatly routed," he reported to Major General Thomas Pinckney. "Five hundred & fifty seven were left dead upon the peninsula, & a great number were killed by the horsemen; It is believed not more than 20 have escaped." The killing continued "for five hours." When the battle was over, about 250 prisoners were taken, "all women & children except two or three." Jackson's casualties numbered 26 killed and 106 wounded. The Battle of Horseshoe Bend was a stunning victory for the American, Cherokee, and loyal Creek forces. "The power of the creeks is I think forever broken," Jackson surmised.[37]

Months later, in August 1814, as he dictated a peace settlement to the Creek nation, Jackson made it clear to all that he intended to see his musings in the aftermath of the victory at Horseshoe Bend become reality on the ground of the Old Southwest. The prospect of American Indian dispossession, implicit in the words of Thomas Jefferson, explicit in the words of Willie Blount, would be made real on the treaty ground of Fort Jackson by Andrew Jackson himself. The agreement that formally ended hostilities between the Creek nation and the United States, the Treaty of Fort Jackson, proved to be a bitter pill for the Creeks to swallow. After Jackson's victory at Tohopeka, Secretary of War John Armstrong deputed Thomas Pinckney and Benjamin Hawkins to begin negotiations with the Creeks. In preliminary talks with the Creek leaders, Pinckney and Hawkins presented generous terms of settlement to the Creeks. The Creeks would have to pay an indemnity for the war's costs, sever all ties with the Spanish and British, and surrender Red Stick military and religious leaders. The Creek communities and individuals who had remained loyal to the United States and assisted the war effort would be rewarded. The Creeks were very willing to accept such a treaty. However, the nature of the potential settlement changed when Armstrong relabeled the upcoming treaty as a military capitulation. Hawkins, the longtime agent to the Creeks, was shunted to the side, and when Jackson received promotion to the rank of major general, he replaced Pinckney in the role of treaty commissioner.[38]

The terms Jackson presented to the Creek who assembled at Fort Jackson in August 1814 were most different from what Hawkins and Pinckney had discussed with them in the aftermath of Tohopeka. Jackson had outlined his view of what the proper course of action toward the Creek Indians should be in a lengthy letter to Colonel John Williams of Knoxville. Williams had queried Jackson as to the extent of land claimed by the Creeks that would constitute a proper indemnity for the cost of the war. While Jackson felt that "the country west of the Coossee [Coosa] and North of the Alabama" would provide raw compensation, Jackson had fixed on an even larger set of goals. While he believed that the loyal, allied Creeks needed to be compensated and protected, "the hostile Creeks have forfeited all right to the Territory we have conquered." Furthermore, he wanted to completely transform the geopolitics of the southwestern borderlands—he wanted to limit the ability of a future group of Creeks to start a new rebellion, and he wanted a marchland that could be policed between the Creek nation and Spanish Florida. He explained to Williams that "the grand policy of the government ought to be, to connect the settlements of Georgia with that of the Territory of Tennessee, which at once forms a bulwark against foreign invasion, and prevents the introduction of foreign influence to corrupt the minds of the Indians." The former rebellious Creeks would be relocated into the remainder of the Creek nation. Jackson further hoped that the federal government would adopt policies to "populate speedily" these newly acquired lands. He also hoped that the close of the Red Stick War would allow the federal government to effect a revolution in the Old Southwest and "extinguish the Cherokee and Chickasaw Claim within the state of Tennessee," that is, portions of western and eastern Tennessee still under the sovereignty of the Cherokee and the Chickasaw. Jackson's dreams for the Old Southwest were similar to those of his friend and colleague Willie Blount from five years previous. Jackson wanted secure borders for the established settlements and open lands to create new white settlements. Jackson told Williams he was "truly astonished" at Hawkins's attempt to return to the *status quo ante*. For Jackson, the Red Stick War, and the War of 1812 of which it was a part, offered an enormous opportunity to change the geopolitics of the North American interior and place the interactions between the United States and the polities on its western borders on an entirely new footing. And this was what the Treaty of Fort Jackson did. Although astonished and upset, the Creek Indians agreed to a land cession of over 20 million acres—land that would eventually form about a fifth of the state of Georgia and a third of the future state of Alabama.[39]

In the decade following the War of 1812, American political leaders would defend the sovereignty of the United States unapologetically, demanding recognition and equality in the eyes of the European powers and also asserting the inviolable sovereignty of the United States' newly independent neighbors in the Western Hemisphere.[40] The demand for European noninterference in the Western Hemisphere—the Monroe Doctrine—was promulgated in 1823 by President James Monroe, but was largely the work of Secretary of State John Quincy Adams.[41] As much as the United States' hemispheric diplomacy for the remainder of the nineteenth century would be guided by a Monroe Doctrine in which John Quincy Adams had a hand in drafting, it is not improper to see the United States' American Indian diplomacy guided by a "Jackson Doctrine" that was fully articulated as the War of 1812 drew to a close. Certainly Jackson himself laid out the tenets of the Jackson Doctrine during the course of 1814—both at the treaty ground at Fort Jackson as well on the battlefield at Horseshoe Bend. American diplomatic energies, as well as military energies if necessary, needed to be directed toward isolating the American Indian polities of the North American interior from the commercial and political networks of the wider European-Atlantic world. Security for the United States as a whole, and especially for the settler polities on the American borderlands (the states of the "West"), depended on controlling Native communities' access to Atlantic markets and denying these communities independent and unfiltered communications with the other European powers of the Westphalian states system. The Jackson Doctrine sought to undermine the sovereignty of the Indian nations and render them dependent. Ironically, everything the United States had sought for themselves in the first War for Independence—recognition and sustained dialogue with the European powers in order to facilitate commerce—they now sought to deny to the American Indian nations in the "Second War for Independence" that some imagined the War of 1812 to be. In reflecting on the notion of a Jackson Doctrine, two additional parallels between it and the Monroe Doctrine present themselves. The first is that what the United States wanted to do to the Indian nations within its borders from the War of 1812 onward—that is, limit the ability of the European powers to interfere in the nations' internal affairs and the United States' diplomacy with them—is almost exactly what the United States wanted in terms of European relations with the new Latin American states, as outlined by the Monroe Doctrine. Second, and more ironic, is the role that John Quincy Adams played in articulating both the Monroe and Jackson doctrines. While Andrew Jackson was extracting ruinous concessions from the Creeks at Fort Jackson and, in the process, outlining a new order in the Old Southwest, John Quincy Adams and a team of American diplomats were beginning negotiations with their British counterparts in Ghent, Belgium, to end the War of 1812 itself. Just as it had before the Treaty of Fort Jackson, the position of American Indian nations relative to the European-Atlantic world would emerge as a major problem.[42]

The tangled nature of polity relations within the Atlantic world reared its head as soon as the Ghent negotiations began. The responsibility of returning peace to North America fell to seven men. Great Britain had commissioned three men—James Lord Gambier, Henry Goulburn, and Dr. William Adams—to serve as peace commissioners, while the United States had sent John Quincy Adams of Massachusetts, James Bayard of Delaware, Henry Clay of Kentucky, Albert Gallatin of Pennsylvania, and Jonathan Russell of Massachusetts as their negotiating team. For the British side, it was Henry Goulburn who would emerge as the leading, and most strident, voice in demanding a measure of justice from the Americans. The fastidious Goulburn had spent the duration of the War of 1812 as undersecretary of state for war and the colonies. As his superior, Henry Bathurst, Earl of Bathurst, was predominantly concerned with the war against Napoleon, it fell to Goulburn to oversee the war effort in America and understand the nature of the political and commercial relationships in which the British Empire was involved in North America. Goulburn saw the United States as the aggressor in the conflict and was determined that any peace treaty would contain the United States and protect the integrity and viability of the British colonial settlements in Canada.[43]

Goulburn seized upon one aspect of the British commissioners' instructions and fought his American counterparts in order to include it in the final treaty. Goulburn, Adams, and Gambier demanded that "the Indian allies of Great Britain be included in the pacification" and that a boundary be drawn "between the dominions of the Indians and those of the United States." This delineation would have created a so-called "Indian buffer state" in the Great Lakes basin, and it was this British proposal that caused the most consternation among the Americans. The United States government would not be able to purchase land from the Indian communities inside this territory, although individuals would have had the right to do so. Responding to Goulburn's request to include the Indians in the current treaty, Albert Gallatin responded that it was unnecessary since treaties were already under way to negotiate peace with the Indians (indeed, the Treaty of Fort Jackson concluded almost as the discussions at Ghent began). Gallatin also argued that the notion of Great Britain and the United States settling on an Indian boundary line was unprecedented. While Goulburn pointed out that every European power with a presence in the Americas had made treaties with the Indians, Gallatin countered that boundary lines between Indian nations and European settler polities had been the province of those particular parties. It was not the place of two European countries to set an Indian boundary line. Queried by Bayard as to what their purpose in drawing this line was, Goulburn responded "that it was intended as a barrier between the British possessions and the territories of the United States." Upon hearing this, the American commissioners adjourned the negotiating session.[44]

For the remainder of August 1814, the British and American diplomats went back and forth, exchanging notes and holding conferences, with neither party giving much ground. It was at an unofficial meeting, on 1 September, that John Quincy Adams and Henry Goulburn laid out the assumptions behind and the stakes of Goulburn's proposed Indian buffer state. Goulburn had proposed to Adams that the relationship of the Indian nations to the United States was similar to that between Great Britain and Portugal—they were great and small powers, bound together by treaties of alliance and commerce. Using this as a model, Goulburn "insisted that the Indians must be considered as independent nations." The fact that the United States made treaties with them was proof of it. That Goulburn's rhetoric echoed that of Henry Knox a quarter century before was lost to Adams, for he responded using the same arguments and assumptions that had motivated the policies of Thomas Jefferson, the fantasies of Willie

Blount, and the hardheaded negotiations of William Henry Harrison and Andrew Jackson.

Wherever the Indians "would form settlements and cultivate lands," Adams said, "their possessions would undoubtedly be respected." A classic example was the Cherokee, who "had become civilized in a considerable degree." Their property and position would be allowed to continue by the United States. "But the greater part of the Indians could never be prevailed upon to adopt this mode of life," Adams claimed. Living as hunters, they saw the land as a hunting ground, not as property. Exchanging the right to hunt on these lands for money or goods was "an improvement upon the former practice of all European nations, including the British," Adams asserted. But the growing population of the United States needed room to expand. And leaving the land in possession of Indian hunters was, in Adams's view (and the view of most white Americans) a waste. The stakes of this issue were enormous.[45] As Adams expounded:

> To condemn vast regions of territory to perpetual barrenness and solitude that a few hundred savages might find wild beasts to hunt upon it, was a species of game law that a nation descended from Britons would never endure. It was as incompatible with the moral as with the physical nature of things. If Great Britain meant to preclude forever the people of the United States from settling and cultivating these territories, she must not think of doing it by a treaty. She must formally undertake, and accomplish, their utter extermination.[46]

For Adams, Goulburn's proposed Indian buffer state was not a plan for perpetual peace, but perpetual war. As the United States' settler population grew and expanded westward, they would push up against the boundary of the buffer state, challenging it and contesting it all the time, leading to new wars between the peoples of the United States and British North America. As Adams imagined the future of the American nation, the options posited for it were diametrically opposed—expand or die. That the notion of "extermination" came so readily to the lips and pens of these men—be it Adams at Ghent or Jackson at Tohopeka—reveals the degree to which the perceptions, assumptions, and ideologies informing American diplomatic negotiation had changed from the decades before the Imperial Crisis, through the

Revolution and Federalist period, to the era of the Napoleonic Wars. As national boundaries became less permeable, as war became total, as consumption, rather than negotiation or union, became the driving imperative behind American diplomacy, and as the United States' membership in the community of nation-states was more certain, the desires and assumptions behind American diplomatic negotiation were transformed.

Completed in December 1814, and signed on Christmas Eve, the Treaty of Ghent returned the United States and Great Britain to the *status quo ante bellum*, although to forestall future conflict, the treaty provided a framework for negotiating a future British-American commercial treaty, a treaty that would demilitarize the Great Lakes, and a bilateral commission to firmly establish the boundary line between the United States and British North America (Canada). (This last point was a pressing one, since the boundary lines drawn at the Treaty of Paris [1783], which ended the Revolutionary War, were done on inaccurate, contemporary maps, and a new boundary convention was needed in order to accommodate new surveys.) But the biggest challenge to the status quo had been Goulburn's desire to create an Indian buffer state. The American negotiators had successfully defeated this proposal, but in the course of the negotiations, diplomats on both sides had to take stands about the kind of diplomacy Indians engaged in, what the nature of Indian treaties were, and where Native peoples fit within the framework of the Westphalian states system and the law of nations. The British diplomats had been asking for formal codification of the customary practices of the old imperial, Atlantic system and its attendant borderlands diplomatic regime that had existed for a century. Ironically, in finally openly discussing the prospect of welcoming American Indian nations into the European-centered states system, the British negotiators made sure it would never happen. The Americans were forced to formally reject these claims, and the act of doing so essentially marked the removal of American Indian nations from contact with the Westphalian system. The reality that played out on the ground during the War of 1812 and beyond, from Horseshoe Bend and the Treaty of Fort Jackson forward to the Trail of Tears, witnessed the withering away of the old norms of negotiation. The forms remained the same, but the realities of power behind them were markedly different. There was also an increasing willingness of federal government in general, and Jackson in particular, to use force, rather than negotiation, to get what was wanted out of the Indian country. The Jackson Doctrine of 1814 was just as important as the 1823 Monroe Doctrine, which warned the European powers to stay out of the Western Hemisphere and that laid the groundwork for United States' pretensions of hemispheric hegemony for the remainder of the nineteenth century. Interestingly, and tellingly, the Jackson Doctrine was finally put to the test, and faced its toughest challenge, not in the council house or on the battlefield, but in the courtroom.

Epilogue

The Cherokee Lawyer

Our story concludes, fittingly (as this is a book about America), with a lawsuit. In the spring of 1830, the Baltimore attorney William Wirt was approached by a delegation from the government of the Cherokee Indian nation asking him to serve as their counsel. The Cherokee had not approached Wirt randomly—he was recommended by some of the most powerful opponents of President Andrew Jackson, and his opinion of the situation of the Cherokee Nation was a matter of some record. Six years before, in 1824, when Wirt was attorney general of the United States, he had authored an opinion for the secretary of war about the legality of taxes the Cherokee nation had been imposing on white traders who operated within its boundaries. While he found the Cherokees' taxes to be in violation of federal law, Wirt had also noted that the extent of development and "civilization" among the Cherokees was a sign that the federal government should probably rethink its "paternalistic" relationship with the Indian nation. While it is unclear how many would have been aware of Wirt's sympathies with the Cherokee cause, nearly every American was familiar with Wirt from his service as the federal government's prosecutor in the 1807 trial of Aaron Burr for treason. Despite Burr's acquittal, Wirt's performance had won him a national reputation as an orator, which, combined with his subsequent twelve years of service as the attorney general of the United States, had solidified his reputation as one of the best lawyers in America. The Cherokee were hiring well. And in 1830, the Cherokee nation needed a good lawyer desperately.[1]

In the spring of 1830, the Cherokee nation confronted a crisis in which its very survival was at stake. The inauguration of Andrew Jackson as president a year earlier had effected a revolution in how the United States related to the Indian nations. Desirous of facilitating the transfer of the remaining lands under American Indian sovereignty east of the Mississippi to the hands of the federal government and the states, the Jackson administration had proposed the Indian Removal Bill to Congress in December 1829, and it had been formally introduced by the Tennessee delegation a month later. The Removal Bill gave the secretary of war the power and the imperative to begin negotiating with all the remaining Indian nations on the eastern side of the Mississippi River to arrange their relocation to the western side of the river. The bill also required that Congress fund the negotiations, compensate the Indian nations for their lands, and pay for the transportation of the Indian peoples and their property to the westward. The debate over the bill had raged for months, with divisions emerging along party and sectional lines. The National Republicans (the future Whig Party) generally opposed the bill, with Jackson's Democrats supporting it. Westerners and southerners tended to support the bill (the southerners almost unanimously), with northeasterners generally opposed. Passed by Congress and signed into law by President Jackson on 28 May 1830, the Indian Removal Act accomplished two main objectives, one ideological and the other practical. Ideologically and intellectually, the act changed the guiding principle behind the United States government's interaction with American Indian peoples in the East from the promotion of "civilization" to forced removal and relocation. No matter how much an Indian nation had acculturated and accommodated itself to Euro-American norms (the ostensible goal of American policy from the administrations of George Washington through John Quincy Adams), it would no longer have a place in eastern North America. At the same time, the Indian Removal Act had immediate practical effects. For years, the state of Georgia had wanted to take possession of lands within its boundaries held by the Cherokee and Creek Indians (as had been promised it by the federal government in the Georgia Compact of 1802). The government of Georgia saw the Removal Act as a green light, and in accordance with previously enacted state laws providing for the organization and distribution of the Cherokee lands, Georgia dispatched 320 surveyors into the Cherokee nation, where they began to survey and map tracts of land for sale to white settlers. Georgia refused to recognize the political and legal institutions of the Cherokee nation and the legal rights of individual Cherokees. The governing council of the Cherokee nation quickly realized that Georgia's actions needed to be stopped if the nation was to survive. Led by the principal chief of the Cherokee nation, John Ross, the Cherokee now sought one of the most famous lawyers in America to take their case to the United States Supreme Court.[2]

After some reflection, William Wirt agreed to take the case. It was not an easy decision. As he told his friend, Virginia judge Dabney Carr, he knew that taking the Cherokees' case would make him "instrumental in thwarting or impeding a project on which the President and the State of Georgia were bent," but that if the Cherokees were devoid of counsel it would in all probability render them subjects of "immediate" removal. He confessed that "the delicacy of the situation in which such an engagement would place me, glanced through my mind," but that "he was strongly impressed with the injustice about to be done to" the Cherokee, and thus accepted the case and joined the emerging Cherokee legal team. (John Ross and the Cherokees had also hoped to hire Daniel Webster, but ended up retaining John Sergeant, who would run for vice president on the Whig ticket in 1832.) For Wirt, the legal issues at stake were clear. Since the close of the Revolution, the United States had negotiated and contracted several treaties with the Cherokee nation. The act of making treaties was an explicit acknowledgment of the Cherokees' sovereignty, and precedent "held unanimously that these tribes are *alien and sovereign nations*, and their citizens *aliens*." Furthermore, under Article VI of the Constitution, these treaties were part of the supreme law of the land, and state judges were bound to uphold such law. The state of Georgia could not unilaterally violate the law of the land. But seeking to protect the Cherokee nation under these principles required a delicate legal strategy. While Wirt first considered suing Georgia in its own state courts for violating the Cherokees' sovereignty and then taking a case to the Supreme Court via the appellate track, he was aware that Georgia's judges and prosecutors would stall before allowing this to happen. Wirt was left to assert the Cherokee nation could sue Georgia under the Supreme Court's original jurisdiction, as the Supreme Court was the American court of first choice in disputes between a state and a foreign nation. This would be a permissible path for a lawsuit, if the Cherokee nation was considered to be, at least in terms of the Constitution, a foreign nation. Wirt believed he was on solid ground and he held out hope that the Supreme Court might rule in the Cherokees' favor. It was even "possible, (though not very probable)," Wirt conceded, "that the President may bow to the decision of the Supreme Court and cause it to be enforced." Oral arguments began on 12 March 1831, with John Sergeant opening the argument for the Cherokees and Wirt concluding on 14 March.[3]

Interestingly, the arguments that Wirt, the Cherokee nation, and their allies made on one side, and that Georgia and the Jackson administration made on the other, hinged in large part on how one interpreted the history of the previous century or more of interaction and negotiation between the European settlers and their descendants and American Indians. Were the treaties between the Cherokee nation and Georgia or the United States "real" treaties in the eyes of the Constitution? Did treaty making on the part of the United States and its ancestor polities constitute a recognition of full, undeniable, and unqualified sovereignty of the negotiating partner? As Wirt and Sergeant described in their initial bill filed with the Supreme Court, it was unquestioned that "various treaties have been made, from time to time, between the British colony in Georgia, before her confederation with the other states, between the confederated states afterwards, between the United States under their present constitution, and the Cherokee nation, as well as other nations of Indians." Furthermore, "in all of [these treaties] the said Cherokee nation and other nations have been recognized as sovereign and independent states, possessing both the exclusive right to their territory and the exclusive right of self government within that territory." Wirt and Sergeant argued to the Court that the history of treaties and negotiations between the United States and the Indian nations was proof, in the legal sense, that the Indian nations were possessed of full sovereignty, and that the state of Georgia (and the United States), could not violate that sovereignty through positive acts of legislation undertaken unilaterally.[4]

Wirt and Sergeant further buttressed their legal argument in defense of the Cherokee nation's sovereignty by pointing to the success the Cherokee people had exhibited in embracing the plan of "civilization" that the federal government had made the linchpin of federal Indian policy. "Under the promised '*patronage, aid,* and *good neighbourhood*' of the United States, [the Cherokee] have become *civilized, Christians,* and *agriculturalists*," the lawyers recited in their initial brief. Wirt and Sergeant made it clear that the Cherokees believed that whether or not they met the standards of "civilization" was immaterial to their case—the treaties they had signed and ratified were the law of land no matter what, and they also drolly wondered whether "their white brethren around them" could meet the same test of "civilization" that was being so rigorously applied to them. But the lawyers and their client obviously felt that some notice needed to be paid to the revolution that had been wrought among the Cherokee people in recent decades.[5]

As we have already noted, the years just before the War of 1812 saw the rise to prominence of men like Willie Blount and Andrew Jackson in the settler communities of the southern borderlands. The growing settler population and a federal government more attuned to settler interests put the American Indians peoples of trans-Appalachia at greater risk than they had been in the eighteenth century. Not only were Indian nations like the Cherokee under more pressure to sell and cede lands at treaty negotiations, but the spread of white settlement, and with it, the conversion of forests to agricultural land, made eighteenth-century modes of subsistence (the mixture of agriculture and hunting) increasingly untenable. The Cherokee people were confronted with difficult choices. By the middle of the first decade of the 1800s, the Cherokee people had split into factions. A minority of village chiefs—spurred by duplicitous actions by the federal government's Indian agent to the Cherokee, Return Jonathan Meigs—were willing to consider the sale of much of the Cherokee nation's land and voluntary relocation of the nation to the trans-Mississippi region. The majority of the Cherokee wanted nothing to do with this scheme. An internal political struggle between the so-called "old chiefs" and "new chiefs" ensued. The bulk of the Cherokee ultimately chose to remain in their current homeland, and began to politically reorganize their nation, and actively defend their sovereignty, their territory, and their culture. Cherokee nationalism grew during a "ghost dance" movement occurring contemporaneously with the revival movements of the Shawnee Prophet and the Creek Red Sticks. Cherokee nation building acquired greater urgency in the aftermath of the War of 1812, as the Cherokees witnessed the harsh terms imposed on the Creek Indians by Andrew Jackson at the treaty negotiations following his victory at Horseshoe Bend. The Cherokees took hold of the inducements offered by the federal government's "plan of civilization" and deployed it for their own ends, adopting European agricultural and subsistence practices in order to materially strengthen what they now considered to be a singular Cherokee nation. The Cherokees became a nation of European-style farmers, with numerous farming villages, and an additional small number of cotton plantations that used enslaved African American labor. In the 1820s, Sequoyah famously developed a written syllabary for the Cherokee language; and Elias Boudinot began to publish a newspaper. The Cherokees drafted and enacted a formal written constitution, with a separate legislative (the National Council), executive (the Principal Chief), and judicial branches. Indeed, the enactment of the Cherokee Constitution of 1827 was one of the actions that spurred the state of Georgia to enact its law extending its jurisdiction over the Cherokee nation within the boundaries of Georgia. The Georgians feared the Cherokee had crossed a number of thresholds that might prevent them from ever acquiring the land that had been promised them in the Georgia Compact of 1802.[6]

The stakes were thus very high when Chief Justice John Marshall read the Court's opinion to the public on 18 March 1831. The majority opinion in *Cherokee Nation v. Georgia* contained both good news and bad news for the Cherokee nation—the Court found that the Cherokee nation was a separate political entity with rights and prerogatives, but the Court could not hear this case since the Cherokee nation was not a foreign state, but a "domestic dependent nation." The Cherokee had scored a moral victory, but (in another very American turn of events) their case had been essentially dismissed on a technicality.[7]

Cherokee Nation v. Georgia came just months after the hundred-year anniversary of the conclusion of the treaty between the British Board of Trade and the Cherokee warriors who had journeyed to London with the aristocratic confidence man Alexander Cuming. Certainly, one could do worse in illustrating the changes that had come to the North America in the intervening century than examining the changed relations between the Cherokee nation and its neighbors. Where the Cherokee "nation" was once more of a notion than a reality—the Cherokee in 1730 lived in a loose confederation of four subconfederations of villages—by 1830, the villages of the Cherokee had committed to a centralized political union under national council headed by a principal chief and national committee. The customary political and cultural structures and norms of the "middle ground" that had defined the relationships between metropolitan, settler, and Native polities within the First British Empire and the larger early modern Atlantic system had given way to a new reality. Most of the settler polities of North America—now the United States of America—were fully sovereign and independent, and accepted by the European powers and the new Latin American republics as full members of the Westphalian states system. With the extension of the Westphalian system across the Atlantic to the Americas, the older, customary borderlands diplomatic regime, which had acknowledged (at least in part) the sovereignty of the American Indian nations and allowed them a modicum of agency, was passing rapidly into eclipse. A century's worth of contrast was evident here as well. In 1730, the Cherokee approached the British Empire's Board of Trade, which was then (as always) something of a protean body with loosely defined powers and prerogatives. The Board of Trade of 1730 approached diplomacy with the Indian nations with a conflicting set of norms—on the one hand, like provinces, colonies, and countries, Indian nations could be bound by treaty and profess loyalty to the king, but on the other hand, Indian nations had a different status vis-à-vis the British Empire because of their "savage" character. In 1831, the Cherokee, via William Wirt, approached the United States Supreme Court with purpose (where their ancestors had approached the Board of Trade almost accidentally via Alexander Cuming). After three decades of John Marshall's jurisprudence, the Court's place in the American federal government and the American union was clear (if still somewhat controversial), and the power of the American federal government to affect the life of the Cherokee nation was far more real and potent than any power ever claimed by the Board of Trade.

The political structures in which the Cherokee nation (and all of the American Indian nations of North America) were enmeshed had changed with the independence of the United States of America, and this transformation became irrevocable in the aftermath of the War of 1812. Where sovereign power existed on a continuum in the early modern Atlantic world, with metropolitan authorities, settler colonies, and indigenous villages and confederacies utilizing and exploiting slowly evolving customary modes of interaction and negotiation (via the political, legal, and cultural spaces provided by the "middle ground" and the imperial constitution), the American Constitution and federal government had foreshortened the continuum of sovereign power. American federalism gave land-hungry white settlers access to levers of power British imperialism never did nor could have. For frontier whites, the triumph of Andrew Jackson had ensured they had a sympathetic actor not only at the state level but at the federal level as well. Although norms had changed in a century's time, it was the change in power structures that tipped the balance against the Cherokee nation. American federalism, like early modern British imperialism, gave space on paper for American Indian sovereignty to interact with, negotiate with, and exist alongside the sovereign states of the United States of America. This was the assumption that William Wirt was operating under as he interpreted the history of the Cherokee nation's history of treaty making with the United States, it was the viewpoint articulated by the Cherokees' defenders in the American public sphere, and it was the view embraced by the Cherokees themselves. However, a different set of norms, rooted in the early ideas of Indians as a "savage" people, was articulated by the state of Georgia, the Jackson administration and its allies, and by an increasing number of white Americans. This normative construction held that treaties between Indians and Europeans were a lesser political form, that Indian peoples had no real civilization and thus a lesser and imperfect right to the lands they inhabited, and that political agreements with such people were not equal to and could not supersede the charters and constitutions that created the states and the compacts that bound the states and federal government to each other. While the seeds of this view were in evidence in the hundred-year-old notion of the Board of Trade that Indian nations were "savage" nations, nineteenth-century racial science and nineteenth-century American federalism invigorated the notions of distinction between Europeans and Native Americans. New structures of sovereign power enhanced and enabled a different set of norms.

Uncomfortable as many modern intellectuals may be with the notion that "might makes right," one is forced to concede that this seemed to be the operating principle in Jacksonian America's dealing with the Indian nations. The opportunistic intellectual hodgepodge upon which the Georgians based their claims to the Cherokee nation triumphed over the more consistent legal reasoning of the Cherokee. Power, not principle, had settled the matter. For all the intellectual and rhetorical gifts he brought to bear on behalf of the Cherokee nation, William Wirt himself was forced to concede that, even with favorable Supreme Court rulings, their position was a hopeless one. The growing numbers of the white settler population, the power this constituency had over the state governments, the Congress, and the chief executive, and the power these institutions now wielded, rendered hopes for justice moot. Norms changed to accommodate new power structures, and not vice versa. Wirt encouraged the Cherokee nation to seek an accommodation with the United States government, and remove westward under the best terms possible. While a tiny minority ultimately did this at the 1835 Treaty of New Echota, the majority of the Cherokee nation rejected the treaty and only moved west when forced to do so by the federal government between 1838 and 1839.[8] While the Trail of Tears is rightly regarded as a tragic turning point in Cherokee history, its place in United States history is worthy of reconsideration. With the sundering of the final vestige of the eighteenth-century borderlands diplomatic regime and its negotiations rooted in nebulous structures and customary norms, the United States of America had consummated its passage into the Westphalian states system. There was no going back. Europe recognized the United States as an equal, at least in diplomatic terms. The United States' internal powers, now evident in the federal government's ability to forcibly relocate an ethnic/racial minority against its will, continued to approach the Hobbesian, absolutist ideal.[9] And while in moral terms the United States' treatment of the Cherokees remains what William Wirt termed a "disgrace . . . which the waters of the ocean of Time can never wash out," structurally, the United States' conduct revealed a polity well on its way to becoming a modern nation-state.[10]

Notes

Abbreviations

AFC	*Adams Family Correspondence*
ASP-FA	*American State Papers: Foreign Affairs*
ASP-IA	*American State Papers: Indian Affairs*
DHFFC	*Documentary History of the First Federal Congress*
DHRC	*Documentary History of the Ratification of the Constitution*
EAID	*Early American Indian Documents: Treaties and Laws, 1607–1789*
EN	*The Emerging Nation: A Documentary History of the Foreign Relations of the United States under the Articles of Confederation, 1780–1789*
JCC	*Journals of the Continental Congress*
LC	Library of Congress
LDC	*Letters of Delegates to Congress*
PBF	*Papers of Benjamin Franklin*
PCC	Papers of the Continental Congress
PGW-PS	*Papers of George Washington: Presidential Series*
PJA	*Papers of John Adams*
PJM	*Papers of James Madison*
PTJ	*Papers of Thomas Jefferson*
TJW	*Thomas Jefferson Writings*

Introduction

1. Hubert Védrine used the term *hyperpuissance*, or "hyperpower," often in public discussions in 1999 to denote the complex of military, economic, and cultural power perceived to be wielded by the United States, at times without the consent of other world powers. "I believe that since 1992 the word 'superpower' is no longer sufficient to describe the United States. That's why I use the term 'hyperpower,' which American media think is aggressive," Védrine said in November 1999. The United States' deployment of preponderant military power against Serbia during the 1999 Kosovo War, in concert with the seemingly unstoppable force of economic and cultural

globalization in the late 1990s, had Védrine and other French leaders, including President Jacques Chirac, on edge. Védrine opined (again in November 1999) that "the willingness of the United States to accept with anybody, and particularly with Europe, partnership that is anything but momentary or limited, and to move from unilateralism to multilateralism, remains to be demonstrated.... We cannot accept a politically unipolar world, nor a culturally uniform world, nor the unilateralism of a single hyperpower." For all quotes, and context, see Whitney, "France Presses for a Power Independent of the U.S." Needless to say, the use of the term "hyperpower" to describe the United States continued in the aftermath of September 11, 2001, although with a somewhat different context—and more contentious atmosphere—than that of the discussions of 1999–2000. While these discussions and the developments that inform them were ongoing during the composition of this book and continue as it goes to press, what remains interesting to this historian is the fact that the American situation vis-à-vis Europe (and the rest of the world) at the beginning of the twenty-first century is arguably the diametric opposite to that at the end of the eighteenth.

2. Key to this book's argument is the proposition that the unified sovereignty of the United States of America was an emergent phenomenon. Therefore, I use the plural to describe the nation ("the United States *are*") throughout this book except when I am discussing the United States over the course of its lifespan, when I default to the singular ("the United States *is*").

3. Twentieth-century historiography, through the first decade and a half of the Cold War, stressed the isolationist impulse of American foreign policy, usually finding its origins in the colonial and Revolutionary eras. For samples of works locating the sources of isolationist thought in eighteenth-century America, see Savelle, "Colonial Origins of American Diplomatic Principles"; and Savelle, "The Appearance of an American Attitude toward External Affairs, 1750–1775." See also Bemis, *Diplomacy of the American Revolution*. For a more subtle reading of the origins of the isolationist impulse—rooted in American understandings of the European system and culminating in George Washington's Farewell Address of 1796, see Gilbert, *To the Farewell Address*. During the Vietnam War, the historiography of American foreign policy began to be shaped by the perspectives of the New Left, viewing the history of American engagement with the wider world as driven by a quest for markets and a desire to extend imperial power. A classic statement of this view is the scholarship of William Appleman Williams; see, in particular, *The Tragedy of American Diplomacy*. The most recent rejection of the isolationist interpretation of early American diplomacy is Kagan, *Dangerous Nation*.

4. An appreciation for the international context of the American Revolution and the era of the American Founding, and a concomitant rejection of the emphasis on isolationism, has quietly increased in acceptance since the 1960s. Diplomatic historians produced a series of detailed monographs demonstrating the depth of thought and action behind the making of early American foreign policy. See, for example, Ammon, *The Genet Mission*; Combs, *The Jay Treaty*; DeConde, *Entangling Alliance*;

The Quasi-War; and *This Affair of Louisiana*; Morris, *The Peacemakers*; Stagg, *Mr. Madison's War*; and Stinchcombe, *The American Revolution and the French Alliance*. At the same time, works of diplomatic and intellectual history appeared that demonstrated how American diplomats' thoughts and actions did not deviate from contemporary European norms (for example, Stourzh, *Benjamin Franklin and American Foreign Policy*; and Hutson, *John Adams and the Diplomacy of the American Revolution*), and how the actions of European diplomatists played as great role as Americans, if not more, in winning American independence (see Dull, *The French Navy and American Independence*; and *A Diplomatic History of the American Revolution*).

5. The historiography of American Indian diplomacy will be dealt with forthwith. However, an overview of the United States' political interaction with American Indian nations can be found in Prucha, *American Indian Treaties*; and *The Great Father*. Early American interaction with the Islamic world—in particular the states of North Africa (or the Maghreb)—is beyond the scope of this book, and will only be dealt with tangentially. Despite the increased attention in recent years given to early American conflict with the "Barbary States" of North Africa, the best study on this subject remains Allison, *The Crescent Obscured*.

6. The dearth of historical studies of non-European peoples, and the different assumptions that have been brought to bear on those studies, is something historians—particularly those studying Native American peoples—have tried to redress in the last few decades. For a discussion of past biases, see Wolf, *Europe and the People without History*.

7. For an overview of the modern study of the Atlantic world, see Bailyn, *Atlantic History*. Important recent histories that chart the structures of interaction between Europeans and American Indians in North America begin with White, *The Middle Ground*; and have grown to include Hinderaker, *Elusive Empires*; Cayton and Teute, eds., *Contact Points*; Merrell, *Into the American Woods*; Saunt, *A New Order of Things*; Shannon, *Indians and Colonists at the Crossroads of Empire*; Richter, *Facing East from Indian Country*; DuVal, *The Native Ground*; and Taylor, *The Divided Ground*.

8. The articulation of the law of nations in the eighteenth century, in both Europe and North America, was a key stepping-stone in the emergence of modern international law as well as the modern normative systems of international relations, including and especially liberal internationalism and liberal realism (as defined against classical realism). A summary of the history of these ideas with an eye toward the emergence of liberal realism in the form of the work of political theorist Martin Wight is Robert H. Jackson's *Classical and Modern Thought on International Relations*. Like eighteenth-century law-of-nations writers, liberal realists see the state as the fundamental unit and actor in the world system. The promotion of international norms that respect state sovereignty and integrity allow each state to express its citizens' diverse conceptions of the common good, rooted in their history, culture, language, religion, and other societal norms. Jackson himself had articulated modern liberal realist theory in great detail in *The Global Covenant*. One of the major counterpoints to liberal realism is modern liberal internationalism, which also traces its roots

to the law of nations, but stresses natural law–based conceptions of human rights that transcend state boundaries. The scholarship of Robert E. Keohane is the touchstone for much of liberal internationalism—see, in particular, *After Hegemony*. See Power, *"A Problem from Hell": America and the Age of Genocide*, for a discussion of modern policymakers wrestling with contemporary liberal internationalist norms. Another counterpoint is modern realism, often termed neorealism or structural realism, which sees international relations as anarchic and a realm of Hobbesian competition; norms emerge from this process of collision and competition between states. For an overview, see Walz, *Theory of International Politics*. A classic piece of realist analysis (by the most noted practitioner of realism) is Kissinger's study of the emergence of the post-Napoleonic order, *A World Restored*.

9. For American engagement with the eighteenth-century law of nations, see Lang, *Foreign Policy in the Early Republic*; Onuf and Onuf, *Federal Union, Modern World*; and Hendrickson, *Peace Pact*.

10. In this way, I endorse and affirm political scientist Daniel H. Deudney's conception of the early United States as a states system (see Deudney, "The Philadelphian System"). The classic statement of the diplomatic imperative behind the Philadelphia Convention and the Constitution of 1787 is Marks, *Independence on Trial*. The imperatives of making diplomacy were just as important in shaping the vision behind the Constitution as the imperative of centralizing American fiscal and military power, as outlined by Edling in *A Revolution in Favor of Government*.

11. Leading scholars in the field of early American political history recently offered a consensus, working definition of political culture—it is "defined most commonly as the set of assumptions (and less commonly as the set of methods and practices) that people brought with them into the political realm" (see the introduction to Waldstreicher, Pasley, and Robertson, eds., *Beyond the Founders*, quote on 6).

12. For a utilization of this more traditional notion of diplomatic culture, and an argument for the importance of taking it seriously, see Frey and Frey, "The Reign of Charlatans Is Over." In considering diplomatic ceremony and culture, I have found Roosen, "Early Modern Diplomatic Ceremonial, A Systems Approach," most helpful. One of my models in attempting to "read" the culture of diplomacy is Andrew Cayton's study of the Treaty of Greenville of 1795 (Cayton, "'Noble Actors' upon the 'Theatre of Honour': Power and Civility in the Treaty of Greenville," in Cayton and Teute, eds., *Contact Points*, 235–69).

13. For example, see Allgor, *Parlor Politics*; Branson, "*These Fiery Frenchified Dames*"; Freeman, *Affairs of Honor*; Pasley, "*The Tyranny of Printers*"; and Waldstreicher, *In the Midst of Perpetual Fetes*.

14. My definition of a states system is a synthesis of several strains of thinking in the political science literature. Foremost, I am utilizing the notion of states, states systems, and evolving early modern norms described by Deudney in "Philadelphian System" (esp. 191–204); and by Hendrickson in *Peace Pact* (esp. 263–65). Also influential to my thinking have been recent studies incorporating the once moribund field of geopolitics to international relations, thus incorporating discussions of spatial or-

ganization to political power. See, in particular, Agnew and Corbridge, *Mastering Space*. Also instrumental to my spatial understanding of the early modern Atlantic world has been Meinig, *The Shaping of America*, esp. vol. 1, *Atlantic America, 1492–1800*; Hornsby, *British Atlantic, American Frontier*; as well as Wallerstein, *The Modern World-System*.

15. Deudney, "Philadelphian System," 192–200. See also Onuf and Onuf, *Federal Union, Modern World*; and the provocative Tuck, *The Rights of War and Peace*.

16. Seed, "Taking Possession and Reading Text."

17. Daniels and Kennedy, eds., *Negotiated Empires*.

18. I take the notion of an Atlantic states system from the works of several scholars. For the notion of the European empires as "composite states" and the interpretive opportunities and problems arising from the transatlantic extension of the Westphalian system, see Countryman, "Indians, the Colonial Order, and the Social Significance of the American Revolution"; as well as Koenigsberger, "Composite States, Representative Institutions, and the American Revolution"; and Jay Gitlin, "On the Boundaries of Empire: Connecting the West to Its Imperial Past," in Cronon, Miles, and Gitlin, eds., *Under an Open Sky*. Also influential here is Jack P. Greene's conception of the British Empire as an "extended polity," detailed in *Peripheries and Center*. All of these works allow us to consider eighteenth-century imperial structures, and the relationships between governing and subject populations as fluid and negotiated political relationships, rather than ones of outright domination—both the structures and the norms of a system of state/polity interaction are in evidence. At the same time, for divergences in norms between the Atlantic and Westphalian systems, see Gould, "Zones of Law, Zones of Violence." For disjunctures between Westphalian diplomacy and American Indian diplomacy in particular, see Jones, *License for Empire*; and R. A. Williams, *Linking Arms Together*.

19. Many scholars argue that racial animosity made the eventual, extensive dispossession of Indian peoples in the nineteenth century inevitable from the mid-eighteenth century, and the conclusion of the Seven Years' War in particular (see Dowd, *War under Heaven*; and Merritt, *At the Crossroads*). Others see racial animosities harden a little later, during the American Revolution itself (see Knouff, *Soldiers' Revolution*; and Parkinson, "Enemies of the People"). While not dismissing the importance of emergent notions of racial difference in shaping the attitudes and actions of contemporaries, my argument sees political and diplomatic power as definitive, and thus allows for a strong measure of contingency in the interactions between Anglo-Americans and American Indians through the end of the War of 1812. My argument is more in keeping with that made by Colin G. Calloway in *The Scratch of a Pen*; and Patrick Griffith in *American Leviathan*; but again, the question of timing and when to identify the major turning point is a source of disagreement.

20. *Cherokee Nation v. Georgia* 5 Peters 1–80 (1831); reprinted in Peters, ed., *The Case of the Cherokee Nation against the State of Georgia*, 159–63; Marshall, *Papers of John Marshall*, 12:41–61.

PROLOGUE: THE CHEROKEE EMPEROR

1. All biographical notes are taken from the introductory matter to "Journal of Alexander Cuming, 1730," in S. C. Williams, ed., *Early Travels in the Tennessee Country*, 115–43.

2. For an overview of the growth of the British Empire in the Americas, see Greene, *Pursuits of Happiness*; and Taylor, *American Colonies*. For the eighteenth-century migration to British North America of which Cuming was but one example, see Bailyn, *The Peopling of British North America*; and Bailyn, with Barbara DeWolfe, *Voyagers to the West*. For Scotland and Scottish migration in particular, see Eric Richards, "Scotland and the Uses of Atlantic Empire," in Bailyn and Morgan, eds., *Strangers within the Realm*, 67–114; and Fischer, *Albion's Seed*, 605–782.

3. Cuming's exploits do not even come close to those of contemporary Tom Bell (see Bullock, "A Mumper among the Gentle").

4. I am operating in the interpretive framework outlined by the contributors in Daniels and Kennedy, eds., *Negotiated Empires*.

5. White, *The Middle Ground*.

6. See Gallay, *The Indian Slave Trade*.

7. For the detailed history of South Carolina's interactions with its American Indian neighbors, see Merrell, *Indians' New World*, as well as Crane, *The Southern Frontier*. For South Carolina's political history, I have relied on Sirmans, *Colonial South Carolina*. For early South Carolina society and the emergence of the plantation complex based on enslaved African labor, see P. H. Wood, *Black Majority*; and P. D. Morgan, *Slave Counterpoint*.

8. Sirmans, *Colonial South Carolina*, 110–28. For the origins and effects of the Yamasee War, see Merrell, *Indians' New World*, 68–91; and Ramsey, "Something Cloudy in Their Looks." For a detailed discussion of the internal construction and organization of Cherokee politics, see Reid, *A Law of Blood*, 11–71, and, more generally, Reid, *A Better Kind of Hatchet*; Oliphant, *Peace and War on the Anglo-Cherokee Frontier*, 1–8; and Gearing, *Priests and Warriors*. The course of Cherokee-Carolina diplomacy during these years is detailed in Reid, *A Better Kind of Hatchet*, 98–196.

9. Sirmans, *Colonial South Carolina*, 129–63. Additional information on South Carolina's financial woes, and, in particular, the paper money controversies, can be found in Greene, *The Quest for Power*, 108–15.

10. The account of Cuming's financial manipulations comes from an anonymous "Letter from South Carolina," dated 12 June 1730, in *The Echo; or Edinburgh Weekly Journal* (16 September 1730), quoted in S. C. Williams, *Early Travels in the Tennessee Country*, 117–18.

11. Quotes from Alexander Cuming, "Journal of Sir Alexander Cuming, 1730," printed in *Historical Register* (London, 1731), 61:1–18; reprinted in S. C. Williams, *Early Travels in the Tennessee Country*, 122–43. The quotes are from page 124 of the Williams reprint, which is hereafter cited as "Cuming Journal."

12. One of our few firsthand sources for Cuming's "embassy" to the Cherokee nation, other than Cuming's own journal, is a deposition given twenty-six years later by

the trader Ludovick Grant about his personal experiences with the Cherokee, of which the Cuming episode forms a part: "Historical Relation of Facts Delivered by Ludovick Grant, Indian Trader, to His Excellency the Governor of South Carolina," 12 January 1756; reprinted in *South Carolina Historical and Genealogical Magazine* 10 (January 1909): 54–68, quote on 55. Hereafter cited as "Relation of Ludovick Grant."

13. My spellings of Cherokee town names and sense of Cherokee geography are informed by Betty Anderson Smith, "Distribution of Eighteenth-Century Cherokee Settlements," in King, ed., *The Cherokee Indian Nation*, 46–60.

14. "Relation of Ludovick Grant," 55; "Cuming Journal," 124–25, 132–33. For details of Cherokee town governance and the town house structure, see Reid, *A Law of Blood*, 29–33; and Oliphant, *Peace and War on the Anglo-Cherokee Frontier*, 4–5.

15. "Relation of Ludovick Grant," 56; "Cuming Journal," 132–33.

16. "Relation of Ludovick Grant," 56; "Cuming Journal," 132–33.

17. There was no such office or title as "emperor of the Cherokees" until Sir Alexander Cuming's arrival in the nation in 1730. Each Cherokee town was an autonomous political unit; each town also acknowledged the preeminence of certain elders, or "beloved men." Beloved men were authority figures in their community, leading by persuasion and building consensus within each town's council. (The most senior and important of the beloved men was the headman, and second to him in importance was the warrior, or war leader.) While contemporary European observers (like Cuming) labeled the town leaders "kings," modern historians and anthropologists consider such labels to be evidence of gross misunderstanding. No Cherokee leader had the power to coerce others in his town. Similarly, no town had the power to coerce its neighboring towns. Custom (including an individual's clan status, or lineage) gave the voices of the elders more weight in deciding their town's fate, and custom similarly gave more weight to the voices of the beloved men of certain towns. Foremost among the towns was Chota of the Overhill Towns (although there is some debate about Chota's preeminence). Chota was often called the "mother town" of the Cherokee people, and the leading priest of Chota held the title of "Uku" or "Fire King." Again, as with the town's beloved men, the leadership provided by the Uku of Chota was customary and persuasive—he had no capacity for coercion. The Uku of Chota was neither a king nor an emperor (see Reid, *A Law of Blood*, 17–48; Oliphant, *Peace and War on the Anglo-Cherokee Frontier*, 5–7; and Gearing, *Priests and Warriors*, 37–54, 79–84).

18. Oliphant, *Peace and War on the Anglo-Cherokee Frontier*, 6–8.

19. "Relation of Ludovick Grant," 56–57; "Cuming Journal," 133–35.

20. "Cuming Journal," 134–35.

21. Ibid., 135.

22. Ibid., 136. For Attakullakulla, see Kelly, "Notable Persons in Cherokee History: Attakullakulla."

23. "Cuming Journal," 136; the 1730 treaty between the Cherokee and Great Britain is reprinted in S. C. Williams, *Early Travels in the Tennessee Country*, 138–41, quote on 139. Further evidence that the Cherokees did not conceptualize themselves

as surrendering their sovereignty in toto is provided by Ludovick Grant, who subsequently asserted: "I was present the whole time [at the Naquasse congress] and am positive that there was not the least word spoken about Surrendering any lands. I know all the people that went over to England well, I know they had no Commission of authority from the Nation to give away any of their land, and I know they had no power or right in themselves to do it" (see "Relation of Ludovick Grant," 57).

24. S. C. Williams, *Early Travels in the Tennessee Country*, 118–19; Alexander Cuming to the Duke of Newcastle, [1730], *EAID*, 13:133. For an overview of the Board of Trade and bureaucratic machinery of the British Empire, see Ian K. Steele, "The Anointed, the Appointed, and the Elected: Governance of the British Empire, 1689–1784," in P. J. Marshall, ed., *The Eighteenth Century*, vol. 2 of Louis, ed., *The Oxford History of the British Empire*, 105–27.

25. Board of Trade to Duke of Newcastle, Whitehall, 20 August 1730, *EAID*, 13:134–35.

26. Ibid.

27. S. C. Williams, *Early Travels in the Tennessee Country*, 120–21.

28. The nature of subsequent relations between the Cherokee and their neighbors are dealt with in Oliphant, *Peace and War on the Anglo-Cherokee Frontier*; the relations of the new settler colony of Georgia with its Indian neighbors are discussed in Sweet, *Negotiating for Georgia*; see also Hahn, *The Invention of the Creek Indian Nation*; and, more generally, Axtell, *The Indians' New South*.

1. "In the Nature of Ambassadors"

1. James Alexander abstracted an August 1751 letter from the governor of Canada for Governor George Clinton and Cadwallader Colden. Responding to charges from New York that the French construction of fortifications at Niagara was a violation of the Treaty of Utrecht, the Canadian governor was belligerent. In Alexander's rendering: "[H]e advances a number of facts groundless & false in themselves which (Says he) had they been known at the Treaty of Utrecht and Aix La Chapelle the Dominion of England over the five nations would not have been acknowledged by his master the King of France." The implicit design of the French rhetoric was to weaken the British claim to be the sole party with the ability to treat with the nations of the Iroquois Confederacy, a most troubling prospect to the British in New York (see James Alexander, Notes on the Govr. of Canada's Letter of Aug. 10, 1751 to Cadwallader Colden, Govr. Clinton and Dr. Mitchell, 27 August 1751, in Colden, *Letters and Papers of Cadwallader Colden*, 4:288–91.

2. For details of Archibald Kennedy's life and works, see Milton M. Klein, "Archibald Kennedy: Imperial Pamphleteer," in Leder, ed., *Some Eighteenth-Century Commentators*, 2:73–105. For the War of Austrian Succession, see M. S. Anderson, *The War of Austrian Succession*.

3. For commerce in colonial New York, see Matson, *Merchants and Empire*. Kennedy's essays were *Observations on the Importance of the Northern Colonies Under Proper Regulations* (New York, 1750); *The Importance of Gaining and Preserving the*

Friendship of the Indians to the British Interest, Considered (New York, 1751); *An Essay on the Government of the Colonies* (New York, 1752); *Serious Considerations on the Present State of Affairs of the Northern Colonies* (New York, 1754); and *Serious Advice to the Inhabitants of the Northern Colonies, on the Present Situation of Affairs* (New York, 1755).

4. [Kennedy], *Importance of Gaining and Preserving the Friendship of the Indians*; for quote about "Truck or Trading-Houses," see [Kennedy], *Serious Considerations*, 11.

5. The conception of the eighteenth-century British Empire as an extended polity is that of Jack P. Greene. I am indebted to the framework of empire outlined in Greene's *Peripheries and Center*.

6. All quotes and background information regarding the letter are from Benjamin Franklin to James Parker, Philadelphia, 20 March 1750/1, *PBF*, 4:117–18. For the Albany Congress of 1754, see Shannon, *Indians and Colonists at the Crossroads of Empire*. Shannon discusses the connections between Franklin's 1751 letter and his "Short Hints" on union, composed on the eve of the Albany Congress (see 111–12). For the exchange with Kennedy in the context of Franklin's political and intellectual growth, see G. S. Wood, *The Americanization of Benjamin Franklin*, 72–78.

7. [Kennedy], *Importance*, all quotes on 5.

8. For details of the Covenant Chain, see Francis Jennings, "Iroquois Alliances in American History," in Jennings, *History and Culture of Iroquois Diplomacy*, 37–65.

9. For details of the Beaver Wars, see Richter, *Ordeal of the Longhouse*, 50–66.

10. Jennings, "Iroquois Alliances in American History," 38–42. Iroquois political theory, like that of most Native American peoples, had a strong spiritual component that European negotiators discussed little, if at all. For the Iroquois, their league (between the Six Nations) was not just a political unit, but a spiritual union as well. The same held true for the Covenant Chain alliance between the Six Nations and other Indian nations. The Iroquois Confederacy that was presented diplomatically to the Europeans was merely the temporal, political element of a spiritual and cosmological entity, the *Haudenosaunee*, the Longhouse, or the Great League of Peace and Power. This entity had existed in the Iroquois mythos long before the arrival of the French, Dutch, and British, being founded, in part, by Deganawidah, the Peacemaker, a man of spiritual origin. Daniel Richter explains and explores the meaning of the Deganawidah Epic in *Ordeal of the Longhouse*, 30–49. See also Fenton, *Great Law and the Longhouse*, 3–6, 34–103.

11. Jennings, "Iroquois Alliances in American History," 40–44.

12. Ibid., 42–47. For more background on the theory and practice of "covering the dead," see White, *Middle Ground*, 75–82.

13. The elaborate nature of the rituals at the Treaty of Lancaster is discussed in Fenton, *Great Law and the Longhouse*, 416–33. For a larger discussion of Canasatego, see William A. Starna, "The Diplomatic Career of Canasatego," in Pencak and Richter, eds., *Friends and Enemies in Penn's Woods*, 144–63.

14. Alternative spellings are Tachanoontia or Tekanontie.

15. This discussion is drawn from accounts of the Lancaster negotiations pre-

sented in Jennings, "Iroquois Alliances in American History," 44–47; and Fenton, *Great Law and the Longhouse*, 418–25. All quotes from Tachanoontia speech, Lancaster Court-House, 27 June 1744, *EAID*, 2:88–89. See also Kalter, *Benjamin Franklin, Pennsylvania, and the First Nations*, 86–122.

16. For the background of the writing and publishing of *Plain Truth*, as well as a consideration of its immediate aftereffects, see the editorial in *PBF*, 3:180–88. An insightful discussion of the significance of *Plain Truth* as Franklin's first political tract dealing with national security and foreign affairs can be found in Stourzh, *Benjamin Franklin and American Foreign Policy*, 33–82.

17. [Benjamin Franklin], "Plain Truth," 17 November 1747, *PBF*, 3:188–204, quotes on 191, 193, 194.

18. For a brief overview of the geopolitical dynamic in North America before the Seven Years' War, see Bruce P. Lenman, "Colonial Wars and Imperial Instability, 1688–1793," in P. J. Marshall, ed., *The Eighteenth Century*, vol. 2 of Louis, ed., *The Oxford History of the British Empire*, 151–68; and John Shy, "The American Colonies in War and Revolution, 1748–1783," ibid., 300–324. For a discussion of imperial-Indian relations through the mid-eighteenth century, with a specific focus on the differences between French and British policies, see the first four chapters of Hinderaker, *Elusive Empires*, as well as White, *Middle Ground*.

19. Like the French and the Algonkians in the Great Lakes basin and the Ohio-Mississippi Valley, British-Indian diplomacy was rooted in relationships based on mutual misunderstandings and shared, functional fictions about the nature of politics within and between their respective polities. For the power of mutual misunderstanding, see White, *Middle Ground*, x.

20. For the distinct cultural assumptions behind Indian-European commerce, see White's discussion of the fur trade in *Middle Ground*, 94–141. Equally important discussions of the role of commerce in undergirding political interaction on the southern borderlands include Saunt, *A New Order of Things*; and Braund, *Deerskins and Duffels*.

21. Cadwallader Colden to George Clinton, New York, 8 August 1751, in Colden, *Letters and Papers of Cadwallader Colden*, 4:277–78.

22. [Kennedy], *Importance*, 6–7.

23. A French officer, Charles-Michel Mouet de Langlade, and his Chippewa and Ottawa troops attacked the town of Pickawillany, which had become home to many traders from Pennsylvania and Virginia, and eventually killed the town's headman and a trader residing there (see F. Anderson, *Crucible of War*, 28–29; and White, *Middle Ground*, 230–34). For French incursions into Iroquoia, see Colden to Clinton, 8 August 1751, in Colden, *Letters and Papers of Cadwallader Colden*, 4:280–81.

24. Braund, *Deerskins and Duffels*, 36–38.

25. Jacobs, *The Appalachian Indian Frontier: The Edmond Atkin Report and Plan of 1755*; and xvi–xxiii for biographical information; hereafter cited as *Atkin Report*.

26. Edmond Atkin to the Right Honourable the Lords Commissioners for Trade and Plantations, 30 May 1755, printed in Jacobs, *Atkin Report*, 3. All subsequent citations of *Atkin Report* are to this letter.

27. Quotes from Jacobs, *Atkin Report*, 49. For Atkin's discussion of the Cherokee, see 48–54; the Catawbas, 46–48; the Creeks, 54–64; Chickasaws, 64–71; and Choctaws, 71–74.

28. Ibid., 8.
29. Ibid., 9–13.
30. Ibid., 7.
31. Ibid., 8.
32. Ibid., 77.
33. Ibid., 77–89.
34. Ibid., 92–93. For details of the controversial Anglo-Cherokee Treaty of 1730 between Bermuda governor Alexander Cuming and Moitoi of Tellico, see the prologue of this book.
35. Quotes from Douglass, *Summary, Historical and Political, Of the First Planting, Progressive Improvements, and Present State of the British Settlements in North-America*, 155, 160. Many of Douglass's commentaries in the *Summary* are reflective of his own personal idiosyncrasies, although his views on Native Americans were certainly not his alone. For background on Douglass and his views, see David Freeman Hawke, "William Douglass's Summary," in Leder, ed., *Some Eighteenth-Century Commentators*, 2:43–74.
36. The persistence of conflict and misunderstanding between European settlers and Native peoples in eastern North America is explored in detail in Merrell, *Into the American Woods*. Merritt, in *At the Crossroads*, explores similar themes.
37. F. Anderson, *Crucible of War*, is the most recent, and most thorough, treatment of the conflict.
38. Oliphant, *Peace and War on the Anglo-Cherokee Frontier*, 20–68.
39. Ibid., 69–112.
40. Ibid., 140–68.
41. Ibid., 194–201.
42. The impact of the postwar settlement and attempted reworking of the imperial constitution in both the settler colonies and the Indian country is suggestively put forward in F. Anderson, *Crucible of War*, 737–46.
43. The letter is discussed and cited in Oliphant, *Peace and War on the Anglo-Cherokee Frontier*, 200. British imperial ambitions and Indian concerns at the Augusta Congress are elaborated in Jones, *License for Empire*, 42–52.
44. For a list of all participants, see *Journal of the Congress of the Four Southern Governors, and the Superintendent of that District, with the Five Nations of Indians, at Augusta, 1763* (Charles Town, 1764), 22; hereafter cited as *Augusta Congress Journal*. For background on Augusta's life as a frontier entrepôt, see the short essays collected in Cashin, ed., *Colonial Augusta*. The Cherokee experience at the congress is discussed briefly by Oliphant in *Peace and War on the Anglo-Cherokee Frontier*, 201–6. For the Creek experience, see Corkran, *The Creek Frontier*, 237–41.
45. Oliphant, *Peace and War on the Anglo-Cherokee Frontier*, 169–90.
46. For the treaty text, see *Augusta Congress Journal*, 38–42.
47. This speech occurred on either 7 or 8 November 1763 (the journal is not clear,

as Indian speeches occupied both of these days) (see *Augusta Congress Journal*, 28–30). For further details of Attakullakulla, see Oliphant, *Peace and War on the Anglo-Cherokee Frontier*, 208. See also Kelly, "Notable Persons in Cherokee History: Attakullakulla."

48. Stuart's speech was delivered on 5 November 1763 (see *Augusta Congress Journal*, 23).

49. Snapp, *John Stuart*, quotes on 64 and 58.

50. For details of Stuart's plan, see ibid., 54–67. For the intersection of Stuart's vision with the work of the Board of Trade—and its ultimate frustration—see Daniel K. Richter, "Native Americans, the Plan of 1764, and a British Empire That Never Was," in Olwell and Tully, eds., *Cultures and Identities in Colonial British America*, 267–92.

51. See James Wright to John Stuart, Savannah, 5 January 1767, quoted and cited in Snapp, *John Stuart*, 74. For greater detail on the colonial resistance to the Stuart plan, see ibid, 74–76.

52. Ibid., 74–75, quote from a letter from Thomas Gage to the Earl of Shelburne, New York, 26 August 1767, quoted and cited in Snapp, 75. For a wider discussion of the effects of the Proclamation of 1763 on colonial attitudes, see Holton, "The Ohio Indians."

53. See Snapp, *John Stuart*, 68–89.

54. See the discussion in Thomas, *The Townshend Duties Crisis*, 51–59. See also Snapp, *John Stuart*, 76–78.

55. Earl of Hillsborough to General Thomas Gage, 15 April 1768, in Jensen, ed., *American Colonial Documents to 1776*, 705.

56. For the 1768 Treaty of Fort Stanwix, see Fenton, *Great Law and the Longhouse*, 533–47; and Holton, *Forced Founders*, 3–20. The text of the treaty is in Brodhead, O'Callaghan, and Fernow, eds., *Documents Relative to the Colonial History of the State of New York*, 8: 111–37.

57. Thomas, *The Townshend Duties Crisis*. For a detailed overview of the end of the Imperial Crisis, see Gipson, *British Empire*, vol. 12; and Middlekauff, *The Glorious Cause*, 53–226.

2. "In an Odd State"

1. See Ammerman, *In the Common Cause*.

2. For details of the adjournment of the First Continental Congress, see *JCC*, 1:102–3; for the events of late 1774 and early 1775, see Middlekauff, *The Glorious Cause*, 250–311. The response to Lexington and Concord is discussed in Royster, *A Revolutionary People at War*, 25–53; Fischer, *Paul Revere's Ride*, 261–80; Gross, *The Minutemen and Their World*, 133–70; and Montross, *The Story of the Continental Army*, 3–36.

3. For Adams's role in the Boston Massacre trials, see Zobel, *The Boston Massacre*. For a general discussion of Adams's experiences during the Second Continental Congress, see Page Smith, *John Adams*, 1:196–274; and McCullough, *John Adams*, 78–124.

4. John Adams to James Warren, 7 June 1775, Philadelphia, *LDC*, 452–53. Congress's initial resolve not to authorize an incursion into Canada was on 1 June 1775 (see *JCC*, 2:75), and had followed Congress's public address to "the oppressed inhabitants of Canada" of 29 May 1775 (see *JCC*, 2:68–70).

5. Quotes from "The Declaration as Adopted by Congress," 6 July 1775, *PTJ*, 1:217; see also *JCC*, 2:154.

6. I am here, in great part, endorsing the view that stresses continuity between the colonial period and the Revolutionary and post-Revolutionary periods in American history, at least as concerns questions of state power and policy. For an articulation of the historiographic and interpretive problem, see Greene, "Colonial History and National History." While I do not want to discount the disjuncture provided by the American Revolutionary experience (as subsequent chapters will make evident), I would specifically disagree with historians who posit the radical changes wrought by the Revolution occurring at the moment of its inception (see, for example, the argument advanced by Fischer in *Washington's Crossing*).

7. For the correspondence between John Adams and Abigail Adams about Franklin, see AA to JA, 5 July 1775, *AFC*, 1:239–40; JA to AA, 23 July 1775, *AFC*, 1:252–54, quotes on 253. For Franklin's liminal position between England and America, see G. S. Wood, *The Americanization of Benjamin Franklin*, 124–51.

8. My conception of Franklin's political thinking is drawn from a number of sources. For Franklin's understanding of the British Empire as a vehicle for the advancement of mutual self-interest, see Stourzh, *Benjamin Franklin and American Foreign Policy*, 33–82. For the place of affection in the bonds of empire, see Jack Greene, "Pride, Prejudice, and Jealousy: Benjamin Franklin's Explanation of the American Revolution," in Greene, *Understanding the American Revolution*, 18–47. My overall conception of the growth of Franklin's political thinking and identity is in deep agreement with the framework offered by G. S. Wood in *Americanization of Benjamin Franklin*.

9. Stourzh, *Franklin and American Foreign Policy*, 33–82.

10. For the American reception of the Stamp Act and the ensuing crisis in government, see Morgan and Morgan, *The Stamp Act Crisis*. The British policymakers' rationale for the Stamp Act and their response to the colonial uproar are discussed in detail in Thomas, *British Politics and the Stamp Act Crisis*. A widespread belief in parliamentary supremacy had taken hold by the time of the passage of the Townshend Duties (see Thomas, *The Townshend Duties Crisis*). Interestingly, it would be two men, Frederick Howe and William Howe, who most favored conciliation with the American colonists who would be put at the head of the military effort to put down the colonial rebellion in 1776 (see Gruber, *The Howe Brothers and the American Revolution*, esp. 42–88). The Carlisle Commission is discussed in chapter 3 of this book. For Franklin's negotiations and thinking about the provincial-metropolitan relationship during controversies surrounding the governorship of Thomas Hutchinson, see Stourzh, *Benjamin Franklin and American Foreign Policy*; and Bailyn, *The Ordeal of Thomas Hutchinson*, 201–11.

11. Franklin to Joseph Priestley, Philadelphia, 16 May 1775, *PBF,* 22:44; Franklin to William Strahan, Philadelphia, 5 July 1775, *PBF,* 22:85; Franklin to Priestley, Philadelphia, 7 July 1775, *PBF,* 22:91–93, quotes on 91; Franklin to Jonathan Shipley, 7 July 1775, Philadelphia, *PBF,* 22: 93–98, quote on 95.

12. Silas Deane initially proposed that any American confederation be constructed along the lines of the New England Confederation of the mid-seventeenth century (see Silas Deane to Patrick Henry, Wethersfield, 2 January 1775, *LDC,* 1:291–92). For a comparative discussion of Deane's and Franklin's proposals for the Articles of Confederation, see Rakove, *The Beginnings of National Politics,* 135–51.

13. Franklin, "Proposed Articles of Confederation," 21 July 1775, *PBF,* 22:122–23.

14. Ibid., 22:124.

15. Ibid., 22:125.

16. "The King's Speech on the Opening of the Session," 26 October 1775, in Cobbet, ed., *Parliamentary History of England,* 18:695–97, quotes on 695–96; Gipson, *British Empire,* 12:337–45. For George III's agency in shaping British policy during the American Revolution, see O'Shaughnessy, "If Others Will Not Be Active, I Must Drive."

17. Johan Adams to Abigail Adams, 23 July 1775, *AFP,* 1:253.

18. See *JCC,* 2:89–90, 96, 103.

19. My discussion in this section in particular, and to a lesser extent in this chapter as whole, parallels the excellent work of Jerrilyn Greene Marston in *King and Congress.* Marston charts the growing acceptance of the Continental Congress as the legitimate governing body of the Thirteen Colonies from late 1774 through the end of 1776 and compellingly argues that the transfer of allegiance and acceptance of congressional legitimacy was a gradual process. Here I am less concerned with the concept of legitimacy and more interested in the Thirteen Colonies' position in the international/Atlantic system, and how the Congress's gradual assumption of sovereign powers was a product of the American polities' need to articulate and define their position within that system. For additional treatment of the move toward independence during this period, see the brief Pole, *The Decision for American Independence.* For deliberations in the Continental Congress, see Rakove, *The Beginnings of National Politics,* 63–86.

20. "King's Speech," 26 October 1775, *Parliamentary History,* 18:695–97.

21. Joseph Ward to John Adams, Roxbury, 23 October 1775, *PJA,* 3:236–38, quotes on 237.

22. Joseph Palmer to John Adams, Watertown, 11 November 1775, *PJA,* 3:264–66, quotes on 265.

23. James Warren to John Adams, Watertown, 14 November 1775, *PJA,* 3:301–6, quotes on 304.

24. Massachusetts's trade had been embargoed since the passage of the Boston Port Bill by Parliament, word of which arrived in America in May 1774 (see Gipson, *British Empire,* 12:138–67; and Ammerman, *Common Cause,* 1–17).

25. Benjamin Hinchborn to John Adams, Lexington, 10 December 1775, *PJA,* 3:320–27, quote on 325.

26. For details of the American invasion, see Middlekauff, *The Glorious Cause*, 304–8. For Jefferson's hopes about Canada's incorporation into the union, see Thomas Jefferson to John Randolph, Philadelphia, 29 November 1775, *PTJ*, 1:268–70; *LDC*, 2: 402–3.

27. Congress's speech to the Iroquois was approved on 13 July 1775 (see *JCC*, 2:178–83). For the German Flats and Albany Conferences of August–September 1775, see Item 134, 1–46, PCC.

28. Philip Schuyler to John Hancock, Albany, 14 December 1775, Item 153, 1:362–64, PCC, quote on 362.

29. See Samuel Adams to John Adams, Philadelphia, 22 December 1775, *PJA*, 3:374–76; *LDC*, 2:506–8; for publication, see Robert Smith's Diary, 22 December 1775, *LDC*, 2:512–13; and *JCC*, 3:456.

30. John Adams to James Warren, Philadelphia, 7 June 1775, *LDC*, 1:452–53, quotes on 452.

31. Marston, *King and Congress*, 224–27; *JCC*, 2:174–83.

32. *JCC*, 2: 174–77, quotes on 174–76. See also Marston, *King and Congress*, 226–27.

33. *JCC*, 2:174. For the Albany Conference, see Item 134, 8–46, PCC.

34. For the dispute between America and Britain as a "family quarrel," see "Speech to the Six Confederate Nations," in *JCC*, 2:178–83, quote on 182. The delivery of this part of Congress's speech to the Iroquois at the Albany Conference occurred on 28 August 1775 (see Item 134, 25, PCC).

35. See Dull, *Diplomatic History*, 49–51; and Bemis, *The Diplomacy of the American Revolution*, 29–33.

36. See Bemis, *The Diplomacy of the American Revolution*, 32–34; and Dull, *Diplomatic History*, 50. Francis Wharton described the history of the Committee of Secret Correspondence/Committee of Foreign Affairs in detail in *Revolutionary Diplomatic Correspondence of the United States*, 1:456–72. The resolution of Congress creating the Committee of Secret Correspondence is in *JCC*, 3:392, quote on 392.

37. Committee of Secret Correspondence to Arthur Lee, Philadelphia, 13 December 1775, *PBF*, 22:296–97, quote on 297.

38. Benjamin Franklin to Charles-Guillaume-Frédéric Dumas, Philadelphia, 9 December 1775, *PBF*, 22:287–91, quotes on 287–88.

39. Franklin to Dumas, 9 December 1775, *PBF*, 22:287–91, quotes on 288–89.

40. Franklin's letter to Dumas had a dual functionality—i.e., it was both communicative and performative of the American position at that moment—similar to that identified by David Armitage (reading J. L. Austin) in the Declaration of Independence (see Armitage, "The Declaration of Independence and International Law").

41. Committee of Secret Correspondence to Silas Deane, Philadelphia, 2 March 1776, *PBF*, 22:369–74, quote on 371.

42. Dull, *Diplomatic History*, 57–65; Bemis, *Diplomacy of the American Revolution*, 34–40.

43. "Resolution of Independence," 7 June 1776, *PTJ*, 1:298; *LDC*, 4: 158–60; *JCC*, 5: 425–26.

44. "Resolution of Independence," 7 June 1776, *PTJ*, 1:298.

45. For the drafting and composition of the Declaration of Independence, generally, see Becker, *The Declaration of Independence*; Boyd, *The Declaration of Independence*; Wills, *Inventing America*; Rakove, *The Beginnings of National Politics*, 87–110; and Maier, *American Scripture*.

46. Jefferson, "Notes of Proceedings in the Continental Congress," 7 June–1 August 1776, in *PTJ*, 1:299–329, quotes on 309–10. See also John Dickinson, Notes for a Speech in Congress, [8–10 June] 1776, *LDC*, 4:165–69. Dickinson still held out hopes for reconciliation with Great Britain, but also rooted his unease with a declaration of independence in that such an act would be a formal declaration of war and thus "one of the highest Powers of Sovereignty." Dickinson felt that congressional appropriation of sovereign power required clear statements of support by all of the Congress's constituents. Quote ibid., on 166.

47. *JCC*, 5:431, 433.

48. See both David Hendrickson's brief treatment (in the larger context of discussing the American Founding period, and especially the Constitution in terms of international relations) in Hendrickson, *Peace Pact*, 124–26, as well as David Armitage's recent works: "The Declaration of Independence and International Law"; and *The Declaration of Independence: A Global History*.

49. Quotes from Armitage, "The Declaration of Independence and International Law."

50. "Declaration of Independence as Adopted by Congress," *PTJ*, 1:429–33, quote on 432.

51. For the context of the Model Treaty, see Dull, *Diplomatic History*, 55; and Bemis, *The Diplomacy of the American Revolution*, 45–47. For the drafting of the Model Treaty, see the editorial note and apparatus accompanying the two drafts and one final text of the Plan in *PJA*, 4:260–302. The politics of the drafting of the Articles of Confederation is discussed in Rakove, *The Beginnings of National Politics*, 135–91; and Hendrickson, *Peace Pact*, 115–57. See also Jensen, *The Articles of Confederation*.

52. "Plan of Treaties" Editorial Note, *PJA*, 4:260–65. For a summary of American commercial diplomacy during the Revolution and the assumptions behind it, see Crowley, *The Privileges of Independence*, 50–66.

53. See Rakove, *The Beginnings of National Politics*, 163–91; and Hendrickson, *Peace Pact*, 115–49.

54. Onuf, *The Origins of the Federal Republic*; Rakove, *The Beginnings of National Politics*, 163–215.

55. Hendrickson, *Peace Pact*, 161–93; Martin and Lender, *A Respectable Army*, esp. 29–99.

56. The delegation of the Six Nations to Philadelphia is mentioned in Glathaar and Martin, *Forgotten Allies*, 116–17, although it is not discussed in Fenton's generally excellent survey of Iroquois history, *Great Law and the Longhouse*.

57. Glathaar and Martin, *Forgotten Allies*, 115–17.

58. Caesar Rodney to Thomas Rodney, Philadelphia, 29 May 1776, *LDC*, 4:99–100, quote on 99.
59. *JCC*, 5:430–31; Glathaar and Martin, *Forgotten Allies*, 117.
60. "Josiah Bartlett's and John Dickinson's Draft Articles of Confederation," [17 June–1 July 1776], *LDC*, 4:233–55, quote on 239; "Declaration of Independence as Amended and Adopted by the Committee and Congress," *PTJ*, 1:429–33, quote on 431.
61. "Draft Articles of Confederation," *LDC*, 4:240.
62. Marston, *King and Congress*, 225–27.
63. Articles of Confederation, in Bailyn, ed., *The Debate on the Constitution*, 2:926–36, quotes on 931–32.

3. "Are We Not . . . Independant States?"

1. [Gouverneur Morris], *Observations on the American Revolution*, quote on 120.
2. Ibid., 121–22.
3. For Morris as a conservative Revolutionary, see Brookhiser, *Gentleman Revolutionary*.
4. For the Carlisle Commission, see Van Doren, *Secret History of the American Revolution*, 59–116; Ritcheson, *British Politics and the American Revolution*, 233–86; W. Brown, *Empire or Independence*, 169–292; Robson, *The American Revolution in Its Political and Military Aspects*, esp. 200–219.
5. For the significance of the Declaration of Independence in the context of international relations, see Armitage, "The Declaration of Independence and International Law."
6. Quotes from Caron de Beaumarchais to Silas Deane, Paris, 22 July 1776, in Deane, *Deane Papers*, 1:158–59. For Deane's pose as a merchant from Bermuda, see Deane to the Secret Committee of Congress, 18 August 1776, ibid., 1:199–200. Interestingly, Deane's original instructions from the Secret Committee suggested that he represent himself as a merchant "engaged in the business of providing goods for the Indian trade" (see Secret Committee to Deane, Philadelphia, 3 March 1776, in Deane, *Deane Papers*, 1:123).
7. Dull, *The French Navy and American Independence*.
8. See Deane to Secret Committee, Paris, 18 August 1776, in Deane, *Deane Papers*, 1:198.
9. Deane to Secret Committee, 18 August 1776 (postscript of 15 August 1776 letter), in Deane, *Deane Papers*, 1:212.
10. Deane to Secret Committee, postscript of 15 August 1776 to letter of 18 August 1776, in Deane, *Deane Papers*, 1:217. For an overview of the American diplomatic mission to France leading to the Treaty of Alliance, see Schiff, *A Great Improvisation*.
11. See, for example, the hierarchy of printed political "weaponry" in Freeman's discussion of the "paper war" in early national America in *Affairs of Honor*, 105–58.
12. See Morris to Deane, Philadelphia, 5 June 1776, Box 1, Folder 28, Papers of Silas Deane. Such division of labor between letters varied by individual writer as well as by nationality.

13. For letters as semi-public and public documents in eighteenth-century America, see R. D. Brown, *Knowledge Is Power*.

14. Deane noted that his lengthy "Memoir on the Commerce of America, and its Importance to Europe" received a good deal of circulation, as "it has had a great run among the Ministers of this and some other Courts in a private way" (see Deane to Secret Committee, postscript of 15 August 1776 to letter of 18 August 1776, in Deane, *Deane Papers*, 1:217). Deane would communicate to Gerard, who would then carry *memoires* and other correspondence to Vergennes. As Deane's written French was poor, the *memoires* would presumably circulate in English (see Silas Deane, "Essay on the Policy of France toward the American Colonies in the Revolutionary Era," n.d., Box 7, Folder 34, p. 17, Papers of Deane. Quoted with permission of the Connecticut Historical Society).

15. The use of written *memoires* by American diplomats would continue into the 1780s—a classic example of such a *memoire* was Thomas Jefferson's *Observations on the Whale-Fishery* (1788). See editorial note for Jefferson, *Observations on the Whale Fishery* in *TJP*, 14:217–68.

16. See Van Doren, *Benjamin Franklin*, 574–75.

17. See J. Adams, *Letters from a Distinguished American*.

18. Benjamin Franklin to Richard Price, Passy, 13 June 1782, *PBF*, 37:472. As a former printer, Franklin understood the power of newspapers in shaping public opinion and political outcomes, a power his American successors would deploy to good use in the decades to come (see Pasley, *"The Tyranny of Printers"*).

19. All quotes from "Memorandum" enclosed in Deane to Conrad Alexandre Gérard, Paris, 18 July 1776, in Deane, *Deane Papers*, 1:147–53

20. Deane, "Memoir on the Commerce of America, and its Importance to Europe," 15 August 1776, in Deane, *Deane Papers*, 1:184–95, quotes on 185, 189.

21. Franklin, "Comparison of Great Britain and America as to Credit, 1777," [before 8 September 1777], *PBF*, 24:508–14, quotes on 512.

22. See Dull, *French Navy and American Independence*; and Orville T. Murphy, "The View from Versailles: Charles Gravier Comte de Vergennes's Perceptions of the American Revolution," in Hoffman and Albert, eds., *Diplomacy and Revolution*, 107–49. More generally, see Stinchcombe, *The American Revolution and the French Alliance*. For a recent study of Vergennes's career, see Price, *Preserving the Monarchy*.

23. Eden was the third son of Sir Robert Eden, third baronet, of Windstone Hall, Durham. At Eton, Eden befriended Frederick Howard, the fifth Earl of Carlisle, forming a mutually beneficial relationship that would last the rest of their lives. Taking both a bachelor's and a master's degree from Christ Church College at Oxford by 1768, he entered the bar at the Middle Temple the following year. Eden became a Member of Parliament in 1774, and in 1776 was appointed to the Board of Trade. This post, in concert with a personal interest in commerce and economics, found Eden concerned with the British trade in America, the Caribbean, and Africa, all of which necessarily involved him heavily in the questions of American Revolution (see "Eden, William," in *Dictionary of National Biography*, 6:362–64).

24. All quotes from William Eden to Lord North, Greenwich, 7 December 1777, British Library, Additional Manuscripts 34414:395–98. The papers of Eden, later Baron Auckland, are held in the British Library, London, Additional Manuscripts 34412–34471, 46490–46491. Eden's papers from the period of the American Revolution (Add. Mss. 34412–17) have been microfilmed as *Materials Related to the American Revolution from the Auckland Papers in the British Museum*, in W. E. Minchton, ed., *British Records Relating to America in Microform* (East Ardsley, UK, 1974). I have consulted the microfilm edition for my research. I hereafter cite material from the Auckland Papers, per convention, as Add. Mss. Much of this correspondence has also been reproduced in Stevens, ed., *Facsimiles of Manuscripts in European Archives Relating to America, 1773–1783*. I cite this as Stevens, *Facsimiles*. My reading of the Carlisle Commission is indebted to the treatment in Ritcheson, *British Politics and the American Revolution*, 255–86.

25. The most detailed description of Eden's spy network remains Van Doren, *Secret History of the American Revolution*, 59–86.

26. Biographical sketches of Paul Wentworth can be found in Wharton, *Revolutionary Diplomatic Correspondence*, 1:661; and under "Paul Wentworth," in *Dictionary of American Biography*, 10:659. Wentworth's duties as a colonial agent for the province of New Hampshire are mentioned briefly in Kammen, *A Rope of Sand*, 283–87.

27. See Paul Wentworth to Silas Deane, Paris, 15 December 1777, in Add. Mss. 34414:531; and Wentworth's notes to William Eden, 12 December 1777, in Add. Mss. 34414: 529–30.

28. Wentworth to Eden, Paris, 17 December 1777, Add. Mss. 34414:433–43.

29. [Paul Wentworth], untitled report on America, n.d., Add. Mss. 34415:170–85. The report is in Wentworth's hand and is filed among Eden's papers of early 1778, before his departure to America, indicating that Eden at least referred to it while he was preparing the Carlisle Commission's instructions. Internal evidence indicates it was composed after the Declaration of Independence. Given the volume of Wentworth's correspondence with Eden increases through 1777, fixing composition at some point in 1777 or very early 1778 seems reasonable.

30. Wentworth went on to identify each of the said "Zealots" in each state, coding them "R." for "Rich"; "M." for "Mediocrity"; "S." for "Small fortune"; "E." for "Embarrassed"; and "R.R." for "Rank & Riches from the Rebellion." For example, Samuel Adams was awarded an "E." and was described as "an unprincipled Man in his Morals; Steady to one point in his Politicks, Independancy was his constant prayer" (see Add. Mss. 34415:170–85).

31. Eden to North, 7 February 1777, Add. Mss. 34415: 108–11.

32. For the role of William Howe and Frederick Howe in attempting to promote reconciliation of the American Revolutionary conflict, see Gruber, *The Howe Brothers and the American Revolution*.

33. "Hints," Add. Mss. 34415:200–203.

34. Ritcheson, *British Politics and the American Revolution*, 265–71.

35. Ibid., 271–74.

36. William Eden to Morton Eden, Philadelphia, 15 June 1778, Add. Mss. 34415:424–25.

37. George Washington to Henry Laurens, 9 June 1778, Item 152, 6:87–93, PCC.

38. See Joseph Reed to Esther Reed, 9 June 1778, *LDC*, 10:62.

39. For draft report of the committee, see Committee of Congress Draft Report, [11 June 1778], *LDC*, 10:71–72. On debate, see Josiah Bartlett to Nathaniel Folsom, York Town, 12 June 1778, *LDC*, 10:76–77; and Samuel Adams to James Warren, York Town, 13 June 1778, *LDC*, 10:85.

40. George Johnstone to Joseph Reed, 11 April 1778, *LDC*, 10:98–99.

41. Henry Laurens to Horatio Gates, 13 June 1778, *LDC*, 10:87.

42. Commissioners for Quieting Disorders to Henry Laurens and Congress, Philadelphia, 9 June 1778, in Davies, ed., *Documents of the American Revolution*, 15:136.

43. Richard Henry Lee to Thomas Jefferson, York, 16 June 1778, in *LDC*, 10:106–7.

44. Charles Thomson, Notes, 16 June 1778, *LDC*, 10:111–12.

45. *JCC*, 11:616.

46. Laurens to George Washington, York, 18 June 1778, *LDC*, 10:131–32.

47. Although there is no evidence of this proposal's author, the modern editors of *The Letters of the Delegates to Congress* believe that it was Drayton (see *LDC*, 10:115–16).

48. Laurens to Washington, 18 June 1778, *LDC*, 10:131–32.

49. Thomas McKean to Caesar Rodney, York, 17 June 1778, *LDC*, 10:129–30.

50. William Henry Drayton to the Carlisle Commissioners, York Town, 17 June 1778, *LDC*, 10:116–21.

51. Francis Dana's Notes, [16 June 1778], *LDC*, 10:104–5.

52. Commissioners to Lord George Germain, New York, 5 July 1778, in Davies, ed., *Documents of the American Revolution*, 15:159.

53. Earl of Carlisle to William Eden, private, 29 September [1778], Add. Mss. 34416:33–34.

54. Ibid.

55. For an overview of the events after early 1779, both on the battlefield and in the realm of politics, that led to American victory, see Middlekauff, *The Glorious Cause*, 396–581; Higginbotham, *The War for American Independence*; Bemis, *Diplomacy of the American Revolution*, 58–256; and Dull, *Diplomatic History of the American Revolution*, 97–163.

56. For the events of 1782, see Morris, *The Peacemakers*, 246–410; and Dull, *Diplomatic History of the American Revolution*, 137–63. John Adams's mission to the Netherlands is critically analyzed in Hutson, *John Adams and the Diplomacy of the American Revolution*, 102–16. For the opening of negotiations, see Bemis, *John Adams and the Diplomacy of the American Revolution*, 189–205.

57. Quote from Comte de Vergennes to Joseph Matthias Gérard de Rayneval, Versailles, 4 December 1782, *EN*, 1:706. For the final negotiations, see Dull, *Diplomatic History*, 144–51; Bemis, *The Diplomacy of the American Revolution*, 215–42. For

further background on the Peace of Paris, see DeConde, "Historians, the War for American Independence, and the Persistence of the Exceptionalist Ideal"; Kaplan, "The Treaty of Paris, 1783"; and the essays in Hoffman and Albert, eds., *Peace and the Peacemakers*.

58. For Vergennes's calculations in the making of the peace settlements, see Dull, *A Diplomatic History of the American Revolution*, 152–63. The Russian theater is discussed on 128–33.

59. Chevalier de la Luzerne to Comte de Vergennes, Philadelphia, 2 March 1781, *EN*, 1:150.

60. See Ritcheson, *The Aftermath of Revolution*, 33–34.

4. "Rendering Us Great and Respectable in the Eyes of the World"

1. Chevalier de la Luzerne to Comte de Vergennes, Philadelphia, 2 March 1781, *EN*, 1:150

2. The role of state-level debates in pushing Americans to embrace or reject the Philadelphia Constitution is a subject of much recent and classic literature. See, for example, Holton, *Unruly Americans and the Origins of the Constitution*; Bouton, *Taming Democracy*; Beeman, Botein, and Carter, eds., *Beyond Confederation*; Peter S. Onuf, *The Origins of the Federal Republic*; and G. S. Wood, *The Creation of the American Republic*.

3. A Plain Citizen, "To the Honorable the Convention of the State of Pennsylvania," *Independent Gazetteer*, 22 November 1787, DHRC 2:289.

4. Cumberland County Petition to the Pennsylvania Convention, 28 November 1787, DHRC, 2:299.

5. Hendrickson, *Peace Pact*; Marks, *Independence on Trial*.

6. This belief had informed the Plan of Treaties of 1776, which Adams had taken the lead in drafting, as well as a series of anonymous newspaper essays, *Letters from a Distinguished American*, Adams had authored and published. For the Plan of Treaties, see *PJA*, 4:260–302 and the discussion in chapter 2 of this book. For the newspaper essays, see [John Adams], *Letters from a Distinguished American*. Letters IV, VI, VII, VIII, IX, and XI are the essays most primarily concerned with commerce.

7. For Adams's conversation with Jay and Oswald, see "John Adams Diary," 9 December 1782, in John Adams, *Diary and Autobiography of John Adams*, 3:91–93, quotes on 91. For Jay's apartment location, see entry of 26 October 1782, ibid., 37.

8. These events are summarized briefly in Crowley, *The Privileges of Independence*, 68–75, and more extensively in Morris, *The Peacemakers*, 411–37. A more detailed treatment of British political developments in the period of the peace negotiations can be found in Ritcheson, *Aftermath of Revolution*, 3–32.

9. John Adams to Robert Livingston, Paris, 23 June 1783, in John Adams, *The Works of John Adams*, 8:74–75; hereafter cited as *Works*.

10. John Adams to Robert Livingston, Paris, 3 July 1783, in John Adams, *Works*, 8:77–81, quotes on 79.

11. John Adams to Robert Livingston, Paris, 14 July 1783, in John Adams, *Works*, 8:97–99, quote on 98.

12. For the reports and resolutions in Congress on this subject, see *JCC*, 25:626–32, quotes on 630. For more background on commercial competition between the states, see Matson and Onuf, *A Union of Interests*, 67–81.

13. All quotes from John Adams to John Jay, London, 19 July 1785, in John Adams, *Works*, 8:279–83.

14. All quotes from John Adams to John Jay, Auteuil, 8 May 1785, in John Adams, *Works*, 8:242–46.

15. John Adams to John Jay, Auteuil, 5 May 1785, in John Adams, *Works*, 8:240–41.

16. Jefferson's diplomatic mission to France has been a subject of many works; for a summary of his diplomatic activities, see W. H. Adams, *The Paris Years of Thomas Jefferson*, 159–206. For further background, see D. Malone, *Jefferson and the Rights of Man*, vol. 2 of *Jefferson and His Time*; and Kimball, *Jefferson: The Scene of Europe*.

17. Quotes from John Adams to Thomas Jefferson, London, 31 July 1786, in John Adams, *Works*, 8:412. For further details on the conflict between the United States and the North African Barbary States, see Allison, *The Crescent Obscured*, esp. 3–34.

18. "Report of the Committee on Indian Affairs," 15 October 1783, *JCC*, 25:681–95. Quote from *EAID*, 18:290.

19. This a somewhat overgeneralized portrait, as decisions about which side to take in the conflict often came down to a village or even individual level, rather than a national one, and many individual villages sought to maintain neutrality until absolutely necessary (see Fenton, *Great Law and the Longhouse*, 582–98; and Alan Taylor, *The Divided Ground*, 77–108).

20. The council fire at the Onondaga village symbolized the unity of the Iroquois League and Confederacy (see Fenton, *Great Law and the Longhouse*, 3–16).

21. Robert J. Surtees, "The Iroquois in Canada," in Jennings et al., eds., *The History and Culture of Iroquois Diplomacy*, 67–83; Taylor, *Divided Ground*, 111–41. For the complexity of Iroquois loyalties during the American Revolution, see Tiro, "A 'Civil War'?"; for Brant's Grand River settlement, see Taylor, *Divided Ground*, 122–28; Fenton, *Great Law and the Longhouse*, 582–603; Calloway, *The American Revolution in Indian Country*, generally, 26–64, and specifically, 129–57.

22. "Report of the Committee on Indian Affairs," 15 October 1783, *EAID*, 18:290.

23. See, for example, E. Douglass to General [Philip] Schuyler, Albany, 2 August 1783, *EAID*, 18:284–85; and Philip Schuyler to the Six Nations, Saratoga, 29 July 1783, ibid., 18:286–87.

24. "Report of the Committee on Indian Affairs," 15 October 1783, *EAID*, 18:291.

25. Quotes from "Report of the Committee on Indian Affairs," 15 October 1783, *EAID*, 18:292–93. For a summary of the Federalist Indian policies of the 1790s, see Bernard W. Sheehan, "The Indian Problem in the Northwest: From Conquest to Philanthropy," in Hoffman and Albert, eds., *Launching the "Extended Republic,"* 190–222; and Sheehan, *Seeds of Extinction*.

26. James Duane (1733–1797) was a delegate to the Continental Congress from

the state of New York "almost continuously" until 1783. A member of Governor George Clinton's council when Clinton and Washington received New York from the British in November 1783, Duane was appointed mayor of New York City on 4 February 1784. He served as mayor until September 1789. He married into the Livingston family (marrying Mary, daughter of Robert Livingston Jr. in 1759), and throughout his career was involved in land speculation and development, primarily in the Mohawk Valley and Vermont (Source: "Duane, James," in *Dictionary of American Biography*, 3:465–66).

27. All quotes from James Duane to George Clinton, [July–August 1784], in Clinton, *Papers of George Clinton*, 8:328; also printed in *EAID*, 18:299. For further background, see Taylor, *Divided Ground*, 142–45.

28. All quotes from James Duane to George Clinton, [July–August 1784], *EAID*, 18:299–300.

29. George Clinton to U.S. Indian Commissioners, Albany, 13 August 1784, *EAID*, 18:301.

30. U.S. Commissioners to George Clinton, New York, 19 August 1784, *EAID*, 18:303.

31. For the growth of Congress as an arbiter between jurisdictions, see Onuf, *The Origins of the Federal Republic*, esp. 3–20. For further background on Clinton's role in the diplomacy, see Taylor, *Divided Ground*, 142–54.

32. See "Extracts from the Proceedings of the Treaty of Fort Stanwix between New York and the Six Nations," 4–10 September 1784, *EAID*, 18:305–12. For background on the state negotiations, see Taylor, *Divided Ground*, 154–57.

33. "Extracts from the Proceedings of the Treaty of Fort Stanwix Between New York and the Six Nations," 4–10 September 1784, *EAID*, 18:305–12.

34. "Proceedings of the United States and the Six Nations at Fort Stanwix," 3–22 October 1784, *EAID*, 18:313–26; Fenton, *Great Law and the Longhouse*, 615–20. For more details of the dismissal of Schuyler from the site of the negotiations, see Taylor, *Divided Ground*, 157–58.

35. "Proceedings of the United States and the Six Nations at Fort Stanwix," 3–22 October 1784, *EAID*, 18:313–26; Fenton, *Great Law and the Longhouse*, 615–20.

36. Quotes from "Proceedings of the United States and the Six Nations at Fort Stanwix," 3–22 October 1784, *EAID*, 18:313–26; Fenton, *Great Law and the Longhouse*, 615–20. For the Iroquois desire to preserve their sovereignty and resist American claims to preemption, see Taylor, *Divided Ground*, 157–62.

37. "Proceedings of the United States and the Six Nations at Fort Stanwix," 3–22 October 1784, *EAID*, 18:323–25; Fenton, *The Great Law and the Longhouse*, 618–20.

38. For Hill's claims of coercion at Fort Stanwix, see Taylor, *Divided Ground*, 158–59. For the State of New York's continuing attempts to acquire Iroquois lands during the remainder of the 1780s, see 169–202.

39. The movement of Anglo-Americans into the Ohio Valley began in the middle of the eighteenth century, but accelerated in the years before the American Revolution. Conflict between settlers and American Indians often resulted, and such con-

flicts were folded into and exacerbated by the War for Independence. Violence did not abate in the years immediately after the Treaty of Paris. An overview of the conflict for the region is available in White, *Middle Ground*: 366–412 for the War for Independence, and 413–486 for the immediate aftermath and the period under discussion in this chapter. Also valuable is the imperial perspective on events provided in Hinderaker, *Elusive Empires*, 185–267. The settlement of Kentucky is discussed in Aron, *How the West Was Lost*, esp. 5–57. For the American Indian perspective, see Calloway's account of the fate of the Maquachake villages of the Shawnee in "Maquachake: The Perils of Neutrality in the Ohio Country," in his *American Revolution in Indian Country*, 158–81. As Calloway's account makes clear, sporadic violence between the settler communities in Kentucky and various American Indian villages and confederations of villages in the Great Lakes basin persisted after the formal end of the war in 1783.

40. All quotes from Barthélemi Tardiveau to Josiah Harmar, Post Vincennes, 6 August 1787, in Thornbrough, ed., *Outpost on the Wabash*, 26–31.

41. For an overview of Madison's and Jefferson's correspondence with each other during this period, and the subjects discussed, see Koch, *Jefferson & Madison*, 15–96. Also valuable, for an overview, are the introductory essays to the relevant sections of J. M. Smith, *The Republic of Letters*.

42. This gradual change in Madison's thought is described in Banning, *Sacred Fire of Liberty*, 34–75; and Rakove, *Original Meanings*, 35–56.

43. James Madison, "Notes on Ancient and Modern Confederacies," ca. April-June 1786, in *PJM*, 9:3–24. For the composition of the "Notes," see also Miller, *The Business of May Next*, 14–21.

44. Madison, "Notes on Confederacies," *PJM*, 9:7–8.

45. Ibid., 9:8–11.

46. Ibid., 9:11–18.

47. Rakove, "Solving a Constitutional Puzzle:" The Treatymaking Clause as a Case Study"; Marks, *Independence on Trial*, 142–66.

48. Quotes from John Jay, *Federalist* No.3, in Cooke, ed., *The Federalist* (Middletown, Conn.: 1961), 16–17.

49. Quotes from John Jay, *Federalist* No. 4, in Cooke, ed., *The Federalist*, 20–21.

50. Jay's full discussion of the necessity of a strong federal union to serve the United States' interests in the realm of foreign affairs is in Cooke, ed., *The Federalist* Nos. 3–5, 13–27. For Hamilton's essays outlining the hazards of interstate conflict, as well as the dangers of standing armies, see ibid., Nos. 6–9, 29–56.

51. Quotes from Alexander Hamilton, in Cooke, ed., *The Federalist*, No.9, 55.

52. The phrase is from Madison's famous letter to Thomas Jefferson of 24 October 1787, in which Madison outlined in great detail his thoughts on the proper organization of the American government, and specifically his unhappiness with the Philadelphia Convention's rejection of his proposal to give Congress a veto over state legislation. For the letter and a discussion of it, see *PJM*, 10:206–15, quote on 214. The best discussion of Madison's constitutional thinking during the Confederation

and Federal periods is Banning's *The Sacred Fire of Liberty*, specifically his chapters on the Philadelphia Convention (111–91) and those dealing with his collaboration with Hamilton and participation in the Virginia Convention (195–264). As I hope the remainder of this discussion bears out, I am in substantial agreement with much of what Banning argues, foremost that a coherent vision of republicanism informed Madison's thinking on constitutional questions throughout the 1780s and 1790s, and that there is a great deal of consistency between the stances of Madison, the architect of the Constitution, and Madison, the opposition leader. The key to seeing this consistency is understanding that the vision of the opposition that Madison and Jefferson would head was a vision premised not simply on how a republic functioned, but on how a system of republics functioned—that is, how republican governments interlocked and interacted with one another.

53. Patrick Henry, Virginia Convention Debates, 4 June 1788, DHRC, 9:929–30.
54. Edmund Randolph, Virginia Convention Debates, 4 June 1788, DHRC, 9:935.
55. George Mason, Virginia Convention Debates, 18 June 1788, DHRC, 10:1380–81.
56. Patrick Henry, Virginia Convention Debates, 4 June 1788, DHRC, 9:930.

5. "To Be Considered as Foreign Nations"

1. Quotes from George Washington to John Jay, New York, [8] June 1789, *PGW-PS*, 2:455. For Washington's notes, see Washington, "Notes and Minutes," 4–8 June 1789, Series 4, General Correspondence, Papers of George Washington, LC. For Knox's memoranda, see Henry Knox to Washington, 6 July 1789, *PGW-PS*, 3:123–29; Knox to Washington, 7 July 1789, *PGW-PS*, 3:134–41, 141–43, 143–45.

2. Elbridge Gerry, speech of 16 June 1789, House of Representatives, in *Documentary History of the First Federal Congress*, 9:878–79; series hereafter cited as *DHFFC*.

3. The Foreign Affairs Bill passed the House by a vote of 29 to 22 on 24 June 1789; was passed by the Senate on 18 July 1789; and its amended version passed the House again two days later. President Washington signed the Foreign Affairs Act into law on 27 July 1789. The text of the bill and its legislative history can be found in *DHFFC*, 4:689–97.

4. James Madison, speech of 16 June 1789, House of Representatives, *DHFFC*, 9:866–69. The quotes are from 868–69.

5. Egbert Benson, speech of 17 June 1789, House of Representatives, *DHFFC*, 9:931–34.

6. For an overview of Jefferson's experiences in France, see Kimball, *Jefferson: The Scene of Europe*; D. Malone, *Jefferson and the Rights of Man*, vol. 2 of *Jefferson and His Time*; Ellis, *American Sphinx*, 64–117; W. H. Adams, *The Paris Years of Thomas Jefferson*; and Halliday, *Understanding Thomas Jefferson*.

7. Jefferson, "Opinion on the Powers of the Senate Respecting Diplomatic Appointments," New York, 24 April 1790, *PTJ*, 16:378–79.

8. Jefferson, "Opinion on the Powers of the Senate Respecting Diplomatic Appointments," New York, 24 April 1790, *PTJ*, 16:379–80.

9. My reading of Federalist statecraft and state building is indebted to three works

of slightly different interpretative casts: Kohn, *Eagle and Sword*; Walling, *Republican Empire*; and Edling, *A Revolution in Favor of Government*.

10. Henry Knox to William Blount, 22 April 1792, *ASP-IA*, 1:252–53, quote on 253. The view of human nature as primarily self-interested was a staple of Scottish Enlightenment thought and in particular of the writings of David Hume, a philosopher whose influence on Hamilton and the Federalists has been often noted. For Hume's influence, see Elkins and McKitrick, *The Age of Federalism*, 105–13.

11. The best description of Federalist Indian policy, to which I am deeply indebted, is Bernard W. Sheehan, "The Indian Problem in the Northwest: From Conquest to Philanthropy," in Hoffman and Albert, eds., *Launching the "Extended Republic,"* 190–222. Also important are Sheehan's early work, *Seeds of Extinction*; and Prucha, *American Indian Policy in the Formative Years*.

12. Henry Knox to George Washington, War Office, 7 July 1789, in *PGW-PS*, 3:137–38.

13. Henry Knox to George Washington, War Office, 7 July 1789, in *PGW-PS*, 3:138–39.

14. Much of the material discussed in the following paragraphs and my thinking on early Federalist Indian diplomacy are drawn from research done on the Treaty of New York of 1790. These findings made their initial public appearance as an unpublished paper: "'In the White Town of the Grand Council': Indian Images and Geopolitical Realities in the Treaty of New York, 1789–1790," presented to the Society for Historians of the Early American Republic in Lexington, Kentucky, July 1999. A discussion of this material can also be found in Onuf and Sadosky, *Jeffersonian America*, 190–94.

15. Jefferson queried Knox on the proper etiquette for the ratification ceremony for the Treaty of New York (Jefferson to Knox, New York, 12 August 1790, *PTJ*, 17:340–41).

16. This opinion was articulated in the context of the status of Georgia lands, but in a matter officially separate from the treaty negotiations. In May 1790, Jefferson committed to writing his opinion of the first round of land sales the government of Georgia made to the various Yazoo companies, under an act of the legislature dated 21 December 1789. In Jefferson's understanding, the sales of these huge tracts of land were made to "certain companies" even though "the Indian right has never yet been acquired." The sales were also made "with a proviso in the grant which implies that those individuals may take measures for extinguishing the Indian right under the authority of [the state] government." Jefferson found this situation unacceptable.

In Jefferson's understanding, as well as Knox's, only the federal government had the right, under the Constitution, to acquire title to Indian lands. Jefferson's logic was firmly rooted in his conception of the law of the nations. In Jefferson's mind, it was consistent with the laws of nature for a people to claim and occupy a vacant country. However, when, as in the case of North America, such a country was "thinly occupied by another nation, the right of the natives forms an exception to that of the new-comers." The new arrivals, on claiming the land, held sovereignty vis-à-vis any other potential colonizers, and thus held "the exclusive privilege of the acquiring the native right by purchase or other just means." Jefferson elaborated further that "this is called the right or pre-emption; and is become a principle of the law of nations, fundamental with respect to America." Jefferson then quoted the Constitution at length, demonstrating that the state governments, including Georgia, had ceded the right of pre-emption "to the general government." Jefferson thus affirmed that treaties with the Indians nations, and the land sales resulting from them, had to proceed according to strict constitutional principles, which were grounded in a still-evolving law of nations (see Jefferson, "Opinion on Certain Georgia Land Grants," 3 May 1790, *PTJ*, 16:406–9).

17. Jefferson, "Opinion on McGillivray's Monopoly," 29 July 1790, *PTJ*, 17:288–89.
18. Jefferson to Knox, New York, 26 August 1790, *PTJ*, 17:430–31.
19. Jefferson to Knox, Philadelphia, 10 August 1791, *PTJ*, 22:27–28.
20. Summaries of Hamiltonian financial policy can be found in Elkins and McKitrick, *Age of Federalism*, 92–131, 257–82; and Herbert E. Sloan, "Hamilton's Second Thoughts: Federalist Finance Revisited," in Ben-Atar and Oberg, eds., *Federalists Reconsidered*, 61–76. Dimensions of the Republican response can be found in Banning, *The Jeffersonian Persuasion*, 126–60; McCoy, *The Elusive Republic*, 136–65; and Sloan, *Principle and Interest*.
21. The literature on the French Revolution is, as one might imagine, immense. The most recent growth in English-language literature coincided with the 1989 bicentennial of the beginning of the French Revolution. An accessible survey of the Revolution's history produced at this time is Doyle, *The Oxford History of the French Revolution*. Other important recent surveys of the Revolution's history that have shaped my understanding of the Revolution include Schama, *Citizens*; and Furet, *Revolutionary France*. For the National Convention period in particular, see Palmer, *Twelve Who Ruled*. For the diplomatic history of the period, see Palmer, *The Age of Democratic Revolution*; and Doyle, *The Old European Order*, 265–356.
22. According to Jefferson, Hamilton first broached the question of Genet's reception at a cabinet meeting on 25 February 1793. The question hung in the air throughout the month of March, with Hamilton being the greatest proponent against his reception, and Washington and the remainder of the cabinet generally being for it (see Jefferson, "Notes on the Reception of Edmund Charles Genet," 30 March 1793, *PTJ*, 25:469–70). Hamilton's misgivings about the formal reception of Genet hinged on the fact that his formal reception would constitute a recognition of the French National Assembly as the sole legitimate bearer of the sovereignty of the French nation—which was somewhat problematic given the internal political state of France in early 1793—and the fact that many European sovereigns at war with France were pledged to the restoration of the Bourbon dynasty. Hamilton and Knox authored a joint memorandum to Washington outlining these concerns (see Hamilton and Knox to Washington, Philadelphia, 2 May 1793, in Hamilton, *Papers of Alexander Hamilton*, 14:367–96). Despite these continued misgivings, by early April, Hamilton had come to believe that the formal reception of Genet was the only tenable course of action (see

Hamilton to John Jay, 9 April 1793, in Hamilton, *Papers of Alexander Hamilton*, 14:297–99). The question was officially settled in the affirmative during the cabinet meeting of 19 April 1793 (see Jefferson, "Cabinet Opinion on Washington's Questions on Neutrality and the Alliance with France," 19 April 1793, *PTJ*, 25:570–71). Hamilton and Knox submitted their reservation pursuant to this cabinet meeting.

23. Washington to Hamilton, Mount Vernon, 12 April 1793, in Hamilton, *Papers of Alexander Hamilton*, 14:315.

24. A summary of the issues and events involved is available in Elkins and McKitrick, *Age of Federalism*, 303–54. A more extended treatment can be found in Ammon, *The Genet Mission*.

25. The essays are printed in Hamilton, *Papers of Alexander Hamilton* 15:33–43, 55–63, 65–69, 82–86, 90–95, 100–106, 130–35.

26. By the time the third "Pacificus" essay had appeared, Jefferson was horrified that no writer was challenging Hamilton: "Nobody answers him, and his doctrine will therefore be taken for confessed." It was up to Madison to refute Hamilton: "For god's sake, my dear Sir, take up your pen, select the most striking heresies, and cut him to pieces in the face of the public" (Jefferson to Madison, Philadelphia, 7 July 1793, *PTJ* 26:443–44). For a more thorough discussion of the origins of the "Helvidius" essays, see the editorial note in *PJM*, 15:64–66. See also Ketcham, *James Madison*, 345–48; and Banning, *The Sacred Fire of Liberty*, 374–78. The essays are printed in *PJM*, 15:66–74, 80–87, 95–103, 106–10, and 113–20.

27. Madison, "Helvidius, Number 1," 24 August 1793, *PJM*, 15: 66–73, quotes on 72.

28. The classic study of the negotiation of the Jay Treaty is Bemis, *Jay's Treaty*. For the politics of ratification, see Combs, *The Jay Treaty*. For a recent exploration of the dynamics of the public debate over the Jay Treaty, see Estes, *The Jay Treaty Debate*.

29. The classic study of the Treaty of San Lorenzo remains Bemis, *Pinckney's Treaty*.

30. For the negotiation of the Treaty of Greenville, see Andrew R. L. Cayton, "'Noble Actors' upon 'the Theatre of Honour': Power and Civility in the Treaty of Greenville," in Cayton and Teute, eds., *Contact Points*, 235–69. See also Sheehan, "The Indian Problem in the Northwest," in Hoffman and Albert, eds., *Launching the "Extended Republic*," 190–222; Griffin, *American Leviathan*, 240–71.

31. See Jefferson, "Report on Commerce," 16 December 1793, *PTJ*, 27:567–79; as well as the Editorial Note, *PTJ*, 27:532–35.

32. James Madison, *Political Observations*, 20 April 1795, *PJM*, 15:511–34, quotes on 513, 518, and 522, respectively.

33. See DeConde, "Washington's Farewell, the French Alliance, and the Election of 1796."

34. For the text of the Farewell Address, see George Washington, "Farewell Address," 19 September 1796, in Washington, *The Writings of George Washington*, 35:214–39.

35. Benjamin Hawkins, George Clymer, and Andrew Pickens to James McHenry, Colerain, 16 June 1796, in *ASP-IA*, 1:597.

36. These two treaties were the Treaty of Galphinton and the Treaty of Shoulderbone Creek.

37. Henry Knox to George Washington, War Department, 16 December 1793, *ASP-IA*, 1:362.

38. For details of the Yazoo transactions and their aftermath, see Clark and Guice, *The Old Southwest*, 72–81.

39. "An Act for Appropriating a Part of the Unlocated Territory of this State for Payment of Late State Troops, and for Other Purposes Therein Mentioned," enclosure to George Washington to the Congress, 17 February 1795, *ASP-IA*, 1:551–55.

40. Benjamin Hawkins and George Clymer to Henry Gaither, Coleraine, 26 May 1796, *ASP-IA*, 1:589.

41. Hawkins, Clymer, and Pickens to James McHenry, Colerain, 30 May 1796, and Hawkins, Clymer, and Pickens to Commissioners of Georgia, Colerain, 30 May 1796, both in *ASP-IA*, 1:590.

42. James Hendricks to Commissioners of the United States, Colerain, 31 May 1796, *ASP-IA*, 1:591.

43. Hawkins, Clymer, and Pickens to Commissioners of Georgia, Colerain, 1 June 1796, *ASP-IA*, 1:592.

44. Treaty Journal, 16–18 June 1796, *ASP-IA*, 1:597–98.

45. Treaty Journal, 22–30 June 1796, *ASP-IA*, 1:599–610.

46. Hawkins, Clymer, and Pickens to James McHenry, Colerain, 1 July 1796, *ASP-IA*, 1:610–11.

47. Hawkins, Clymer, and Pickens to Jared Irwin, Colerain, 1 July 1796, *ASP-IA*, 1:612–13.

48. The Federalists also undermined their own cause with the establishment of the Indian factory system, as provided for in the Indian Trade and Intercourse Acts. James Seagrove, the federal Indian superintendent, hinted this when appointed factor Edward Price arrived to take charge of the new Creek factory during the winter of 1795–96. The factory system was not popular with local Indian merchants, who were actually sympathetic to Federalist aims of maintaining a regular Indian trade and slowing expansion. By taking the Indian trade out of the hands of local, state-level traders, the Federalists alienated the only "natural" white constituency for their plan of trade and "civilization" (see Edward Price to Tench Frances, Savannah, 26 December 1795, in "Letter-Book of the Creek Trading House," Record Group 75, Microcopy 4, Roll 1, National Archives, Washington, D.C.).

49. See DeConde, *The Quasi-War*; and Kurtz, *The Presidency of John Adams*.

6. Enlarging "Our Association"

1. For all quotes, see E. S. Brown, ed., *William Plumer's Memorandum of Proceedings in the United States Senate, 1803–1807*, 211–14; hereafter cited as *Plumer's Memorandum*. For Jefferson's practice of politics at the presidential dinner table, see Allgor, *Parlor Politics*, 23–27. The home of the president of the United States was known as the "President's House" through Jefferson's presidency. It was first informally called the "White House" in 1811 and not officially labeled as such until 1901.

2. *Plumer's Memorandum*, 212–13. For a description and analysis of politics of the Mammoth Cheese, see Jeffrey L. Pasley, "The Cheese and the Words: Popular Politi-

cal Culture and Participatory Democracy in the Early American Republic," in Waldstreicher, Pasley, and Robertson, *Beyond the Founders*, 31–56. For the diplomacy of the Louisiana Purchase, see Lewis, *The Louisiana Purchase*; DeConde, *This Affair of Louisiana*; and E. S. Brown, *The Constitutional History of the Louisiana Purchase*.

3. For consumption as a driving force in the politics of the era of the American Revolution, see Breen, *The Marketplace of Revolution*; and for eighteenth-century consumption more generally, see Bushman, *The Refinement of America*; and Brewer and Porter, eds., *Consumption and the World of Goods*.

4. For a summary of Jeffersonian Republican thought about political economy, see McCoy, *The Elusive Republic*.

5. See Onuf and Sadosky, *Jeffersonian America*, 124–71, for an overview. My view of the Jeffersonians' view of commerce and politics owes much to Ben-Atar, *The Origins of Jeffersonian Commercial Policy and Diplomacy*.

6. D. Malone, *Jefferson the President: Second Term, 1805–1809*, vol. 5 of *Jefferson and His Time*, 3–5.

7. Thomas Jefferson, Second Inaugural Address, 4 March 1805, *TJW*, 518–23, quotes on 518.

8. Quotes from Jefferson, Second Inaugural Address, 4 March 1805, *TJW*, 519; Jefferson, First Inaugural Address, 4 March 1801, ibid., 494. My reading of Jefferson's political and diplomatic polices generally, and the Louisiana Purchase and the second inaugural address particularly, is deeply indebted to Peter S. Onuf's scholarship on Jefferson (see Onuf, *Jefferson's Empire*, esp. 53–79; Onuf, "The Expanding Union," in Konig, ed., *Devising Liberty*, 50–80; Onuf, "The Revolution of 1803," and "The Louisiana Purchase and American Federalism," in Onuf, *The Mind of Thomas Jefferson*, 99–108, 121–36).

9. Jefferson, Second Inaugural Address, 4 March 1805, *TJW*, 520. For the origins of the Knoxian "civilization" program, as well as Jefferson's formulation of United States' Indian policy during the Mississippi Crisis, see chapter 5 of this book. Further background on Jefferson's engagement with the question of place of the American Indian in American political development and world history can be found in Wallace, *Jefferson and the Indians*; and Sheehan, *Seeds of Extinction*.

10. Rather than favoring the interests of one or two sections (the South and West) ahead of the interests of the nation as a whole, as his opponents feared, Jeffersonian political economy had a strong unionist streak, one that recognized the inherent interdependence of each section on transatlantic markets. Jefferson saw each part of the union engaging with the transatlantic market in its own way (the South by providing staples, the West and Mid-Atlantic by providing agricultural foodstuffs, the Northeast by providing the merchant marine and merchant capital) contributing to good of the whole. Jefferson's commercial policy and diplomacy sought to facilitate this division of labor within the union, rather than set sections against each other (see Onuf and Sadosky, *Jeffersonian America*, 128–48 and passim; and Spivak, *Jefferson's English Crisis*, 1–12).

11. For an overview of the diplomatic history of this period, see McKay and Scott,

The Rise of the Great Powers, 272–311. For Haiti in particular, see Dubois, *A Colony of Citizens*.

12. In the *Essex* decision, and a similar case involving the ship *Aurora*, "English judges held that the goods' ultimate destination determined their national character, and if the ultimate destination was a French or Spanish port, the Rule of 1756" applied. My discussion is drawn largely from Spivak, *Jefferson's English Crisis*, which has one of the most comprehensive discussions of the diplomacy and politics surrounding these issues (see, in particular, 12–30, quote on 24). The foremost advocate for the American position that "free ships made free goods" was Secretary of State James Madison, who published a nearly two-hundred-page pamphlet on the subject: [James Madison], *An Examination of the British Doctrine, Which Subjects to Capture a Neutral Trade, not Open in Time of Peace* (Washington, 1806), reprinted in Madison, *Writings of James Madison*, 8:204–375. See also B. Perkins, *Prologue to War*, esp. 32–100; Stagg, *Mr. Madison's War*; and Egan, *Neither Peace nor War*.

13. McKay and Scott, *The Rise of the Great Powers*, 311–25; Broers, Europe *under Napoleon*, 94–97. For the Napoleonic conflicts as the first modern "total" war, see Bell, *The First Total War*.

14. For James Stephen and *War in Disguise*, see B. Perkins, *Prologue to War*, 15, 77–79.

15. For America's friends in the British public and political spheres, brewer Samuel Whitbread and banker Alexander Baring, see B. Perkins, *Prologue to War*, 18–20. For a sketch of Perceval, see ibid., 12–13.

16. See Broers, *Europe under Napoleon*, 94–97; for the Continental System and the larger schema of Napoleon's governance of Europe, see ibid., generally, as well as Connelly, *Napoleon's Satellite Kingdoms*. For Britain's response, see Mori, *Britain in the Age of the French Revolution*, 205–10; and Hilton, *A Mad, Bad, and Dangerous People?* 210–21.

17. For the Monroe-Pinkney-Auckland negotiations, see B. Perkins, *Prologue to War*, 101–39.

18. For the *Chesapeake*–*Leopard* Affair, see Spivak, *Jefferson's English Crisis*, 70–101; and Tucker and Reuter, *Injured Honor*. For the embargo, see Spivak, *Jefferson's English Crisis*, 102–36; and B. Perkins, *Prologue to War*, 40–183.

19. George W. Campbell, *Report on Foreign Relations*, 22 November 1808, *Annals of Congress*, 10th Cong., 2nd sess., 514–18.

20. All quotes from George W. Campbell, *Report on Foreign Relations*, 22 November 1808, *Annals of Congress* 10th Cong., 2nd sess., 514–18.

21. For Jackson's remarks, see Andrew Jackson, "Address to the Citizens of Nashville," [16 January 1809], in Jackson, *The Papers of Andrew Jackson*, 2:210–11; hereafter cited as *Jackson Papers*. For details of Jackson's life and career during these years, see Remini, *Andrew Jackson and the Course of American Empire*. For the Jeffersonian Republicans' drive to preserve section unity during the embargo, see Spivak, *Jefferson's English Crisis*, 156–97.

22. For all quotes, see Willie Blount to Andrew Jackson, Knoxville, 28 December 1809, in Jackson, *Jackson Papers*, 2:226–27.

23. For the end of the embargo and the beginning of nonimportation, see B. Perkins, *Prologue to War*, 178–83; and Spivak, *Jefferson's English Crisis*, 180–225.

24. Blount to Jackson, 28 December 1809, in Jackson, *Jackson Papers*, 2:226–27. The emergence of Knoxian Indian policy and its persistence into the Jefferson administration was discussed in the previous chapter.

25. For the evolution and persistence of the idea of removal in the thinking of Jefferson and other Jeffersonian Republicans, see Horsman, *Expansion and American Indian Policy*; Sheehan, *Seeds of Extinction*; and Wallace, *Jefferson and the Indians*.

26. Blount to Jackson, 28 December 1809, in Jackson, *Jackson Papers*, 2:227.

27. The ground truly was contested (see DuVal, *The Native Ground*).

28. The Georgia Compact was the result of a federal commission led by three of Jefferson's cabinet members—James Madison, Albert Gallatin, and Levi Lincoln—to resolve the controversial Yazoo land fraud. After the state of Georgia had sold claims to its entire western domain to four private companies in 1795, it was revealed that nearly every member of the Georgia legislature was either involved with one of the companies or had taken a bribe from parties who were. Subsequent legislation repealed the sale, but in turn sparked litigation on behalf of the original shareholders. Despite the compact, the Yazoo litigation was not ultimately resolved until the Supreme Court case of *Fletcher v. Peck* (1810) (see C. Peter Magrath, *Yazoo, Land and Politics in the New Republic*, Georgia Compact on 34–36).

29. Jefferson to Henry Dearborn, "Hints on the subject of Indian boundaries," 29 December 1802, Series 1, General Correspondence, Thomas Jefferson Papers, LC.

30. Jefferson to Dearborn, 15 February 1803, Series 1, General Correspondence, Thomas Jefferson Papers, LC. This letter had a wish list of sorts, as Jefferson prioritized the five Indian nations with which he wanted treaties concluded as quickly as possible.

31. My argument here is influenced deeply by the argument put forward by Wallace, *Jefferson and the Indians*, 206–40. For additional background see Prucha, *American Indian Treaties*, 105–28; Prucha, *The Great Father*, 1:61–158; and Onuf, *Jefferson's Empire*, 1–52.

32. Jefferson to Dearborn, 29 December 1802, Series 1, General Correspondence, Jefferson Papers, LC.

33. Jefferson to William Henry Harrison, 27 February 1803, *TJW*, 1118.

34. For Harrison's Indian diplomacy, see Owens, "Jeffersonian Benevolence on the Ground," fur trade detail on 428. The Treaty of Fort Wayne (1809) can be found in *ASP-IA*, 1:760–62. Further background on Indian diplomacy during Jefferson's presidency can be found in Prucha, *American Indian Treaties*, 105–28. In calling the policies of Jefferson and Harrison "Machiavellian," I am taking my cue from Merrill Peterson who, as editor of the Library of America's edition of Jefferson's writings, captioned the 27 February 1803 letter from Jefferson to Harrison, "Machiavellian Benevolence and the Indians" (see *TJW*, 1117).

35. For background on Jackson's campaign against the Creeks, I have relied on Remini, *Andrew Jackson and His Indian Wars*, 50–93. The religious revival of

Tecumseh and Tenskwatawa is discussed in Edmunds, *The Shawnee Prophet*. It is fit into the framework of American Indian religious revivals more generally in Dowd, *A Spirited Resistance*. For the Red Sticks, see Martin, *Sacred Revolt*. The Creeks' accommodation and resistance to European market relations is cataloged in Saunt, *A New Order of Things*. The Creek nation's development from the perspective of Benjamin Hawkins is charted in Etheridge, *Creek Country*. For Fort Mims, see Martin, *Sacred Revolt*, 156–57.

36. Remini, *Jackson and His Indian Wars*, 62–74; for quotes, see Andrew Jackson to Thomas Pinckney, Bend of the Tallapoosa, 28 March 1814, in Jackson, *Jackson Papers*, 3:52–53.

37. Jackson to Thomas Pinckney, 28 March 1814, in Jackson, *Jackson Papers*, 3:52–53; Remini, *Jackson and His Indian Wars*, 75–79.

38. Remini, *Jackson and His Indian Wars*, 83–87.

39. All quotes from Jackson to John Williams, Nashville, 18 May 1814, in Jackson, *Jackson Papers* 3:3–75; Remini, *Jackson and His Indian Wars*, 84–93.

40. Lewis, *The American Union and the Problem of Neighborhood*.

41. See D. Perkins, *A History of the Monroe Doctrine*. For John Quincy Adams's role, see Bemis, *John Quincy Adams and the Foundations of American Foreign Policy*; and Lewis, *John Quincy Adams*.

42. For an overview of the War of 1812, see Hickey, *The War of 1812*; Stagg, *Mr. Madison's War*; and Reginald Horsman, *The War of 1812*.

43. For a description of Goulburn's life and early career, see Zuehlke, *For Honour's Sake*, 140–46.

44. For details of the negotiation, see John Quincy Adams, Diary, 9 August 1814, *Memoirs of John Quincy Adams*, 3:7–10, quote on 8. For official notes of this meeting, see *ASP-FA*, 3:708.

45. John Quincy Adams, Diary, 1 September 1814, *Memoirs of John Quincy Adams*, 3: 27–28.

46. John Quincy Adams, Diary, 1 September 1814, *Memoirs of John Quincy Adams*, 3: 28.

Epilogue: The Cherokee Lawyer

1. For the hiring of Wirt by the Cherokees, see Editorial Note on *Cherokee Nation v. Georgia* in Marshall, *Papers of John Marshall*, 12:43. For Wirt's role in the 1824 taxation controversy, see McLoughlin, *Cherokee Renascence in the New Republic*, 322–24.

2. McLoughlin, *Cherokee Renascence in the New Republic*, 428–38; Marshall, *Papers of John Marshall*, 12:41–43; Prucha, *American Indian Treaties*, 156–65.

3. All quotes from William Wirt to Dabney Carr, Baltimore, 21 June 1830, in Kennedy, *Memoirs of the Life of William Wirt*, 2:290–96. For details of Wirt's legal strategy and the origins of the *Cherokee Nation v. Georgia* case, see Marshall, *Papers of John Marshall*, 12:43–51. For Ross's attempt to hire Webster, see John Ross to Jeremiah Evarts, Head of Coosa, Cherokee Nation, 24 July 1830, in Ross, *The Papers of Chief John Ross*, 1:195–96.

4. "Bill Filed on Behalf of the Cherokee Nation v. the State of Georgia," in Peters, ed., *The Case of the Cherokee Nation against the State of Georgia*, 2–31, quote on 5–6.

5. Ibid., both quotes on 12.

6. The story of the transformation of the Cherokee in these years is told in detail in McLoughlin, *Cherokee Renascence in the New Republic*, 109–365. See also Perdue, *Cherokee Women*, 115–34; Perdue, *Slavery and the Evolution of Cherokee Society*; and H. T. Malone, *The Cherokees of the Old South*.

7. "Cherokee Nation v. Georgia," in Marshall, *Papers of John Marshall*, 12:41–61

8. McLoughlin, *Cherokee Renascence in the New Republic*, 448–51.

9. For the notion of the Hobbesian "real-state," see Deudney, "The Philadelphian System," 195–200.

10. Wirt quote from Kennedy, *Memoirs of the Life of William Wirt*, 2: 297. For a wider discussion of the equivocal record of the modern state, see Onuf and Onuf, *Nations, Markets, and War*; and Scott, *Seeing Like a State*.

Bibliography

Archival Sources

"Letter-Book of the Creek Trading House." National Archives, Washington, D.C.
Papers of the Continental Congress. National Archives, Washington, D.C.
Papers of Silas Deane. Connecticut Historical Society, Hartford.
Papers of Thomas Jefferson. Library of Congress, Washington, D.C.
Papers of George Washington. Library of Congress, Washington, D.C.

Other Sources

Adams, John. *Diary and Autobiography of John Adams.* Edited by L. H. Butterfield. 4 vols. New York: Atheneum, 1964.
———. *Letters from a Distinguished American: Twelve Essays by John Adams on American Foreign Policy, 1780.* Edited by James H. Hutson. Washington: Library of Congress, 1978.
———. *The Papers of John Adams.* Edited by Robert J. Taylor, Mary-Jo Kline, and Gregg L. Lint. 14 vols. to date. Cambridge: Harvard University Press, 1977– .
———. *The Works of John Adams, Second President of the United States.* Edited by Charles Francis Adams. 10 vols. Boston: Little, Brown, 1850–56.
Adams, John Quincy. *Memoirs of John Quincy Adams.* Edited by Charles Francis Adams. 12 vols. Philadelphia, 1874.
Adams, William Howard. *The Paris Years of Thomas Jefferson.* New Haven: Yale University Press, 1997.
Adams Family Correspondence. Edited by L. H. Butterfield, Marc Friedlaender, Richard Alan Ryerson, Margaret A. Hogan, Wendell D. Garrett, and Marjorie E. Sprague. 8 vols. to date. Cambridge: Harvard University Press, 1963– .
Agnew, John, and Stuart Corbridge. *Mastering Space: Hegemony, Territory, and International Political Economy.* London: Routledge, 1995.
Allgor, Catherine. *Parlor Politics: In Which the Ladies of Washington Help Build a City and a Government.* Charlottesville: University of Virginia Press, 2000.
Allison, Robert. *The Crescent Obscured: The United States and the Muslim World, 1776–1815.* New York: Oxford University Press, 1995.

American State Papers. 38 vols. Washington: Gales and Seaton, 1832–61.

Ammerman, David. *In the Common Cause: American Response to the Coercive Acts of 1774.* Charlottesville: University of Virginia Press, 1974.

Ammon, Harry. *The Genet Mission.* New York: Norton, 1973.

Anderson, Fred. *Crucible of War: The Seven Years' War and the Fate of Empire in British North America, 1754–1766.* New York: Knopf, 2000.

Anderson, M. S. *The War of Austrian Succession, 1740–1748.* London: Longman, 1995.

Annals of Congress. 42 vols. Washington: Gales and Seaton, 1834–56.

Armitage, David. *The Declaration of Independence: A Global History.* Cambridge: Harvard University Press, 2007.

———. "The Declaration of Independence and International Law." *William and Mary Quarterly*, 3rd ser., 59 (2002): 39–64.

Aron, Stephen. *How the West Was Lost: The Transformation of Kentucky from Daniel Boone to Henry Clay.* Baltimore: Johns Hopkins University Press, 1996.

Auckland, Baron, William Eden. *Papers.* Filmed and published as *Materials Related to the American Revolution from the Auckland Papers in the British Museum.* In *British Records Relating to America in Microform*, edited by W. E. Minchon. East Ardsley, U.K., 1974.

Axtell, James. *The Indians' New South: Cultural Change in the Colonial Southeast.* Baton Rogue: Louisiana State University Press, 1997.

Bailyn, Bernard. *Atlantic History: Concept and Contours.* Cambridge: Harvard University Press, 2005.

———, ed. *The Debate on the Constitution: Federalist and Antifederalist Speeches, Articles, and Letters during the Struggle over Ratification.* 2 vols. New York: Library of America, 1993.

———. *Ideological Origins of the American Revolution.* 1967. Cambridge: Harvard University Press, 1992.

———. *The Ordeal of Thomas Hutchinson.* Cambridge: Harvard University Press, 1974.

———. *The Peopling of British North America: An Introduction.* New York: Knopf, 1986.

———. *Voyagers to the West: A Passage in the Peopling of America on the Eve of the Revolution.* With Barbara DeWolfe. New York: Knopf, 1986.

Bailyn, Bernard, and Philip D. Morgan, eds. *Strangers within the Realm: Cultural Margins of the First British Empire.* Chapel Hill: University of North Carolina Press, 1991.

Banning, Lance. *The Jeffersonian Persuasion: Evolution of a Party Ideology.* Ithaca, N.Y.: Cornell University Press, 1978.

———. *The Sacred Fire of Liberty: James Madison and the Founding of the Federal Republic.* Ithaca, N.Y.: Cornell University Press, 1995.

Becker, Carl. *The Declaration of Independence: A Study in the History of Political Ideas.* New York: Harcourt, Brace, 1922.

Beeman, Richard, Stephen Botein, and Edward C. Carter II, eds. *Beyond Confedera-*

tion: Origins of the Constitution and American National Identity. Chapel Hill: University of North Carolina Press, 1987.

Bell, David A. *The First Total War: Napoleon's Europe and the Birth of Warfare as We Know It*. Boston: Houghton Mifflin, 2007.

Bemis, Samuel Flagg. *The Diplomacy of the American Revolution*. New York and London: D. Appleton-Century, 1935.

———. *Jay's Treaty: A Study in Commerce and Diplomacy*. New Haven: Yale University Press, 1962.

———. *John Quincy Adams and the Foundations of American Foreign Policy*. New York: Knopf, 1949.

———. *Pinckney's Treaty: America's Advantage from Europe's Distress, 1783–1800*. New Haven: Yale University Press, 1960.

Ben-Atar, Doron S. *The Origins of Jeffersonian Commercial Policy and Diplomacy*. New York: St. Martin's, 1993.

Ben-Atar, Doron, and Barbara B. Oberg, eds. *Federalists Reconsidered*. Charlottesville: University of Virginia Press, 1998.

Bouton, Terry. *Taming Democracy: "The People," the Founders, and the Troubled Ending of the American Revolution*. Oxford: Oxford University Press, 2007.

Boyd, Julian P. *The Declaration of Independence: The Evolution of the Text*. Princeton: Princeton University Press, 1945.

Branson, Susan. *"These Fiery Frenchified Dames": Women and Political Culture in Early National Pennsylvania*. Philadelphia: University of Pennsylvania Press, 2001.

Breen, T. H. *The Marketplace of Revolution: How Consumer Politics Shaped American Independence*. New York: Oxford University Press, 2004.

Brewer, John, and Roy Porter, eds. *Consumption and the World of Goods*. London: Routledge, 1993.

Broers, Michael. *Europe under Napoleon, 1799–1815*. London and New York: Arnold, 1996.

Brookhiser, Richard. *Gentleman Revolutionary: Gouverneur Morris, the Rake Who Wrote the Constitution*. New York: Free Press, 2003.

Braund, Kathryn E. Holland. *Deerskins and Duffels: The Creek Indian Trade with Anglo-America, 1685–1815*. Lincoln: University of Nebraska Press, 1993.

Brodhead, John Romeyn, E. B. O'Callaghan, and Berthold Fernow, eds. *Documents Relative to the Colonial History of the State of New York*. 15 vols. Albany, N.Y.: Weed, Parsons, 1853–87.

Brown, Everett Somerville. *The Constitutional History of the Louisiana Purchase, 1803–1820*. Berkeley: University of California Press, 1920.

———, ed. *William Plumer's Memorandum of Proceedings in the United States Senate, 1803–1807*. New York: Macmillan, 1923.

Brown, Richard D. *Knowledge Is Power: The Diffusion of Information in Early America, 1700–1865*. Oxford: Oxford University Press, 1989.

Brown, Weldon A. *Empire or Independence: A Study in the Failure of Reconciliation, 1774–1783*. Port Washington, N.Y.: Kennikat Press, 1966.

Bullock, Stephen C. "A Mumper among the Gentle: Colonial Confidence Man Tom Bell." *William and Mary Quarterly*, 3rd ser., 55 (April 1998): 231–58.

Bushman, Richard L. *The Refinement of America: Persons, Houses, Cities*. New York: Knopf, 1992.

Calloway, Colin G. *The American Revolution in Indian Country: Crisis and Diversity in Native American Communities*. Cambridge: Cambridge University Press, 1995.

———. *The Scratch of a Pen: 1763 and the Transformation of North America*. Oxford: Oxford University Press, 2006.

Cashin, Edward J., ed. *Colonial Augusta: "Key of the Indian Countrey."* Macon, Ga.: Mercer University Press, 1986.

Cayton, Andrew R. L., and Fredrika J. Teute, eds. *Contact Points: American Frontiers from the Mohawk Valley to the Mississippi, 1750–1830*. Chapel Hill: University of North Carolina Press, 1998.

Clark, Thomas D., and John D. W. Guice. *The Old Southwest, 1795–1830*. Norman: University of Oklahoma Press, 1996.

Clinton, George. *Public Papers of George Clinton, First Governor of New York*. Edited by Hugh Hastings. 10 vols. Albany: State of New York, 1899–1914.

Cobbet, William, ed. *Parliamentary History of England, From the Earliest Period to the Year 1803*. 36 vols. London, 1806–20.

Colden, Cadwallader. *The Letters and Papers of Cadwallader Colden, 1711–1775*. 9 vols. New York: New York Historical Society, 1918–37.

Combs, Jerald A. *The Jay Treaty: Political Battleground of the Founding Fathers*. Berkeley and Los Angeles: University of California Press, 1970.

Connelly, Owen. *Napoleon's Satellite Kingdoms*. New York: Free Press, 1966.

Cooke, Jacob E. ed. *The Federalist*. By Alexander Hamilton, John Jay, and James Madison. Middletown, Conn.: Wesleyan University Press, 1961.

Corkran, David H. *The Creek Frontier, 1540–1783*. Norman: Oklahoma University Press, 1967.

Countryman, Edward. "Indians, the Colonial Order, and the Social Significance of the American Revolution." *William and Mary Quarterly*, 3rd ser., 53 (1996): 342–62.

Crane, Verner W. *The Southern Frontier, 1670–1732*. Durham, N.C.: Duke University Press, 1928.

Cronon, William A., George A. Miles, and Jay Gitlin, eds. *Under an Open Sky: Rethinking America's Western Past*. New York: Norton, 1992.

Crowley, John E. *The Privileges of Independence: Neomercantilism and the American Revolution*. Baltimore: Johns Hopkins University Press, 1993.

Daniels, Christine, and Michael V. Kennedy, eds. *Negotiated Empires: Centers and Peripheries in the Americas, 1500–1820*. New York: Routledge, 2002.

Davies, K. G., ed. *Documents of the American Revolution, 1770–1783*. 21 vols. Shannon: Irish University Press, 1972–81.

Deane, Silas. *The Deane Papers*. Edited by Charles Isham. 5 vols. New York, 1887–91. Published in *Collections of the New York Historical Society*, vols. 19–23.

DeConde, Alexander. *Entangling Alliance: Politics and Diplomacy Under George Washington.* Durham, N.C.: Duke University Press, 1958.
———. "Historians, the War for American Independence, and the Persistence of the Exceptionalist Ideal." *International History Review* 3 (August 1983): 399–430.
———. *The Quasi-War: The Politics and Diplomacy of the Undeclared War with France, 1797–1801.* New York: Scribner's, 1966.
———. *This Affair of Louisiana.* Baton Rouge: Louisiana State University Press, 1976.
———. "Washington's Farewell, the French Alliance, and the Election of 1796." *Mississippi Valley Historical Review* 43 (March 1957): 641–58.
Deudney, Daniel H. "The Philadelphian System: Sovereignty, Arms Control, and Balance of Power in the American States-Union, circa 1787–1861." *International Organization* 49 (Spring 1995): 191–228.
Dictionary of American Biography. 22 vols. New York: Scribner's, 1928–58.
Documentary History of the First Federal Congress. Edited by Linda Grant DuPauw, Charlene Bangs Bickford, and Helen E Veit. 17 vols. Baltimore: Johns Hopkins University Press, 1972–2004.
Douglass, William. *Summary, Historical and Political, Of the First Planting, Progressive Improvements, and Present State of the British Settlements in North-America.* Boston, 1749. Reprint, New York: Arno Press, 1972.
Dowd, Gregory Evans. *A Spirited Resistance: The North American Indian Struggle for Unity.* Baltimore: Johns Hopkins University Press, 1992.
———. *War under Heaven: Pontiac, the Indian Nations, and the British Empire.* Baltimore: Johns Hopkins University Press, 2002.
Doyle, William. *The Old European Order, 1660–1800.* Oxford: Oxford University Press, 1992.
———. *The Oxford History of the French Revolution.* Oxford: Oxford University Press, 1989.
Dubois, Laurent. *A Colony of Citizens: Revolution and Slave Emancipation in the French Caribbean, 1787–1804.* Chapel Hill: University of North Carolina Press, 2006.
Dull, Jonathan R. *A Diplomatic History of the American Revolution.* New Haven: Yale University Press, 1985.
———. *The French Navy and American Independence: A Study of Arms and Diplomacy, 1774–1787.* Princeton: Princeton University Press, 1975.
DuVal, Kathleen. *The Native Ground: Indians and Colonists in the Heart of the Continent.* Philadelphia: University of Pennsylvania Press, 2006.
Edling, Max M. *A Revolution in Favor of Government: Origins of the U.S. Constitution and the Making of the American State.* Oxford: Oxford University Press, 2003.
Edmunds, R. David. *The Shawnee Prophet.* Lincoln: University of Nebraska Press, 1983.
Egan, Clifford L. *Neither Peace nor War: Franco-American Relations, 1803–1812.* Baton Rouge: Louisiana State University Press, 1983.
Elkins, Stanley, and Eric McKitrick. *The Age of Federalism: The Early American Republic, 1788–1800.* New York: Oxford University Press, 1993.

Ellis, Joseph J. *American Sphinx: The Character of Thomas Jefferson.* New York: Knopf, 1997.

The Emerging Nation: A Documentary History of the Foreign Relations of the United States under the Articles of Confederation, 1780–1789. Edited by Mary A. Giunta, J. Dane Hartgrove, Norman A. Graebner, Peter P. Hill, Lawrence S. Kaplan, Richard B. Smith, and Mary-Jane M. Dowd. 3 vols. Washington, D.C.: National Historical Publications and Records Commission, 1996.

Estes, Tood. *The Jay Treaty Debate, Public Opinion, and the Evolution of Early American Political Culture.* Amherst: University of Massachusetts Press, 2006.

Etheridge, Robbie. *Creek Country: The Creek Indians and Their World.* Chapel Hill: University of North Carolina Press, 2003.

Fenton, William N. *The Great Law and the Longhouse: A Political History of the Iroquois Confederacy.* Norman: University of Oklahoma Press, 1998.

Fischer, David Hackett. *Albion's Seed: Four British Folkways in America.* New York: Oxford University Press, 1989.

———. *Paul Revere's Ride.* New York: Oxford University Press, 1994.

———. *Washington's Crossing.* New York: Oxford University Press, 2004.

Franklin, Benjamin. *The Papers of Benjamin Franklin.* Edited by Leonard W. Labaree. 39 vols. to date. New Haven: Yale University Press, 1959– .

Freeman, Joanne B. *Affairs of Honor: National Politics in the New Republic.* New Haven: Yale University Press, 2001.

Frey, Linda, and Marsha Frey. "'The Reign of Charlatans Is Over': The French Revolutionary Attack on Diplomatic Practice." *Journal of Modern History* 65 (December 1993): 706–44.

Furet, François. *Revolutionary France.* Translated by Antonia Nevill. Oxford: Blackwell, 1992.

Gallay, Alan. *The Indian Slave Trade: The Rise of the English Empire in the American South, 1670–1717.* New Haven: Yale University Press, 2002.

Gearing, Fred. *Priests and Warriors: Social Structures for Cherokee Politics in the Eighteenth Century.* Memoir 93 of the American Anthropological Association. *American Anthropologist* 64, no. 5, pt. 2 (October 1962).

Gilbert, Felix. *To the Farewell Address: Ideas of Early American Foreign Policy.* Princeton: Princeton University Press, 1961.

Gipson, Lawrence Henry. *The British Empire before the American Revolution.* 15 vols. Caldwell, Id.: Caxton Printers, 1936–70.

Glathaar, Joseph T., and James Kirby Martin. *Forgotten Allies: The Oneida Indians and the American Revolution.* New York: Hill and Wang, 2006.

Gould, Eliga H. *Persistence of Empire: British Political Culture in the Age of the American Revolution.* Chapel Hill: University of North Carolina Press, 2000.

———. "Zones of Law, Zones of Violence: The Legal Geography of the British Atlantic, circa 1772." *William and Mary Quarterly,* 3rd ser., 60 (2003): 471–510.

Grant, Ludovick. "Historical Relation of Facts Delivered by Ludovick Grant, Indian Trader, to His Excellency the Governor of South Carolina." 12 January 1756. Re-

printed in *South Carolina Historical and Genealogical Magazine* 10 (January 1909): 54–68.
Greene, Jack P. "Colonial History and National History: Reflections on a Continuing Problem." *William and Mary Quarterly*, 3rd ser., 64 (April 2007): 235–50.
———. *Peripheries and Center: Constitutional Development in the Extended Polities of the British Empire and the United States, 1607–1788*. Athens: University of Georgia Pres, 1986.
———. *Pursuits of Happiness: The Social Development of Early Modern British Colonies and the Formation of American Culture*. Chapel Hill: University of North Carolina Press, 1988.
———. *The Quest for Power: The Lower Houses of Assembly in the Southern Royal Colonies, 1689–1776*. Chapel Hill: University of North Carolina Press, 1963.
———. *Understanding the American Revolution: Issues and Actors*. Charlottesville: University of Virginia Press, 1995.
Griffith, Patrick. *American Leviathan: Empire, Nation, and Revolutionary Frontier*. New York: Hill and Wang, 2007.
Gross, Robert A. *The Minutemen and Their World*. New York: Hill and Wang, 1976.
Gruber, Ira D. *The Howe Brothers and the American Revolution*. New York: Norton, 1975.
Hahn, Steven C. *The Invention of the Creek Indian Nation*. Lincoln: University of Nebraska Press, 2004.
Halliday, E. M. *Understanding Thomas Jefferson*. New York: HarperCollins, 2001.
Hamilton, Alexander. *The Papers of Alexander Hamilton*. Edited by Harold C. Syrett (gen. ed.), Jacob E. Cooke (assoc. ed.) et al. 27 vols. New York: Columbia University Press, 1961–87.
Hendrickson, David C. *Peace Pact: The Lost World of the American Founding*. Lawrence: University Press of Kansas, 2003.
Hickey, Donald R. *The War of 1812: A Forgotten Conflict*. Urbana: University of Illinois Press, 1989.
Higginbotham, Don. *The War for American Independence: Military Attitudes, Policies, and Practice, 1763–1789*. New York: Macmillan, 1971.
Hilton, Boyd. *A Mad, Bad, and Dangerous People?: England, 1783–1846*. Oxford: Oxford University Press, 2006.
Hinderaker, Eric. *Elusive Empires: Constructing Colonialism in the Ohio Valley, 1673–1800*. Cambridge: Cambridge University Press, 1997.
Hoffman, Ronald, and Peter J. Albert, eds. *Diplomacy and Revolution: The Franco-American Alliance of 1778*. Charlottesville: University of Virginia Press, 1981.
———. *Launching the "Extended Republic": The Federalist Era*. Charlottesville: University of Virginia Press, 1996.
———. *Peace and the Peacemakers: The Treaty of 1783*. Charlottesville: University of Virginia Press, 1986.
Holton, Woody. *Forced Founders: Indians, Debtors, Slaves, and the Making of the American Revolution in Virginia*. Chapel Hill: University of North Carolina Press, 1999.

———. "The Ohio Indians and the Coming of the American Revolution in Virginia." *Journal of Southern History* 60 (1994): 453–78.

———. *Unruly Americans and the Origins of the Constitution.* New York: Hill and Wang, 2007.

Hornsby, Stephen J. *British Atlantic, American Frontier: Spaces of Power in Early Modern British America.* Hanover, N.H.: University Press of New England, 2005.

Horsman, Reginald. *Expansion and American Indian Policy, 1783–1812.* 1967. Norman: University of Oklahoma Press, 1992.

———. *The War of 1812.* New York: Knopf, 1969.

Hutson, James H. *John Adams and the Diplomacy of the American Revolution.* Lexington: University Press of Kentucky, 1980.

Jackson, Andrew. *The Papers of Andrew Jackson.* Edited by Samuel B. Smith, Harriet Chappell Owsley, Harold D. Moser, Sharon Macpherson, David H. Roth, and George H. Hoemann. 7 vols. to date. Knoxville: University of Tennessee Press, 1980– .

Jackson, Robert H. *Classical and Modern Thought on International Relations: From Anarchy to Cosmopolis.* New York: Palgrave Macmillan, 2005.

———. *The Global Covenant: Human Conduct in a World of States.* Oxford and New York: Oxford University Press, 2000.

Jacobs, Wilbur R. *The Appalachian Indian Frontier: The Edmond Atkin Report and Plan of 1755.* Lincoln: University of Nebraska Press, 1967.

Jefferson, Thomas. *Thomas Jefferson Writings.* Edited by Merrill D. Petersen. New York: Library of America, 1984.

———. *The Papers of Thomas Jefferson.* Edited by Julian P. Boyd, Charles T. Cullen, John Catanzariti, and Barbara B. Oberg (gen. eds.) et al. 34 vols. to date. Princeton: Princeton University Press, 1950– .

Jennings, Francis, William N. Fenton, Mary A. Druke, and David R. Miller, eds. *The History and Culture of Iroquois Diplomacy: An Interdisciplinary Guide to the Treaties of the Six Nations and Their League.* Syracuse, N.Y.: Syracuse University Press, 1985.

Jensen, Merrill, ed. *American Colonial Documents to 1776.* Vol. 9 of *English Historical Documents,* edited by David C. Douglas. New York: Oxford University Press, 1969.

———. *The Articles of Confederation: An Interpretation of the Social-Constitutional History of the American Revolution, 1774–1781.* 1940. Madison: University of Wisconsin Press, 1948.

Jensen, Merrill, John P. Kaminski, and Gaspare J. Saladino, gen. eds. *Documentary History of the Ratification of the Constitution.* 14 vols. to date. Madison: State Historical Society of Wisconsin, 1976– .

Jones, Dorothy V. *License for Empire: Colonialism by Treaty in Early America.* Chicago: University of Chicago Press, 1982.

Journal of the Congress of the Four Southern Governors, and the Superintendent of that District, with the Five Nations of Indians, at Augusta, 1763. Charles Town, 1764.

The Journals of the Continental Congress. Edited by Worthington Chauncey Ford, Peter Timothy, Gaillard Hunt, John Clement Fitzpatrick, Roscoe R. Hill, Kenneth E. Harris, and Steven D. Tilley. 34 vols. Washington: U.S. Government Printing Office.

Kagan, Robert. *Dangerous Nation: America's Place in the World from Its Earliest Days to the Dawn of the Twentieth Century*. New York: Knopf, 2006.

Kalter, Susan. *Benjamin Franklin, Pennsylvania, and the First Nations: The Treaties of 1736–62*. Urbana: University of Illinois Press, 2006.

Kammen, Michael G. *A Rope of Sand: The Colonial Agents, British Politics, and the American Revolution*. New York: Vintage, 1974.

Kaplan, Lawrence S. "The Treaty of Paris, 1783: A Historiographical Challenge." *International History Review* 3 (August 1983): 431–42.

Kelly, James C. "Notable Persons in Cherokee History: Attakullakulla," *Journal of Cherokee Studies* 3 (Winter 1978): 2–34.

[Kennedy, Archibald]. *An Essay on the Government of the Colonies*. New York, 1752.

———. *The Importance of Gaining and Preserving the Friendship of the Indians to the British Interest, Considered*. New York, 1751.

———. *Observations on the Importance of the Northern Colonies under Proper Regulations*. New York, 1750.

———. *Serious Advice to the Inhabitants of the Northern Colonies, on the Present Situation of Affairs*. New York, 1755.

———. *Serious Considerations on the Present State of Affairs of the Northern Colonies*. New York, 1754.

Kennedy, John P. *Memoirs of the Life of William Wirt*. 2 vols. Philadelphia, 1849.

Keohane, Robert E. *After Hegemony: Cooperation and Discord in the Contemporary World Political Economy*. Princeton: Princeton University Press, 1984.

Ketcham, Ralph. *James Madison: A Biography*. 1971. Charlottesville: University of Virginia Press, 1990.

Kimball, Marie G. *Jefferson: The Scene of Europe, 1784–1789*. New York: Coward-McCann, 1950.

King, Duane H., ed. *The Cherokee Indian Nation: A Troubled History*. Knoxville: University of Tennessee Press, 1979.

Kissinger, Henry A. *A World Restored: Metternich, Castlereagh, and the Problems of Peace, 1812–22*. Boston: Houghton Mifflin, 1957.

Knouff, Gregory T. *Soldiers' Revolution: Pennsylvanians in Arms and the Forging of Early American Identity*. University Park: Pennsylvania State University Press, 2003.

Koch, Adrienne. *Jefferson and Madison: The Great Collaboration*. Oxford: Oxford University Press, 1964.

Koenigsberger, H.G. "Composite States, Representative Institutions, and the American Revolution." *Historical Research* 63 (1989): 135–53.

Kohn, Richard H. *Eagle and Sword: The Federalists and the Creation of the Military Establishment in America, 1783–1802*. New York: Free Press, 1975.

Konig, David Thomas, ed. *Devising Liberty: Preserving and Creating Freedom in the New American Republic.* Stanford: Stanford University Press, 1995.

Kurtz, Stephen G. *The Presidency of John Adams: The Collapse of Federalism, 1795–1800.* Philadelphia: University of Pennsylvania Press, 1957.

Lang, Daniel G. *Foreign Policy in the Early Republic: The Law of Nations and the Balance of Power.* Baton Rouge: Louisiana State University Press, 1985.

Leder, Lawrence H., ed. *Some Eighteenth-Century Commentators.* Vol. 2 of *The Colonial Legacy.* New York: Harper and Row, 1971.

Letters of Delegates to Congress, 1774–1789. Edited by Paul H. Smith, Gerald W. Gawalt, Rosemary Fry Plakas, and Eugene Sheridan. 26 vols. Washington: Library of Congress, 1976–2000.

Lewis, James E., Jr. *The American Union and the Problem of Neighborhood: The United States and the Collapse of the Spanish Empire, 1783–1829.* Chapel Hill: University of North Carolina Press, 1998.

———. *John Quincy Adams: Policymaker for the Union.* Wilmington, Del.: SR Books, 2001.

———. *The Louisiana Purchase: Jefferson's Noble Bargain?* Chapel Hill: University of North Carolina Press, 2003.

Louis, Wm. Roger, ed. *The Oxford History of the British Empire.* 5 vols. Oxford: Oxford University Press, 1998.

Madison, James. *The Papers of James Madison.* Edited by William T. Hutchinson, William M. E. Rachal, Robert A. Rutland, J. C. A. Stagg, Thomas A. Mason, Jeanne K. Sisson, David B. Mastern, and Jean Schneider. 17 vols. Chicago: University of Chicago Press; Charlottesville: University of Virginia Press, 1962–91.

———. *The Writings of James Madison.* Edited By Gaillard Hunt. 9 vols. New York: G. P. Putnam's Sons, 1900–1910.

Magrath, C. Peter. *Yazoo, Land and Politics in the New Republic: The Case of Fletcher v. Peck.* New York: Norton, 1966.

Maier, Pauline. *American Scripture: Making the Declaration of Independence.* New York: Knopf, 1997.

Malone, Dumas. *Jefferson and His Time.* 6 vols. Boston: Little, Brown, 1948–81.

Malone, Henry Thompson. *The Cherokees of the Old South: A People in Transition.* Athens: University of Georgia Press, 1956.

Marks, Frederick W., III. *Independence on Trial: Foreign Affairs and the Making of the Constitution.* Baton Rouge: Louisiana State University Press, 1973. Reprint, Wilmington, Del.: Scholarly Resources, 1986.

Marshall, John. *The Papers of John Marshall.* Edited by Herbert A. Johnson. 12 vols. Chapel Hill: University of North Carolina Press, 1974–2006.

Marston, Jerrilyn Greene. *King and Congress: The Transfer of Political Legitimacy, 1774–1776.* Princeton: Princeton University Press, 1987.

Martin, James Kirby, and Mark Edward Lender. *A Respectable Army: The Military Origins of the Republic, 1763–1789.* 1982. Wheeling, Ill.: Harlan Davidson, 2006.

Martin, Joel W. *Sacred Revolt: The Muskogees' Struggle for a New World.* Boston: Beacon, 1991.

Matson, Cathy D. *Merchants and Empire: Trading in Colonial New York*. Baltimore: Johns Hopkins University Press, 1998.
Matson, Cathy D., and Peter S. Onuf. *A Union of Interests: Political and Economic Thought in Revolutionary America*. Lawrence: University of Kansas Press, 1990.
McCoy, Drew R. *The Elusive Republic: Political Economy in Jeffersonian America*. Chapel Hill: University Of North Carolina Press, 1980.
McCullough, David. *John Adams*. New York: Simon and Schuster, 2001.
McKay, Derek, and H. M. Scott. *The Rise of the Great Powers, 1648–1815*. London and New York: Longman, 1983.
McLoughlin, William G. *Cherokee Renascence in the New Republic*. Princeton: Princeton University Press, 1986.
Meinig, D. W. *The Shaping of America: A Geographical Perspective on 500 Years of History*. 4 vols. New Haven, 1986–2004.
Merrell, James H. *The Indians' New World: Catawbas and Their Neighbors from European Contact through the Era of Removal*. Chapel Hill: University of North Carolina Press, 1989.
———. *Into the American Woods: Negotiators on the Pennsylvania Frontier*. New York: Norton, 1999.
Merritt, Jane T. *At the Crossroads: Indians and Empires on a Mid-Atlantic Frontier, 1700–1763*. Chapel Hill: University of North Carolina Press, 2003.
Middlekauff, Robert. *The Glorious Cause: The American Revolution, 1763–1789*. 1982. Oxford: Oxford University Press, 2005.
Miller, William Lee. *The Business of May Next: James Madison and the Founding*. Charlottesville: University of Virginia Press, 1992.
Montross, Lynn. *The Story of the Continental Army, 1775–1783*. 1952. New York: Barnes and Noble, 1967.
Morgan, Edmund S., and Hellen M. Morgan. *The Stamp Act Crisis: Prologue to Revolution*. 1953. Chapel Hill: University of North Carolina Press, 1992.
Morgan, Philip D. *Slave Counterpoint: Black Culture in the Eighteenth-Century Chesapeake and Lowcountry*. Chapel Hill: University of North Carolina Press, 1998.
Mori, Jennifer. *Britain in the Age of the French Revolution, 1785–1820*. Harlow, UK: Longman, 2000.
[Morris, Gouverneur]. *Observations on the American Revolution*. Philadelphia, 1779.
Morris, Richard B. *The Peacemakers: The Great Powers and American Independence*. New York: Harper and Row, 1965.
Oliphant, John. *Peace and War on the Anglo-Cherokee Frontier, 1756–63*. Baton Rouge: Louisiana University Press, 2001.
Olwell, Robert, and Alan Tully, eds. *Cultures and Identities in Colonial British America*. Baltimore: Johns Hopkins University Press, 2006.
Onuf, Peter S. *Jefferson's Empire: The Language of American Nationhood* Charlottesville: University of Virginia Press, 2000.
———. *The Mind of Thomas Jefferson*. Charlottesville: University of Virginia Press, 2007.

———. *The Origins of the Federal Republic: Jurisdictional Controversies in the United States, 1775–1787*. 1983. Philadelphia: University of Pennsylvania Press, 2001.

Onuf, Peter, and Nicholas Greenwood Onuf. *Federal Union, Modern World: The Law of Nations in an Age of Revolutions, 1776–1814*. Madison, Wisc.: Madison House, 1993.

———. *Nations, Markets, and War: Modern History and the American Civil War*. Charlottesville: University of Virginia Press, 2006.

Onuf, Peter S., and Leonard J. Sadosky. *Jeffersonian America*. Houndsmills, UK; and Malden, Mass.: Blackwell, 2002.

O'Shaughnessy, Andrew J. "'If Others Will Not Be Active, I Must Drive': George III and the American Revolution." *Early American Studies* 2 (2004): 1–46.

Owens, Robert M. "Jeffersonian Benevolence on the Ground: The Indian Land Cession Treaties of William Henry Harrison." *Journal of the Early Republic* 22 (2002): 405–35.

Palmer, Robert R. *The Age of Democratic Revolution: A Political History of Europe and America, 1760–1800*. 2 vols. Princeton: Princeton University Press, 1959–64.

———. *Twelve Who Ruled: The Year of the Terror in the French Revolution*. 1941. Princeton: Princeton University Press, 1989.

Parkinson, Robert G. "Enemies of the People: The Revolutionary War and Race in the New American Nation." Ph.D. diss., University of Virginia, 2005.

Pasley, Jeffrey L. *"The Tyranny of Printers": Newspaper Politics in the Early American Republic*. Charlottesville: University Press of Virginia, 2001.

Pencak, William A., and Daniel K. Richter, eds. *Friends and Enemies in Penn's Woods: Indians, Colonists, and the Racial Construction of Pennsylvania*. University Park: Pennsylvania State University Press, 2004.

Perdue, Theda. *Cherokee Women: Gender and Culture Change, 1700–1835*. Lincoln: University of Nebraska Press, 1998.

———. *Slavery and the Evolution of Cherokee Society, 1540–1866*. Knoxville: University of Tennessee Press, 1979.

Perkins, Bradford. *Prologue to War: England and the United States, 1805–1812*. Berkeley and Los Angeles: University of California Press, 1968.

Perkins, Dexter. *A History of the Monroe Doctrine*. Boston: Little, Brown, 1955.

Peters, Richard, ed. *The Case of the Cherokee Nation against the State of Georgia, Argued and Determined at the Supreme Court of the United States, January Term 1831*. Philadelphia, 1831.

Pole, J. R. *The Decision for American Independence*. Philadelphia: Lippincott, 1975.

Power, Samantha. *"A Problem from Hell": America and the Age of Genocide*. New York: Basic Books, 2002.

Price, Munro. *Preserving the Monarchy: The comte de Vergennes, 1774–1787*. Cambridge: Cambridge University Press, 1995.

Prucha, Francis Paul. *American Indian Policy in the Formative Years: The Indian Trade and Intercourse Acts, 1790–1834*. Cambridge: Harvard University Press, 1962.

———. *American Indian Treaties: The History of a Political Anomaly*. Berkeley and Los Angeles: University of California Press, 1994.

———. *The Great Father: The United States Government and the American Indians.* 2 vols. Lincoln: University of Nebraska Press, 1984.
Rakove, Jack N. *The Beginnings of National Politics: An Interpretive History of the Continental Congress.* New York: Knopf, 1979.
———. *Original Meanings: Politics and Ideas in the Making of the Constitution.* New York: Knopf, 1996.
———. "Solving a Constitutional Puzzle": The Treatymaking Clause as a Case Study." *Perspectives in American History,* n.s., 1 (1984): 233–81.
Ramsey, William L. "'Something Cloudy in Their Looks': The Origins of the Yamasee War Reconsidered." *Journal of American History* 90 (2003): 44–75.
Reid, John Philip. *A Better Kind of Hatchet: Law, Trade, and Diplomacy in the Cherokee Nation during the Early Years of European Contact.* University Park: Pennsylvania State University Press, 1976.
———. *A Law of Blood: The Primitive Law of the Cherokee Nation.* Dekalb: Northern Illinois University Press, 2006.
Remini, Robert V. *Andrew Jackson and His Indian Wars.* New York: Viking, 2001.
———. *Andrew Jackson and the Course of American Empire, 1767–1821.* New York: Harper and Row, 1977.
Richter, Daniel K. *Facing East from Indian Country: A Native History of Early America.* Cambridge: Harvard University Press, 2001.
———. *The Ordeal of the Longhouse: The Peoples of the Iroquois League in the Era of European Colonization.* Chapel Hill: University of North Carolina Press, 1992.
Ritcheson, Charles R. *The Aftermath of Revolution: British Policy toward the United States, 1783–1795.* New York: Norton, 1971.
———. *British Politics and the American Revolution.* Norman: University of Oklahoma Press, 1954.
Robson, Eric. *The American Revolution in Its Political and Military Aspects, 1763–1783.* New York: Norton, 1955, 1966.
Roosen, William. "Early Modern Diplomatic Ceremonial: A Systems Approach." *Journal of Modern History* 52 (1980): 452–76.
Ross, Chief John. *The Papers of Chief John Ross.* Edited by Gary E. Moulton. 2 vols. Norman: University of Oklahoma Press, 1985.
Royster, Charles. *A Revolutionary People at War: The Continental Army and the American Character, 1775–1783.* Chapel Hill: University of North Carolina Press, 1979.
Sadosky, Leonard J. "'In the White Town of the Grand Council': Indian Images and Geopolitical Realities in the Treaty of New York, 1789–1790." Paper presented to the Society for Historians of the Early American Republic, Lexington, Ky., July 1999.
Saunt, Claudio. *A New Order of Things: Power, Property, and the Transformation of the Creek Indians, 1733–1816.* Cambridge: Cambridge University Press, 1999.
Savelle, Max. "The Appearance of an American Attitude toward External Affairs, 1750–1775." *American Historical Review* 52 (July 1947): 655–66.
———. "Colonial Origins of American Diplomatic Principles." *Pacific Historical Review* 3 (1934): 334–50.

Schama, Simon. *Citizens: A Chronicle of the French Revolution.* New York: Knopf, 1989.
Schiff, Stacy. *A Great Improvisation: Franklin, France, and the Birth of America.* New York: Henry Holt, 2005.
Scott, James C. *Seeing Like a State: How Certain Schemes to Improve the Human Condition Have Failed.* New Haven: Yale University Press, 1998.
Seed, Patricia. "Taking Possession and Reading Texts: Establishing the Authority of Overseas Empires." *William and Mary Quarterly,* 3rd ser., 49 (1992): 183–209.
Shannon, Timothy J. *Indians and Colonists at the Crossroads of Empire: The Albany Congress of 1754.* Ithaca, N.Y.: Cornell University Press, 2000.
Sheehan, Bernard W. *Seeds of Extinction: Jeffersonian Philanthropy and the American Indian.* New York: Norton, 1974.
Sirmans, M. Eugene. *Colonial South Carolina: A Political History, 1663–1763.* Chapel Hill: University of North Carolina Press, 1966.
Sloan, Herbert E. *Principle and Interest: Thomas Jefferson and the Problem of Debt.* New York: Oxford University Press, 1995.
Smith, James Morton, ed. *The Republic of Letters: The Correspondence between Thomas Jefferson and James Madison, 1776–1826.* 3 vols. New York: Norton, 1995.
Smith, Page. *John Adams.* 2 vols. Garden City, N.Y.: Doubleday, 1962.
Snapp, J. Russell. *John Stuart and the Struggle for Empire on the Southern Frontier.* Baton Rouge: Louisiana State University Press, 1996.
Spivak, Burton. *Jefferson's English Crisis: Commerce, Embargo, and the Republican Revolution.* Charlottesville: University of Virginia Press, 1979.
Stagg, J.C.A. *Mr. Madison's War: Politics, Diplomacy, and Warfare in the Early American Republic, 1783–1830.* Princeton: Princeton University Press, 1983.
Stephen, Sir Leslie, and Sir Sidney Lee, gen. eds. *Dictionary of National Biography.* 66 vols. London: Smith, Elder, and Co., 1885–1901.
Stevens, Benjamin Franklin, ed. *Facsimiles of Manuscripts in European archives Relating to America, 1773–1783,* 24 vols. London, 1889–95. Reprint, Wilmington, Del.: Scholarly Resources, 1970.
Stinchcombe, William C. *The American Revolution and the French Alliance.* Syracuse: Syracuse University Press, 1969.
Stourzh, Gerald. *Benjamin Franklin and American Foreign Policy.* 1954. 2nd ed. Chicago: University of Chicago Press. 1969.
Sweet, Julie Anne. *Negotiating for Georgia: British-Creek Relations in the Trustee Era, 1733–1752.* Athens: University of Georgia Press, 2005.
Taylor, Alan. *American Colonies: the Settling of North America.* New York: Penguin, 2001.
———. *The Divided Ground: Indians, Settlers, and the Northern Borderland of the American Revolution.* New York: Knopf, 2006.
Thomas, Peter D. G. *British Politics and the Stamp Act Crisis: The First Phase of the American Revolution, 1763–1767.* Oxford: Oxford University Press, 1975.
———. *Tea Party to Independence: the Third Phase of the American Revolution, 1773–1776.* Oxford: Oxford University Press, 1991.

———. *The Townshend Duties Crisis: The Second Phase of the American Revolution, 1767–1773*. Oxford: Oxford University Press, 1987.

Thornbrough, Gayle, ed. *Outpost on the Wabash, 1787–1791*. Indianapolis: Indiana Historical Society Publications, 1957.

Tiro, Karim. "A 'Civil War'?: Rethinking Iroquois Participation in the American Revolution." *Explorations in Early American Culture* 4 (2000): 148–65.

Tuck, Richard. *The Rights of War and Peace: Political Thought and International Order from Grotius to Kant*. Oxford: Oxford University Press, 1999.

Tucker, Robert W., and David C. Hendrickson. *Empire of Liberty: The Statecraft of Thomas Jefferson*. New York: Oxford University Press, 1990.

Tucker, Spencer C., and Frank J. Reuter, *Injured Honor: The Chesapeake–Leopard Affair, June 22, 1807*. Annapolis: Naval Institute Press, 1996.

Van Doren, Carl. *Benjamin Franklin*. New York: Viking, 1938.

———. *Secret History of the American Revolution*. New York: Viking, 1941.

Vaughan, Alden T. *Early American Indian Documents: Treaties and Laws*. 20 vols. Washington, D.C.; Fredrick, Md.; and Bethesda, Md.: University Publications of America, 1979–2004.

Waldstreicher, David. *In the Midst of Perpetual Fetes: The Making of American Nationalism, 1776–1820*. Chapel Hill: University of North Carolina Press, 1997.

Waldstreicher, David, Jeffrey L. Pasley, and Andrew W. Robertson, eds. *Beyond the Founders: New Approaches to the Political History of the Early American Republic*. Chapel Hill: University of North Carolina Press, 2004.

Walling, Karl-Friedrich. *Republican Empire: Alexander Hamilton on War and Free Government*. Lawrence: University of Kansas Press, 1999.

Wallace, Anthony F. C. *Jefferson and the Indians: The Tragic Fate of the First Americans*. Cambridge: Harvard University Press, 1999.

Wallerstein, Immanuel. *The Modern World-System*. 3 vols. New York and San Diego: Academic Press, 1974–89.

Walz, Kenneth N. *Theory of International Politics*. New York: McGraw Hill, 1979.

Washington, George. *The Papers of George Washington: Presidential Series*. Edited by Dorothy Twohig, William W. Abbot, Jack D. Warren Jr., Mark A. Mastromarino, Philander D. Chase, Frank E. Grizzard Jr., Beverly H. Runge, Edward G. Lengel, and Christine Sternberg Patrick. 14 vols. to date. Charlottesville: University of Virginia Press, 1988– .

———. *The Writings of George Washington, from the Original Manuscript Sources*. Edited by John C. Fitzpatrick. 39 vols. Washington: U.S. Government Printing Office, 1931–44.

Wharton, Francis, ed. *Revolutionary Diplomatic Correspondence of the United States*. 6 vols. Washington, 1888.

White, Richard. *The Middle Ground: Indians, Empires, and Republics in the Great Lakes Region, 1650–1815*. Cambridge: Cambridge University Press, 1991.

Whitney, Craig. "France Presses for Power Independent of the U.S." *New York Times*, November 7, 1999.

Williams, Robert A. *Linking Arms Together: American Indian Treaty Visions of Law and Peace, 1600–1800.* New York: Oxford University Press, 1997.

Williams, Samuel Cole, ed. *Early Travels in the Tennessee Country, 1540–1800.* Johnson City, Tenn.: Watauga Press, 1928.

Williams, William Appleman. *The Tragedy of American Diplomacy.* New York: Dell, 1962.

Wills, Garry. *Inventing America: Jefferson's Declaration of Independence.* Garden City, N.Y.: Doubleday, 1978.

Wolf, Eric R. *Europe and the People without History.* 1982. Berkeley: University of California Press, 1997.

Wood, Gordon S. *The Americanization of Benjamin Franklin.* New York: Penguin, 2004.

———. *The Creation of the American Republic, 1776–1787.* 1969. Chapel Hill: University of North Carolina Press, 1993.

Wood, Peter H. *Black Majority: Negroes in Colonial South Carolina from 1670 through the Stono Rebellion.* New York: Norton, 1996.

Zobel, Hiller B. *The Boston Massacre.* New York: Norton, 1970.

Zuehlke, Mark. *For Honour's Sake: The War of 1812 and the Brokering of an Uneasy Peace.* Toronto: Knopf Canada, 2006.

Index

Act of Union (1707), 15
Adams, Abigail (Smith), 59, 63
Adams, John, 59–60, 62–63, 70–73, 82–84, 89, 97, 99, 122–27, 150, 175
Adams, John Quincy, 200–205, 208
Adams, Samuel, 105, 110, 112
Adams, William, 201–5
Addington, Henry, 185
African Americans, 196–97, 212
Alabama, 194, 196, 199–200
Albany Congress (1754), 34, 68
Algiers, 127, 150
Alien Acts (1798), 175
American Indians: policy of British Empire toward, 25–29, 32–35, 37–48, 50–58, 129, 133–34, 137–38, 201–5, 212–15; policy of France toward, 22, 42–43, 45–47, 194–95; policy of U.S. toward, 60–63, 66–69, 73–77, 85–89, 127–40, 156–61, 165–74, 178–80, 182–83, 191–205, 207–15. *See also under names of individual Indian nations*
American role in European system, French/British views of, 100–101
Anglo-Cherokee War (1758–61), 50–51
Annapolis Convention (1786), 141
Armitage, David, 83
Armstrong, John, 198–99

Articles of Confederation, 83–89, 118, 119–22; diplomatic ineffectiveness of, 119–22, 124–27, 138–39, 146–47; drafted by Dickinson, 86–89; proposed by Franklin, 66–68
Atkin, Edmond, 40, 44–48, 50–51, 64
Attakullakulla (Cherokee leader), 24, 27, 52–53
Auckland, 1st Baron of, 187. *See also* Eden, William
Austerlitz, Battle of (1805), 185
Austria, 183, 185

Barbary States, 3, 127
Barbeu-Duborg, Jacques, 93
Barrington, 2nd Viscount (William Wildman), 55
Bathurst, Earl of (Henry Bathurst), 201
Bayard, James, 201–5
Beaumarchais, Caron de (Pierre-Augustin), 94–95
Benson, Egbert, 152–53
Berlin Decree, 186–89, 190
Big Warrior (Creek leader), 172
Blount, William (governor of Southwest Territory), 157
Blount, Willie (governor of Tennessee), 190–94, 211

268 Index

Board of Trade (Lords Commissioners for Trade and Plantations), 25–27, 54–57, 212–14
Bonaparte, Napoleon (Napoleon I, Emperor of France), 183, 185–86, 196, 201
Boston Massacre (1770), 60
Boudinot, Elias (Cherokee), 212
Brant, Joseph (Thayendanegea, Mohawk leader), 129, 133–34
British Empire, 98–100, 102–9; expansion across Atlantic Ocean, 14–16; reintegration of American colonies into, proposed by William Eden, 106–8; relations with American colonies, 31–34, 49–50, 53–58; relations with France, 31, 39–43, 48–49; relations with Indian nations, 25–29, 32–35, 37–48, 50–58, 129, 133–34, 137–38, 212–15
British North America, 59–61; metropolitan administration of, 51, 53–58; proposals for reorganization of, 32–34, 39–48, 51, 53–55; rivalry between colonies, 33–34
Burgoyne, John, 101–2
Burke, Edmund, 123
Burr, Aaron, 207
Butler, Richard, 129, 135–38

Campbell, George Washington, 188–89
Canada, 60, 73, 79, 89, 180, 201, 204
Canasatego (Iroquois leader), 38–39
Carleton, Guy, 74
Carlisle, Earl of (Frederick Howard), 91, 106, 108, 110, 114, 115
Carlisle Commission, 91–92, 106–15, 187
Carr, Dabney, 209
Catawba Nation, 16–17
Cayuga Nation, 129
Charleston (Charles Town), S.C., 13, 18–19, 23–24
Cherokee Nation, 19–27, 44–45, 47, 149–50, 160, 166, 168, 191–93, 198–99, 203, 207–15; "emperor" created, 21–24; government of, 19–20, 22–25, 25–26, 207–15, 223; relations with British Empire, 49–54; relations with U.S., 149–50, 166, 198–99, 203, 207–15
Cherokee Nation v. Georgia (1831), 8, 208–12
Cherokee Treaty (1730), 25–27, 213
Chesapeake–Leopard incident, 187–88
Chickasaw Nation, 149, 168, 191–93
Chippewa (Ojibwa) Nation, 138
Choctaw Nation, 149, 168
Chota (Cherokee town), 22, 24, 27
"civilization" of Indians, U.S. government policy of, 157–59, 182–83, 193–96, 203, 208–12
Clark, William, 177, 195
Clay, Henry, 201–5
Clinton, George, 131–35, 138
Clymer, George, 165–74
Coercive Acts (1774), 58, 59
Coffee, John, 198
Colden, Cadwallader, 40, 43–44, 64
Colerain, Georgia, 165–73
commerce (transatlantic): disruptions of during Napoleonic Wars, 180–89; as lynchpin of French-American relations, 98–101
Concord, Battle of (1775), 59–61
Confederation Congress. *See* Continental Congress
Congress (U.S.), 151–54, 156, 162–63, 175, 180–81, 187–89, 196
Congress of Augusta (1763), 51–54
"conquest theory," 128–29, 130, 135–38, 180–89
Constitution (U.S.), 2, 4, 8, 119–22, 143–47, 149–50, 151–55, 159–60, 164, 168, 170, 171, 209–14
consumption, as factor in American political economy, 178–79

Continental Army, 70, 73, 109, 111, 115
Continental Congress, 59–63, 69–70, 74–89, 90–93, 97–101, 109–15, 151, 156; attempts to open negotiations with France, 93–95, 97–101; Committee on Indian Affairs, 74–76, 128–31; Committee of Secret Correspondence, 77–80; policy toward British America/British Empire, 60–63; policy toward Great Britain, 77–78; policy toward Indian nations, 60–63, 74–77, 85–89, 127–40; receives French-American alliance, 91–92; responds to Carlisle Commission, 109–15
"Continental System," 186
Cornplanter (Seneca leader), 129, 133
Cornwallis, Lord Charles, 116
Craven, Charles (South Carolina governor), 17
Creek Nation, 17–19, 22, 49–54, 149–50, 159–60, 165–74, 180, 196–99, 201, 208, 211; Red Stick movement, 180, 196–99; relations with British Empire, 49–54; relations with U.S., 159–60, 165–74
Cuming, Sir Alexander, 13–27, 212–14

Dana, Francis, 90, 113–14
Deane, Silas, 92–101, 103–4, 111, 114; establishes American diplomatic contact with French court, 92–95; imagines future French-American relationship, 98–99
Dearborn, Henry, 194–95
Declaration of Independence (1776), 61–62, 81–84, 86, 92, 107
Declaration of the Causes and Necessity of Taking up Arms (1775), 61, 66
Declaratory Act (1766), 65
Definitive Articles of Peace (1783). See Treaty of Paris (1782–83)
Delaware (Indian) Nation, 138, 196

Delaware River, 109
Democratic Party, 208
Deudney, Daniel, 7–8
Dickinson, John, 62, 78, 81–82, 84, 86–89
diplomatic communication, forms of, 95–97
diplomatic culture/culture of diplomacy, 5, 153–55
Douglass, William, 48
Drayton, William Henry, 112–15
Duane, James, 124, 128, 130–32
Dumas, Charles-Guillaume-Frédéric, 78–80

Eden, William (later, 1st Baron Auckland), 101–10, 114–15
Egremont, 2nd Earl of (Charles Wyndham), 51, 55
Embargo of 1807–1809, 187–90
"Emperor of the Cherokees," office created and Moitoi of Tellico crowned, 21–24
Emuckfaw, Battle of (1814), 197
England. *See* British Empire; Great Britain
Essex case (1805), 184–85

Fallen Timbers, Battle of (1794), 163
federal Constitution. *See* Constitution, U.S.
federal-state rivalry over Indian diplomacy, 159–60, 166–74, 207–9
Federalist, The, 144–45, 181
Federalist movement (1787–88), 143–47
Federalist Party, 149–51, 156–63, 165–74, 176–77, 182, 189
Ferguson, Adam, 107, 109–10
Five Nations. *See* Iroquois Confederacy
First Continental Congress. *See* Continental Congress
Fletcher v. Peck (1810), 167
Florida, 180, 197, 199

Index

Foreign Affairs Act (1789), 151–55
Fort Jackson, 198–200
Fort Mims, 196–97
Fox, Charles James, 123
France, 71–72, 77–78, 91–101, 103, 107, 111, 114, 115–18, 120, 122–24, 146, 149, 150, 161, 175; colonial expansion in North America, 22; relations with American Indian nations, 22, 42–43, 45–47, 194–95; relations with Great Britain, 31, 39–43, 48–49, 150, 183–89; relations with U.S., 77–78, 91–101, 117–18, 149–50, 154, 161, 175, 183–89, 190–91, 193–95
Franco-American Alliance. *See* French-American Alliance
Franklin, Benjamin, 31, 33–34, 39–44, 48, 54, 58, 63–69, 78–80, 82, 86, 88, 92–93, 96–97, 99–101, 104; imagines future French-American relationship, 99–101; proposes Articles of Confederation, 66–68, 86
French-American Alliance, 91–93, 99–101, 107, 111–16, 120, 146
French Revolution, 149, 150, 160–61; perception of in U.S., 160–61
Friedland, Battle of (1807), 185–86

Gage, Thomas, 54, 58, 59–60, 66
Gaither, Henry, 165, 167, 169–70
Gallatin, Albert, 201–5
Gambier, Lord James, 201–5
Gates, Horatio, 101–2
Genêt, Edmund Charles, 161
George II (king of Great Britain), 15
George III (king of Great Britain), 65, 69–70, 74, 98, 108
Georgia, relations with Indian nations, 49, 51–54, 56–57, 165–74, 207–12
Georgia Compact, 175, 194, 208
Gérard, Conrad-Alexandre, 94
Germain, Lord George, 106, 108–9, 114
German Flats Conference (1775), 73

Germantown, Pa., 111
Giles, William Branch, 176–77
Goulburn, Henry, 201–5
Grand River Iroquois Reserve, 129, 137
Grant, Ludovick (South Carolina Indian trader), 19–23
Grasse, Comte de (François-Joseph Paul de Grasse), 116
Graves, Thomas, 116
Great Britain, 120–27, 129; relations with France, 183–89; relations with Indian nations, 201–5; relations with U.S., 150–51, 162, 163–64, 183–89, 190–91, 196, 201–5. *See also* British Empire
Great Tellico (Cherokee town), 19, 21–23, 27

Haldimand, Frederick, 129
Hamilton, Alexander, 143, 145, 148, 156, 157, 160–62, 164
Hancock, John, 74, 86
Harmar, Josiah, 138–39
Harrison, William Henry, 195–96, 203
Hawkins, Benjamin, 165–74, 195, 198–99
"Helvidius" (James Madison), 161–62
Hendricks, James, 166–73
Henry, Patrick, 145–46
Hill, Aaron (Mohawk leader), 136
Hillsborough, 1st Earl of (Wills Hill), 55–56
Horseshoe Bend, Battle of (1814), 197–98, 211
House of Representatives (U.S.), 188–89
Howe, Admiral Lord Richard, 106, 108
Howe, Sir William, 106, 108–9
human nature, Federalist vision of, 156–57, 174
hyperpower (*hyperpuissance*), 1, 217–18

Indiana, 195
Indian "buffer state," proposed by Goulburn at Ghent, 202–3

Indian departments created by Continental Congress, 75–77
Indian Removal (as concept), 190–94
Indian Removal Act (1830), 207–9
Indians. *See* American Indians; *and also under names of individual Indian nations*
international history, defined, 2–3
Intolerable Acts. *See* Coercive Acts
Iroquois Confederacy, 26, 61, 67–68, 129–38; Covenant Chain alliance of, 36–37, 45–46; diplomacy of, 34–39, 225n10; government of, 35–37, 225n10; participation in Treaty of Lancaster (1744), 37–39; relations with British Empire, 37–39, 73–75, 129, 137; relations with France, 43; relations with Thirteen Colonies/U.S., 73–75, 85–88, 129–38. *See also under names of individual Iroquois nations* (Cayuga Nation; Mohawk Nation; Oneida Nation; Onondaga Nation; Seneca Nation; Tuscarora Nation)
isolationism, 2, 218–19

Jackson, Andrew, 189–94, 196–201, 204–5, 207–14
Jackson, James, 166–73
Jackson, Richard, 106
Jacob the Conjurer (Cherokee religious leader), 23
Jay, John, 116–17, 122, 125, 126, 144–45, 148–49, 150, 162
Jay Treaty (1794–95), 150, 162–63
Jefferson, Thomas, 73–74, 81–83, 86, 111, 127, 140, 148–49, 153–55, 156, 159–60, 162, 163, 175, 176–83, 187–89, 191–95, 198, 202; first inaugural address, 181–82; second inaugural address, 176, 180–82, 195
Jeffersonian Republican Party, 149–51, 160–64, 174–75, 176–78

Jena, Battle of (1806), 185–86
Johnson, Guy, 73, 74
Johnson, Robert (South Carolina governor), 18, 27
Johnson, Sir William, 40, 50, 55–58

Keith, Sir William, 27
Kennedy, Archibald, 31–36, 39–40, 42–44, 48–49, 50, 54, 58, 64
Keowee (Cherokee town), 19–21
Knox, Henry, 139, 148–49, 156–60, 166–67, 182, 192–93, 202; formulates Washington administration Indian policy, 156–59

Lafayette, Marquis de, 135
Laurens, Henry, 110–14, 116
Law of Nations, The (Vattel), 78
law of nations/international law, defined, 4
Leclerc, Charles, 183
Lee, Arthur, 92, 96, 101, 104, 129, 135–38
Lee, Richard Henry, 62, 81–82, 110, 111, 112, 146
Lewis, Merriwether, 177
Lexington, Battle of (1775), 59–61
London, 16, 23, 25
Louis XVI (king of France), 83, 94, 100, 150, 160
Louisiana Purchase (1803), 150, 175, 177, 179, 181–83, 194
Luzerne, Chevalier de la (Anne-César), 118, 119

Madison, James, 135, 140–47, 151–54, 161–64, 178, 180, 187, 189–90, 196; "Notes on Confederacies Ancient and Modern," 141–43; *Political Observations*, 163–64
Mammoth Cheese, 177–78
Marchant, Henry, 110
Marie Antoinette (queen of France), 150
Marks, Frederick W., 143

Marshall, John, 8, 212
Maryland, relations with Indian nations, 34–39
Mason, George, 146
Massachusetts, 59–61, 65–66, 70–72, 119
McGillivray, Alexander (Creek leader), 159, 166, 173
McHenry, James, 165, 173
McKean, Thomas, 113
Meigs, Return Jonathan, 195, 211
Menawa (Creek leader), 197
Miami Nation, 196
"middle ground," 121–22, 127–28
Milan Decree, 186–87
Mississippi Crisis (1802–1803), 182–83, 194–95
Mississippi River, 177–83, 189–94
Model Treaty. See Plan of Treaties (1776)
Mohawk Nation, 129
Moitoi of Tellico, 21–25, 27
Monahee (Creek leader), 197
Monroe, James, 187
Monroe Doctrine, 201–2, 205
Morris, Gouverneur, 90–91, 93, 111, 114–15
"most-favored nation" status, 121

Napoleon I (emperor of France). See Bonaparte, Napoleon
Napoleonic Wars, 179–80, 183–84, 186–87
Naquasse (Cherokee town), 23–25
Nashville, Tenn., 189–90
Native Americans. See American Indians; and also under names of individual Indian nations
neomercantilism, 123–24, 185–87
Netherlands, 78–80, 116, 120, 141, 142; recognizes American independence, 116, 120
New Orleans, La., 177, 183, 193–94
New York (colony/state), 31–32, 130–37; relations with Indian nations, 32, 37, 130–37
New York City, 102, 108, 114, 116, 151, 166, 172
Newcastle, Duke of (Thomas Pelham-Holles), 25–27
North, Lord Frederick, 102, 103, 106, 109, 116; ministry of, 91–93, 101–9, 116

Observations on the American Revolution (Morris, 1779), 90–91, 115
Observations on the Commerce of the American States (Lord Sheffield, 1783), 123
Oconee River, 172–73
Ohio Valley, Indian nations of, 150, 163, 166, 195–96
Olive Branch Petition (1775), 61, 66, 69–70
Oneida Nation, 129
Onondaga Nation, 67, 129, 132
Orders in Council, 123–25, 186–89, 190
Oswald, Richard, 116–17, 122
Ottawa Nation, 138
Ottoman Empire, 117

"Pacificus" (Alexander Hamilton), 161–62
Palmer, Joseph, 71–72
Parliament, 60, 62, 65–66, 69, 70
Parris, Alexander (South Carolina treasurer), 18
Pennsylvania, relations with Indian nations, 34–39, 56–57, 131
Pennsylvania Ratifying Convention, 119–20
Pensacola, Fla., 197
Perceval, Spencer, 186, 196
Philadelphia, 109–11
Philadelphia Convention (1787), 119–21, 143–45, 149
Philadelphian System, 7–8, 121–22

Pickens, Andrew, 165–74
Pinckney, Thomas, 199
Pinkney, William, 187
Pitt, William, the Elder (later, 1st Earl of Chatham), 47
Pitt, William, the Younger, 126, 185
Plan of Treaties (1776), 62, 83–84, 99
Plumer, William, 176–78
political culture, defined, 5, 220n11
Polly case (1800), 184, 186, 187
Potowatomi Nation, 196
precedence (diplomatic culture), 154–55
Preliminary Articles of Peace (1782). See Treaty of Paris (1782–83)
President (U.S.), role in making diplomacy, 151–55, 160–64
President's House (White House), 176–78, 180
Price, Richard, 97
Priestley, Joseph, 66
Proclamation of Neutrality (1793), 161–62
Prussia, 185
"Publius," 144–45

Quasi-War (1797–1800), 175
Quebec, 60, 68, 73
Quebec Act (1774), 58, 60

race, as factor in study of Indian-white relations, 3, 8, 221
Rakove, Jack N., 143
Red Jacket (Seneca leader), 129
Red Sticks, 211
Red Stick War (1812–14), 196–200
Republican Party (1790s–1820s). See Jeffersonian Republican Party
Revolutionary War (1775–83), 93, 101, 109–10, 115–17, 119–21
Rochambeau, Comte de (Jean-Baptiste Donatien de Vimeur), 116
Rockingham, 2nd Marquess of (Charles Watson-Wentworth), 116

Rodney, Caesar, 113
Ross, John (Cherokee leader), 209–12
"Rule of 1756," 184
Russell, Jonathan, 201–5
Russia, 117, 185

Saint-Domingue (Haiti), 183
Saratoga, Battle of (1777), 101–2
Savannah (Indians), 17
Schuyler, Peter, 135
Schuyler, Philip, 73–74, 77, 85
Seagrove, James, 165, 167
Second Continental Congress. See Continental Congress
Sedition Act (1798), 175
Senate (U.S.), role in making diplomacy, 143–44, 151–55, 160–64
Seneca Nation, 129
Sequoyah (Cherokee lexicographer), 212
Sergeant, John, 209–12
Seven Years' War (1754–63), 28–29, 48–49, 184
Shawnee Nation, 138, 180, 196
Shawnee Prophet, 180, 196, 211
Shays' Rebellion (1786–87), 119
Sheffield, Lord (John Holroyd), 123, 185
Shelburne, 2nd Earl of (William Petty-Fitzmaurice), 55, 116–17, 122–23
Shipley, Jonathan, 66
Simms, James, 166–73
Six Nations. See Iroquois Confederacy
South Carolina, 13–27, 44; early history and growth of, 16–18; place of African slavery in, 17; relations with Indian nations, 16–18, 49–54
sovereignty: defined by George III, 69–70; division of, within American federal union, 149–51, 156–59, 161–65, 168–71, 173–75
Spain, 71–72, 115–16, 150, 159, 162, 180, 194
spying, conducted by British in France, 93–95, 103–6

274 Index

Stamp Act (1765), 58, 65
State Department, creation of, 151–55
states system, defined, 5–6
Stephen, James, 185–86
Strahan, William, 66
Stuart, John, 34, 49, 51–54, 56, 57
Supreme Court (U.S.), 208–15
Swiss Confederation, 141–42

Tardiveau, Bartélemi, 139
Tasetche (Cherokee town), 23
Tecumseh, 180, 196
Tennessee, 188, 189–94, 196–200
Tenskwatawa. See Shawnee Prophet
Thayendanegea. See Brant, Joseph
Thirteen Colonies (United Colonies), 59, 62–63, 66–74, 77–81; relations with Indian nations, 66–69, 73–77
Tohopeka (Creek town), 197–98, 203
Townshend Duties, 58, 65
Trail of Tears, 204, 215
Transcontinental Treaty (1819), 180
Treaty of Alliance (U.S.-France, 1778), 91–92, 101, 113–14, 120, 146, 150, 160. See also French-American Alliance
Treaty of Amiens (1802), 179, 183
Treaty of Aranjuez (1779), 115–16
Treaty of Colerain (1796), 165–74
Treaty of Fort Jackson (1814), 198–200, 202
Treaty of Fort McIntosh (1785), 138
Treaty of Fort Stanwix (1768), 56–57
Treaty of Fort Stanwix (1784), 121, 129–38; September negotiations (New York), 133–35; October negotiations (U.S. Congress), 135–38
Treaty of Galphinton (1785), 166–67, 172
Treaty of Ghent (1814–15), 180, 201–5
Treaty of the Great Miami River (1786), 138
Treaty of Greenville (1795), 163, 166
Treaty of Holston (1791), 166

Treaty of Lancaster (1744), 37–39
Treaty of Lunéville (1801), 183
Treaty of Mortefontaine (1800), 183
Treaty of New Echota (1835), 215
Treaty of New York (1790), 159, 166–67, 172–73
Treaty of Paris (1763), 49, 51
Treaty of Paris (1782–83), 116–18, 119, 120, 122, 127, 128, 129, 130, 131, 133, 134, 135, 137, 159, 204
Treaty of Philadelphia (Cherokee, 1794), 166
Treaty of San Lorenzo (1795), 162, 165
Treaty of Shoulderbone Creek (1786), 166–67, 172
Tuscarora Nation, 129

United Colonies. See Thirteen Colonies
United States, 90–101, 109–18; relations with France, 91–101, 117–18, 149, 160–61, 175, 178–80, 181, 183–89, 190–91, 193–95; relations with Great Britain, 109–17, 150–51, 162, 163–64, 178–80, 183–89, 190–91, 196, 201–5; relations with Indian nations, 156–61, 165–74, 178–80, 182–83, 191–205, 207–15

Valley Forge, Pa., 109
Vergennes, Comte de (Charles Gravier), 92, 94–97, 100–101, 115–18
Vincennes (Northwest Territory), 138–39
Virginia, 140–41; relations with Indian nations, 34–39, 48, 49–53, 56–57
Virginia Capes, Battle of the (1781), 116
Virginia Land Cession (1784), 137
Virginia Ratifying Convention, 145–47

War of Austrian Succession (1740–48), 31, 39–43
War of 1812 (1812–15), 196–205
Ward, Joseph, 70

Warren, James, 60, 71–72, 74
Warren, Mercy Otis, 71–72
Washington, George, 2, 70, 109–10, 113, 116, 148–50, 152–57, 160–62, 164–66, 169, 174; Farewell Address, 2, 164–65
Wayne, Anthony, 163
Webster, Daniel, 209
Wedderburn, Alexander, 106–7
Wentworth, Paul, 103–6
West Indies, 123–24
Westphalia, Peace of (1648), 6
Westphalian System, defined, 6–7
Whig Party, 208

White House. *See* President's House
Williams, John, 199
Wirt, William, 207–15
Wolcott, Oliver, 129, 135–38
Wright, James (colonial governor of Georgia), 52, 54
Wyandot Nation, 138

Yamasee Nation, 16–18
Yamasee War (1715–17), 17–18
Yazoo land speculation, 160, 167–68
York, Pa., 109, 111
Yorktown, Battle of (1781), 116

JEFFERSONIAN AMERICA

Jan Ellen Lewis and Peter S. Onuf, editors
*Sally Hemings and Thomas Jefferson: History,
Memory, and Civic Culture*

Peter S. Onuf
Jefferson's Empire: The Language of American Nationhood

Catherine Allgor
*Parlor Politics: In Which the Ladies of Washington
Help Build a City and a Government*

Jeffrey L. Pasley
*"The Tyranny of Printers": Newspaper Politics
in the Early American Republic*

Herbert E. Sloan
*Principle and Interest: Thomas Jefferson and
the Problem of Debt* (reprint)

James Horn, Jan Ellen Lewis, and Peter S. Onuf, editors
The Revolution of 1800: Democracy, Race, and the New Republic

Phillip Hamilton
*The Making and Unmaking of a Revolutionary Family:
The Tuckers of Virginia, 1752–1830*

Robert M. S. McDonald, editor
Thomas Jefferson's Military Academy: Founding West Point

Martha Tomhave Blauvelt
The Work of the Heart: Young Women and Emotion, 1780–1830

Francis D. Cogliano
Thomas Jefferson: Reputation and Legacy

Albrecht Koschnik
"Let a Common Interest Bind Us Together": Associations, Partisanship, and Culture in Philadelphia, 1775–1840

John Craig Hammond
Slavery, Freedom, and Expansion in the Early American West, 1787–1820

David Andrew Nichols
Red Gentlemen and White Savages: Indians, Federalists, and the Search for Order on the American Frontier

Douglas Bradburn
The Citizenship Revolution: Politics and the Creation of the American Union, 1774–1804

Clarence E. Walker
Mongrel Nation: The America Begotten by Thomas Jefferson and Sally Hemings

Timothy Mason Roberts
Distant Revolutions: 1848 and the Challenge to American Exceptionalism

Peter J. Kastor and François Weil, editors
Empires of the Imagination: Transatlantic Histories of the Louisiana Purchase

Eran Shalev
Rome Reborn on Western Shores: Historical Imagination and the Creation of the American Republic

Leonard J. Sadosky, Peter Nicolaisen, Peter S. Onuf, and Andrew J. O'Shaughnessy, editors
Old World, New World: America and Europe in the Age of Jefferson

Leonard J. Sadosky
Revolutionary Negotiations: Indians, Empires, and Diplomats in the Founding of America